THE SACRED BOOKS OF THE EAST

F. MAX MULLER (ED.)

LIST OF THE 50 VOLUMES

1. Upanishads.
2. Sacred Laws of Aryas.
3. Texts of Confucianism.
4. Zend-Avesta.
5. Pahlavi Texts.
6. Qur'an.
7. Institutes of Vishnu.
8. Bhagavadgita, & c.
9. Qur'an.
10. (i) Dhammapada.
10. (ii) Sutta-Nipata.
11. Buddhist Suttas.
12. Satapatha-Brahmana.
13. Vinaya Texts.
14. Sacred Laws of Aryas.
15. Upanishads.
16. Texts of Confucianism.
17. Vinaya Texts.
18. Pahlavi Texts.
19. Fo-sho-hing-tsanking.
20. Vinaya Texts.
21. Saddharma Pundarika.
22. Gaina-Sutras.
23. Zend-Avesta.
24. Pahlavi Texts.
25. Laws of Manu.
26. Satapatha-Brahmana.
27. Texts of Confucianism (Li Ki).
28. Texts of Confucianism (Li Ki).
29. Grihya-Sutras.
30 Grihya-Sutras.
31. Zend-Avesta.
32. Vedic Hymns.
33. Minor Law-Books.
34. Vedanta-Sutras.
35. Milinda.
36. Milinda.
37. Pahlavi Texts.
38. Vedanta-Sutras.
39. Texts of Taoism
40. Texts of Taoism
41. Satapatha-Brahmana
42. Atharva-veda.
43. Satapatha-Brahmana.
44. Satapatha-Brahmana.
45. Gaina-Sutras.
46. Vedic Hymns.
47. Pahlavi Texts.
48. Vedanta-Sutras.
49. (i) Buddhakarita.
49. (ii) Mahayana Texts.
50. A General Index

The Sacred Books of the East, Vol. 33

THE MINOR LAW-BOOKS

Edited by

F. MAX MULLER

Translated by

JULIUS JOLLY

PART I

NARADA. BRIHASPATI

GYAN

Published by

GYAN

Gyan Publishing House
5, Ansari Road
Daryaganj, New Delhi-110002
Phone: 011-47034999, 9811692060
E-mail: books@gyanbooks.com

Distribution Network
gyanbooks.com
India, USA, Canada, UK, Australia, France

ISBN : 978-81-212-2937-1 (Set)
ISBN : 978-81-212-2790-2 (PB)
First Published, 1889

2nd Impression 2021

Printed at: Gyan Press, Delhi.

The Sacred Books of the East, Vol. 33

The Minor Law-Books, Part-I
Edited by: F. Max muller, Translated by: Julius Jolly

THE

SACRED BOOKS OF THE EAST

TRANSLATED

BY VARIOUS ORIENTAL SCHOLARS

AND EDITED BY

F. MAX MÜLLER

VOL. XXXIII

Oxford

AT THE CLARENDON PRESS

1889

THE

MINOR LAW-BOOKS

TRANSLATED BY

JULIUS JOLLY

PART I

NÂRADA. B*RI*HASPATI

Oxford

AT THE CLARENDON PRESS

1889

CONTENTS.

INTRODUCTION

TO

NÂRADA.

Supposed origin of the Code of Manu.

The Nârada-smriti or Nâradîya Dharmasâstra first attracted attention nearly a century ago by being quoted in the Preface to Sir W. Jones's celebrated translation of the Code of Manu. What caused it to be brought before the notice of the learned world, was its bearing on the origin and history of the authoritative law-book of ancient India. The statements extracted by Sir W. Jones from the opening chapter of Nârada's law-book require some modification at present, as he was not acquainted with the larger and more authentic of the two versions of Nârada's work, which is now translated. It appears from the present work (pp. 1–4) that Nârada, the reputed compiler of the Nâradîya Dharmasâstra, refers to four, instead of three, successive versions of the Code of Manu, in 100,000 slokas or 1,080 chapters, in 12,000, 8,000, and 4,000 slokas. The authorship of these four versions is assigned, respectively, to Manu, Nârada, Mârkandeya, and Sumati, the son of Bhrigu, and the Nârada-smriti is described as an abridgment, made by Nârada, of the ninth or Vyavahâra (legal) chapter of the original Code in 100,000 slokas. The first part of Nârada's abridgment of the ninth chapter of Manu's Code is designed as a mâtrikâ or vyavahâra-mâtrikâ, 'summary of proceedings-at-law' or 'general rules of procedure.'

Explanation of the legend.

Though the mythical nature of the Preface to the Nârada-smriti is sufficiently apparent, some facts which recently have come to light impart a higher degree of probability to the alleged connexion between Manu and Nârada, than was formerly allowed by myself. Thus the contents of Nârada's Preface to his Smriti appear to have been known to such an early author as Medhâtithi, who quotes it, rather loosely it is true, in his Commentary on the Code of Manu, where he says that 'this work, consisting of one hundred thousand (*s*lokas), was composed by Pra*g*âpati and abridged successively by Manu and the rest [1].' This goes far to prove that the Preface to the Nârada-sm*ri*ti had attained notoriety as early as the ninth century A.D., and must be nearly or quite as old as the remainder of the work. The antiquity of the account given by Nârada of the origin and history of the principal code of ancient India is supported to some extent by the Paurâ*n*ik statement regarding four successive remodellings of the original composition of Svâya*m*bhuva (Manu), by Bh*ri*gu, Nârada, B*ri*haspati, and Aṅgiras [2], and by a curious tradition preserved in the Mahâbhârata, to the effect that the original Dharma*s*âstra, produced by Brahman in 100,000 chapters, was successively reduced to 10,000, 5,000, 3,000, and 1,000 chapters by *S*a*m*kara, Indra, B*ri*haspati, and Kâvya [3]. What is more, in a colophon of the ancient Nepalese MS. of the Nârada-sm*ri*ti, that work is actually designed as the Mânava Dharma*s*âstra in the recension of Nârada (mânave dharma*s*âstre nâradaproktâyâ*m* sa*m*hitâyâm), just as the Code of Manu in the colophons is usually called the Mânava Dharma*s*âstra in the recension of Bh*ri*gu (mânave dharma*s*âstre bh*ri*guproktâyâ*m* sa*m*hitâyâm, or mânave dharma*s*âstre bh*ri*guprokte). Again, the chapter on theft (*k*aurapratishedha), which has come to light in Mr. Bendall's Nepalese Palm-leaf MS. of Nârada, and in a Nepalese paper MS. recently discovered by the same scholar, forms an appendix to the body of the Nârada-sm*ri*ti, exactly in the same way as an analogous chapter on robbery and other criminal offences is tacked on at the close of the eighteen titles of law in the Code of Manu, IX, 252–293. It also deserves to be noted, perhaps, that the Dhamathats of Burma, while professing to be founded

[1] Manu*t*îkâsaṅgraha, p. 39, gloss on Manu I, 58; Bühler, Sacred Books of the East, vol. xxv, p. xv.

[2] Mandlik's Hindu Law, p. xlvii.

[3] Mahâbhârata XII, 59, 22, and 80 foll.; Bühler, ibid. p. xcvi.

on the laws of Manu, contain several rules and maxims which may be traced to the Nârada-sm*ri*ti, whereas they do not occur in the Code of Manu [1].

Manu anterior to Nârada.

Although, therefore, there appears to be an element of truth in Nârada's account of the history of the Code of Manu, and of his own Sm*ri*ti, there can be no doubt that the actual position of the two works has been inverted by him. The composition of Bh*ri*gu, or of Sumati, the son of Bh*ri*gu, i.e. the now extant Code of Manu, is not posterior, but decidedly anterior, in date to the Nârada-sm*ri*ti, as may be gathered easily from a comparison of both works. Thus e.g. Nârada mentions twenty-one modes of acquiring property, fifteen sorts of slaves, fourteen species of impotency, three kinds of women twice married, and four kinds of wanton women, twenty women whom a man must not approach, thirty-two divisions of the law of gift, eleven sorts of witnesses, five or seven ordeals, four or five losers of their suit, two kinds of proof and two kinds of documents, seven advantages resulting from a just decision, eight members of a lawsuit, one hundred and thirty-two divisions of the eighteen principal titles of law. The first germs of some of these theories may be traced to the Code of Manu, and it is interesting to note how these germs have been developed by Nârada. As a rule, his judicial theories show an infinitely advanced stage of development as compared to Manu's, and his treatment of the law of procedure, in particular, abounding as it does in technical terms and nice distinctions, and exhibiting a decided preference for documentary evidence and written records over oral testimony and verbal procedure, exhibits manifest signs of recent composition.

Nârada acquainted with the Code of Manu.

An analogous inference may be drawn from the fact that Nârada was apparently acquainted with a work either identical with, or closely allied to, the now extant Code of Manu. His analysis of the contents of the original Code composed by Manu in 100,000 *s*lokas corresponds in the main to the topics

[1] Forchhammer, The Jardine Prize Essay, pp. 54-58.

treated in that work as it now stands. He quotes the opening verse of the original gigantic work of Manu, and it is a remarkable coincidence that this verse agrees with Manu I, 5, 6, i.e. with the actual exordium of the Code of Manu, as vv. 1–4 serve as an introduction only, and may be a subsequent addition. Forensic law is alleged to have formed the subject of the ninth chapter of the original composition of Manu. In the Code of Manu, law and judicature are discussed in the eighth and ninth chapters. The twenty-four chapters, divided into one thousand and eighty, i. e. 45 × 24 sections, of the original Code, seem to represent double the twelve chapters of the Code of Manu. On the other hand, Sumati, the son of Bh*ri*gu, who is alleged to have reduced the original Code of Manu to its present size, and to have produced the law-book now current among mankind, may be identified with Bh*ri*gu, the supposed author of the actual Manu-sm*ri*ti ; and the number of 4,000 *s*lokas, which is assigned to his composition, may be taken to be a rough statement of the actual extent of the Manu-sm*ri*ti, which in reality runs up to 2,685 *s*lokas only.

A consideration of these facts leaves but little doubt that the compiler of the Nârada-sm*ri*ti, whoever he was, must have been acquainted with a work closely akin to the now extant Manu-sm*ri*ti. This is so much the more probable because several of his references to the authoritative enunciations of Manu may be actually traced to the Manu-sm*ri*ti [1], and because a number of verses either occurring in the MSS. of the Nârada-sm*ri*ti, or attributed to him by the digest-writers, recur in the Code of Manu.

Discrepancies between Manu and Nârada.

However, though acquainted with the Code of Manu, the so-called Nârada was far from offering a mere slavish reproduction of its doctrines in his own work. On the contrary, the Nârada-sm*ri*ti must be considered as an independent, and therefore specially valuable, exposition of the whole system of civil and criminal law, as taught in the law schools of the period. It is in fact the only Sm*ri*ti, completely preserved

[1] See e. g. Appendix 26 (p. 227) and Manu VIII, 320; Appendix 34 (p. 228) and Manu VIII, 334; Appendix 36, 37 (p. 228) and Manu VIII, 124, 125.

in MSS., in which law, properly so-called, is treated by itself, without any reference to rules of penance, diet, and other religious subjects; and it throws a new and an important light on the political and social institutions of ancient India at the time of its composition. Several of the doctrines propounded by Nârada are decidedly opposed to, and cannot be viewed in the light of developments from, the teaching of Manu. Thus e.g. Nârada advocates the practice of Niyoga, or appointment of a widow to raise offspring to her deceased husband; he declares gambling to be a lawful amusement, when carried on in public gaming-houses; he allows the remarriage of widows; he virtually abrogates the right of primogeniture by declaring that even the youngest son may undertake the management of the family property, if specially qualified for the task; he ordains that, in a partition of the family property, the father may reserve two shares for himself, and that, in the case of a partition after his death, the mother shall divide equally with the sons, and an unmarried sister take the same share as a younger son; he lays down a different gradation of fines from those laid down by Manu, &c.[1]

Their probable origin.

It may be argued that Nârada would not have ventured to differ from the Code of Manu on such essential points as these, unless he had found good authority for doing so in other early works or dicta attributed to the primeval legislator of India, and that this fact furnishes another reason for attaching some credit to what Nârada relates of the original Code in 100,000 verses, and of its successive abridgment. Thus much is certain, that a great many floating proverbs and authoritative enunciations of Manu and of V*ri*ddha or B*ri*han-Manu must have existed by the side of the Code of Manu in the times of Nârada as well as before and after his period, when they were quoted in the Mahâbhârata[2] and in the Com-

[1] See the foot-notes, passim.

[2] See Nârada XII, 80-88, and Manu IX, 65-68; Nârada XVII, 1-8, and Manu IX, 221-228; Nârada XII, 97, and Manu V, 162; Nârada XIII, 5, and Manu IX, 105-109; Nârada XIII, 13, 14, and Manu IX, 104, 131; Nârada, Appendix 30, 31, and Manu VIII, 138.

mentaries and Dharmanibandhas from Medhâtithi's Manubhâshya down to *G*agannâtha's Digest, translated by Colebrooke. The compiler of the Nârada-sm*ri*ti may have incorporated a number of these dicta in his own composition. At the same time, it is far from improbable that a work on law, called the Code of Manu in the version of Nârada, may have existed by the side of the celebrated Code of Manu in the version of Bh*ri*gu, and that the unknown compiler of the Nârada-sm*ri*ti may have utilised that work for his own composition, and enhanced the value and authority of the latter by referring to, and arranging in his own way, the reports current with regard to Manu and Nârada. The precise nature of the origin of such a work as the Nârada-sm*ri*ti must needs remain a matter for speculation; but it certainly was an established practice with Sanskrit writers to graft their own compositions on earlier works attributed to fabulous personages of the heroic age of India, and indeed to fabricate an authority of this kind for the productions of their own pen.

Date of the Nârada-sm*ri*ti.

The probable date of the Code of Manu may be turned to account for determining the date of the Nârada-sm*ri*ti; just as the presumable date of the latter work has been used in its turn for fixing the chronological position of Manu. The composition of the two works is separated, apparently, by a considerable interval of time. If, therefore, the date of Manu has been rightly placed between the second centuries B.C. and A.D. by Professor Bühler[1], it would seem to follow that the Nârada-sm*ri*ti can hardly belong to an earlier period than the fourth or fifth century A.D. The same conclusion may be arrived at by other, and independent considerations.

Compared with other Sm*ri*tis,

Thus the Nârada-sm*ri*ti agrees on many important points, especially in the law of evidence, with the Dharma*s*âstras or Sm*ri*tis of Yâ*gñ*avalkya, Vish*n*u, B*ri*haspati, Kâtyâyana, and Vyâsa. It may be a little older than the three last-named works,

[1] Loc. cit. p. xcvii.

which belong to the latest productions of the Smr*i*ti epoch of Hindu Law, but its legal rules and judicial theories have a decidedly more advanced character than either Vish*n*u's or Yâ*g*ñavalkya's. The Smr*i*ti of Vish*n*u cannot belong to an earlier period than the third century A. D. [1], and the Yâ*g*ñavalkya Smr*i*ti is not likely to be anterior to it in date [2].

and with the drama M*r*ikk*h*aka*t*ikâ.

Again, the judicial trial which is described in the well-known drama M*r*ikk*h*aka*t*ikâ corresponds in all essential features to the rules laid down in Nârada's chapter on 'The Plaint [3].' If, then, the Nâradîya Dharma*s*âstra and the M*r*ikk*h*aka*t*ikâ are contemporaneous productions, we have a further reason for assigning the composition of the former work to the fifth or sixth century A. D. It may also be noted that Nârada (XII, 74) regards sexual intercourse with a female ascetic, pravra*g*itâ, as a kind of incest. In the earlier Indian dramas likewise, such as Kâlidâsa's Mâlavikâgnimitra and *S*ûdraka's M*r*ikk*h*aka*t*ikâ, the position of nuns and monks is highly dignified.

The term Dînâra.

Last, not least, the European term Dînâra, i. e. denarius or δηνάριον, which is so important for the purposes of Indian chronology, occurs repeatedly in the Nârada-smr*i*ti. In the first passage (Introd. II, 34, p. 32), Dînâras are mentioned among other objects made of gold, and it would seem that a gold coin used as an ornament is meant, such as e. g. the necklaces made of gold mohurs, which are being worn in India at the present day. 'A string of Dînâras' (dînâra-mâlaya) used as a necklace occurs in a well-known Jain work, the Kalpa-sûtra of Bhadrabâhu [4]. It is, however, possible that the 'Dînâras or other golden things' may be gold coins simply, and that Nârada means to refer to forged or otherwise counterfeit coins. The second passage (Appendix v. 60, p. 232) is specially valuable, because it contains an exact

[1] Sacred Books of the East, vol. vii, p. xxxii.

[2] Tagore Law Lectures, p. 49.

[3] See, particularly, p. 27, note on 18.

[4] See Dr. Jacobi's edition, par. 36 (p. 44), and the same scholar's translation of the Kalpa-sûtra, Sacred Books of the East, vol. xxii, p. 232.

statement of the value of a Dînâra which, it says, is called a Suvar*n*a also. The reception of Dînâras among the ordinary coins of that period shows that their circulation in India must have commenced some time before the Nârada-sm*r*i*t*i was written. The first importation of gold Dînâras into India cannot be referred to an earlier period than the time of the Roman emperors, and the gold Dînâras most numerously found in India belong to the third century A.D.[1]

References to Nârada.

The earliest reference to a work called Nâradîya Dharma*s*âstra seems to be contained in a work of the sixth century, Bâ*n*a's Kâdambarî[2]. Whether the compiler of the Pa*ñk*atantra was acquainted with the Nârada-sm*r*i*t*i appears to be doubtful. The Pa*ñk*atantra in Kosegarten's edition contains a legal text which is attributed to Nârada, though it is not to be found in the Nârada-sm*r*i*t*i. The standard Bombay edition of the Pa*ñk*atantra has that very text, but the name of Nârada is omitted[3]. Medhâtithi's Manubhâshya, which seems to belong to the ninth century, contains several references to the Nârada-sm*r*i*t*i, and Asahâya, who appears to have preceded Medhâtithi, is the reputed author of the ancient Commentary on it, which has largely been used for the present work[4].

Result.

These considerations tend to show that the composition of the Nârada-sm*r*i*t*i cannot be referred to a more recent period than the fifth century A.D., or the sixth century at the very latest. Nor can it belong to a much earlier age than that. This estimate of its age agrees with the results arrived at, thirteen years ago, from the very scanty data then available.

---

[1] Bühler, S. B. E., vol. xxv, p. cvii; West and Bühler, p. 48; Max Müller, History of Ancient Sanskrit Literature, p. 245; Jolly, Tagore Law Lectures, p. 36; Hörnle, Proceedings of the Seventh Congress of Orientalists, p. 134.

[2] P. 91 in Peterson's edition. See Bühler, Sacred Books of the East, vol. xxv, p. cvii, note 1.

[3] See Kosegarten's Pa*ñk*atantra III, 94; Bombay ed., III, 2. It is true that the two texts immediately preceding the text in question in the Pa*ñk*atantra may be compared with Nârada XI, 2 and I, 5, 79.

[4] The fact that Asahâya refers to a coin called dramma, i. e. the Greek δραχμή, may be used for fixing the earlier limit of his date.

The present translation, unlike the Institutes of Nârada previously published by myself (London, Trübner & Co., 1876), is based in the main on what may be termed the large version of Nârada, and accords throughout with the editio princeps of the Nârada-smriti in the Bibliotheca Indica. The reasons which have induced me to consider the large version as the original and authentic composition of Nârada, and to make it the basis of my edition of the Sanskrit text in the Bibliotheca Indica, have been stated in my volume of Tagore Law Lectures, pp. 54–56. In those parts of the work also where both versions agree, or where the only extant MS. of the large version is deficient and has to be supplied from the MSS. of the minor version, the present translation will be found to differ not inconsiderably from my previous rendering of the 'Institutes of Nârada.' The discovery of five valuable MSS. of the minor version, besides the three used in preparing the 'Institutes of Nârada,' the recovery of Asahâya's ancient and valuable Commentary on the Nârada-smriti, and the dies diem docet have united to produce a considerable number of new results. Among the new MSS. discovered, the fifteenth-century Nepalese Palm-leaf MS. of Mr. Bendall is the most important, and has furnished an entire new chapter, the authenticity of which is proved by numerous references in the mediaeval and modern Digests of Law. The chapter in question has been termed an Appendix in the present work (pp. 223–232). It is found, likewise, in a Nepalese paper MS. of the minor version, discovered very recently by Mr. Bendall among the Nepalese MSS. of the British Museum, where it had been labelled wrongly as *K*aurapratishedha.

The present translation.

The Commentary of Asahâya, as far as it goes, has furnished the substance of the foot-notes to the present translation, in which it has been quoted constantly as 'A.' Asahâya was a standard writer in the province of Hindu Law, and his Nâradabhâshya is a very valuable production indeed. He shares with other early commentators of law-books the peculiarity of indulging every now and then in illustrations

*Asahâya and Kalyâ*n*abha*tt*a.*

taken from the every-day life of his period, which help to throw some light on the practical working of Indian Law in those times. As an instance of this tendency I would cite his remarks on a rule concerning liability for debts (pp. 43, 44). Of course it would be dangerous to trust his philological skill everywhere, and some of his interpretations are decidedly artificial. What is worse, the Commentary of Asahâya has not been preserved in its original shape, but in a recast due to one Kalyâ*n*abha*tt*a, whose name is entirely unknown to fame. It is just possible that Kalyâ*n*abha*tt*a, instead of confining his activity to supplying deficiencies and correcting mistakes in the copies of Asahâya's Commentary, may have inserted some new verses in the text of the Nârada-sm*ri*ti as well. Such might be conjectured, for example, to be the origin of the four verses, Introd. I, 21–24 (pp. 9–13), which are quoted in none of the authoritative Digests, and objectionable as to grammar and metre. It should be remembered, however, that Kalyâ*n*abha*tt*a declares the original work of Asahâya to have been spoiled by negligent scribes, and so the grammatical blunders may be charged to their account.

Other auxiliary writings.

The latter half of Asahâya's Commentary being lost, I had to avail myself for the corresponding portion of the Nârada-sm*ri*ti, of the glosses of other mediaeval writers, by whom the texts of Nârada have been quoted and discussed a great deal. Their opinions have been adverted to very fully, in the chapter on inheritance especially, both on account of the practical importance of inheritance for the law-courts of modern India, and because each of the various schools of Sanskrit lawyers has been anxious to interpret the sayings of Nârada to its own advantage. For the curious and somewhat obscure disquisition on fourteen kinds of impotency (XII, 11–18, pp. 167–169), I have been able to use the advice of my late lamented friend Dr. Haas, the well-known student of Indian medical science. A somewhat analogous passage in the canonical literature of the Buddhists has been kindly pointed out to me by Mr. Rhys Davids[1].

[1] *K*ullavagga X, 17, 1. See Sacred Books of the East, vol. xx, p. 349.

Nârada's repute as a legal writer.

The sign of an asterisk (*) has been prefixed to those texts of Nârada which were found to be quoted in one or several of the Sanskrit Commentaries or Digests of Law. The same method has been observed previously in the Bibliotheca Indica edition of the Sanskrit text, but a considerable number of quotations has come to light since then. The repute of Nârada as a legal writer appears to have been so great that upwards of half his work has been embodied in the authoritative compositions of the mediaeval and modern writers in the province of Sanskrit law.

'Quotations from Nârada.'

Under the heading of Quotations from Nârada, all those texts have been collected at the close of the present translation which are attributed to Nârada in one or several of the Digests and Commentaries, without being traceable in the MSS. of the Nârada-sm*ri*ti. Between these quotations have been inserted, for the sake of completeness and in order to fill up the gaps between the single texts contained in the quotations, a number of unpublished texts from the MSS. of the minor version, and from the final chapter on Ordeals in the ancient Nepalese MS. of the Nârada-sm*ri*ti [1]. A complete edition of that chapter will, I trust, be published by Dr. A. Conrady. The quotations have been taken from all the principal Sanskrit works on law, from Medhâtithi's Manubhâshya downwards. For a detailed statement of the particular work and chapter from which each text has been quoted, I may refer to the foot-notes. Most texts being quoted in more than one work at a time, it has not been thought necessary to give complete references to every such work in each particular case, but I have made a point of referring as much as possible to those law-books which exist in English, both for convenience of reference and in order to facilitate a comparison of the present translation with previous renderings of the texts of Nârada. All the unpublished texts have been given in the foot-notes in the original Sanskrit, together with the names of the works from which they have been taken. The MSS.

[1] Regarding that chapter, see Preface to Nârada-sm*ri*ti, pp. 6, 7.

of these works were obtained principally from the India Office and Deccan College libraries; for some of them I was able to use copies of my own. A peculiar source of difficulties lies in the fact that these works differ considerably as to the names of the authors of the single texts. Many texts were no doubt proverbial sayings, and appropriated therefore by several writers. In other cases, the mutually conflicting statements of various writers regarding the authorship of the texts may be attributed to carelessness. Grammatical blunders and faulty readings, as well as the varietas lectionis, have been referred to in important cases only. I subjoin a list of the abbreviations used in the foot-notes to the present translation.

ABBREVIATIONS.

Aparârka=Aparârka's Commentary on the Yâgñavalkya-smriti, Deccan College MS.

Âpastamba, see Manu.

Baudhâyana, see Manu.

Col. Dig.=Colebrooke's Digest of Hindu Law (translation of Gagannâtha's work).

Dâyabhâga=Colebrooke's translation of the Dâyabhâga on Inheritance, or the Sanskrit text of the D., in the Calcutta edition of 1829.

Dâyakramasaṅgraha=Wynch's translation in Stokes's Hindu Law-Books, or the Calcutta edition.

Gagannâtha=Gagannâtha's Vivâdabhaṅgârnava (the work translated by Colebrooke), Bengali MS. in my possession.

Gautama, see Manu.

M. or Mitâksharâ=Mitâksharâ, the Calcutta edition of the Vyavahârâdhyâya, or Colebrooke's version of the Mitâksharâ on Inheritance.

M. Macn.=Macnaghten's translation of the Mitâksharâ on Administration of Justice.

Manu=the Code of Manu, ed. Jolly, London, 1887; or Professor Bühler's translation of the same. For the principal editions and translations of Âpastamba, Baudhâyana, and the other old law-books, I may refer to my volume of Tagore Law Lectures.

May.=Mandlik's translation of the Vyavahâra Mayûkha, in his Hindu Law, Bombay, 1880.

May. (text)=Mandlik's edition of the same, ibid.

Mayûkha=the same work.

Minor Nârada=The Institutes of Nârada, transl. by J. Jolly, London, 1876; or the unpublished Sanskrit original of the same work.

Nârada=the present translation.

Nârada-smriti=The Institutes of Nârada, edited by J. Jolly, in the Bibliotheca Indica series.

Nepalese Nârada=Mr. Bendall's Nepalese Palm-leaf MS. of Nârada.

Raghunandana=Raghunandana's Vyavahâratattva, the Calcutta edition.

Ratn.=Vivâda Ratnâkara, in the Bibliotheca Indica.

Sm*ri*ti*k*.=Deva*nn*abha*tt*a's Sm*ri*ti*k*andrikâ, India Office MS.

Sm*ri*ti*k*andrikâ=the same, or the chapter on Inheritance, transl. by Iyer.

Tod. or *Tod*arânanda=Vyavahârasaukhya in *Tod*ar Mall's *Tod*arânanda, Deccan College MS.

(Uncertain)=texts quoted as 'Sm*ri*ti' generally, without the name of the author being given.

Vasish*th*a, see Manu.

Vîram.=Vîramitrodaya, in Jîbânanda Vidyâsâgara's edition.

Vish*n*u, see Manu.

Viv.=Vivâda*k*intâma*n*i, translated by Tagore, Calcutta, 1863.

Vivâda*k*intâma*n*i=the Sanskrit text, Calcutta edition of 1837.

V. T.=Vivâdatâ*nd*ava by Kamalâkara, India Office MS.

Vy. *K*.=Vyavahâra*k*intâma*n*i by Vâ*k*aspatimi*s*ra, Devanâgarî MS. in my possession.

Yâ*gñ*avalkya, see Manu.

NÂRADA.

THE AUTHOR'S PREFACE.

1. Holy Manu, in order to promote the welfare of all beings, composed a book here, which was to become the foundation of the established rule of conduct. It was made up of twenty-four sections, on (1) the creation of the world; (2) the various kinds of living beings; (3) the extent of the virtuous

1. Regarding the historical value and bearing of this Preface, see Introduction. The table of contents, which is here given for the original Code of Manu, corresponds in the main to the contents of the now extant version of that work. Thus the creation of the world is treated of, Manu I, 5–57; the various kinds of living beings, I, 34–50; the virtuous countries, II, 17–23; the constitution of a judicial assembly, XII, 108–114; the performance of offerings, III, 69–286; IV, 21–28, &c.; established usage (Â*k*âra), passim, all the multifarious rules of private morals and social economy falling under this head; forensic law, chapters VIII and IX; the extirpation of offenders, IX, 252–293; the mode of life of a king, chapter VII; the system of the four castes and four orders, I, 87–101; IX, 325–336, &c.; marriage laws, III, 1–62; the mutual relations between husband and wife, IX, 1–103; the order of succession, IX, 103–220; the performance of obsequies, III, 122–286; rules of purification, V, 57–146; rules of diet, V, 1–56; saleable commodities, and those which may not be sold, X, 85–94; the classification of offences, XI, 55–71; the twenty-one hells, IV, 88–90; penances, XI, 72–266. The Upanishads are frequently referred to, e.g. II, 165; VI, 29. Secret or mysterious doctrines are e.g. those taught in the twelfth chapter of the Code of Manu. A somewhat analogous table of contents of the Code of Manu is given in that work itself, I, 111–118.

country; (4) the constitution of a judicial assembly; (5) the performance of offerings according to the Vedas and Vedâṅgas; (6) established usage; (7) forensic law; (8) the extirpation of offenders; (9) the mode of life of a king; (10, 11) the system of the (four) castes and (four) orders; (12) marriage laws; (13) the mutual relations between husband and wife; (14) the order of succession; (15) the performance of obsequies; (16) the elucidation of difficult points regarding purification; (17) the rule as to what may be eaten and what not; (18, 19) the law regarding vendible commodities, and those which must not be sold; (20) the various kinds of crime; (21) heaven and hell; (22) penances; (23) the Upanishads; (24) secret doctrines.

2. Holy Manu, after having thus (composed) that (book) in a hundred thousand *s*lokas, and in one thousand and eighty chapters, delivered it to the divine sage Nârada. He having learnt it from him, reflecting that a work of this kind could not be remembered easily by mortals on account of its size, abridged it in twelve thousand (*s*lokas) and delivered it to the great sage Mârka*nd*eya.

3. He having learnt it from him, and reflecting on

2. The Manu who is referred to in this place is no doubt Manu Svâya*m*bhuva, or 'Manu sprung from the self-existent Being,' to whom the Code of Manu is said to have been revealed by Brahman; see Manu I, 58. Nârada is one of the seven principal *Ri*shis. He is also reckoned among the Pra*g*âpatis, 'lords of creatures' or 'creators,' and is viewed as the chief of heavenly musicians. Mârka*nd*eya is elsewhere called 'the long-lived,' and is celebrated for his austerities. He is the reputed author of a well-known Purâ*n*a, called after him the Mârka*nd*eya Purâ*n*a.

3. Bh*ri*gu, one of the great *Ri*shis of antiquity, is in the Code of Manu introduced as a son of Manu, and as the compiler of the

the (limited duration and) capacity of human life, reduced it to eight thousand (*s*lokas), and delivered this (abridgment) to Sumati, the son of Bh*ri*gu.

4. Sumati, the son of Bh*ri*gu, after having learnt (this book) from him and considered what human capacity had been brought down to through the (successive) lessening of life (in the four ages of the world), reduced it to four thousand (*s*lokas).

5. It is this (abridgment) which Manes and mortals read, whilst the gods, Gandharvas, and other (exalted beings) read in extenso the (original) code, consisting of one hundred thousand (*s*lokas). There the first *s*loka runs as follows: 'This universe was wrapped up in darkness, and nothing could be discerned. Then the holy, self-existent Spirit issued forth with his four faces.'

6. After this exordium, chapter follows chapter

---

present version of the Code of Manu; see Manu I, 35, 59, 60. The fact of his being mentioned here as the father of Sumati, the compiler of the final recension of the Code of Manu, renders it probable that this work may have closely resembled the now extant Code of Manu. However, the latter work has not more than 2684 *s*lokas, instead of the 4000 attributed to the version of Sumati.

4. As for the successive lessening of life, and general deterioration of the world, in the four ages, K*ri*ta, Tretâ, Dvâpara, and Kali, see Manu I, 81–86.

5. A. observes expressly that the term 'there' refers to the original Code in 100,000 *s*lokas. The *s*loka here quoted is nearly identical with Manu I, 5 a, 6 a.

6. The Mât*ri*kâ or 'Introduction' (compare divyamât*ri*kâ, a 'general introduction to the law regarding ordeals,' in the Mitâksharâ, p. 139) which is here attributed to Nârada, appears to have formed part of the abridgment in 12,000 *s*lokas, which was originally composed by him. It was composed in the Sûtra style, i.e. it was made up of aphorisms. The *s*lokas are frequently designed as Sûtras by the commentators of law-books. Supposing this work to have consisted of twelve chapters, like the present Code

continuously. There the ninth chapter is headed, 'Judicial Procedure.' There Nârada, the divine sage, composed an Introduction in the Sûtra style, as follows. It begins with the following *s*loka.

---

of Manu, each chapter would have contained about 1000 *s*lokas. The Nârada-sm*ri*ti actually has about 1000 *s*lokas. In the Code of Manu, forensic law is treated in the eighth and ninth chapters. The compiler of the present work declares his composition to be the ninth chapter of Nârada's abridged version of the Code of Manu. In the above enumeration of twenty-four subjects treated in the original Code of Manu, judicial procedure is introduced as the seventh and eighth subject. This coincidence indeed might be accidental.

INTRODUCTION.

I. Legal Procedure.

*1. When mortals were bent on doing their duty alone and habitually veracious, there existed neither lawsuits, nor hatred, nor selfishness.

*2. The practice of duty having died out among mankind, lawsuits have been introduced; and the king has been appointed to decide lawsuits, because he has authority to punish.

3. Documents and (the testimony of) witnesses are declared to be the two methods for clearing up doubtful matters, where two parties are quarrelling with one another.

*4. Proceedings at law are of two kinds; attended by a wager, or not attended by a wager. A lawsuit

---

I, 1. Where the sun shines, there is no shade. Where there is shade, there the sun does not shine. Similarly, where virtue reigns, there are neither lawsuits, nor hatred, nor selfishness. On the other hand, where these three are, there virtue is not to be found. A. The object of this introductory portion is to show how far judicial procedure is connected with Dharma 'Virtue,' or 'Duty,' the principal subject of an Indian law-book. The Vîramitrodaya and other compilations attribute a further hemistich to Nârada, in which the happy age here alluded to is referred to the period 'when Manu, the father of mankind, was reigning on earth.'

3. Yâg*ñ*avalkya II, 22; Vasish*th*a XVI, 10; Vish*n*u VI, 23.

4. 'A lawsuit attended by a wager' is where one of the parties promises in writing to pay a certain sum to the king, over and above the amount in dispute. 'A lawsuit not attended by a wager' is one devoid of a stipulation of this sort. Vîramitrodaya. This is apparently the correct explanation. Asahâya observes that the amount staked may be much smaller than the amount in dispute.

attended by a wager is where (either of the two parties) stakes in writing a certain sum which has to be paid besides the sum in dispute (in case of defeat).

5. In a lawsuit attended by a wager, he of the two who is cast must pay his stake and a fine when his defeat has been decided.

* 6. The plaint is declared to be the essential part of a proceeding-at-law. If he succumbs with it, the defendant loses the whole suit. If he can prove the charge, he gains the suit.

* 7. Gatherings (kula), corporations (*s*re*n*i), assemblies (ga*n*a), one appointed (by the king), and the king (himself), are invested with the power to decide

---

Thus, although the sum in dispute be very considerable, one may stake two hundred Pa*n*as, or a hundred Pa*n*as, or fifty Pa*n*as only.

5. According to Asahâya, the wager must not be laid till the two first stages of the trial, the charge and the answer, are over. The wager may be laid either by the plaintiff or by the defendant. The plaintiff, whose declaration has been refuted by the defendant, stakes a certain sum on the issue of the case. Or the defendant, after having denied the correctness of the charge, stakes a certain sum on the correctness of his own statements, to be proved by the issue of the case. Asahâya does not say to whom the sum staked has to be paid in his opinion. It may be observed that, according to Burmese law, which is an offshoot of the early law of India, ten per cent. of the sum staked should be given to the judge and to the pleaders, and the remainder to the victorious party; see Richardson's Dhammathat, p. 73. Yâg*ñ*avalkya II, 18 (see Mitâksharâ).

6. Yâg*ñ*avalkya II, 8.

7. Kula means an assemblage consisting of a few persons. *S*re*n*i denotes an assemblage of eminent merchants, &c. Ga*n*a denotes a fellowship, such as e.g. the Brahman caste. A. Other commentators take kula to mean a family meeting; *s*re*n*i, a company of artizans; ga*n*a, an assembly of cohabitants. These three stages of private arbitration may be compared to the modern Panchayats of India.

lawsuits; and of these, each succeeding one is superior to the one preceding him in order.

* 8. Judicial procedure has four feet, four bases, four means, it benefits four, reaches four, and produces four results. This has been declared.

* 9. It has eight members, eighteen topics, a hundred branches, three efficient causes, two modes of plaint, two openings, and two issues.

* 10. Virtue, a judicial proceeding, documentary evidence, and an edict from the king are the four feet of a lawsuit. Each following one is superior to the one previously named.

* 11. There virtue is based on truth; a judicial proceeding (rests) on the statements of the witnesses; documentary evidence (rests) on declarations reduced

---

11. Where both parties adhere strictly to truth in their statements, there is virtue or justice clearly enough, judicial procedure, written proof, and a royal edict being quite unnecessary in that case. Where either of the two parties is suspected to have made a false statement, judicial procedure has to be resorted to, which depends on the evidence given by witnesses. Documentary evidence (*k*aritra) is where the statements of witnesses are consulted, written in their own hand, on a leaf, or on birch-bark, or on a strip of rind, or some other writing material. That suit, however, which has been decided by an edict from the king himself, is superior to all the rest, according to the saying, 'What has been decided in a village, goes into the town. What has been decided in the town, goes before the king. What has been decided by the king, though wrongly decided, cannot be tried anew.' A. The term *k*aritra has been rendered in conformity with this interpretation, which is confirmed by the remarks of *K*andes*v*ara on this *s*loka. Other commentators and several MSS. of the Nârada-sm*ri*ti read svîkara*n*e or pra*s*nakara*n*e for pustakara*n*e. These commentators explain the term *k*aritra in conformity with a text of B*ri*haspati, 'Whatever is practised by a man, proper or improper, in accordance with local usage, is termed *k*aritra (custom).'

to writing; an edict (depends) on the pleasure of the king.

*12. Because the four means, of conciliation and the rest, are adopted, it is said to have four means. Because it protects the four orders, therefore it is said to benefit four.

*13. Because it affects criminals, witnesses, the assessors of the court, and the king, to the amount of one quarter each, therefore it is said to reach four.

*14. Because it produces these four, justice, gain, renown, and esteem among men, therefore it is declared to produce four results.

*15. Because it consists of these eight, the king,

---

12. Because a lawsuit is decided by resorting, as the case may be, to any one of the four means of success, viz. conciliation, division, bribery, and force, therefore it is said to have four means. Because it protects or guards the four castes and the four orders, therefore it is said to benefit four. A. The four orders are the four stages in the life of a twice-born man: student, householder, hermit, and ascetic.

13. If unjustly decided, it brings evil on the four persons mentioned in this *s*loka. If justly decided, it confers good on them. A.

15. The several functions of the eight (or ten) 'members' of a judicial proceeding are thus described in a *s*loka attributed to Br*i*haspati. 'The chief judge publishes the sentence. The king passes it. The assessors investigate the facts of the case. The law-book dictates the judgment, i.e. the victory of the one party, and the fine imposed on the other party. Gold and silver serve the purpose of administering ordeals. Water is used for relieving thirst or appeasing hunger. The accountant has to compute the sums. The scribe has to record the proceedings. The attendant must compel the defendant and the witnesses to appear in court, and detain both plaintiff and defendant, if they have given no sureties.' According to Asahâya, the term 'the king's righteous officer' has to be referred to the king's chief judge, and by 'law-

his dutiful officer, the assessors of the court, the law-book, the accountant and scribe, gold, fire, and water; therefore it is said to have eight members.

*16. Recovery of a debt, deposits, partnership, resumption of gift, breach of a contract of service,

*17. Non-payment of wages, sales effected by another than the rightful owner, non-delivery of a sold chattel, rescission of purchase,

*18. Transgression of a compact, boundary disputes, the mutual duties of husband and wife, law of inheritance, heinous offences,

*19. Abuse, assault, games, and miscellaneous, these are (the eighteen titles of law) on account of which (judicial procedure) is said to have eighteen topics.

*20. Their branches amount to one hundred and

---

books' are meant the compositions of Manu, Nârada, Visvarûpa, and others.

16–19. Manu VIII, 4–8.

20–25. The 132 divisions of the eighteen titles of law are stated as follows by Asahâya:—

1. Recovery of a debt.

1. Which debts have to be paid, and which not, &c.; 2. debts (in general); 3. property; 4. means of livelihood of a Brahman in times of distress; 5. modes of proof; 6. lending money at interest; 7. usurers; 8. sureties; 9. pledges; 10. documents; 11. incompetent witnesses; 12. witnesses for the plaintiff; 13. witnesses for the defendant; 14. six cases where witnesses are unnecessary; 15. validity of testimony, how long retained; 16. false witnesses; 17. exhorting the witnesses; 18. valid evidence; 19. invalid evidence; 20. what has to be done, where both witnesses and documents are wanting; 21. ordeal by balance; 22. ordeal by fire; 23. ordeal by water; 24. ordeal by poison; 25. ordeal by sacred libation.

2. Deposits.

1. Nyâsa (common deposits); 2. aupanidhika (sealed deposits);

thirty-two. On account of the multifariousness of human concerns, (a judicial proceeding) is said to have a hundred branches.

21. 'Recovery of a debt' has twenty-five divisions; 'deposits' has six; 'partnership' has three; 'resumption of gift' has four;

---

3. yâkitaka (loans for use); 4. anvâhitaka (deposits for delivery); 5. silpihastagata (bailments with an artizan); 6. pogandadhana (property of a minor).

3. Partnership.

1. The common undertakings of partners in business; 2. sacrifices offered by officiating priests; 3. tolls.

4. Resumption of gift.

1. What may be given; 2. what may not be given; 3. valid gifts; 4. invalid gifts.

5. Breach of a contract of service.

1. Service; 2. impure work; 3. conduct of a student; 4. rules of conduct for an apprentice; 5. rules of conduct for a manager; 6. fifteen sorts of slaves; 7. emancipation from slavery; 8. legal position of a slave; 9. release of a slave by the favour of his master.

6. Non-payment of wages.

1. The wages of servants; 2. cowherds and the rest; 3. fee of a public woman; 4. questions arising in regard to the payment of rent.

7. Sales effected by another than the rightful owner.

1. Sale without ownership; 2. treasure-trove.

8. Non-delivery of a sold chattel.

9. Rescission of purchase.

1. Time; 2. worn clothes; 3. loss on metals (caused by working them); 4. preparing cloth.

10. Transgression of a compact.

11. Boundary disputes.

1. Quarrels regarding a field; 2. quarrels regarding a house; 3. quarrels regarding a garden; 4. quarrels regarding a well; 5.

22. 'Breach of service' consists of nine divisions; 'wages' has four divisions; there are two divisions of 'sales effected by another than the rightful owner;' 'non-delivery of a sold chattel' has a single division only;

23. 'Rescission of purchase' has four divisions; 'transgression of compact' is onefold; 'boundary disputes' is twelvefold; there are twenty divisions in 'mutual duties of husband and wife;'

---

quarrels regarding a sanctuary; 6. quarrels regarding (the boundary of) a village; 7. prohibition to decorate (to cause nuisance in?) a cross-road, &c.; 8. making a dike; 9. waste land; 10. protection of grain; 11. compensation for grain (destroyed by cattle); 12. the foundation (of a householder's existence).

12. Mutual duties of husband and wife.

1. Examination of a man's virile potency; 2. gift of a maiden in marriage; 3. the offence of insulting an officiating priest; 4. the right time for giving a maiden in marriage; 5. the offence of casting a blemish on an unblemished maiden, or suitor; 6. marriage forms; 7. rule regarding incontinent females and other (unchaste women); 8. what constitutes legitimate issue; 9. illicit intercourse; 10. punishment of adultery; 11. incest; 12. intercourse with cattle, and other crimes of this sort; 13. raising issue where there is no husband; 14. the offspring of adulterous intercourse; 15, 16. authorised and unauthorised intercourse of a woman with one not her husband; 17, 18. rule regarding bad wives and husbands; 19. conduct prescribed for a woman whose husband is absent; 20. definition of a rendezvous.

13. Law of inheritance.

1. Definition of heritage; 2. its distribution; 3. indivisible property; 4. what constitutes strîdhana; 5. descent of strîdhana after the death of the proprietress; 6. rules regarding the property of brothers; 7. division of the property between parents and sons; 8. case of a daughter whose father is unknown, &c.; 9. case of a father unauthorised (to raise issue); 10. share of a son suffering from a chronic or agonising disease, or otherwise (incapable of inheriting); 11. division among the sons of a reunited coparcener;

24. 'Law of inheritance' consists of nineteen divisions; 'heinous offences' of twelve; of both 'abuse' and 'assault' there are three divisions;

25. 'Gambling with dice and betting on animals' has a single division; 'miscellaneous' has six divisions. Thus, adding up all these branches (of the principal titles of law), there are one hundred and thirty-two of them.

---

12. management of the property of a deceased or absent brother; 13. work done by one to whom the management of the family property has been entrusted, &c.; 14. decision in the case of a contested partition; 15. enumeration of the divers kinds of sons. [There ought to be nineteen subdivisions of the law of inheritance, instead of fifteen. That number might be obtained by counting each reason of exclusion from inheritance as a separate division.]

14. Heinous offences.

1. What constitutes a heinous offence; 2. punishments ordained for heinous offences; 3. robbery; 4. distinction between articles of inferior, middling, and superior value; 5, 6. the two kinds of robbers; 7. seizure of robbers; 8. granting food or shelter (to thieves), &c.; 9. thieves; 10. punishment of heinous offences and larceny; 11. tracing a thief by the foot-marks; 12. confiscation of the property of thieves or others, when the stolen goods have not been recovered.

15, 16. Abuse and assault.

1. Abuse; 2. assault; 3. punishments ordained for both offences.

17. Gambling with dice, and betting on animals.

18. Miscellaneous.

1. Protection of the (four) castes and (four) orders by the king in person; 2. dignity of a king; 3. maintenance of Brahmans by the king; 4. authorisation from the king to bestow one's property (on Brahmans); 5. description of the various modes of subsistence permitted to a Brahman; 6. eight things worthy of reverence.

It should be noted that Asahâya himself, in the sequel of his commentary, does not adhere strictly to this division, and gives

* 26. Because it proceeds from one of these three motives, carnal desire, wrath, and greed; therefore it is said to have three efficient causes. These are the three sources of lawsuits.

* 27. It is said to have two modes of plaint, because a plaint may be either founded on suspicion or on fact. It is founded on suspicion, when the defendant has been seen to move in bad company. It is founded on fact, when the stolen chattels or the like have come to light.

* 28. Because it is based on the statements of the two litigants, therefore it is said to have two openings. There the accusation is called the plaint; the answer is called the declaration of the defendant.

* 29. Because it may be founded either on truth or on error, therefore it is said to have two issues. Truth is what rests on true facts. Error is what rests on mistake of facts.

30. Ordeals even are rendered nugatory by artful men. Therefore let no mistake be committed in regard to place, time, quantity, and so on.

---

a number of different headings, which will be quoted in the notes to this translation.

27. Supposing that the owner of a lost chattel casts his suspicion on a man who is constantly seen in the company of well-known thieves and other bad characters, or who lives with prostitutes, or is addicted to gambling, if he impeaches that man, it is called a charge founded on suspicion. If a man is impeached, after having been taken with the maner, the stolen goods having been found among his property, it is called a charge founded on fact. In a charge founded on suspicion, the decision must be referred to the gods (i.e. to an ordeal). In a charge founded on fact, the decision rests with the king's judge. A.

29. The issue of a lawsuit, like its beginning, may be twofold. Either a just decision is given, in accordance with fact, or the decision is erroneous. A.

31. There a king who acts justly must neglect error when it is brought forward, and seek truth alone, because prosperity depends on (the practice of) duty.

32. As seven flames rise from fire, even so will seven good things become manifest in a self-restrained king who passes just sentences at trials.

33. Religious merit, gain, fame, esteem among men, reverence on the part of his subjects, conquests, and an everlasting residence in paradise.

34. Therefore let a king, after having seated himself on the judgment seat, be equitable towards all beings, discarding selfish interests and acting the part of (Yama) Vaivasvata, (the judge of the dead).

* 35. Attending to (the dictates of) the law-book and adhering to the opinion of his chief judge, let him try causes in due order, adhibiting great care.

36. The connection (âgama) must be examined

---

31. 'Brought forward,' i.e. stated by the plaintiff. The king shall neglect it, i.e. not accept it as correct. A. Yâ*gñ*avalkya II, 19.

32. The idea that fire is composed of seven rays or flames is derived, no doubt, from the seven rays of the sun-god Sûrya, who is represented down to the present day as riding in a chariot drawn by seven horses.

34. 'Discarding selfish motives,' i. e. free from love or wrath (sine ira et studio). 'The part of Yama,' the king of righteousness, i.e. the distribution of the rewards and punishments due to good and bad actions. A. Yâ*gñ*avalkya II, 1; Vish*n*u III, 92, &c.

35. While consulting the law-book, he should take heed at the same time of whatever is brought forward by the assessors of the court conjointly with the chief judge. He should abide by the opinion delivered by the latter. He should try causes in due order, i.e. so that the four feet of a judicial proceeding follow one another in due succession. A. Manu VIII, 1, 8, 9; Yâ*gñ*avalkya II, 1, &c.

36. Âgama, 'the connection,' i.e. the relation of the case in hand to the entire system of law; 'the title of law,' its appertaining to a subdivision of this or that title of law; its 'cure,' i.e. it must

first of all; then the title of law must be ascertained; thereupon follows the cure; and the decision comes at the end. These are the four parts of a trial.

37. Avoiding carefully the violation of either the sacred law or the dictates of prudence, he should conduct the trial attentively and skilfully.

38. As a huntsman traces the vestiges of wounded deer in a thicket by the drops of blood, even so let him trace justice.

* 39. Where the rules of sacred law and the dictates of prudence are at variance, he must discard the dictates of prudence and follow the rules of sacred law.

40. When it is impossible to act up to the precepts of sacred law, it becomes necessary to adopt a method founded on reasoning, because custom decides everything and overrules the sacred law.

41. Divine law has a subtile nature, and is occult

---

be cured like an illness, by carrying it through the four parts of a judicial proceeding. A.

38. As deer in a thick forest is difficult to catch, even so justice is difficult of attainment. A huntsman traces the game by following up the drops of blood to the spot, though the soil may be covered by thick grass, where the wounded deer is seen by him. Similarly a king, following the course of the lawsuit, traces law to the point where justice shines forth clearly. A. Manu VIII, 44.

39. Yâg*ñ*avalkya II, 21.

40. According to A., this verse inculcates the superiority of custom to written law. Thus both the practice of raising offspring to a deceased or disabled brother, and the remarriage of widows (see twelfth title of law) are specially sanctioned in the sacred law-books. Yet these two customs are opposed to established practice. Therefore subtle ratiocination is required. A. quotes a verse to the effect that the immemorial usages of every province, which have been handed down from generation to generation, can never be overruled by a rule of the sacred law. Vasish*th*a XVI, 4; Gautama XI, 23.

41. 'The visible path' means either ratiocination founded on

and difficult to understand. Therefore (the king) must try causes according to the visible path.

*42. One who has never committed robbery may be charged with robbery. An actual robber, on the other hand, may be acquitted of the charge of robbery. Mâ*nd*avya was tried and declared to be a robber.

*43. In the case of a woman, at night, outside of

---

internal or circumstantial evidence, or it may mean a sound decision. A. Gautama XI, 24.

42. 'Justice has been stated (in 41) to be difficult to attain, because a man may be suspected to be a thief merely on account of stolen chattels being found amongst his property. Thus the great sage Mâ*nd*avya even was reproached with theft by an injudicious king, because, faithful to his vow of silence, he did not make a reply when he was charged with theft. Therefore it is necessary to adhibit great care in discerning righteous men from evil-doers.' A. The history of Mâ*nd*avya is related in the Mahâbhârata I, 4306 foll. A gang of robbers (Dasyus) being pursued by a guard, dropped their booty in the habitation of Mâ*nd*avya the ascetic, and hid themselves in his hermitage. Soon after, their pursuers arrived, and asked Mâ*nd*avya in which direction the robbers had proceeded. The saint made no reply, whereupon the guard took to searching the hermitage, in which they discovered both the robbers and the stolen chattels. The thing looking suspicious, they conducted both the saint and the robbers before the tribunal of the king, who ordered the saint to be tied to a stake. However, though tied to the stake and left without food, the saint remained alive. After some time, the king ordered him to be released, and asked his forgiveness for the ill-usage offered to him.

43. 'In the case of a woman,' i. e. if the lawsuit has been instituted by a wife or daughter; or if it has been decided by a woman. 'At night,' as the night is the proper time for sleeping, and not the proper time for attending to judicial business; for it is obviously impossible to try a cause at night. 'Outside of the village,' means 'in the wood.' A lawsuit, when decided in one of these places (or special circumstances), is not finally decided and settled; the cause has therefore to be tried anew. Such is the meaning of this rule. A.

the village, in the interior of a house, and by enemies; a sentence passed under any one of these various circumstances may be reversed.

*44. Owing to the recondite nature of lawsuits, and the weakness of memory, the answer may be delayed at pleasure in lawsuits relating to a debt or other subject, with a view to ascertain the true facts.

*45. Let him answer at once in charges concerning a cow, landed property, gold, a woman, robbery, abuse, an urgent affair, a heinous offence, or a calumny.

*46. One who tries to right himself in a quarrel, without having given notice to the king, shall be severely punished and his cause must not be heard.

*47. A defendant who absconds when the cause is about to be tried, and he who does not take heed of what (the claimant) says, shall be arrested by the plaintiff until the legal summons has been declared.

*48. Local arrest, temporary arrest, inhibition

---

44. Owing to the recondite nature of lawsuits, and on account of the weakness of men's memory, which renders them unable to remember distinctly any event that has occurred long ago, the defendant in a lawsuit must be allowed sufficient time to prepare his answer. A. Read *rin*âdishu in the text.

45, 46. The first rule constitutes an exception to the preceding one. In the cases here mentioned the answer should be tendered at once. A. Gautama XIII, 40, 41; Yâ*gñ*avalkya II, 12, 16.

48. Local arrest is in this form: 'If you move from this place, the king will arrest you.' Temporary arrest is in this form: 'You must not leave this house for a certain period.' Inhibition from travelling consists of a prohibition not to undertake a journey on which one has determined. Arrest relating to karman is in this form: 'You must not persevere in performing this or that karman (religious ceremony).' Thus according to A. and Vîramitrodaya, p. 55. When placed under arrest of any one out of these four kinds, the person arrested must not break the arrest. Otherwise he will become guilty of an offence against the king. A.

from travelling, and arrest relating to karman; these are the four sorts of arrest. One arrested must not break his arrest.

* 49. One arrested while crossing a river, or in a forest (kântâra), or in a bad country, or during a great calamity, or in another such predicament, commits no fault by breaking his arrest.

[50. Those causes which have been tried in the king's court, (or) by friends, connections, or relations, shall be tried anew, after a fine of twice the original amount (of the sum in dispute) has been imposed.]

* 51. If one arrested at a proper time breaks his arrest, he shall be punished. One who arrests improperly is (equally) liable to punishment.

* 52. One about to marry; one tormented by an illness; one about to offer a sacrifice; one afflicted by a calamity; one accused by another; one employed in the king's service;

---

49. Kântâra, 'a fearful forest,' 'a bad country,' a dangerous place, 'a great calamity,' a public disaster or a heavy affliction and the like. One who breaks an arrest which has been put on him in one of the places or on one of the occasions hitherto mentioned, does not commit a criminal offence by doing so. A.

50. A. observes that this verse, though it ought not to come in here, has been inserted from the original work (of Nârada?). It means, according to him, that both those lawsuits which have been decided by the king in person, and those which have been decided by friends, connections, or relatives, shall be tried anew, in case the double amount of the fine ordained has been paid. Yâ*gñ*avalkya II, 305. Perhaps the word '(or)' had better be omitted.

51. 'A proper time' means 'a suitable time,' i. e. any other time besides the various occasions mentioned in paragraph 45. 'One who arrests improperly,' is either one who arrests on one of the prohibited occasions, or one who arrests without sufficient reason. A.

52. Artizans, i. e. manual labourers, while engaged in their work. A.

* 53. Cowherds engaged in tending cattle; cultivators in the act of cultivation; artizans, while engaged in their own occupations; soldiers, during warfare;

* 54. One who has not yet arrived at years of discretion; a messenger; one about to give alms; one fulfilling a vow; one harassed by difficulties: a person belonging to any of these categories must not be arrested, nor shall the king summon him (before a court of justice).

* 55. One accused of an offence must not lodge a plaint himself, unless he have refuted the charge raised by the other party. Neither (is he allowed to accuse) one who has already been accused by a different party. It is wrong to strike one again who has already been struck (by another).

56. When he has proffered a charge, he must not

53, 54. 'One who has not yet arrived at years of discretion,' i.e. a boy. 'A messenger,' whether employed in the affairs of the king, or by a private person. 'One about to give alms,' at one of the 'Parvan' days (the days of the four changes of the moon). 'One fulfilling a vow,' performing a special religious observance. 'One harassed by difficulties,' i.e. one who has been befallen, at the time being, by a calamity from the king or from fate. All persons in any such situation must not be arrested. A.

55. The defendant, after having been accused by the plaintiff, must not proffer a counter plaint against the plaintiff, without having previously cleared himself of the charge raised against himself, because two different causes cannot be tried at one and the same time. Neither must a new plaint be lodged against one who has already been impeached by another, because one already hit must not be hit again. If a deer has been first hit by one huntsman, and is again hit by another hunter, the effort of the latter is to no purpose. The first huntsman may justly claim the deer, and not the second. A. Yâ*gñ*avalkya II, 9.

56. 'He must not alter the charge,' as e.g. by claiming a larger or a smaller sum afterwards than he had done before If e.g. after

again alter it. He must not recede from his previous claim. By doing so he will lose his suit.

57. He must not lodge a false plaint. He is a sinner who proffers a false charge (against any one). Whatever fine is declared in a suit of this sort has to be paid by the claimant.

58. If a man delays his answer under false pretences, or if he stands mute at the trial, or if he revokes his own former statements: these are the signs by which a loser of his cause may be known.

59. One who absconds after having received the summons, or who does not make any defence after having arrived in court, shall be punished by the king, because his cause is lost.

60. If a man being questioned does not uphold

---

having first claimed, as being his due, a sum amounting to 20 Gadyâ*n*akas of gold, he says afterwards: This man has to give 50 drammas (drachmas) to my son, it is called 'receding from one's first claim and proffering another claim.' A. Yâ*gñ*avalkya II, 9.

58. Delaying one's answer under false pretences is e.g. if a man says, 'I am unwell just now,' or 'I am unclean just now. I make no answer.' Likewise, if a man, after having been asked by the judges, does not speak, or if having made a statement previously he revokes it; by such signs as these a man may be known to have lost his cause. A.

59. He who, after having been summoned by the king, makes off; or who, having decamped and having been seized with difficulty by the king's officers, does not make any reply to the questions put to him, shall be fined by the king, because he loses his suit. A. Manu VIII, 55, 56; Yâ*gñ*avalkya II, 16.

60. If, being questioned by the judges, he does not uphold, i.e. maintain, a statement previously made by himself. A. The commentators of Manu, in commenting on an analogous passage of the Code of Manu (VIII, 54), give the following example. A man has made a certain statement regarding the money in dispute. The judge asks him afterwards, 'Why did you tender or accept the money at night?' The man thereupon does not abide by his own former statement. (See Jolly, translation of the eighth chapter of

a statement duly made by himself (at a former stage of the trial); or if he ends by admitting what had been previously negatived by himself;

61. Or if he is unable to produce any witnesses, after having declared that they are in existence and having been asked to produce them: by all such signs as these persons devoid of virtue may be known.

* 62. When a lawsuit has been decided evidence becomes useless, unless a document or witnesses can be produced who or which had not been announced at a former stage of the trial.

* 63. As the (fertilizing) power of rain is thrown away on ripe grain, even so evidence becomes useless when the suit has been decided.

---

the Code of Manu.) 'He who, after having answered a question in the negative previously, makes an opposite statement afterwards.' The meaning is as follows: He is cast, if, having been interrogated by the judges, 'Can you adduce any witnesses or documents?' he replies at first by saying 'I have none,' and goes on to say 'I have witnesses and documents.' A. The reading seems faulty. See Manu.

61. If a man says he has documents or witnesses, and the judges, having heard this, say to him, 'If you have witnesses, show them,' i. e. exhibit them; if thereupon he does not adduce them, he loses his suit. A. Manu VIII, 57.

62. 'This wicked debtor owes me money. He declines to restore it, though I can prove his obligation to pay me by witnesses and documentary evidence. Therefore I must cite him before the tribunal of the king.' If the claimant says so and does not produce evidence at the time when he proffers his claim, but produces it afterwards, it does not make evidence. If, however, a statement of this kind had been previously made, and the claimant, owing to some unfortunate accident, or to forgetfulness, &c., has merely failed to repeat it at the third stage of the trial (i. e. during the judicial inquiry), it may be renewed, and shall be examined by the judges; although the case had already been decided, and sureties been given and taken. A. Yâg*ñ*avalkya II, 20.

64. False statements even have to be examined if they have been made in due season. That, on the other hand, which has been passed over in silence through inadvertency, fails to produce any result, even though it be true.

* 65. If a man is of opinion that the suit has been decided and punishment declared in a way contrary to justice, he may have the cause tried once more, provided he should pay twice the amount of the fine inflicted.

* 66. If a verdict contrary to justice has been passed, the assessors of the court must pay that fine; because nobody certainly can act as a judge without incurring the risk of being punished (eventually).

67. When a member of a court of justice, actuated by wrath, ignorance, or covetousness, has passed an

---

64. Yâ*gñ*avalkya II, 19.

65. A lawsuit is 'decided' at the time when the judges, after having come to a unanimous agreement about the verdict to be passed on the plaintiff and defendant, give them a written record of their respective victory and defeat. The 'punishment has been declared' when the judges, after passing the verdict, dictate a certain punishment, in accordance with the comparative heaviness or lightness of the offence committed. In both cases, if a man considers himself to have lost his cause through an unjust sentence, he may have the cause tried anew, if he pledges himself to pay twice the amount of the fine to the king's judge. A. Yâ*gñ*avalkya II, 305.

66. 'Where an unjust sentence has been passed, the blame attaches to the assessors of the court. Therefore they have to pay that fine.' A. Yâ*gñ*avalkya II, 4.

67. 'Wrath' is when he bears him an old grudge. 'Ignorance' means folly. That is done 'through covetousness' which is done in consideration of a bribe. 'He who passes an unjust sentence,' i.e. who says what is opposed to justice. Such an assessor has to be considered as 'no assessor of the court,' i.e. he is unworthy to sit in the court. A.

unjust sentence, he shall be declared unworthy to be a member of the court, and the king shall punish him for his offence.

* 68. That king, however, who is intent on doing his duty, must be particularly anxious to discover what is right and what is wrong, because there is a variety of dispositions among mankind.

69. There are some who give false evidence from covetousness. There are other villainous wretches who resort to forging documentary evidence.

70. Therefore both (sorts of evidence) must be tested by the king with great care: documents, according to the rules regarding writings; witnesses, according to the law of witnesses.

* 71. Liars may have the appearance of veracious men, and veracious men may resemble liars. There are many different characters. Therefore it is necessary to examine (everything).

* 72. The firmament has the appearance of a flat surface, and the fire-fly looks like fire. Yet there is no surface to the sky, nor fire in the fire-fly.

* 73. Therefore it is proper to investigate a matter, even though it should have happened before one's own eyes. One who does not deliver his opinion till he has investigated the matter will not violate justice.

---

68. The two following paragraphs show what is meant by 'the diversity of men's minds.' A.

72. As the sky has the appearance of a level plain like the earth, yet there is nothing like earth about it; and as there is no fire in the fire-fly, although it sparks like fire; even so the utterances of men are often untrue, though they may have the appearance of true statements. Therefore it is necessary to examine strictly even what a man professes to have seen with his own eyes. A.

* 74. Thus a king, constantly trying lawsuits with attention, will acquire widespread and brilliant renown in this life and the abode of Indra after his death.

II. The Plaint.

1. The claimant, after having produced a pledge the value of which has been well ascertained, shall cause the plaint to be written. (He must have been impelled) to proffer his claim, by the nature of the claim, and must be intent on promoting the victory of his cause.

* 2. The defendant (creditor), immediately after having become acquainted with the tenour of the plaint, shall write down his answer, which must correspond to the tenour of the plaint.

* 3. Or let him (the defendant) deliver his answer on the next day, or three days, or seven days later.

II, 1. The term suniskitabalâdhânas, which has been taken to mean 'after having produced a pledge the value (or competence) of which has been well ascertained,' is by no means clear, and admits of several different interpretations. Thus it might be rendered, 'after having carefully explored the nature of the wrong offered to him.' A. does not explain this obscure term 'Impelled by the nature of his claim;' not by the king, or by an enemy, but merely by his own cause. 'Intent on promoting the victory of his cause,' i.e. absolutely determined not to embark in any other undertaking, previous to having gained his cause. A.

2. The creditor is called plaintiff. The debtor is called defendant. The defendant, after having heard the tenour of the plaint which has been tendered in writing by the plaintiff, shall write an answer, i.e. make a reply, which corresponds to the tenour of the plaint. A. Read pratyarthî in the text.

3. The defendant may tender his written answer on the next day, or three days, or seven days after he has heard the accusation. The plaintiff, on the other hand, is not allowed any time to reply to the statements of the defendant. His victory (or defeat) is

The plaintiff no doubt duly obtains his victory at once, when the trial has reached the third stage (the examination of the evidence).

* 4. An answer is fourfold ; a denial, a confession, a special plea, and that which is based on a plea of former judgment.

* 5. A denial is fourfold (being couched in any one out of the four forms hereafter mentioned). 'This is false,' or 'I do not know anything about it,' or 'I was not present at the transaction,' or 'I was not in existence at the time when this event took place.'

6. A contradiction, the reverse, a retort, and a friendly counsel; in one out of these four forms should the answer be given, and it should be in conformity with the tenour of the plaint.

* 7. Before the answer to the plaint has been tendered by the defendant, the plaintiff may amend his own statements as much as he desires.

---

decided at once, by examining the proofs that have been adduced. A. Yâ*gñ*avalkya II, 7.

4. A special plea is when the defendant admits a fact, but qualifies or explains it so as not to allow it to be matter of accusation. A plea of former judgment is when the defendant pleads that the very same cause has been previously tried at the tribunal of this or that judge, and that his adversary has been cast. A.

6. This paragraph, says A., occurs in the original work, and has therefore been inserted in this place, though it is difficult of explanation and a mere paraphrase of the preceding paragraph. It has been rendered in accordance with his interpretation. 'The reverse' means confession. 'A retort' means a special plea. 'A friendly counsel' means plea of former judgment. A.

7. The plaintiff may go on altering and improving his written declaration, till the defendant gives in his answer. When, however, the plaint has been answered, he is no longer at liberty to make any further amendments. A.

* 8. These are called the defects of a plaint: (1) if it relates to a different subject; (2) if it is unmeaning; (3) if the amount (of the sum claimed) has not been properly stated; (4) if it is wanting in propriety; (5) if the writing is deficient; (6) or redundant; (7) if it has been damaged.

9. By whomsoever a claim is raised, whatever and from whomsoever it may have been claimed: from that very person must the claimant receive that very thing, and it must not be (claimed) mutually, or (claimed) from a stranger. Thus 'a claim relating to a different subject' may be of three kinds.

10. Thy friend here has thought in his mind, that I am his enemy. On account of this great intolerance I have impeached thee here.

11. If he omits to state the amount of the thing (claimed), and forgets to aim at brevity(?): this fault of a plaint is called omission of the amount (claimed), and it should be avoided.

12. Let him avoid improper statements in the plaint (e.g. an accusation which is raised) by a plurality of persons against one single-handed; or

---

8. A. does not explain the rather obscure terms occurring in several of the following paragraphs. He confines himself to stating that they contain an accurate definition of the 'seven defects of a plaint,' as enumerated in paragraph 8, to which the defect described in paragraphs 15, 16 has to be added as an eighth.

9. The three kinds of 'a claim relating to a different subject' appear, therefore, to be these: where it proceeds from a different person than the creditor; where the amount of the sum claimed has not been stated correctly; and where the plaint has been addressed to a wrong person.

10. This is an instance of an unmeaning or frivolous accusation. A.

11. The reading of this paragraph is uncertain.

(a cause which) is opposed to (the interests of) the city or kingdom (in which he lives).

13. A plaint in which a mere dot is omitted, or where a word or a syllable has been obliterated, or where too little or too much has been written, or which is absurd; such a plaint should be carefully avoided.

14. He should (equally) avoid a plaint which has been destroyed or damaged (by an accident), or which has been soiled by water, oil, or other (liquids), even though the purport and meaning of the plaint be quite plain.

*15. A plaint, though otherwise established, is not correct, if it is contrary to established law and usage.

16. A claim which is proffered in this form—'I gave this to him while he was in a state of intoxication with fragrance (through a smell of perfume)'—cannot succeed, because it is contrary to established usage.

*17. Where different words are (subsequently) inserted (in the plaint), and where the sense becomes different (in consequence), there the judicial investigation becomes confused, and the evidence itself is thrown into confusion.

*18. When the claimant, in a passion, and actuated

17. A. illustrates this rule by the following example. The claimant has claimed a certain sum. At the time of the trial he names a larger sum than he did before. Thus the judicial investigation becomes confused.

18. If a man actuated by one of the three passions, sexual desire, wrath, and covetousness, mentions some special (important) circumstance at the trial, the scribe shall enter it at once in writing on a board, or leaf, or Bhûrga-bark, or box, or wall. A. This rule seems to relate to incidental statements, which escape one of the parties through inadvertency. Thus in the well-known drama M*rikkh*aka*t*ikâ, the wicked prince Sa*m*sthânaka, when informing the

by one of the immoral motives, such as partiality, makes some special statement, it shall at once be completely reduced to writing on a board or other (writing material).

19. Other statements than those (taken down at first) regarding the plaintiff on a board or other (writing material) shall be removed, after careful consideration, by persons versed in law, (when reporting on the trial) for the information of the king's judge.

20. Let such persons reduce to writing the statements of each party, and whatever else has been written on the board, together with the names of the

---

judge that Vasantasenâ has been murdered, adds, 'not by myself.' The judge pounces upon the latter statement, suspicious as it looks, and causes the scribe to put it down in writing on the floor. The prince, perceiving that he has committed himself, effaces the writing with his foot. The custom of writing the statements of the parties on the floor is repeatedly referred to in the Indian dramas. From what B*ri*haspati says, it would seem that in the time of this law-writer the statements of the parties had first to be written on a board, and then on a leaf, after all the required corrections had been entered. Nârada seems to refer to the same custom in paragraphs 19 and 20.

According to Dr. Burnell, the boards referred to in the law-books must have been a sort of black wooden boards. See Burnell, South Indian Palæography, 2nd ed., p. 87.

20. In translating this paragraph, the obscurity of which is only surpassed by the preceding paragraph, I have deviated from the interpretation proposed by the commentator.

A. takes this paragraph as containing four independent clauses: 1. what has been stated or admitted by both parties; 2. whatever else has been written on the board; 3. the depositions of the witnesses; 4. what each party has conceded to the other. These four things should be reduced to writing by the persons entrusted with the judicial investigation. 'Whatever else has been written on the board,' i. e. whatever the plaintiff amends or adds, while the plaint is being reduced to writing. Such statements, as shown in the next paragraph, are called Pratyâkalita.

witnesses, as well as those statements in which both parties concur.

21. Additional statements of the plaintiff (or defendant), which are not contained in the writings of both parties, shall be (subsequently) entered into his (their) declaration. They are called Pratyâkalita ('what is interposed').

* 22. If one deputed by the claimant, or chosen as his representative by the defendant, speaks for his client in court, the victory or defeat concerns the party (himself and not the representative).

* 23. He deserves punishment who speaks in behalf of another, without being either the brother, the father, the son, or the appointed agent; and so does he who contradicts himself at the trial.

* 24. He who forsakes his original claim and produces a new one, loses his suit, because he confounds two plaints with one another.

* 25. A verbal error does not annul the claim in

---

21. A. infers from the use of the term 'both parties' that a Pratyâkalita statement may proceed from the defendant as well as from the plaintiff, though the plaintiff alone is specially mentioned. A. adds that this rule applies equally to all those kinds of statements, which are mentioned in paragraph 20.

22. This rule applies equally where a party is prevented from appearing before the court by illness, and where the party is not a good speaker, and has appointed an agent or attorney for that reason. A.

23. This prohibition relates to those who, from love, anger, or avarice, meddle with the affairs of strangers, and pretend to act in their behalf at court. A.

24. If a claimant, on finding himself unable to prove his claim at the trial, proffers a different claim, he must be pronounced the losing party, on account of the confusion caused by him. A.

25. An erroneous statement does not necessarily cause the defeat

actions of any kind. So if the case relates to cattle, or to a woman, or to land, or to a debt, he is liable to punishment, but his claim is not annulled.

26. Where the defendant denies the charge, the claimant has to prove his accusation, unless the denial should have been in the form called Pratyavaskandana.

* 27. What the claimant has fully declared word for word in the plaint that he must substantiate by adducing evidence at the third stage of the trial.

* 28. Proof is said to be of two kinds, human and divine. Human proof consists of documentary and oral evidence. By divine proof is meant the ordeal by balance and the other (modes of divine test).

29. Where a transaction has taken place by day,

---

of the plaintiff. This is particularly the case in one of the following important actions: a case relating to a cow, female buffalo, or other cattle; a case relating to a woman; a case relating to landed property, i.e. a house, field, &c.; and a case relating to one of the twenty-five subdivisions of the law of debt. In any case he is not defeated, merely on account of an erroneous statement contained in the suit. He does not lose the suit instituted by him, though he is liable to punishment. A. The Mitâksharâ (p. 23) has a long gloss on this rule of Nârada, from which it appears that the 'erroneous statements' here referred to are statements made through inadvertency, and that this rule applies to civil, as opposed to criminal actions. Read vâk*kh*ale in the Sanskrit text.

26. An answer in the form called Pratyavaskandana is where the defendant admits the facts adduced by the plaintiff, but explains them so as not to be matter of accusation.

27. The claimant must prove, at the judicial investigation, whatever he has committed to writing in the plaint. A.

29. The divers kinds of divine test will be declared below. In the case of all those transactions which take place during day-time eye- and ear-witnesses are present. Documentary evidence, likewise, is generally available in such cases. Therefore, divine proof should not be resorted to. Where a transaction is known to have

in a village or town, or in the presence of witnesses, divine test is not applicable.

* 30. Divine test is applicable (where the transaction has taken place) in a solitary forest, at night, or in the interior of a house, and in cases of violence, or of denial of a deposit.

31. Where the defendant has evaded the plaint by means of a special plea, it becomes incumbent on him to prove his assertion, and he is placed in the position of a claimant.

* 32. One who takes to flight after having received the summons; one who remains silent; one who is convicted (of untruth) by (the deposition of) the witnesses; and one who makes a confession himself: these are the four kinds of Avasannas (losers of their suit).

* 33. One who alters his former statements; one

---

taken place in the presence of witnesses, divine proof is also not applicable. A.

30. In all the places and occasions mentioned in this paragraph human proof is not applicable, wherefore divine test has to be resorted to. A.

31. Where the defendant has recourse to the mode of defence called Pratyavaskandana, i.e. where he admits the charge, but adduces a special circumstance to exonerate himself, the plaint becomes purposeless. To the defendant, however, belongs the onus probandi in regard to the special circumstance mentioned by him. He is, therefore, reduced to the position of a claimant, in that it is incumbent on him to prove his assertion at the time of the judicial investigation (kriyâ). A.

32. One who, though summoned by the king's officers, absconds through fear of the accusation brought against him; one who stands mute in the assembly when he is asked to make his declaration; one who is cast by the depositions of the witnesses; and one who confesses to be in the wrong himself: these four persons are non-suited. A. Yâgñavalkya II, 16; Manu VIII, 55–58.

33. Two out of the four 'losers of their suit,' who are referred

who shuns the judicial investigation; one who does not make his appearance (before the tribunal); one who makes no reply; and one who absconds after receiving the summons: these five kinds of persons are called Hîna (cast in their present suit).

34. Precious stones, such as rubies, golden ornaments, such as Dînâras, pearls, coral, shells, and other (jewels and precious metals) shall be returned

---

to in the preceding paragraph, may be said to have lost their cause for once and all, viz. one who is convicted of untruth by the deposition of the witnesses, and one who confesses his wrong himself. The two others, viz. one who remains silent and one who absconds, are liable to punishment, but they do not entirely lose their suit, as their cause may be tried anew. Similarly, the five persons mentioned in par. 33, though non-suited in the case in hand, may have their cause tried anew. 'One who alters his statements,' i.e. one who, from forgetfulness, says something different from what he had stated before. 'One who shuns the judicial investigation,' i.e. one who, from repugnance against judicial investigation, throws the proceedings into confusion. 'One who does not make his appearance before the tribunal,' i.e. on account of a calamity which has befallen him through the king or through fate, &c. 'One who makes no reply,' i.e. one who does not give in his answer at once, and asks for delay to prepare it. 'One who absconds' from fear of an enemy. A. This interpretation has evidently been called forth by a desire to reconcile par. 33 with the preceding paragraph, as the persons called Hîna are partly identical with those designed as Avasannas. It may be doubted, however, whether par. 32 belongs to the original work of Nârada, as the identical rule is elsewhere attributed to B*ri*haspati (see Vîram., p. 102), and as it is certainly difficult to reconcile the two paragraphs with one another.

34. If the owner of the articles mentioned in this rule sells them for genuine, and the purchaser, putting belief in his statements, accepts them as such, and pays for them, but finds out afterwards that they are not genuine, the seller must take them back, and must give other articles in exchange for them which are really valuable, or he must make good their value to the purchaser. A. As for the meaning of the term Dînâra, which corresponds to the Latin denarius, see the Introduction.

to their owner, in case they turn out to be imitations only.

35. If a man seizes perfumes, or garlands—other than those which have been given to him—or ornaments, or clothes, or shoes, which belong to the king, he deserves to be corporally punished.

* 36. The price or value of a commodity, wages, a deposit, a fine, what has been abandoned (by one and found by another), what has been idly promised, and what has been won at play; none of these articles yields interest, except under a special agreement to the purpose.

37. Men of the *S*ûdra caste, who proffer a false accusation against a member of a twice-born (Aryan) caste, shall have their tongue slit by (the officers of) the king, and he shall cause them to be put on stakes.

38. A royal edict, a (private) document, a written

35. One who, from pride, seizes (or uses) one of the above articles, shall be corporally punished, if they belong to the king. A. The reading of this paragraph is quite uncertain.

36. 'The price of a commodity,' the price paid for a saleable commodity which has been sold. 'A deposit,' a trust. 'A fine,' an amercement which has been inflicted by the king's judges. 'What has been abandoned,' what has been seized after its dereliction (by the original owner). 'What has been idly promised' to bards or other worthless persons.

37. If the *S*ûdras, by whom this crime has been committed, are punished by the king, he becomes free from blame. Otherwise, the blame falls on him, as it is his duty to reward the honest, and to punish evil-doers. A.

38: The divers forms in which a plaint is instituted in each of these several cases (excepting a single case, a transaction of sale) are stated as follows by A.: '1. This man has not taken notice of a certain royal edict. 2. This man has (unduly) availed himself of a certain document relating to its owner. 3. This man, by virtue of a certain written title, has appropriated a slave girl belonging to

title, a grant, a pledge, a (promise reduced to) writing, a sale, or purchase: one who brings a claim in regard to any one of these before the king is known as defendant among those conversant with the rules (of legal pleading).

* 39. Where the deposition of the witnesses has been objected to, it becomes necessary first of all to clear the witnesses from suspicion. When the witnesses themselves have been cleared from suspicion, he may undertake to remove the doubts which have been raised against their deposition.

* 40. When a man has lost his cause through the dishonesty of witnesses or judges, the cause may be tried anew. When, however, a man has been cast through his own conduct, the trial cannot be renewed.

41. One convicted by his own confession, one

---

myself. 4. This man raises the revenue of a certain village which has been granted to myself. The grant relates to myself only. 5. This property has first been pledged to me by the debtor. How can any one else enjoy it? 6. Why does not this man deliver this chattel to me, which has been promised to me in writing? 7. I have purchased this commodity from him, and paid for it. He does not make the commodity over to me.'—Read âgñâ.

39. Where the defendant raises groundless objections against the trustworthiness of the depositions of witnesses, he is liable to punishment, like one who shuns the judicial investigation, and loses his suit in consequence. After the witnesses have been cleared from suspicion, their statements have to be examined in order to remove what looks suspicious in them. A.

40. Those who have lost their cause, either through the statements of their own witnesses, or through the decision of the judges, may have their cause tried anew, according to a rule previously laid down. If, however, a man has been convicted by his own conduct, or if the witnesses adduced by him should turn out to have been corrupted by him, the case cannot again be opened. A.

41. 1. One who pleads guilty; 2. one convicted by his own

cast through his own conduct, and one whom the judicial investigation has proved to be in the wrong: (these three) deserve to have their final defeat declared at the hand of the judges.

42. Whenever the (false) assertions have been removed, the judges shall pass a decree. If they pass a judgment, before the false statements have been removed, they will cause evil in the next world and in this.

43. One condemned by the judges shall be punished by the king according to law. The victorious party shall receive a document recording his victory, and couched in appropriate language.

44. This has been formerly declared by the self-existent Being to be the mouth of a lawsuit. If the mouth of a lawsuit is in order, the whole suit is in order, but not otherwise.

---

conduct, as e.g. by adducing false witnesses or forged documents; 3. one convicted by the witnesses: those three shall not be punished till they have been condemned by the judges. A.

42. When the time for passing a decree has arrived, the judges shall carefully remove all mere assertions of either party. Should they omit to do so, they would be in danger of condemning an innocent man, and might produce evil in this world by causing loss of money, and in the next world by barring the way to paradise to themselves, as it is the duty of kings to restrain evil-doers and to protect the righteous. A.

43. According to B*ri*haspati, the document of victory which has to be given to the victorious party shall contain an accurate record of the plaint, of the answer, and of the judicial investigation.

44. The general rules regarding judicial proceedings, which have been laid down in the preceding section, are declared to be the mouth of a lawsuit, because they are applicable to the trial of every suit. 'The self-existent Being,' i.e. Brahman. A.

III. Courts of Justice.

* 1. One who has not been authorized must not speak on any account at the trial. But authorized persons must deliver their opinion in an unbiassed spirit.

* 2. Whether unauthorized or authorized, one acquainted with the law shall give his opinion. He passes a divine sentence who acts up to the dictates of law.

3. If he delivers a fair opinion, a member of the court will incur neither hatred nor sin. But if he speaks otherwise he at once incurs both.

* 4. Let the king appoint, as members of a court

III, 1. Courts of justice are generally thronged by a large attendance. Some of the persons present are intelligent, others are not, and others are wise in their own estimation only. Such persons, if unrestrained, would disturb the judges by interpreting idle speeches between the legal proceedings, and by quarrelling amongst themselves. Therefore, the first half of this paragraph relates to the punishment ordained for those who speak without authorization. Authorized persons, i.e. the judges who sit on the seat of judgment, shall strive to be just, i.e. they shall deliver a judgment in accordance with justice, and shall not show partiality for either of the parties. A.

2. Where all the assessors of the court pass an unjust sentence, from ignorance of the law, or from interested motives, there a Brahman versed in the sacred law and acquainted with legal proceedings, who happens to be present, shall point out the law to them, and restrain the judges from their sinful course. He shall speak, though he has not been appointed to deliver judgment. Law is called the voice of the deity. A.

3. That is called 'a fair opinion' which is not contrary to written law and to custom. A judge who delivers a sentence of this kind incurs neither enmity nor sin, i.e. he does not become unhappy either in this world or in the next. A.

4. As young bulls are able to carry a heavy burden, even so

of justice, honourable men, of tried integrity, who are able to bear, like good bulls, the burden of the administration of justice.

* 5. The members of a royal court of justice must be acquainted with the sacred law and with rules of prudence, noble, veracious, and impartial towards friend and foe.

6. Justice is said to depend on them, and the king is the fountain head of justice. Therefore the king should try causes properly, attended by good assessors.

7. When lawsuits are decided properly, the members of the court are cleared from guilt. Their purity depends on the justice (of the sentences passed by them). Therefore one must deliver a fair judgment.

8. Where justice is slain by injustice, and truth by falsehood, the members of the court, who look on with indifference, are doomed to destruction themselves.

---

competent judges are able to discharge the onerous duties of their responsible office. They must be men of ripe wisdom, acquainted with sacred law and with the ways of the world, and the king must have tested their qualifications. A. Vish*n*u III, 74, &c.

5. The law-books contain many utterances of the sages, which are obscure and difficult to make out. Therefore slow-minded persons, who are unable to understand them, and to refer their contents to each case in hand, must not be appointed. Well-descended persons shall be appointed, because they will avoid partiality from family pride. 'Veracious' persons have a natural abhorrence against untruthfulness. Ạ. Yâ*gñ*avalkya II, 2.

6. 'On them,' i.e. on the judges, whose qualities have been previously described. A. Vish*n*u III, 72; Manu VIII, 1; Yâ*gñ*avalkya II, 1, &c.

7. If the king decides lawsuits justly, the assessors obtain their own absolution through the just decision. A.

8. Identical with Manu VIII, 14.

9. Where justice, having been hit by injustice, enters a court of justice, and the members of the court do not extract the dart from the wound, they are hit by it themselves.

10. Either the judicial assembly must not be entered at all, or a fair opinion delivered. That man who either stands mute or delivers an opinion contrary to justice is a sinner.

11. Those members of a court who, after having entered it, sit mute and meditative, and do not speak when the occasion arises, are liars all of them.

* 12. One quarter of the iniquity goes to the offender; one quarter goes to the witness; one quarter goes to all the members of the court; one quarter goes to the king.

13. The king is freed from responsibility, the

---

9. Virtue is here compared to one wounded with a weapon, who goes to a physician in order to be cured by him. The judges are compared to physicians who, by means of a careful judicial investigation, deliver justice from the attacks of iniquity. If they do not extract the dart of iniquity, they are killed themselves by the dart of iniquity, which has been spared by them. A. Nearly identical with Manu VIII, 12.

10. Either the judicial assembly must not be entered at all, not even a single time, or an opinion conformable to justice must be delivered. A judge who remains silent, or who, when asked to pass a sentence, says what is contrary to justice, is criminal, i. e. a great sinner. A. Nearly identical with Manu VIII, 13.

11. Those judges who sit mute in the judicial assembly, being apparently engaged in meditating over an altogether different affair than that for which the parties have appeared before the tribunal, and who fail to declare at the proper time the victory of the one party and the defeat of the other, all such persons shall be looked upon by the king as equally criminal with those who pass a false sentence. A.

12, 13. These two paragraphs belong together. If the judges

members of the court obtain their absolution, and the guilt goes to the offender, when the guilty person is punished.

14. He who, having entered the court, delivers a strange opinion, ignoring the true state of the case, resembles a blind man who regardless swallows fish together with the bones.

15. Therefore let every assessor of the court deliver a fair opinion after having entered the court, discarding love and hatred, in order that he may not go to hell.

* 16. As an experienced surgeon extracts a dart by means of surgical instruments, even so the chief

---

were to acquit the criminal, and unjustly to condemn the innocent party, the iniquity or sinful action committed by the unjust decree would go into four parts, i. e. a quarter of it would go respectively to the shares of the perpetrator of the deed, of the witnesses, of all the assessors of the court, and of the king. If, however, the guilty person alone is condemned, i.e. if the criminal party loses his cause, the king becomes free from guilt, the judges are free from responsibility, and the whole guilt falls on the perpetrator of the iniquitous deed. A. Medhâtithi, in commenting on the identical rule of Manu (VIII, 18), observes that the guilt goes to the king, in case the sentence had been passed by him in person. Otherwise it goes to his chief judge. Identical with Manu VIII, 18, 19, &c.

14. One whose eyesight is unimpaired, does not eat fish without having previously removed the bones, which would injure his mouth, his tongue, and his palate. A blind man, on the contrary, eats fish together with the bones, because he is unable to remove them. The case is similar with the eye of knowledge. A.

15. Considering all this, let a judge, after having entered the court of judicature, reject every kind of bias, and deliver a fair, i.e. an impartial opinion, in order that he may not go to hell burdened with the crime of a guilty person (acquitted by him). A.

16. As a skilful surgeon conversant with the art of extracting a dart, extracts it, though it may be difficult to get at and invisible, by the application of surgical instruments, of spells, and other manifold artful practices, even so a judge shall extract the dart of

judge must extract the dart (of iniquity) from the lawsuit.

* 17. When the whole aggregate of the members of a judicial assembly declare, 'This is right,' the lawsuit loses the dart, otherwise the dart remains in it.

18. That is not a judicial assembly where there are no elders. They are not elders who do not pass a just sentence. That is not a just sentence in which there is no truth. That is not truth which is vitiated by error.

---

iniquity which has entered a lawsuit, by employing the artful expedients of judicial investigation. A.

17. 'The members of a judicial assembly' are those who have come together for the trial of a cause. A.

18. This paragraph, in the original, is a verse composed in the Trish*t*ubh metre, and has the look of an old versus memorialis. Though the author of the Nârada-sm*ri*ti has incorporated it in his work, its contents do not quite fit in with his own ideas regarding the constitution of a judicial assembly, and the prominent place which he assigns to the chief judge of the king.

FIRST TITLE OF LAW.

THE LAW OF DEBT.

1. Payment of a Debt.

* 1. Which debts must be paid, which other debts must not be paid; by whom, and in what form (they must be paid); and the rules of gift and receipt, (all that) is comprised under the title of 'Recovery of a Debt.'

* 2. The father being dead, it is incumbent on the sons to pay his debt, each according to his share (of the inheritance), in case they are divided in interests. Or, if they are not divided in interests, the debt must

---

The twenty-five sections into which the law of debt has been divided in this translation correspond in the main, though not throughout, to the headings proposed by Asahâya in different portions of his work. Asahâya, as pointed out before, is not consistent with himself in this respect. It is curious to note that the whole law of evidence, excepting the general rules laid down in the preceding chapters, has been inserted by Nârada between the divers rules of the law of debt. He seems to have followed in this respect, as in other particulars, the example set to him by the earlier legislators, such as Manu and Yâ*g*ñavalkya.

I, 1, 2. If a debt contracted by the father has not been repaid during his lifetime, by himself, it must be restored, after his death, by his sons. Should they separate, they shall repay it according to their respective shares. If they remain united, they shall pay it in common, or the manager shall pay it for the rest, no matter whether he may be the senior of the family or a younger member, who, during the absence of the oldest, or on account of his incapacity, has undertaken the management of the family estate. A.

be discharged by that son who becomes manager of the family estate.

* 3. That debt which has been contracted by an undivided paternal uncle, brother, or mother, for the benefit of the household, must be discharged wholly by the heirs.

* 4. If a debt has been legitimately inherited by the sons, and left unpaid by them, such debt of the grandfather must be discharged by his grandsons. The liability for it does not include the fourth in descent.

* 5. Fathers wish to have sons on their own account, thinking in their minds, 'He will release me from all obligations towards superior and inferior beings.'

---

3. A debt contracted for the household, by an unseparated paternal uncle or brother, or by the mother, must be paid by all the heirs. If they are separate in affairs they must pay for it according to their shares. If they live in union of interests, they must repay it in common. A.

2, 3. Manu VIII, 166; Vish*n*u VI, 27, 35, 36; Yâg*ñ*avalkya II, 45, 50.

4. A. proposes an explanation of this paragraph which is not in accordance with its literal meaning, and decidedly opposed to the principles of a sound method of interpretation. He says that the term 'grandsons' must be taken to relate to the grandsons of the debtor's sons, i.e. to the great-grandsons of the debtor, and that the term 'the fourth descendant' signifies the fourth in descent from the debtor's sons, i.e. the fifth in descent from the debtor himself. This assumption, he says, is necessary in order to reconcile the present rule with the statements of all other legislators, and with Nârada's own rule (par. 6). Vish*n*u VI, 27, 28; Yâg*ñ*avalkya II, 50.

5. A. uses this paragraph in support of his theory that the obligation to pay the debts of an ancestor extends to the fourth in descent. As the great-grandson has to discharge 'the debt to superior beings,' i.e. as he has to offer the customary *S*râddhas to his great-grandfather, so he is liable for debts contracted by him, which have not been repaid.

6. Three deceased (ancestors) must be worshipped, three must be reverenced before the rest. These

6. Three deceased ancestors, i.e. the father, grandfather, and great-grandfather, may claim the discharge of their terrestrial and celestial liabilities from the fourth in descent. This rule is illustrated by the history of an action which was brought before a court in Patna. A merchant of the Brahman caste, by the name of *S*rîdhara, had lent the whole of his wealth, consisting of 10,000 drammas (drachmas), which he had gained through great labour, to a trader, by the name of Devadhara, on condition that interest amounting to two per cent. per mensem of the principal stock should be paid to him. The interest was duly paid to *S*rîdhara at the end of the first month. In the second month, however, Devadhara met his death through an accident. His son died of an attack of cholera. Devadhara's great-grandson alone was left. His name was Mahîdhara. As he was addicted to licentious courses, the management of the estate was undertaken by his sons and maternal uncles. They got into the hands of a cunning Brahman called Smârtadurdhara, who advised them not to pay a single rupee to *S*rîdhara, as he was able to prove from the law-books that he had no claim to the money. The uncles of Mahîdhara, much pleased with this piece of advice, promised to give 1,000 drammas to the Brahman if they need not pay the money to *S*rîdhara. Thus, when at the close of the second month, the uncles and guardians of Devadhara's great-grandson, Mahîdhara, were asked by *S*rîdhara to pay 200 drammas, being the amount of interest due on the sum lent to Devadhara, they refused payment. They said: 'We do not owe you the principal, much less any amount of interest. The Brahman Smârtadurdhara has pointed out to us that the obligation to pay stops with the fourth in descent.' *S*rîdhara was struck dumb with grief and terror on hearing this announcement made to him. When he had regained his senses, he repaired to the court of justice, attended by his family, friends, and servants, and impeached Mahîdhara, together with his uncles, for their dishonesty. Both parties took sureties. The uncles of Mahîdhara engaged Smârtadurdhara to plead for them. After pretending his clients to be connected with his family by a friendship of long standing, he went on to refer to a text of Nârada (above, par. 4), as proving that the obligation to pay the debts of ancestors stops with the fourth in descent. All his arguments, however, were refuted, and held out to derision by a learned

three ancestors of a man may claim the discharge of their twofold debt from the fourth in descent.

* 7. If a man fails to pay on demand what had been borrowed or promised by him, that sum (together with the interest) goes on growing till it amounts to a hundred krores (= one milliard).

* 8. A hundred krores having been completed, he is born again, in every successive existence, in his (creditor's) house as his slave, in order to repay the debt (by his labour).

* 9. If an ascetic or an Agnihotrî dies without

Brahman, by the name of Smârta*s*ekhara, who, at the end of his address, charged him openly with having taken a bribe from his clients. The consequence was that Mahîdhara and his uncles lost their cause. A. I have quoted this story in full, because it presents a vivid picture of the way in which judicial proceedings used to be transacted in ancient India. The doctrine which the story is intended to illustrate, viz. that the liability to pay debts contracted by an ancestor extends to the great-grandson, is opposed to the teaching of such an eminent authority as Vi*gñ*âne*s*vara, who maintains in the Mitâksharâ that the great-grandson is not liable for debts contracted by his great-grandfather, and, conversely, that he does not inherit his property. See the author's Tagore Law Lectures (Calcutta, 1885). The same opinion was apparently held by the author of the Nârada-sm*ri*ti, as may be gathered from par. 4, and by other Sm*ri*ti writers. It appears quite probable that the present paragraph, which is not quoted in any of the standard compilations on civil law, may have been inserted by the author of the commentary, who wanted to make the contents of the Nârada-sm*ri*ti agree with his personal views. The shorter recension and the quotations, instead of the present paragraph, exhibit another paragraph, in which the obligation of the son only to release his father from debt is inculcated.

7. This paragraph has been translated according to the explanation given in Vîramitrodaya, p. 358.

9. The ample heavenly reward due to an Agnihotrî, i.e. one who has kept the three sacred fires from the date of his birth, or who has practised austerities without interruption, shall belong to the creditor, and not to the debtor. A.

having discharged his debt, the whole merit collected by his austerities and by his Agnihotra belongs to his creditors.

* 10. A father must not pay the debt of his son, but a son must pay a debt contracted by his father, excepting those debts which have been contracted from love, anger, for spirituous liquor, games, or bailments.

* 11. Such debts of a son as have been contracted by him by his father's order, or for the maintenance of the family, or in a precarious situation, must be paid by the father.

* 12. What has been spent for the household by a pupil, apprentice, slave, woman, menial, or agent, must be paid by the head of the household.

13. When the debtor is dead, and the expense has been incurred for the benefit of the family, the debt must be repaid by his relations, even though they be separated from him in interests.

10, 11. A debt contracted by one blinded by love, or incensed by wrath against his own son, or in an outrageous state of intoxication, or mad with gambling, or who has become surety for another, must not be paid by the son. If, however, a debt has been contracted, even by the son, for the benefit of the household, or in a dangerous situation, it is binding on the father. A. According to Kâtyâyana, a debt contracted from love is a promise made to a dissolute woman, and a debt contracted from anger is a reward promised by an angry man to a ruffian for injuring the person or estate of his enemy. 'A debt contracted in a precarious situation,' i. e. a debt contracted in danger of life. A. Yâgñavalkya II, 45, 46, 47; Vishnu VI, 33, 39.

12. 'A pupil,' one engaged in studying science. 'An apprentice,' a pupil who resides with his preceptor for a certain fixed period. 'A slave,' whether born in the house or purchased. A. Vishnu VI, 39.

13. Where the debtor has gone abroad and met his death through illness, or accident, the debtor may claim his due from his relatives, should they even be separated in interests. A.

* 14. The father, uncle, or eldest brother having gone abroad, the son, (or nephew, or younger brother) is not bound to pay his debt before the lapse of twenty years.

* 15. Every single coparcener is liable for debts contracted by another coparcener, if they were contracted while the coparceners were alive and unseparated. But after their death the son of one is not bound to pay the debt of another.

* 16. The wife must not pay a debt contracted by her husband, nor one contracted by her son, except if it had been promised by her, or contracted in common with her husband.

* 17. A sonless widow, and one who has been enjoined by her dying husband (to pay his debt), must pay it. Or (it must be paid) by him who inherits the

---

14. Necessary debts, such as those enumerated in paragraph 11, must be paid at once by the other family members. Where, however, the father, uncle, or eldest brother resides abroad, and is known to be alive, the son, &c. need not pay his debt till after the lapse of twenty years. A. Vish*n*u VI, 27; Yâ*gñ*avalkya II, 50.

15. After the death of those who have contracted the debt jointly, the son of one is not bound to pay the debt of another than his father. His liability does not extend beyond his father's share of the debt. A. Vish*n*u VI, 34; Yâ*gñ*avalkya II, 45.

16. A woman need not pay a debt contracted by her son, unless she has promised herself to repay it. Similarly, she is not bound to pay a debt contracted by her husband, unless she should have contracted it jointly with him, or if he should have enjoined her on his deathbed to pay his debts, or if she has inherited his property. A. Vish*n*u VI, 31, 38; Yâ*gñ*avalkya II, 46, 49.

17. A widowed woman who has no son is bound to pay the debt of her husband, if he has commissioned her to do so on his deathbed, or if his property has escheated to her. If she is unfit to take the estate, her husband's debt must be repaid by those who have inherited the estate. The property and the liabilities go together. A. Vish*n*u VI, 29; Yâ*gñ*avalkya II, 51, &c.

estate. (For) the liability for the debts goes together with the right of succession.

* 18. A debt contracted by the wife shall never bind the husband, unless it had been contracted at a time when the husband was in distress. Household expenses are indispensably necessary.

* 19. The wives of washermen, huntsmen, cowherds, and distillers of spirituous liquor are exempt from this rule. The income of these men depends on their wives, and the household expenses have also to be defrayed by the wives.

* 20. If a woman who has a son forsakes her son and goes to live with another man, that man shall take her (separate) property. If she has no property of her own, her son (shall take the property of her husband).

* 21. If, however, a woman repairs to another

---

18. A debt contracted by the wife, for the purpose of saving from distress her husband, son, daughter, or other family members, must be discharged by the family head. A. Vish*n*u VI, 32, &c.

19. Yâ*g*ñavalkya II, 48; Vish*n*u VI, 37.

20. If a widow who has a son, blinded by love forsakes her son and betakes herself to another husband, taking her Strîdhana (separate property) with her, the Strîdhana shall belong to her second husband, and not to her sons. If, however, a woman who has no separate property goes to live with another man and takes her first husband's property with her, it shall not belong to the second husband. It shall escheat to her son by the first husband. A. This interpretation has been followed in the text. It is hardly reasonable, however, to explain the term dravya, in the first instance, as denoting Strîdhana, and then again, as denoting property inherited from the husband. It would seem that the reading adopted by Asahâya is erroneous. The Vîramitrodaya and other compilations read *ri*n*am* for dravya*m*, '(the son) must pay the whole debt, if she has no property of her own.' Vish*n*u VI, 30; Yâ*g*ñavalkya II, 51.

21. If a widow who has a young son takes her deceased hus-

man, carrying her riches and offspring with her, that man must pay the debt contracted by her husband, or he must abandon her.

* 22. He who has intercourse with the wife of a dead man who has neither wealth nor a son, shall have to pay the debt of her husband, because she is considered as his property.

* 23. Among these three, the heir of the wealth, the protector of the widow, and the son, he is liable for the debts who takes the wealth. The son is liable, on failure of a (protector of the) widow and of an heir; the protector of the widow, on failure of an heir and of a son.

* 24. Debts contracted by the husbands of the last

---

band's property and goes to live with another man, the latter is bound to pay the debts contracted by her first husband. His conduct is unimpeachable, likewise, if he lets her go, she taking the whole of her property with her. A.

23. This rule contains the answer to the question : Who is liable for the debts of a deceased person, whose property has been taken by his heirs, whilst his wife through poverty has acceded to another man, and whilst his son remains both penniless and deprived of the protection of his mother? The decision is as follows. Between those three, the heir of the wealth and no other is liable for the debt. Where, however, there is no heir, owing to the want of assets, there the son is liable, if there is no widow ; and the widow's husband, if there is no son. The respective liability of the son and of the taker of the widow depends on the circumstances of the case. If the widow is a young and handsome woman of high origin, her second husband has to discharge the debt of her first husband, according to the maxim that she is considered as his property (see above, paragraph 22). If, however, she is kept like a handmaid and receives a mere livelihood from the man who has taken her, the son is bound to pay the debt. A. Yâ*gñ*avalkya II, 51.

24. The term uttamâ 'the first,' besides its ordinary meaning, conveys a secondary meaning. It implies that when any of the seven Svairi*n*îs and Punarbhûs happens to be specially handsome or

Svairiṇî and of the first Punarbhû, must be paid by him who lives with them.

25. A wife, a daughter-in-law, a woman entitled to maintenance, and the attendants of the wife: by these have debts to be paid, as also by one who lives on the produce of land (inherited from the debtor).

[If among such brothers as have come to a division and are separate in wives, affairs, and wealth, one should die without leaving issue, his wife inherits his wealth.]

2. Valid and Invalid Transactions.

26. The sages declare that the transactions of a woman have no validity, especially the gift, hypothecation, or sale of a house or field.

27. Such transactions are valid when they are sanctioned by the husband; or, on failure of the husband, by the son; or, on failure of husband and son, by the king.

* 28. What has been given to a wife by her loving

gifted, her second husband is bound to pay the debts contracted by the first. A. This, no doubt, is a highly artificial interpretation. A definition of the seven Punarbhûs and Svairiṇîs is given further on, XII, 46–53. A. refers to XII, 48 and 52. However, the meaning of the term 'the first Punarbhû' is defined in XII, 46. The Mitâksharâ (p. 77) and Vîramitrodaya (p. 347) explain the term 'the last of the Svairiṇîs' as referring to one who, overwhelmed with distress, delivers herself to another man. See XII, 51, and note.

25 b. This paragraph, which contains a rule relative to the law of inheritance, seems to be a marginal gloss, which has somehow crept into the text by mistake.

28. 'Immovables,' such as houses, fields, and the like. A. This rule is frequently quoted in the mediaeval and modern compilations on the law of inheritance, as indicating the extent of a woman's power over her property.

husband, that she may spend or give away as she likes after his death even, excepting immovables.

* 29. In the same way the transactions of a slave are declared invalid, unless they have been sanctioned by his master. A slave is not his own master.

* 30. If a son has transacted any business without authorization from his father, it is also declared an invalid transaction. A slave and a son are equal in that respect.

* 31. A youth who, though independent, has not yet arrived at years of discretion, is not capable of contracting valid debts. (Real) independence belongs to the eldest son (only); (the right of) seniority is based on both capacity and age.

* 32. Three persons are independent in this world: a king, a spiritual teacher, and in all castes successively a householder in his own household.

* 33. All subjects are dependent; the ruler of the country is independent; a student is pronounced to be dependent; independence belongs to the teacher.

---

30. A son who has not come to a partition of the family estate with his father, continues dependent on him till the father dies. A.

31. This rule constitutes an exception to the general independence of the son after the death of his father. During the period of his minority, he is unable to contract a valid debt. A. The rule that seniority is based both on capacity and age, is certainly remarkable. It is, however, in accordance with the view enounced further on (XIII, 5) by Nârada, that the management of the family property may be undertaken by the youngest brother even, if capable, because the prosperity of a family depends on ability.

32. The king is independent of his subjects. A teacher is independent of his pupils. The head of a household is independent of his family and attendants. A.

33, 34. These two paragraphs are intended to show the respective dependence and independence of wives, sons, householders, &c. A.

* 34. Wives, sons, slaves and other attendants are dependent. The head of the family, to whom the property has descended by right of inheritance, is independent with regard to it.

* 35. A child is comparable to an embryo up to his eighth year. A youth, who has not yet reached the age of sixteen, is called Poga*nd*a.

* 36. Afterwards he is no longer a minor and independent, in case his parents are dead. While they are alive he can never acquire independence, even though he may have reached a mature age.

* 37. Of the two (parents), the father has the greater authority, because the seed is superior (to the womb); on failure of the begetter, the mother; on failure of the mother, the eldest son.

* 38. All these persons are independent at all times of those who depend on others. They have

---

34. Colebrooke (Dig. II, 4, 15) has translated a different reading of paragraph 34, thus, 'A householder is not uncontrolled in regard to what has descended from an ancestor.' See, as to the distinction between inherited and self-acquired wealth, Yâ*gñ*avalkya II, 121.

35. 'Comparable to an embryo' is one who is not yet allowed to perform purificatory and other rites. From his eighth year onwards a boy may perform purificatory ceremonies and commence sacred study. He is called Poga*nd*a (a young man), because he is not yet capable of transacting legal business. A. This rule of Nârada has become the foundation of the modern law regarding the duration of minority. A controversy has recently arisen as to whether minority terminates at the end or at the beginning of the sixteenth year. Most, if not all, Indian writers seem to agree in taking the latter view. A. seems to be of the same opinion, though he does not express himself very clearly.

36. He remains dependent during the lifetime of his parents, i.e. if he continues to live in union of interests with them. A.

38. 'Coercion,' i.e. punishment or beating; 'relinquishment,' i.e. renouncing. A.

authority in regard to coercion, the relinquishment and the sale (of property).

* 39. If a boy or one who possesses no independence transacts anything, it is declared an invalid transaction by persons acquainted with the law.

* 40. That also which an independent person does, who has lost the control over his actions, is declared an invalid transaction, on account of his want of (real) independence.

* 41. Those are declared to have lost the control over their actions who are actuated by love or anger, or tormented (by an illness), or oppressed by fear or misfortune, or biassed by friendship or hatred.

42. That is declared a valid transaction which is done by the senior or head of a family and by one who has not lost the control over his actions. That is not valid which has been transacted by one who does not enjoy independence.

3. Property.

43. All transactions depend on wealth. In order to acquire it, exertion is necessary. To preserve it,

---

39. Both what a minor does, and the transactions of one grown up but dependent on others, as e.g. of a slave, are declared invalid by those conversant with law. A.

40. 'One who has lost the control over his actions,' i.e. one whose natural disposition has been perverted, owing to possession by a demon, or to his addiction to gambling or other vicious propensities. A.

42. Here ends the second section of the law of debt, which treats of valid and invalid transactions. A.

43. 'All transactions,' whether originating in virtue, interest, or love. The rule regarding the acquisition (and enjoyment) of wealth is said to be threefold: protection against bipeds, quadrupeds,

to increase it, and to enjoy it: these are, successively, the three sorts of activity in regard to wealth.

44. Again, wealth is of three kinds: white, spotted, and black. Each of these (three) kinds has seven subdivisions.

* 45. White wealth is (of the following seven sorts): what is acquired by sacred knowledge, valour in arms, the practice of austerities, with a maiden, through (instructing) a pupil, by sacrificing, and by inheritance. The gain to be derived from exerting oneself to acquire it is of the same description.

* 46. Spotted wealth is (of the following seven sorts): what is acquired by lending money at interest, tillage, commerce, in the shape of *S*ulka, by artistic performances, by servile attendance, or as a return for a benefit conferred on some one.

* 47. Black wealth is (of the following seven

&c.; increase, through agriculture, lending at interest, trading, and other modes of acquisition; enjoyment of terrestrial and celestial pleasures. A.

44–54. Vish*n*u, chapter LVIII.

45. 'What is acquired by sacred knowledge,' i.e. the gains of sacred study. What is gained by 'the practice of austerities,' i.e. by one who duly performs greater and minor observances, optional and regular rites, and on whom worthy people bestow alms for that reason. What is received 'with a maiden,' i.e. as her marriage portion. The fruit derived from relinquishing white property is of the same kind, i.e. it is pure likewise. Thus A.

46. 'Commerce,' the sale of merchandise. '*S*ulka,' the price obtained for giving a damsel in marriage, whether the transaction be lawful or otherwise. 'Artistic performances,' the art of painting or another art. 'Servile attendance,' waiting upon, and paying homage to, another man. Wealth obtained by one of these seven modes is called spotted, i.e. of a middling kind. A. Others explain the ambiguous term *S*ulka differently, as denoting tolls, or a fare for crossing a river, &c.

47. 'Gambling,' with dice or otherwise. 'One afflicted with

sorts): what is acquired as a bribe, by gambling, by bearing a message, through one afflicted with pain, by forgery, by robbery, or by fraud.

48. It is in wealth that purchase, sale, gift, receipt, transactions of every kind, and enjoyment, have their source.

49. Of whatever description the property may be, with which a man performs any transaction, of the same description will the fruit be which he derives from it in the next world and in this.

50. Wealth is again declared to be of twelve sorts, according to the caste of the acquirer. Those modes of acquisition, which are common to all castes, are threefold. The others are said to be ninefold.

51. Property obtained by inheritance, gifts made from love, and what has been obtained with a wife (as her dowry), these are the three sorts of pure wealth, for all (castes) without distinction.

52. The pure wealth peculiar to a Brahman is

pain,' one pained by an attack of disease. 'Forging,' falsification, of gold, silver, or other metals. 'Robbery,' such as theft. 'Fraud,' deception. What has been acquired by one of these seven kinds is called 'black wealth,' i.e. wealth of the lowest kind. A.

48. From these three kinds of wealth, with their twenty-one subdivisions, spring all the various kinds of transactions, and all kinds of enjoyment. A.

49. The difference between this and the previous classification of the divers modes of acquisition seems to lie in this, that the one system of classification is solely based on the respective legitimacy or illegitimacy of each mode of acquisition, whereas the diversity of caste represents the principle of classification in the other system. It should be borne in mind that an occupation, according to Indian notions, may be perfectly lawful for one caste, though it is unlawful for all others.

52–54. Manu I, 88–91, X, 74–80; Yâg*ñ*avalkya II, 118–120; Vish*n*u II, 4–14; Âpastamba I, 1, 1, 5–6; Gautama X, 2, 7, 49, 56; Vasish*th*a II, 13–20; Baudhâyana I, 18, 1–5.

declared to be threefold: what has been obtained as alms, by sacrificing, and through (instructing) a pupil.

53. The pure wealth peculiar to a Kshatriya is of three sorts likewise: what has been obtained in the shape of taxes, by fighting, and by means of the fines declared in lawsuits.

54. The pure wealth peculiar to a Vaisya is also declared to be threefold: (what has been acquired) by tillage, by tending cows, and by commerce. For a Sûdra it consists of what is given to him by the members of the three higher castes.

55. These are the legitimate modes of acquisition of wealth for all the (four) castes severally. If one caste should take to the occupations of another caste, it is a criminal proceeding, except in extreme cases of distress.

4. Means of Livelihood for a Brahman in Times of Distress.

56. In times of distress, a Brahman is allowed to gain his substance in the mode prescribed for the caste next to him in rank; or he may gain his substance like a Vaisya. But he must never resort to

55. Here ends the section of the divers kinds of wealth in the law of debt. A.

56. 'The class next to him in rank,' i.e. the Kshatriya or warrior caste. If he should find himself unable to support his family by the mode of livelihood of his own caste, he may gain his substance like a Kshatriya. At the time of a drought or famine, he may gain his substance like a Vaisya even. 'The lowest caste,' i.e. the Sûdra caste. A. Manu X, 81, 82; Vishnu II, 15; Yâgña-valkya III, 35; Gautama VII, 6, 7; Baudhâyana II, 4, 16, &c.

the mode of livelihood prescribed for a member of the lowest caste.

57. At no time must a Brahman follow the occupations of a man of vile caste, or a vile man the occupations of a Brahman. In either case, expulsion from caste would be the immediate consequence.

* 58. For neither of them are such occupations permitted as are either far above or far below their own rank. Those two occupations are lawful for them which lie between these two extremes; for they are common to all (castes).

59. When a Brahman has lived through the times of distress, with the wealth acquired by following the occupations of a Kshatriya, he must perform a penance and relinquish the occupations of a Kshatriya.

60. When, however, a Brahman takes delight in those occupations and persists in them, he is declared a Kâ*nd*ap*ri*sh*th*a (professional soldier) and must be expelled from society, because he has swerved from the path of duty.

---

57. By the term 'a vile man,' a member of the *S*ûdra caste is referred to. The occupations of such a man, i.e. the acceptance of food from everybody and the sale of all sorts of commodities, must never be resorted to by a Brahman, even in times of distress. And so must a *S*ûdra avoid the occupation of a Brahman, such as wearing the sacred thread, study of the Vedas, pronouncing sacred benedictions, offering burnt-oblations, and the rest. A.

58. 'Such occupations as are either far above or far below their own rank,' i.e. the occupations of a Brahman and of a *S*ûdra respectively. 'Those two occupations,' i.e. those peculiar to the Kshatriya and Vai*s*ya. A. hitvâ seems a faulty reading (for hite).

59. Yâ*gñ*avalkya III, 35.

60. 'Ejected from society,' i.e. he must not be admitted to obsequial repasts and other religious ceremonies. A.

61. When a Brahman is living by the occupations of a Vais*y*a, he must never sell milk, sour milk, clarified butter, honey, beeswax, lac, pungent condiments, liquids used for flavouring, spirituous liquor,

62. Meat, boiled rice, sesamum, linen, the juice of the Soma plant, flowers, fruit, precious stones, men, poison, weapons, water, salt, cakes, plants,

63. Garments, silk, skins, bone, blankets made of the hair of the mountain-goat, animals whose foot is not cloven, earthen pots, buttermilk, hair, dregs, vegetables, fresh ginger, and herbs.

64. A Brahman may sell dry wood and (dry) grass, excepting fragrant substances, Erakâ grass, ratan, mulberry, roots, and Ku*s*a grass.

65. (He may sell) twigs of bamboo that have fallen spontaneously, of fruits, the fruits of the jujube tree,

---

61–66. Manu X, 85–90; Yâg*ñ*avalkya III, 36–39; Gautama VII, 8–22; Vasish*th*a II, 24–31; Âpastamba I, 7, 20, 11 foll.

61. 'Pungent condiments,' such as sugar. 'Liquids,' such as clarified butter and oil. A.

62. A. explains the term Soma, 'the juice of the Soma plant,' which is offered to the gods at a sacrifice, as denoting sacrificial implements generally; 'men,' i.e. servants; 'plants,' i.e. shrubs, creeping plants, and others. A.

63. 'Blankets,' i.e. what is made of wool. 'Animals whose foot is not cloven,' i.e. whole-hoofed animals, such as horses. 'Dregs,' i.e. the deposit of oil. 'Vegetables,' i.e. fresh pot-herbs. A.

64. 'Fragrant substances,' such as the fragrant root of the plant Andropogon Muricatus, Bâlaka, the root of the Musta grass, and others. A. If the reading of a single MS. be followed, the sale of the articles enumerated in pars. 64 and 65 is also prohibited for a Brahman. Several of these articles are included among those substances the sale of which is prohibited by other legislators. See Manu X, 86–89; Yâg*ñ*avalkya III, 36–39. However, the reading translated above is distinctly supported by the Commentary of Asahâya, and by the analogous rules of Vasish*th*a.

and of the Iṅguda plant, ropes, and thread of cotton, if its shape has not been altered (by working it up).

66. If it is for a medicament used to cure a disease, or for an offering, or if necessity can be shown, he may sell sesamum for a corresponding quantity of grain.

67. A Brahman who swerves from the path of duty by selling prohibited articles, must be reminded of his duty by the king by inflicting a severe chastisement on him.

5. Modes of Proof.

* 68. Those invested with legal authority must pay strict attention to the (various) modes of proof. That even which is provable fails to be proved, if the (prescribed) modes of proof are not attended to.

69. Documents, witnesses, and possession are the traditional three means of proof, by which a creditor endeavouring to recover his loan may obtain what he has lent.

70. If the Creator had not created writing as an

69. The term pramâ*n*a, which has been translated 'means of proof,' is both a philosophical and a law term. A. explains it etymologically, as denoting anything which may be known or discerned accurately. Thus, what is counted or reckoned, may be known by figures. What is capable of measurement, may be known by its measure. Similarly, where a lawsuit is pending, the truth may be known by having recourse to one of the ordinary modes of proof, viz. documents, witnesses, possession, and ordeals. Therefore, these means of proof should be duly applied by holy men, kings, and assessors of the court, and others endowed with legal authority, because that which is doubtful cannot be proved otherwise.

70. The term 'documents' in this section seems to relate principally to the well-known land grants which have been found in many

excellent eye (as it were), the affairs of this whole world would not take their proper course.

71. Writing is an excellent eye (as it were), because it solves all doubts which may have arisen in regard to place, time, profit, matter, quantity, or stipulated period.

72. He who, having received a chattel in a certain place, tries to deny the fact, is liable to be confronted with witnesses and convicted, difficult as it may be to prove his guilt.

73. A document is subject to many blemishes; witnesses are neither exempt from old age nor from death; possession, which has been continually held, is the only sure mode of proof, as it is not connected with any material object (liable to decay).

74. Thus have these three modes of proof been declared, by means of which a creditor may recover an outstanding debt, which has not been paid to him and called into doubt (by the debtor).

75. A document is valid at all times; witnesses (may give valid evidence) as long as they live; possession acquires legal validity through the lapse of a certain period. This is a legal maxim.

---

parts of India. Yâ*g*ñavalkya II, 22; Vish*n*u VI, 23; Vasish*th*a XVI, 10.

75. Witnesses can give evidence while they live only, whereas a document which has been carefully preserved, remains evidence even after the death of the creditor, debtor, and witnesses, and is capable of substantiating a claim raised by the son, grandson, great-grandson, or more remote descendant of the original owner. On the other hand, even after a lapse of time, i.e. when four or five generations have passed away, and an immeasurable period has elapsed, a creditor may recover his loan by dint of uninterrupted possession. 'This is a legal maxim,' i.e. this is the relative value of the divers kinds of proof. A.

76. Of the three modes of proof here enumerated in order, each previous one is superior to the one named after it; but possession is the most decisive of all.

* 77. Though a document be in existence and witnesses living, that is no (true) property of which possession is not actually held. This is specially true as regards immovables.

* 78. If a man is foolish enough to allow his goods to be enjoyed by strangers in his own eyesight, they shall belong to the possessor, even in the presence and during the lifetime of the rightful owner.

* 79. Whatever the owner looking on quietly suffers to be enjoyed by strangers for ten years,

---

76. The apparent contradiction between the first and second parts of this paragraph is thus removed by A.: 'Possession of immovables without a title does not create proprietary right, as stated in par. 84. Therefore, the possessor of landed property becomes its lawful owner, if his right or title is established by witnesses, but not otherwise. Thus far possession is more important than witnesses. In the same way documents with a title are superior to witnesses, and possession with a title is superior to witnesses, documents, and ordeals.'

77. This paragraph is intended to show the weakness of proof by witnesses or documents, where it is not accompanied by possession. Generally speaking, any of the three kinds of proof is invalid, where it is not accompanied by one of the other kinds. A. Yâ*gñ*avalkya II, 27; Manu VIII, 200.

78. If a man suffers his movable or immovable property to be enjoyed by another, the latter will become its lawful owner after the lapse of a long period, no matter whether it has been bestowed on him through affection, or forcibly seized by him, or abandoned by its previous owner. A.

79. Where, however, the owner, though unable to recover his property, owing to special reasons, proffers his claim to it every day, or every month, or every year, it is not lost to him, even after the lapse of a longer period than ten years. A. Identical with Manu VIII, 147.

though he is present, that cannot be recovered by him.

* 80. If he is neither an idiot nor a minor, and the enjoyment takes place before his eyes, his right to it is extinct by law, and the possessor is allowed to keep it.

* 81. A pledge; a boundary; the property of a child; an open deposit, an Upanidhi deposit; women; and what belongs to the king or to a learned Brahman, none (of these descriptions of property) is lost (to the owner) by adverse possession.

82. Pledges and the rest, excepting the property of a woman and of the king, are however lost to the owner if they have been enjoyed in his presence for twenty years.

---

80. 'If he is not an idiot,' nor afflicted by a chronic or agonising disease, nor dumb, blind, or deaf. A. Identical with Manu VIII, 148.

81. 'The property of children' is not lost, though it has been enjoyed for a long time by their guardian. 'An Upanidhi deposit,' i.e. a valuable article which has been delivered under cover to another person. 'A woman,' one who has been delivered to a stranger as a deposit, and enjoyed by him. 'The property of a king,' i.e. land. 'The property of a learned Brahman,' i.e. cows. A. Kullûka, in commenting on the identical verse of Manu, refers the term 'woman' to 'female slaves,' &c. The rules laid down in pars. 79–81, which recur literally in the code of Manu, seem to belong to an older order of ideas than those contained in pars. 84 foll. It may be presumed that the harsh law under which adverse possession of ten years' standing was constituted a source of proprietary right, was mitigated at a subsequent period, and has been inserted here as a sort of historical reminiscence only. According to B*ri*haspati, thirty years is the ordinary period of prescription. Identical with Manu VIII, 149; Vasish*th*a XVI, 18.

82. In this paragraph, as in the preceding one, the term 'a king's property' is referred to landed property by A. The correctness of this interpretation seems questionable.

* 83. The property of a woman and of a king is never lost (to the owner), should it even have been enjoyed for hundreds of years without a title (by strangers).

84. Where there is enjoyment, but no title of any sort, there a title is required in order to produce proprietary right. Possession is not sufficient to create proprietary right in that case.

* 85. A clear title having been produced, possession acquires validity. Possession without a clear title does not make evidence (of ownership).

*86. He who can only plead possession, without being able to adduce any title, has to be considered as a thief, in consequence of his pleading such illegitimate possession.

* 87. He who enjoys without a title for ever so many hundred years, the ruler of the land should inflict on that sinful man the punishment ordained for a thief.

* 88. If a man holds the property of a stranger without a title, it is not legitimate enjoyment. However, after the death of the occupant, it may be enjoyed legitimately by his descendants.

* 89. In cases falling within the memory of man,

---

88. While the possessor is alive, the property which he is enjoying without a title cannot become his. The owner may claim it at any time. When, however, the possessor dies, unmolested by the owner, the property continues to be enjoyed by his heirs. Therefore, the owner should not fail to assert his own right. A.

89. The Mitâksharâ explains the term 'what falls within the memory of man' as denoting a period of 100 years, in accordance with a text from the Veda, 'The life of men extends over a hundred years.' If this explanation be correct, the present rule agrees in substance with the rule laid down in 89 b and 91, a period of a hundred years being about equal in duration to three lives. It is

possession with a title creates ownership. In cases extending beyond the memory of man, and on failure of documents, the hereditary succession of three ancestors (has the same effect).

* 90. If the occupant is impeached (by the legitimate owner), he cannot escape defeat (without refuting the charge). That possession only can create proprietary right, which has been legitimately inherited from the father.

* 91. When possession has been successively held, even unlawfully, by the three ancestors of the father (of the present possessor), the property cannot be taken away from him, because it has gone through three lives in order.

* 92. What has been deposited with a third person to be delivered ultimately to the owner (Anvâhita), stolen goods, ordinary deposits, what is held by force, loans for use, and what is being enjoyed during the absence of the owner, these are six (things possessed) without a title.

---

true that another legislator, Vyâsa, mentions sixty years as the duration of continued possession extending over three generations.

90. If the owner claims his own property from the possessor, the former has to make good his claim. That enjoyment, however, which has passed from the father to the sons by right of inheritance, constitutes a legal title for them. A. Yâ*gñ*avalkya II, 28.

91. If the great-great-grandfather has held possession, be it even without a title, of a certain thing, and if it has been enjoyed, after his death, by the great-grandfather and by the grandfather, it cannot be claimed from the father by any one. Vish*n*u V, 187.

92. The term Anvâhita is usually explained, like Anvâdhi, as denoting what has been deposited with a third person to be delivered ultimately to the owner. A., however, explains Anvâhita as denoting a valuable object received from another in exchange for a worthless article.

* 93. If a litigant dies before a lawsuit (regarding property enjoyed by him) has been decided, the son is required to prove his title. The enjoyment is not legitimate (otherwise).

* 94. After the death of a creditor, witnesses, though available, cannot give valid evidence, except if a statement made by the creditor himself on his deathbed (has been preserved).

95. After the death of the defendant, the deposition of witnesses ceases to make evidence. An attested document retains its validity during his lifetime only.

* 96. Where a pious act is announced by a diseased

---

93. Supposing a man were to have obtained possession of the property of a stranger by one of the previously mentioned illegitimate modes of acquisition, if the rightful owner were to impeach him for it, and if the possessor were to die before the case has been decided, in that case the son would have to substantiate his claim, and would not be allowed to continue his enjoyment of the property without doing so. A. Yâ*gñ*avalkya II, 29.

94. A man says after the death of his creditor, 'I have restored this or that cow, female buffalo, bull, or field to my creditor; certain honest men have witnessed the transaction.' Another man says, 'Your father owes me one hundred drachmas; certain persons have witnessed the transaction.' He dies, however, before his claim has been examined. In either of these two cases trustworthy witnesses even are of no avail. If, however, the creditor has stated his claim before witnesses on his deathbed; or if a man has given evidence as witness on his deathbed regarding a certain loan, about which the creditor has asked him; the testimony of the witnesses has to be considered as valid even after his death. A.

95. 'The defendant,' i.e. the debtor. An attested document is valid while he lives only. It loses its validity after his death. A.

96. When a diseased father has stated his intentions regarding a religious endowment or other matters of this kind during the absence of his sons, but in the presence of witnesses, the deposition of the latter will be valid even after his death. Similarly, when a man

man, the testimony of the witnesses retains its validity even after his death. The case is the same with the six (things possessed without a title), viz. an Anvâhita deposit and the rest.

97. In all transactions relative to a debt or to any other (among the eighteen titles of law), the last act is the decisive one. In the case of a gift, a pledge, or a purchase, the prior act settles the matter.

6. Lending Money at Interest.

* 98. A contract of delivery and receipt may be made with a view to the profit arising from Sthâna. It is called Kusîda (lending money at interest), and money-lenders make a living by it.

---

during an attack of illness, repents of his former act, and declares before witnesses that he has deposited with a friend a worthless object in exchange for a valuable one, and wishes to restore the former; or that he has stolen something and wishes to restore it to the owner; or that he wishes to restore a deposit, which had been delivered to him by the owner; or that he intends to make restoration of what he had obtained by forcible means; or of a loan for use; or of what he had been enjoying in secret: in any one out of these six cases the deposition of the witnesses is valid even after his death. A. See par. 92 and note.

97. In all the eighteen titles of law, beginning with the law of debt, the latest act is considered decisive. The law is different in cases of acceptance, where e.g. a village belongs to him who has been the first to receive it; in the case of a pledge or mortgage, and in the case of a purchase, where the pledge or mortgage, and the article sold belong likewise to the first taker. A. Nearly identical with Yâgñavalkya II, 23.

98. According to A., Sthâna, 'continued abode,' may be threefold: relating to the matter, as when profit arises from (the continuance of) victuals remaining well kept in a certain place; or relating to one's own abode, as when a dealer derives profit from business transactions in his own country; or relating to a different place, as when a dealer earns money through foreign trade.

* 99. Let a money-lender take, in addition to the principal, the interest fixed by Vasish*th*a, viz. an eightieth part of a hundred in every month.

* 100. Two, three, four, or five (in the hundred) is the legitimate (rate of interest). Let him take as much in the shape of interest, every month, in the direct order of the (four) castes.

* 101. Or let him take two in the hundred, remembering the practice of the virtuous. By taking two in the hundred, he does not commit the crime of covetousness.

* 102. Interest is declared fourfold in this law-book: periodical interest; stipulated interest; kâyikâ interest; and compound interest.

* 103. That which runs by the month is termed

99. Identical with Manu VIII, 140. This rule, which fixes the rate of interest at $1\frac{1}{4}$ per cent. by the month, or 15 per cent. per annum, is actually found in the Dharmasûtra of Vasish*th*a II, 51.

100. Identical with Manu VIII, 142. The meaning is that he shall take 2 per cent. from a Brahman, 3 per cent. from a Kshatriya, 4 per cent. from a Vai*s*ya, and 5 per cent. from a *S*ûdra. A. It appears, from the commentaries on the code of Manu, that the present rule is applicable in those cases where no security has been given, whereas the preceding paragraph refers to loans secured by a pledge.

101. Identical with Manu VIII, 141. The meaning is that he shall take 2 per cent. only from honest men, to whatever caste they may belong. A. In the code of Manu, the present rule precedes par. 100, instead of following it. The author of the Nârada-sm*ri*ti would seem to have erroneously inverted the original position of the two verses.

102. Manu VIII, 153; Gautama XII, 34, 35. See, too, Colebrooke's Digest I, XXXV–XLV.

103, 104. 'Periodical interest' means monthly interest, at the rate of from 2 to 5 per cent., according to the caste of the debtor. 'Stipulated interest' is interest at the rate of more than 10 per cent., which has been promised by the debtor himself in times of great distress. Kâya means principal. If a Pa*n*a, or quarter of a Pa*n*a, has to be

periodical interest. That interest is termed stipulated interest which has been promised by the debtor himself.

* 104. Interest at the rate of one Pa*n*a or quarter of a Pa*n*a, paid regularly without diminishing the principal, is denoted kâyikâ interest. Interest upon interest is called compound interest.

* 105. This is the general rule for interest to be paid on loans. There are special rules according to the local usages of the country where the loan has been made.

* 106. In some countries the loan may grow till twice the amount of the principal has been reached. In other countries it may grow till it becomes three, or four, or eight times as large as the principal.

107. The interest on gold, grain, and clothes may rise till it amounts to two, three, or four times the principal. On liquids, the interest may become octuple; of women and cattle, their offspring (is considered as the interest).

---

paid every day, without diminishing the principal, i.e. if the whole principal has to be restored, though ever so much interest may have been paid on it, it is called kâyikâ interest. Where interest at the rate of 5 per cent. per mensem has been paid for twenty months, it will reach the same amount as the sum originally due, so that the principal is doubled. After twenty months more it becomes quadruple; twenty months later it becomes octuple, and so on. This is called compound interest. A. Bri*h*aspati and Vyâsa derive the term kâyikâ from kâya 'a body,' and explain that it denotes bodily labour, or the use of a pledged slave.

105. Where local customs obtain, differing from the rules previously given, they have to be followed. A.

106, 107. Manu VIII, 151; Vish*n*u VI, 11–17; Yâ*gñ*avalkya II, 39; Gautama XII, 36.

107. Gold borrowed at whatsoever rate of interest shall grow till it becomes double; grain, till it becomes treble; cloth, till it becomes

*108. No interest must ever be raised on loans made from friendship, unless there be an agreement to the purpose. Without an agreement even, interest accrues on such loans after the lapse of half a year.

*109. A loan made from friendship can never yield any interest, without being reclaimed by the creditor. If the debtor refuses to restore it on demand, it shall yield interest at the rate of five per cent.

7. Usurers.

*110. Thus has the rule been declared for the interest to be paid on loans offered through friendship. If, however, interest be demanded on grain, at the rate which has been mentioned, it is termed usury.

*111. A Vaisya is at liberty to get over a period of distress by practising usury. A Brahman must never resort to usury, not even in the extremity of distress.

---

quadruple; liquids (and condiments), till they become octuple. The offspring of pledged females and cattle shall belong to the creditor. A.

108. The chattels, which have been mentioned in the preceding paragraph, if lent in amicable intercourse, shall not yield any interest before the expiration of six months, without a special stipulation to that effect. Even without a stipulation to that effect, however, they shall yield interest after the lapse of six months. A.

109. A loan which is not restored, on demand even, shall yield interest at the rate of 5 per cent. from that day forward, even though six months are not yet over. A.

110. The term karman is sometimes used as an equivalent for gold. A. This interpretation has not been followed.

111. Agriculture, the tending of cattle, &c., are lawful occupations for a Vaisya. Lending money at interest is also permitted to him. Therefore it is said here that a Vaisya may practise usury in times of distress, whereas a Brahman must not resort to usury even in times of overwhelming distress. A.

*112. If a debt is due to a (dead) Brahman creditor, whose issue is living, (it must be paid to them.) If there be no issue, the king must cause the debt to be paid to his kinsmen; on failure of kinsmen (it must be paid) to his relatives.

*113. Where there are neither kinsmen, nor relatives, nor distant connexions, it shall be paid to (other) Brahmans. On failure of such, he must cast it into the waters.

*114. When a creditor receives payment, he must give a receipt for it to the debtor. If he does not give a receipt, although he has been asked for it, he shall lose the remainder of the sum due to him.

*115. If, though pressed by the debtor, he does not give an acquittance for the sum paid to him by the debtor, that sum shall yield interest to the debtor (henceforth), as (it had done) to the creditor (previously).

---

112. Sakulya, 'kinsman,' is derived from kulya, 'a bone,' and denotes those who have their bones in common (sic), i.e. a father, a paternal uncle, their sons, and other (agnates). Bandhu, 'a relative,' denotes a mother, a sister, a sister's son, and other (agnates). A.

113. This paragraph is intended to show the pre-eminence of the Brahman caste. A.

114. In Colebrooke's Digest (I, 6, 287) the second half of this paragraph is referred to a refusal on the part of the creditor to restore the money, which the debtor had asked him for, on his refusing to give a receipt. This construction is based on the comment of *G*agannâtha, but it is not countenanced by the remarks of Asahâya, and is thoroughly artificial. Yâ*g*ñavalkya II, 93; Vish*n*u VI, 26.

115. If the creditor fails to receipt the sum which has been restored to him, on the back of the document, it shall yield interest to the debtor, in the same way as it had yielded interest to the creditor previously. A.

*116. On payment of the debt, he must restore the bond. On failure of a bond, he must give a written receipt. Thus the creditor and debtor will be quits.

8. Sureties.

*117. The guarantee to be offered to a creditor may be twofold: a surety and a pledge. A document and (the deposition of) witnesses are the two modes of proof on which evidence is founded.

*118. For appearance, for payment, and for honesty, these are the three different purposes for which the three sorts of sureties have been mentioned by the sages.

*119. If the debtors fail to discharge the debt, or

116. Where the bond is no longer in existence, because it has been stolen or destroyed, or met with some calamity, the creditor, instead of it, shall give a written receipt to the debtor. Here ends the sixth section of the law of debt, which treats of lending money at interest and of usurers. A.

117. A surety and a pledge are the two sorts of guarantee for a loan on interest. Documents and witnesses are the two kinds of evidence for each of the four elements, which have to be distinguished in the law of debt, viz. the principal, the interest, the surety, and the pledge. A.

118. A surety for appearance is where the debtor denies the debt, and is asked to prove his denial in a court. In that case, he must produce a man, who becomes surety for the debtor's appearance at the time of the trial. A surety for payment is where the creditor, anxious to obtain a loan, produces one or several sureties, who are either jointly or severally bound. A surety for honesty is where the debtor denies having received a certain sum, or declares that he has restored it to the creditor, and is required thereupon to produce a surety for his veracity. A. Yâ*gñ*avalkya II, 53; Vish*n*u VI, 41.

119. This paragraph is intended to show that the surety for appearance and the surety for honesty are equally responsible as the

if they prove dishonest, the surety (for payment and for honesty) must pay the debt; and (so must the surety for appearance), if he fails to produce the debtor.

120. When there is a plurality of sureties, they shall pay each (proportionately), according to agreement. If they were bound severally, the payment shall be made (by any of them), as the creditor pleases.

*121. Twice as much as the surety, harassed by the creditor, has given (to the creditor), shall the debtor pay back to the surety.

122. By the mode consonant with religion, by legal

---

surety for payment. A. Manu VIII, 158–160; Yâgñavalkya II, 53; Vishnu VI, 41.

120. Where a number of sureties have promised each to pay a certain stipulated share of the debt, in case of the debtor's inability to discharge it himself, the liability of each surety does not extend beyond what has been promised by him. Where, however, all the sureties have declared their joint liability for the whole debt, the creditor may enforce payment from any one among them whom he thinks able to satisfy his demand. A. Yâgñavalkya II, 55; Vishnu VI, 42.

121. When, however, the surety, anxious to obtain twice the amount of the sum for which he has given security, should pay the sum to the creditor of his own accord, without being pressed to do so by the creditor, the debtor shall pay that sum only to him, and not the double sum. A. Yâgñavalkya II, 56; Vishnu VI, 43.

122. Identical with Manu VIII, 49. According to Asahâya, four out of the five modes of recovery of a debt are equivalent to the traditional four means of obtaining success, viz. conciliation, division (bheda), presents, and violence. Thus, 'the mode consonant with religion' means conciliation, i.e. gentle remonstrances. If these should prove of no avail, 'legal proceedings,' or 'division' (bheda), shall be resorted to, i.e. the debtor shall be threatened with a plaint in a court of justice. After that, 'presents' or 'fraud' should be adhibited, i.e. a false hope of fictitious gain shall be held out to the debtor. If this mode also should prove unsuccessful, 'force' or 'violence'

proceedings, by fraud, by the customary mode, and, fifthly, by force, a creditor may recover what he has lent.

*123. A creditor who tries to recover his loan from the debtor must not be checked by the king, both for secular and religious reasons.

9. Pledges.

*124. That to which a title is given (adhikriyate) is called a pledge. There are two kinds of it: a

---

may be used, by fettering the debtor, or confining him, &c. The fifth mode, called the customary mode (â*k*arita), consists of fasting. If the creditor himself, or his son, or his servant, takes to fasting it is no offence; or he may confine his own son or threaten to kill him, or seize the property of a stranger, as a compensation. The commentators of the Code of Manu explain the five modes of recovery of a debt much in the same way as Asahâya. 'Fraud,' according to them, is when the creditor borrows money from the debtor under false pretences, or retains a deposit belonging to him. Vyavahâra, generally interpreted by 'legal proceedings,' means, according to Medhâtithi, 'engaging the debtor in agriculture, trade, or other work, and taking the proceeds of his labour.' The 'customary mode' (â*k*arita) is variously explained as denoting 'fasting,' or 'killing' or 'taking (one's own or the debtor's) family and cattle.' Under the former interpretation, it is identical with the well-known 'sitting in Dharna.' See the translations of Manu, and Jolly, Ind. Schuldrecht, § 7. For an interesting parallel to the custom of Dharna from the Brehon Laws of Ancient Ireland, see Sir H. Maine's Early History of Institutions, p. 297 foll.

123. A dishonest debtor who applies to the king for protection against a creditor enforcing his demand shall not be abetted by the king. 'For secular reasons,' i. e. in order not to disturb the established order of society. 'For religious reasons,' i. e. in order not to offend against religious law. A. Nearly identical with Manu VIII, 50. Vish*n*u VI, 19; Yâ*g*ñavalkya II, 40.

124. According to Asahâya, the pledge to be released within a specified time is again twofold. It may be either deposited with a 'keeper of the pledge' (âdhipâla), who is to return it on the pledge

pledge which must be redeemed within a certain time, and a pledge which must be retained till the debt has been discharged.

*125. A pledge is again twofold: one to be kept only, and a pledge for enjoyment. It must be preserved precisely in the same condition (as at the time of its delivery); otherwise the pledgee loses interest.

*126. The same thing happens when the pledge has been injured owing to the negligence of the pledgee. If it has been lost, the principal is forfeited, provided that the loss was not caused by fate or the king.

*127. A pledge (for custody) must not be used

---

being restored at the time agreed on. Or it may be delivered to the creditor on condition of its being returned after the lapse of a certain period, say five or ten years. The usufruct of a 'pledge to be retained till the debt has been liquidated' shall belong to the creditor for ever, till the debt has been discharged.

125. Asahâya gives a house and a field as instances of a pledge for use. By spoiling a pledge of this kind, the pledgee forfeits interest, i.e. he loses the produce of a field, the use of a dwelling-place, &c.

126. 'Negligence,' with regard to a bull or other pledge for use, means that it is used at an unseasonable time, or too much, for drawing a cart or carrying a burden. With regard to a pledge for custody, it means that it is abandoned. 'When it has been injured,' as e.g. when an animal given as a pledge has lost one eye. 'The king' may cause the loss of the pledge, if he confiscates the whole property of a man and the pledge together with it, on account of a slight offence. The loss is caused 'by fate,' if e.g. a pledge is stolen by a thief. A. Yâg*ñ*avalkya II, 59; Vish*n*u VI, 6.

127. Identical with Manu VIII, 144. According to Medhâtithi and Kullûka, the provision that the pledgee must make good the value of the pledge to the owner refers to those cases where the pledge has been injured or spoiled. According to Nârâya*n*a, whose opinion is apparently shared by Asahâya, it means that the pledgee

forcibly. The pledgee who uses it forfeits the interest due to him. Moreover he must make good the value (of the pledge) to the owner. Otherwise he is (considered as) a thief of the pledge.

128. That foolish person who uses a pledge without authorization from the owner, shall lose one half of his interest, as a compensation for such use.

129. If a pledge for enjoyment has been given, (the creditor) must not take interest on the loan. Neither must he give or sell a pledge (of any sort) before the (stipulated) period has elapsed.

*130. When a pledge, though carefully kept, loses its value after a certain time, (the debtor) must either give another pledge, or discharge the debt to the debtor.

*131. When a debtor has been disabled by a reverse of fortune (from paying the debt), he shall be made to discharge the debt gradually, according to his means, as he happens to gain property.

*132. If a wealthy debtor from malice refuses to

---

must satisfy the owner of the pledge out of the profit derived from the use of the pledge.

128. Nearly identical with Manu VIII, 150. See Professor Bühler's note.

129. 'A pledge for enjoyment' means one where the profit derived from the pledge takes the place of interest. Such a pledge must not be given or sold before the term fixed for its delivery. A.

130. Yâ*gñ*avalkya II, 60.

131. Where the debtor is unable to give another pledge or to restore the loan, he must be made to restore it successively, as best he can, according to his receipts. A. Manu VIII, 177; IX, 229; Yâ*gñ*avalkya II, 43.

132. The king shall take 5 per cent. as a compensation for the assistance rendered by him. A. Manu VIII, 139; Yâ*gñ*avalkya II, 42; Vish*n*u VI, 21.

pay his debt, the king shall compel him to pay it by forcible means, and shall take five in the hundred for himself.

133. If the debtor acknowledges the debt with his own mouth, the king shall take from him ten per cent. (of the debt) as a fine; and twice as much (i. e. twenty per cent.) if he has been convicted (after denial of the debt).

134. If the debtor, owing to a calamity, has not means sufficient to discharge the whole debt, (the claim of the creditor) shall be entered in a legal document, specifying the caste (of the creditor and debtor), their names, and the names of their neighbours.

10. Documents.

* 135. Documents should be known to be of two sorts: (the first), in the handwriting of the party him-

---

133. If the debtor, when impeached by the creditor, acknowledges the debt himself, the king shall take 10 per cent. only. If, however, the debtor had undergone the trouble of proving the correctness of his demand against the creditor, the king shall take from him twice as much, i. e. 20 per cent. A. Manu VIII, 139; Yâ*g*ñavalkya II, 42; Vish*n*u VI, 20, 21.

134. If a debtor, who has been cast in a suit, has not means sufficient to discharge the whole debt, he shall give a written bond. A. The meaning of the obscure terms *g*âti, sa*m*g*ñâ, adhivâsa may be gathered from a text of B*ri*haspati, which is quoted in Nandapa*nd*ita's Vai*g*ayantî (MS.) III, 74. There these three terms occur in an enumeration of ten points which have to be noticed in a written deed concerning landed property. According to Nandapa*nd*ita, *g*âti denotes the caste, Brahmanical or other, of the plaintiff and defendant; sa*m*g*ñâ denotes their names, as e. g. Devadatta; adhivâsa refers to the names of their neighbours.

135. A document in the handwriting of the party himself has the advantage of being valid without subscribing witnesses. The cus-

self; (the second), in that of another person, (the former being valid) without subscribing witnesses, the latter requiring to be attested. The validity of both depends on local usage.

*136. That document is said to be valid which is not adverse to the custom of the country, the contents of which answer to the rules regarding pledges (and other kinds of security), and which is consistent in import and language.

*137. That document is invalid which has been executed by a person intoxicated, by one charged (with a crime), by a woman, or by a child, and that which has been caused to be written by forcible means, by intimidation, or by deception.

138. A bond ceases to be valid in that case also, if the witnesses, creditor, debtor, and scribe be dead,

---

tom of the country, i.e. the usages prevailing in each country with regard to the validity of documents, is supreme. A. Vish*n*u VII, 1–5; Yâg*ñ*avalkya II, 84–88.

136. I have translated the reading vyaktâdhividhilaksha*n*am. That writing is not adverse to the custom of the country which does not record an invalid gift, or a disposition in regard to a minor, &c. If the contents of a document are in accordance with the rules regarding pledges, sureties, &c., and if its import and language is free from obscurity and breaks, it is valid. A. Vish*n*u VII, 11.

137. What has been written by one intoxicated, or charged with the murder of a Brahman or other heavy crime, or by a woman or child; what has been caused to be written by forcible means, the writer not being concerned in the subject matter; and what has been written by one intimidated, or under a delusion; all such documents are invalid. A. Vish*n*u VII, 6–10; Yâg*ñ*avalkya II, 89.

138. The invalidity of those documents, where the creditor, debtor, witnesses, and writer are all dead, is declared for that reason, because such documents may be suspected of forgery. Even after the actual death of all those persons, however, a document retains its validity, where a pledge is in existence and in the possession of the creditor. A.

unless its validity can be established by the existence of a pledge.

*139. Pledges are declared to be of two kinds, movable and immovable pledges; both are valid when there is (actual) enjoyment, and not otherwise.

*140. If a document has been produced in due time, if (the demand recorded in it) has been (repeatedly) urged, and (publicly) proclaimed, it remains valid for ever, even after the death of the witnesses.

141. A document which is unknown and has never been heard of before does not obtain validity when it is brought forward, even though the witnesses be living.

*142. When a document has been transferred

---

139. A pledge which is only mentioned in a document, without being actually enjoyed, has no legal validity. A.

140. A document or bond which the descendants of the creditor have repeatedly shown to the descendants of the debtor whenever interest was due (prârthitam), or which they have again and again read out, retains its validity for the respective descendants of the creditor and debtor, even after the death of the witnesses and all other persons concerned. A. I have translated the term prârthita*m* as an independant clause.

141. A document or bond, the contents of which are unknown to the descendants of the debtor, about which they have never heard from their ancestors, and which has been suddenly presented to them only in a business transaction, is not considered valid, even though the witnesses be living. A.

142. This rule is equally applicable to a plaintiff and to a defendant in a lawsuit. 1. If a creditor suing a debtor is unable to produce the bond on demand, the judge shall give him time to search for it. If the bond has been destroyed by fire or by some other accident, the fact of its former existence may be established by the testimony of honest persons, who have acted as scribe or as subscribing witnesses, or who happened to be present while the bond was being executed. The statements of such persons are equally decisive where the marks or part of the writing in a document has been obliterated. 2. A debtor having been asked in

into another country, or burnt, or badly written, or stolen, a delay must be granted, in case it should exist still; if it be no longer in existence, the evidence of those who have seen it decides the matter.

143. If a doubt should subsist, as to whether a certain document be authentic or fabricated, its authenticity has to be established by examining the handwriting (of the party), the tenour of the document, peculiar marks, circumstantial evidence, and the probabilities of the case.

*144. If a document is signed by a stranger and

---

court to discharge a certain debt, on the strength of a bond signed by himself, says: 'It is true. I had written that document. However, the money was not handed over to me, and I omitted to cause the document to be torn, because it did not happen to be at hand. A few days later the father of my would-be creditor informed me that he had lost the bond and could not find it anywhere; that, however, he was going to give me a written deed recording its loss. So he actually did, and I have deposited that written deed in a certain box while living in that house.' If the debtor pleads an excuse of this sort, he must be allowed some delay to search for the document in question. If it is no longer in existence, the statements of those who saw it shall decide the matter. A.

143. 'The handwriting,' another specimen of the handwriting of the party. 'The tenour of the document,' the names of the subscribing witnesses. 'Peculiar marks,' flourishes in the handwriting of the scribe. 'Circumstantial evidence,' 'these two facts go together,' or 'they do not go together.' 'The probabilities of the case,' 'how has he got hold of this document?' or 'is he nervous or is his manner of speaking composed and quiet?' By such expedients as these shall doubts regarding the genuineness of a document be removed. A. Vish*n*u VII, 12; Yâ*g*ñavalkya II, 92.

144. If a document has passed by purchase or acceptance from the original owner, who signed it, into the possession of a stranger, who claims the loan recorded in it from the debtor, the judge must examine the document. Kalyâ*n*abha*tt*a has composed three verses in explanation of the technical terms âgama, sa*m*bandha, and hetu. Sa*m*bandha, 'connexion,' according to him, may be founded on descent, caste, marriage, friendship, and social intercourse.

meant for a different purpose, it has to be examined, in case its genuineness should be suspected, by inquiring into the connexion (previously existing between the two parties) and into the (probability of) title, and by resorting to reasonable inference.

145. An (obligation which has been stated in) writing can only be annulled by (another) writing, and an attested bond by witnesses. A writing is superior to witnesses; witnesses are not superior to a writing.

*146. If a document is split, or torn, or stolen, or effaced, or lost, or badly written, another document has to be executed. This is the rule regarding documents.

11. Witnesses.

*147. In doubtful cases, when two parties are quarrelling with one another, the truth has to be

---

Âgama, 'a title,' may be founded on inheritance, purchase, mortgaging, seizure, friendship, and acquisition. Hetu, 'reasonable inference,' may be founded on reasoning and an efficient cause. A. For other explanations of the terms âgama and hetu in an analogous passage of Yâ*gñ*avalkya (II, 92), see the Mitâksharâ. The Mayûkha agrees with Kalyâ*n*abha*tt*a.

145. If the debtor states that he has paid the debt, he must be able to produce an acquittance in the creditor's handwriting. In the same way, if the creditor pleads that the bond has been stolen, or lost, or burnt, &c., he must produce a certificate from the debtor stating its loss. Where, however, the bond was attested by subscribing witnesses, the debt has to be discharged in the presence of the same witnesses. A.

146. Where a document has met with any one out of the divers accidents mentioned in this paragraph, the party by whom it was executed may be compelled to give another document instead of it. Yâ*gñ*avalkya II, 91. Here ends the chapter on documents, the eighth section of the law of debt. A.

147. When the plaintiff and defendant in a lawsuit quarrel

gathered from (the deposition of) witnesses, whose knowledge is based on what has been seen, heard, or understood by them.

148. He should be considered as a witness who has witnessed a deed with his own ears or eyes; with his ears, if he has heard another man speaking; with his eyes, if he has seen something himself.

*149. Eleven descriptions of witnesses are distinguished in law by the learned. Five of them are termed appointed, and the other six not appointed.

*150. A subscribing witness, one who has been reminded, a casual witness, a secret witness, and an indirect witness, these are the five sorts of appointed witnesses.

---

about a doubtful affair of any sort, the truth has to be ascertained by examining the statements of the witnesses, who have seen, or heard, or been present at, the transaction. A.

148. Manu VIII, 74; Vishnu VIII, 13.

149. Definitions of the eleven witnesses are given in the following paragraphs. A.

150. 'A subscribing witness,' i.e. one by whom a document is attested. 'A secret witness,' one who concealed in a house or room listens to the discourse of the parties. A. Kâtyâyana defines the technical terms in this paragraph as follows: 'One adduced by the claimant himself, whose name is inserted in the deed, is a subscribing witness. A reminded witness is not entered in a deed. He is called a reminded witness who in order to insure the publicity of a transaction is reminded of it again and again by the claimant. One purposely brought near, and one who happened to be on the spot accidentally, are two witnesses not entered in a deed, by whom a claim may be corroborated. One who standing concealed is caused, for the purpose of establishing the claim, to hear distinctly the statements of the defendant, is termed a secret witness. One who subsequently corroborates the statements of other witnesses, whether from his own knowledge, or from hearsay, is called an indirect witness.'

*151. The witnesses not appointed by (the party) himself have been declared sixfold: viz. the village, a judge, a king,

*152. One acquainted with the affairs of the two parties, and one deputed by the claimant. In family quarrels, members of that family shall be witnesses.

153. They shall be of honourable family, straightforward, and unexceptionable as to their descent, their actions, and their fortune. The witnesses shall not be less than three in number, unimpeachable, honest, and pure-minded.

154. They shall be Brahmans, Vaisyas, or Kshatriyas, or irreproachable *S*ûdras. Each of these shall be (witness) for persons of his own order, or all of them may be (witnesses) for all (orders).

*155. Among companies (of artizans, or guilds of

151, 152. The village or the co-villagers shall be witnesses in a transaction which has taken place within the village. The testimony of the judge shall be heard in regard to a cause tried in a court of justice. The king shall be witness concerning a transaction which has taken place in his presence. These, and one acquainted with the circumstances of both parties, the agent of the claimant, and members of a family in a lawsuit concerning that family, are the six kinds of witnesses not appointed. A.

153. 'Of honourable family,' belonging to a noble race. 'Straightforward,' habitually veracious. 'Less than three,' viz. one or two persons may be witnesses if both parties consent to it. In a dispute regarding landed property, more than three witnesses are required. 'Honest,' free from avarice. 'Pure-minded,' imbued with the precepts of religion. A. Manu VIII, 62, 63; Vish*n*u VIII, 8; Âpastamba II, 11, 29, 7; Gautama XIII, 2; Yâ*gñ*avalkya II, 68, 69; Vasish*th*a XVI, 28.

154. Members of these four castes shall be witnesses for members of their own caste only. Or let members of any caste be witnesses for members of any other caste. A. Manu VIII, 62; Gautama XIII, 3; Yâ*gñ*avalkya II, 69; Vasish*th*a XVI, 29; Baudhâyana I, 19, 13.

155. Companies or guilds are of eighteen kinds. Labourers

merchants, other) artizans or merchants shall be witnesses; and members of an association among other members of the same association; persons living outside among those living outside; and women among women.

*156. And if in a company (of artizans or guild of merchants) or in any other association any one falls out (with his associates), they must not bear witness against him; for they all are his enemies.

12. Incompetent Witnesses.

*157. The incompetent witnesses, too, have in this law-book been declared by the learned to be of five sorts: under a text of law, and on account of depravity, of contradiction, of uncalled-for deposition, and of intervening decease.

*158. Learned Brahmans, devotees, aged persons, and ascetics, are those incapacitated under a text of law; there is no (special) reason given for it.

*159. Thieves, robbers, dangerous characters,

---

for hire shall be witnesses for other members of the same association. Outcasts shall be witnesses for other low-caste persons. Women shall be witnesses where two women quarrel with one another. In all these cases, the qualities of the witnesses need not be tested. A. Manu VIII, 68; Vasish*th*a XVI, 30.

156. If in a company of traders any one member should contract an enmity towards the other members of it, they are unworthy to bear testimony against or about him, on account of their enmity towards him. Here ends the chapter on witnesses, the tenth section of the law of debt. A.

158. The reason why the persons referred to in this paragraph are excluded seems to lie in their entire renunciation of earthly interests, which renders them unfit to appear in a court of justice. See Manu VIII, 65, where 'one dead to the world' is mentioned among the incompetent witnesses, and other parallel passages.

gamblers, assassins, are incompetent on account of their depravity; there is no truth to be found in them.

160. If the statements of witnesses, who have all been summoned by the king for the decision of the same cause, do not agree, they are rendered incompetent by contradiction.

*161. He who, without having been appointed to be a witness, comes of his own accord to make a deposition, is termed a spy in the law-books; he is unworthy to bear testimony.

*162. Where can (any person) bear testimony if the claimant is no longer in existence, whose claim should have been heard? Such a person is an incompetent witness by reason of intervening decease.

*163. If two persons quarrel with one another,

162. Supposing a man were to claim a certain sum from another and to name a witness, whom he states to have witnessed the transaction. If the soi-disant creditor should die, it would be impossible to ascertain whether the statement of the witness is true or false. Therefore such a witness must not be admitted by reason of intervening decease. A.

163. A claimant declares, 'This bull, which you have got, is mine. He was stolen by thieves, who took seven cows along with him. If they are found among your property, they may be known by a red mark on the forehead, or by their white feet, or by other signs. . . . I am able to adduce four witnesses who will declare them to be mine.' The opponent replies, 'Pragâpati (the Creator) has created many two-legged and four-legged beings closely resembling one another. If a superficial likeness is to be considered as evidence, I might take another man's wife into my house, because she has eyebrows, ears, a nose, eyes, a tongue, hand, and feet like my wife. This bull is born and bred in my own house. I am able to adduce four witnesses from the village in which he is being kept; their statements will establish the fact that he belongs to me.' In a dispute of this sort the witnesses of him who was the first to bring the suit into court will decide the suit. A. Yâgñavalkya II, 17; Vishnu VIII, 10.

and if both have witnesses, the witnesses of that party shall be heard which was the first to go to law.

*164. If the claimant should be cast at the trial, his cause proving as the weaker one of the two, it is fit that the witnesses of the defendant should be heard.

*165. No one should converse in secret with a witness summoned by his adversary, neither should he try to estrange him from the cause of his opponent by other means. A party resorting to such practices as these is cast.

166. If a witness dies or goes abroad after having been appointed, those who have heard his deposition may give evidence; for indirect proof (through a second-hand statement) makes evidence (as well as direct proof).

*167. Even after a great lapse of time (the deposition of) a subscribing witness retains its validity;

---

164. Where the plaint is rejected and the defence acknowledged as correct, the witnesses of the defendant have to be examined. A. Yâ*g*ñavalkya II, 17; Vish*n*u VIII, 11.

165. That man who holds secret conversations with a witness produced by his opponent, or who tries to intimidate him by threats, abuse, and the like, or to bribe him, loses his suit. A.

166. If a witness dies or goes abroad, indirect witnesses, i.e. those who have heard him speak of the matter, on his deathbed, or when he was about to start, either in answer to questions of the plaintiff, or of his own accord, shall be examined. A. Vish*n*u VIII, 12.

167. What follows here is intended to show how long the statements of each of the five appointed witnesses mentioned in par. 150 retain their validity. A subscribing witness may give valid evidence after the lapse of a very long period even. Such a witness should subscribe his name with his own hand, at the time when the document is being executed, as e.g. 'I, Devadatta, have witnessed this transaction.' If he is unable to write, he should cause another person to write in his own name. The document will make evidence, whenever the occasion arises. A.

if a man can write, he should write (his name) himself; if he cannot (write himself), he should cause it to be written by another man.

* 168. (The deposition of) a witness who has been reminded (of the transaction) remains valid in this world up to the eighth year, that of a casual witness remains valid up to the fifth year.

* 169. (The deposition of) a secret witness remains valid up to the third year; (the deposition of) an indirect witness is declared to remain valid for one year only.

* 170. Or no definite period is fixed for judging a witness; for those acquainted with law have declared that testimony depends upon memory.

* 171. A witness whose understanding, memory, and hearing have never been deranged, may give evidence even after a very considerable lapse of time.

13. Six Cases where Witnesses are unnecessary.

* 172. However, six different kinds of proceedings have been indicated in which witnesses are not required. (Other) indications of the crime committed are substituted for the evidence of witnesses in these cases by the learned.

* 173. It should be known that one carrying a firebrand in his hand is an incendiary; that one taken with a weapon in his hand is a murderer; and that, where a man and the wife of another man seize one another by the hair, the man must be an adulterer.

* 174. One who goes about with a hatchet in his

170, 171. Under this rule, the validity of any testimony is declared independent of length of time, and to depend on the competence of the witness alone. A.

hand and makes his approach may be recognised as a destroyer of bridges (and embankments); one carrying an axe is declared a destroyer of trees.

*175. One whose looks are suspicious is likely to have committed an assault. In all these cases witnesses may be dispensed with; only in the (last-mentioned) case of assault careful investigation is required.

176. Some one might make marks upon his person through hatred, to injure an enemy. In such cases it is necessary to resort to inductive reasoning, (ascertaining) the fact of the matter, and stratagems, in order to get a (reliable) test.

14. False Witnesses.

177. Those must not be examined as witnesses who are interested in the suit, nor friends, nor associates, nor enemies, nor notorious offenders, nor persons tainted (with a heavy sin).

*178. Nor a slave, nor an impostor, nor one not admitted to *S*râddhas, nor a superannuated man, nor a woman, nor a child, nor an oil-maker, nor one

175. 'Suspicious looks,' as e.g. a sword smeared with blood. Vîramitrodaya. In an analogous text of *S*aṅkha, as quoted in the Vîramitrodaya, &c., the possession of stolen goods is mentioned as a further manifest proof of crime.

177–187, 190. Manu VIII, 64–67, 71; Yâ*gñ*avalkya II, 70, 71; Vish*n*u VIII, 1–5; Gautama XIII, 5. Asahâya observes that the rules regarding incompetent witnesses do not relate to cases of assault only, but to judicial proceedings of every sort.

177. 'Associates,' i.e. partners in business. 'Notorious offenders,' persons formerly convicted of perjury or other crimes. A. For different interpretations of some of the terms occurring in this section, see the notes to Professor Bühler's Manu, and to Burnell-Hopkins's Manu, VIII, 64, foll.

178. 'A slave,' one born in the house. 'An impostor,' a

intoxicated, nor a madman, nor a careless man, nor one distressed, nor a gamester, nor one who sacrifices for a whole village.

*179. Nor one engaged in a long journey, nor a merchant who travels into transmarine countries, nor a religious ascetic, nor one sick, nor one deformed, nor one man alone, nor a learned Brahman, nor one who neglects religious customs, nor a eunuch, nor an actor.

*180. Nor an atheist, nor a Vrâtya, nor one who has forsaken his wife or his fire, nor one who makes illicit offerings, nor an associate who eats from the same dish (as oneself), nor an adversary, nor a spy, nor a relation, nor one connected by the same womb.

*181. Nor one who has formerly proved an evil-doer, nor a public dancer, nor one who lives by

---

fallacious person. 'One not admitted to *S*râddhas,' one who is not allowed to partake of obsequial feasts. 'A superannuated man,' weak or decrepit persons. 'One distressed,' by a calamity. A.

179. 'One who neglects religious customs,' one who fails to perform his religious duties. 'A eunuch,' one incapable of begetting offspring. A.

180. 'An atheist,' a heretic. 'A Vrâtya,' one for whom the ceremony of initiation has not been performed. 'His wife,' his legitimate spouse. 'His fire,' the sacred Vaitâna fire. 'One who makes illicit offerings,' one who performs sacrifices for persons of bad fame. 'An associate who eats from the same dish,' one with whom one keeps up commensality. 'A spy,' employed in the service of the king. 'One connected by the same womb,' a uterine brother.

181. 'One who has formerly proved an evil-doer,' one afflicted with an ugly disease, the consequence of wicked acts committed in a previous existence; or one guilty of robbery or other crimes. 'One who lives by poison,' one who buys or sells poison. 'A snake-catcher,' one who catches venomous reptiles. 'A poisoner,' one who, actuated by hatred, gives poison to other people. 'An incendiary,' one who sets fire to houses, &c. Kînâ*s*a (a ploughman), 'a *S*ûdra,' or 'a miser.' A.

poison, nor a snake-catcher, nor a poisoner, nor an incendiary, nor a ploughman, nor the son of a *S*ûdra woman, nor one who has committed a minor offence.

*182. Nor one oppressed by fatigue, nor a ferocious man, nor one who has relinquished worldly appetites, nor one penniless, nor a member of the lowest castes, nor one leading a bad life, nor a student before his course of study is completed, nor an oilman, nor a seller of roots.

*183. Nor one possessed by a demon, nor an enemy of the king, nor a weather-prophet, nor an astrologer, nor a malicious person, nor one self-sold, nor one who has a limb too little, nor a Bhagav*ri*tti.

*184. Nor one who has bad nails or black teeth, nor one who betrays his friends, nor a rogue, nor a seller of spirituous liquor, nor a juggler, nor an

182. 'A ferocious man,' one who perpetrates illicit acts of violence. 'One who has relinquished worldly appetites,' an ascetic. 'One penniless,' one who has lost his whole wealth through gambling or other extravagance. 'A member of the lowest castes,' a *K*â*nd*âla. 'One leading a bad life,' an infidel. A. The term mûlika denotes 'a seller of roots,' according to A. The Vîramitrodaya interprets it by 'one who practises incantations with roots.'

183. A. explains varshanakshatrasû*k*aka as a single term, denoting 'an astrologer.' The Vîramitrodaya, more appropriately, divides it into two terms: 'one who prophesies rain,' i.e. a weather-prophet, and 'an astronomer,' i. e. an astrologer. The term aghasa*m*sin, 'a malicious person,' is in the Vîramitrodaya interpreted by 'one who makes public the failings of other people.' 'One self-sold,' one who has entered the state of slavery for money. 'One who has a limb too little,' i.e. an arm or a foot. 'A Bhagav*ri*tti,' one who lives by the prostitution of his wife, or one who suffers his mouth to be used like a female part (bhaga). A.

184. 'A cruel man,' a hard-hearted man; or Ugra is used as a proper noun denoting the offspring of a Kshatriya with a *S*ûdra wife. A.

avaricious or cruel man, nor an enemy of a company (of traders) or of an association (of clansmen).

*185. Nor one who takes animal life, nor a leather manufacturer, nor a cripple, nor an outcast, nor a forger, nor a quack, nor an apostate, nor a robber, nor one of the king's attendants.

*186. Nor a Brahman who sells human beings, cattle, meat, bones, honey, milk, water, or butter, nor a member of a twice-born caste guilty of usury.

*187. Nor one who neglects his duties, nor a Kulika, nor a bard, nor one who serves low people, nor one who quarrels with his father, nor one who causes dissension. These are the incompetent witnesses.

*188. The slaves, impostors, and other incompetent witnesses who have been enumerated above, shall be witnesses nevertheless in suits of a specially grave character.

*189. Whenever a heinous crime, or a robbery, or adultery, or one of the two kinds of insult has been committed, he must not inquire (too strictly) into the (character of the) witnesses.

*190. A child also cannot be (made a witness), nor a woman, nor one man alone, nor a cheat, nor a relative, nor an enemy. These persons might give false evidence.

---

185. 'One who takes animal life,' a butcher. 'A forger,' one who falsifies documents or coined money. 'A quack,' one who practises incantations and the like with mysterious formulas, medicines, &c. 'An apostate,' one who has left the order of religious mendicants. 'An attendant of the king,' a menial. A.

187. 'A Kulika,' a judge; or the head of a caste or guild. 'One who causes dissension,' one who causes friends or others to fall out with one another. Vîramitrodaya.

189. Manu VIII, 72; Yâ*g*ñavalkya II, 72; Gautama XIII, 9; Vish*n*u VIII, 6.

*191. A child would speak falsely from ignorance, a woman from want of veracity, an impostor from habitual depravity, a relative from affection, an enemy from desire of revenge.

*192. By consent of both parties, one man alone even may become a witness in a suit. He must be examined in public as a witness, though (he has been mentioned as) an incompetent witness.

*193. One who, weighed down by the consciousness of his guilt looks as if he was ill, is constantly shifting his position, and runs after everybody;

*194. Who walks irresolutely and without reason, and draws repeated sighs; who scratches the ground with his feet, and who shakes his arm and clothes;

*195. Whose countenance changes colour, whose forehead sweats, whose lips become dry, and who looks above and about him;

*196. Who makes long speeches which are not to the purpose as if he were in a hurry, and without being asked: such a person may be recognised as a false witness, and the king should punish that sinful man.

*197. He who conceals his knowledge (at the time

192. One agreeable to both parties shall be examined in an assembly of honourable men. A. Manu VIII, 77; Yâ*g*ñavalkya II, 72; Vish*n*u VIII, 9.

193–196. These rules relate to the trial of a cause by the judge. The time for examining the witnesses having arrived, he should examine their miens and gestures. Incompetent witnesses are not only those previously mentioned, but those here described are equally incompetent. A. Manu VIII, 25, 26; Yâ*g*ñavalkya II, 13–15; Vish*n*u VIII, 18.

197. One who has made a certain statement in the hearing of others, and makes a different statement at the time of the trial, shall receive specially heavy punishment; for he is a greater criminal than a false witness. A. Yâ*g*ñavalkya II, 82.

of trial), although he has previously related (what he knows) to others, deserves specially heavy punishment, for he is more criminal than a false witness even.

15. Exhorting the Witnesses.

*198. (The judge), after having summoned all the witnesses, and bound them down firmly by an oath, shall examine them separately. (They should be men) of tried integrity and conversant with the circumstances of the case.

199. Let him cause a priest to swear by Truth, a Kshatriya by his riding animal and weapons, a Vai*s*ya by his cows, grain, or gold, a *S*ûdra by all sorts of crimes.

*200. By ancient sacred texts, extolling the excellence of Truth, and denouncing the sinfulness of Falsehood, let him inspire them with deep awe.

201. He who gives false testimony as a witness will enter his enemy's house, naked, with his head shorn, tormented with hunger and thirst, and deprived of sight, to beg food with a potsherd.

202. Naked, with his head shorn, with a potsherd (for a begging-bowl), standing hungry before the door

---

198–228. Manu VIII, 79–101; Yâ*g*ñavalkya II, 73–75; Vish*n*u VIII, 19–37; Gautama XIII, 12–23; Âpastamba II, 11, 29, 7–10; Baudhâyana I, 19, 10–12; Vasish*th*a XVI, 32–34. Böhtlingk's Indische Sprüche.

199. Identical with Manu VIII, 113. See, too, Manu VIII, 88. The commentators of the Code of Manu give various explanations of the latter verse. It may mean that a false witness is threatened with the guilt of all offences committed against riding animals, cows, grain, &c.; or with the guilt of stealing riding animals, &c.; or with their loss; or that the judge shall exhort witnesses to touch a cow, &c.

201, 202. Manu VIII, 93; Vasish*th*a XVI, 33.

of his adversary, shall he constantly meet his enemies who give false testimony.

203. A perjured witness shall spend his nights in the same manner as a wife who has been superseded (by another), or as a man who has been worsted in playing at dice, or as one whose body is weighed down by a heavy burden.

204. A witness who wavers in giving evidence is sure to be fettered with a thousand bonds from the chain of Varu*n*a.

205. After the lapse of a hundred years, the cord is taken off him. When he is free from the cord, the man becomes a woman.

206. Thus is a man liberated from this fixed bondage. *Now I will state, in order, how many kinsmen a false witness kills,

*207. If his evidence concerns, respectively, (small) cattle, cows, horses, human beings, gold, and land. Listen to me, my friend.

---

203. This sentiment shows that the condition of a superseded wife under Hindu law must have been far from enviable. This is equally shown by the custom of presenting a certain sum to her on her supersession by another wife. See Vish*n*u XVII, 18; Yâ*gñ*avalkya II, 143.

204. The snaky 'bonds of Varu*n*a' seem to be an equivalent for dropsy, a disease attributed to the influence of the ancient divinity Varu*n*a. See Professor Bühler's note on Manu VIII, 82.

207. 'Kills,' i.e. sends to hell. This interpretation is given by the majority of Manu's commentators. According to others, it means 'causes to fall from heaven and to be reborn in the wombs of animals,' or 'incurs a guilt as great as if he had killed.' See Professor Bühler's note on Manu VIII, 97. The idea that a man, by telling a falsehood, ruins his kinsmen as well as himself, belongs to the remotest antiquity, and recurs in the Zendavesta. See Vendîdâd IV, 24 seq.; Jolly, translation of Book VIII of the Code of Manu, note.

207–209. Nearly identical with Manu VIII, 97–99, &c.

*208. He kills five by false testimony concerning (small) cattle; he kills ten by false testimony concerning kine; he kills a hundred by false testimony concerning horses; (and he kills) a thousand by false evidence concerning a human being.

*209. He kills the born and the unborn by giving false evidence (in a cause) concerning gold; he kills everything by giving false evidence concerning land; beware, then, of giving false evidence with regard to land.

210. Truth is said to be the one unequalled means of purification of the soul. Truth is the ladder by which man ascends to heaven, as a ferry (plies) from one bank of a river to the other.

211. If truth and a thousand horse-sacrifices are balanced against one another (it will be found that) truth weighs more heavily than a thousand horse-sacrifices.

212. A tank is better than a hundred wells, an offering better than a hundred tanks, a son better than a hundred offerings, and truth better than a hundred sons.

213. It is truth which makes the earth bear all beings, truth which makes the sun rise. It is through truth that winds blow, and that the waters flow.

214. Truth is the greatest gift, truth is the most efficacious kind of austerity, truth is the highest duty in the world, thus it has been revealed to us.

215. The gods are truth simply, the human race is falsehood. He whose mind is persistent in truth, obtains a divine state in this world even.

216. Speak truth and discard falsehood. It is through truth that thou shalt attain heaven. By

uttering a falsehood thou wilt precipitate thyself into a most dreadful hellish abode.

*217. And in the hells the merciless attendants of Yama, endowed with great strength, will cut off thy tongue and strike thee with swords, constantly,

*218. And attack and pierce thee with spears, while thou art wailing helpless. When thou art standing, they will fell thee to the ground and fling thee into the flames.

*219. After having sustained thus for a long while the acute tortures of hell, thou shalt enter in this world the horrid bodies of vultures, crows, and other (despicable creatures).

*220. Having discovered these evils with which falsehood is attended, and knowing, on the other hand, the advantages resulting from veracity, thou must speak truth and (thereby) save thyself. Do not ruin thyself wantonly.

221. Neither relatives, nor friends, nor treasures, be they ever so great, are able to protect those who are about to be plunged into the tremendous darkness (of hell).

222. Thy ancestors are in suspense, when thou hast been appointed to give evidence (reflecting in their minds): 'Will he conduct us (into heaven) or will he precipitate us (into hell)?'

223. Truth is the self of man. Everything depends on truth. Therefore thou must be intent on acquiring bliss by thy own effort, by speaking truth.

224. Whatever lies between that night in which thou wast born, and that night in which thou art to die (thy whole life in fact) has been spent in vain by thee, if thou givest false evidence.

225. Those places of abode which are destined

for the murderer of a Brahman, and those which await the murderer of a woman or child, and the regions awaiting an ungrateful man, are reserved for a false witness.

226. There is no higher virtue than veracity, nor heavier crime than falsehood. A man must speak truth therefore, particularly when he has been appointed to give evidence.

* 227. There are two ancient verses (which run as follows): 'If a man is base enough to speak falsely in regard to the affairs of a stranger, what may not such a wretch be expected to do, fearless of hell, where his own welfare is concerned?

* 228. All affairs are connected with speech, have speech for their root, and depend on speech. He who steals a good speech (by violating truth) is capable of committing any theft (or other crime).'

16. Valid Evidence.

229. Where there is conflicting evidence, the plurality of witnesses decides the matter. If the number of witnesses is equal (on both sides), the testimony of those must be accepted as correct,

---

228. 'Theft' is a very wide term under the Hindu law. The Code of Manu includes in the denomination of theft, forgery of documents and of coins, unlawful sales, and dishonesty generally. For hitâ*m* one might read hi tâ*m*, 'For he who steals speech.' Manu IV, 256.

229. Manu VIII, 73; Yâ*gñ*avalkya II, 78; Vish*n*u VIII, 39.

229, 230. Where witnesses endowed with a good memory are found on both sides in equal numbers, evidence based on recollection is incapable of influencing the decision of the suit. The witnesses must not be examined, and the above rule comes into force, that the witnesses become incompetent, because they do not agree with one another. A. See par. 161.

whose veracity is not liable to suspicion. If the number of such witnesses is equal (on both sides) (the testimony of these must be accepted), who are possessed of a superior memory.

17. Invalid Evidence.

230. Where, however, an equal number of witnesses possessed of a good memory is found on both sides, the evidence of the witnesses is entirely valueless, on account of the subtle nature of the law of evidence.

231. But wherever a litigant has been abandoned by his own witnesses through the act of fate, the sages have declared that he cannot be absolved by (the performance of) an ordeal even.

* 232. Where, the time for giving testimony having arrived, a witness does not make a consistent statement with reference to the questions under notice, his testimony is as good as ungiven.

* 233. If the witnesses were to disagree with one another as to place, time, age, matter, quantity, shape, and species, such testimony is worthless likewise.

* 234. If the witnesses wrongly name too low or too high a sum, this too must be known to make no evidence. This is the rule of witnesses.

18. What has to be done in default of both Witnesses and Documents.

* 235. When, owing to the negligence of the creditor, both a written contract and witnesses are missing, and the opponent denies his obligation, three different methods may be adopted.

* 236. A timely reminder, argument, and, thirdly, an oath, these are the measures which a plaintiff should adopt against his adversary.

* 237. He who does not refute his (adversary's) statements, though he has been reminded again and again, three, or four, or five times, may be compelled to pay the debt in consequence.

* 238. If the defendant has rejected a demand (to pay), he shall aggress him with arguments relative to place, time, matter, the connexions (existing between the two parties), the amount (of the debt), the contents (of the written contract), and so forth.

* 239. If arguments also are of no avail, let him cause the defendant to undergo one of the ordeals, by fire, water, proof of virtue, and so forth, (which may seem) appropriate to the place, to the season, and to the strength (of the defendant).

---

236. 'A timely reminder,' timely appeals to the debtor and to the witnesses who have attested the loan. 'Argument,' arguing that the sum in dispute has been previously repaid, or the obligation acknowledged by the debtor. Thirdly, he may attack the defendant with an oath or ordeal, such as e.g. by causing him to swear by his own good actions, or to undergo the ordeal of sacred libation, &c. A. The term 'a reminder' is not correctly explained by Asahâya, as the rule under notice refers to those cases where witnesses are missing.

237. If a debtor has again and again been addressed by his creditor, saying, 'Thou owest me money,' and the debtor does not deny the correctness of the assertion, he shall be bound to pay the debt. Raghunandana's Vyavahâratattva.

238. Asahâya says that the various arguments mentioned in this verse shall be resorted to successively, arguments relative to time having to be proffered when arguments relative to place have failed, and so on.

239. The term *s*apatha denotes both an ordeal and an oath in this place, though some of the commentators deny that *s*apatha may have the former meaning.

240. He whom the waters keep below the surface, and whom blazing fire does not burn, is considered to refute the charge. In the opposite case he is deemed guilty.

*241. Proof by ordeal takes place (if an offence has been committed) in a solitary forest, at night, in the interior of a house, and in the case of a heinous offence, or denial of a deposit.

* 242. (Ordeals) are equally (applicable) in the case of those women, whose morality has been impeached, in cases of theft and robbery, and in all cases of denial of an obligation.

* 243. Of the gods and *Ri*shis even, the taking of oaths is recorded. Vasish*th*a took an oath when he was accused of having assumed the shape of an evil spirit.

---

240. If a man who is performing the ordeal by water does not rise from water, and if blazing fire, which he is holding in his hand, does not burn him, he is freed from the charge, otherwise he is deemed guilty, i.e. criminal. A. Manu VIII, 115. It does not become quite clear whether the divine tests referred to in this paragraph are identical with the ordeals by water and fire as described further on. See the translations of Manu, and Professor Stenzler's and Dr. E. Schlagintweit's papers on Ordeals in Ancient India.

242. Where the conduct of a woman, i.e. her morals, is called into doubt; where theft or robbery is alleged to have been committed; and where anything has been declared false, for all heavy charges in short, this rule regarding the performance of ordeals has been laid down. A.

243, 244. Manu VIII, 110.

243. The great sage Vasish*th*a, being suspected of being an evil spirit, took an oath, and was cleared of suspicion thus. A. The story, to which allusion is made in this place, is told by the commentators of the code of Manu. Vi*s*vâmitra accused his rival Vasish*th*a before King Sudâs as having eaten up his hundred sons, in the shape of a Râkshasa (malignant spirit). Vasish*th*a thereupon exclaimed, 'I will fall dead on the spot if I am a Râkshasa.'

*244. The seven *R*ishis resolutely took an oath together with Indra in order to clear themselves mutually of suspicion, when each was suspected (by the rest) of having taken lotus fibres.

245. The perpetrator of a wrong action, or of a crime, shall be let off with one half of the punishment due to his offence, if he admits the charge or if he makes his guilt known of his own accord.

246. If, on the other hand, a criminal has cunningly concealed his crime, and is convicted of it, the members of the court of justice will not be satisfied with his conduct, and the punishment inflicted on him shall be specially heavy.

---

244. The story here referred to occurs in the Purâ*n*as. The meaning is this: If the great sages even have taken oaths in order to clear themselves from suspicion, how much less should ordinary mortals refrain from taking an oath. A. According to Medhâtithi and Govindarâ*g*a, the two earliest commentators of Manu, the seven *R*ishis had mutually accused one another of the theft of lotus fibres. Indra took an oath when he was suspected with Ahalyâ.

245. One who has committed any wrong or sinful act to the detriment of any one whomsoever, or who has become guilty of robbery or other crimes, shall have to suffer one half only of the punishment ordained for his misconduct, if he acknowledges in a court of law the truth of the charge brought against himself by the injured party. The same rule obtains, if he has denounced himself guilty, though no plaint has been lodged against him. A.

246. If the perpetrator of a wrong act, or of robbery, &c., denies his guilt, on being examined in a court of justice, and is convicted afterwards by means of an ordeal or of another mode of proof, the assessors of the court will be incensed against and a heavy punishment inflicted on him, as e.g. he will have to pay twice as much as in ordinary cases. Here ends that section of the law of debt which consists of 'Rules for those cases where both documents and witnesses are wanting.' A.

19. Proof by Ordeal.

* 247. If no witness is forthcoming for either of the two litigant parties, he must test them through ordeals and oaths of every sort.

* 248. (Let him cause a Brahman to swear by) truth, (a Kshatriya) by his (horse or other) vehicle, and by his weapons, (a Vaisya) by his cows, seeds or gold and so on, (or all) by venerable deities or deified ancestors, by their pious gifts or meritorious deeds.

249. Where a heavy crime has been committed, the ruler shall administer one of the ordeals. In light cases, on the other hand, a virtuous king shall swear a man with (various) oaths.

* 250. Thus have these oaths been proclaimed by Manu for trifling cases. In a suit concerning a heavy crime, divine test should be resorted to.

251. Holy Manu has ordained that five kinds of ordeals should be administered to those involved in a doubtful case (which has become the object of a lawsuit), especially if the matter under dispute is of a recondite nature.

* 252. The balance, fire, water, poison, and, fifthly, consecrated water, are the ordeals ordained for the purgation of high-minded persons.

---

248. In this rule are indicated the various oaths to be administered according to the caste and individual character of the offender. A. Manu VIII, 114.

249, 250. These two verses are intended to indicate the difference in point of applicability between an ordeal and an oath. A.

251. Holy Manu has said that those against whom a charge of an aggravated nature has been brought, shall have to undergo one out of the five ordeals, in order to clear themselves from suspicion, especially when a secret transgression is concerned. A.

252. In this paragraph the author proceeds to enumerate the five ordeals singly. A. Yâgñavalkya II, 95; Vishnu IX, 11.

* 253. (Those ordeals) have been ordained here by Nârada for the purpose of proving the innocence of criminals who are defendants in a lawsuit, (and) in order that right may be discerned from wrong.

* 254. During the rains let the (ordeal by) fire be administered. In the autumn season the balance is declared to be (the proper kind of ordeal). The (ordeal by) water should be applied in summer, and the (ordeal by) poison in the cold weather.

* 255. The distressed shall not be caused to undergo the (ordeal by) water, nor shall poison be given to the bilious, nor shall the ordeal by fire be administered to persons afflicted with white leprosy, or with blindness, or with bad nails.

* 256. An ordeal should never be administered to persons engaged in performing a vow, to those afflicted with a heavy calamity, to the diseased, to ascetics, or to women, if the dictates of justice are listened to.

257. Where no one declares himself ready to

---

253. The five ordeals have been proclaimed by the great sage Nârada, for the justification of those impeached on account of their suspicious conduct, by showing where the wrong lies and where not. A.

254. The five ordeals should be administered, each of them, at those very seasons, and not at any other season. A. Vish*n*u IX, 25, 28, 30.

255, 256. Vish*n*u IX, 23, 25, 27, 29.

255. In the case of the persons here mentioned, the ordeals referred to should be avoided, on grounds of disease and of incapacity to undergo them. A.

256. 'Persons engaged in performing a vow,' those who have performed the ceremony initiatory to a Soma sacrifice. A.

257. An ordeal should not take place, unless there should be a special reason for it, such as an accusation. Therefore an ordeal must not be administered, unless there be a plaintiff who declares himself ready to take the punishment on himself in case of defeat.

undergo punishment, an ordeal cannot take place. An ordeal shall be administered to litigants where there is reason for it, but not otherwise.

258. Therefore an intelligent, virtuous, righteous, and wise (king or chief judge) should abstain carefully from administering any one out of the (five) ordeals, unless both parties consent to it.

*259. The ordeal by water must not take place in the cold weather, nor the ordeal by fire in the hot season, nor must the (ordeal by) poison be administered to any one during the rains, nor the (ordeal by) balance in stormy weather.

20. The Ordeal by Balance.

*260. Wise legislators conversant with every law have proclaimed, after mature consideration, the following rules regarding the mode of performing the ordeal by balance, which may be administered in every season.

*261. The two posts should be dug in every

A. Yâ*gñ*avalkya II, 96; Vish*n*u IV, 20, 21. The reading na divya*m* (for na vinâ?) seems wrong. Or translate, 'but there is no ordeal for plaintiffs.'

258. A king or chief-judge, who is endowed with the qualities here mentioned, should administer an ordeal with the full approval of both parties in a cause, but not otherwise. A.

259. The times or seasons here referred to should be avoided in the case of the ordeal by water and of the other ordeals, because they are illegal. A. Vish*n*u IX, 24, 26, 28, 30.

260–284. Vish*n*u X; Yâ*gñ*avalkya II, 100–102.

260. 'After mature consideration,' after having duly considered that the ordeals by fire, water, and poison are subject to many interruptions or obstacles arising from time, locality, &c., wise men have devised this ordeal by balance, which may be performed during any season. That is the meaning. A.

261. The apparatus for performing the ordeal by balance, which is described in this and the following paragraphs, consists of the

case to the depth of two Hastas below ground. (The whole of) their length is ordained to amount to six Hastas in extent.

* 262. The beam of the balance should be four Hastas in length, and the height of the two posts (above ground) should be the same. The intermediate space between the two posts should measure one and a half Hastas.

* 263. The beam of the balance should be made straight, of Khadira or of Tinduka wood, quadrangular and (provided) with three Sthânas and with hooks (by which the strings supporting the scale are suspended) and with other (contrivances).

* 264. He should cause it to be made of Khadira wood or *Sim*sapa wood, or in default of such, of

---

following elements: 1. Two wooden posts, supporting a transverse beam. The two posts should be fastened in the ground at a distance of one-and-a-half Hastas (1 Hasta = about 18 inches), facing the west and east. The part above ground should be four Hastas long, and the part below ground two Hastas, the whole length of each post amounting to six Hastas. 2. The beam of the balance, by which the scales have to be suspended. The beam itself, which should measure four Hastas, and should be made of Khadira or other strong wood, should be suspended by means of an iron hook and chain in the middle of the transverse beam. 3. The beam of the balance should be surrounded in the middle and at the two extremities, by three Sthânas (belts?) by which two iron hooks should be fastened. 4. The two scales should be suspended at the two ends of the beam, by the iron hooks, and by four strings each. 5. Each of the two scales should move in a wooden arch (tora*n*a), which serves the purpose of marking the position of the scales. See Mitâksharâ and Stenzler's paper on Ordeals (vol. ix of the Journal of the German Oriental Society), to which a drawing has been added for the purpose of illustrating the statements of the Sm*ri*ti writers regarding this kind of ordeal.

263. Read *rig*vî in the text.

264. Wood of the Khadira tree is the most eligible sort of wood. Then comes Tinduka wood, and lastly *Sim*sapa wood. A.

*S*âla wood, (which must be) without notches and withered portions, and devoid of rents.

* 265. These kinds of timber should be used for preparing the beam of the balance, (which should be erected) either in the midst of a public assembly, or before the gates of the royal palace, or in sight of a temple, or in a cross-road.

266. (The balance) must be dug firmly into the earth, after having been covered with perfumes, garlands, and unguents, and after the performance of purificatory and auspicious ceremonies with sour milk, whole grain, clarified butter, and perfumes.

267. This ordeal should always be administered in the presence of the guardians of the world, who must be invoked to be present for the protection (of virtue and justice), and in sight of everybody (who cares to look on).

* 268. It is ordained that all ordeals should be

---

265. The various places here mentioned are the favourite abodes of Dharmarâ*g*a (the king of justice), when he appears on earth. A. The Vîramitrodaya and other compositions quote two verses of Kâtyâyana, to the effect that ordeals should be administered to felons in sight of a temple; to those who have offended against the king, before the gates of his palace; to low-caste persons, in a cross-road; and to other offenders, in the midst of a public assembly, or court of justice.

266. It appears from the statements of other legislators, that the ceremonies to be performed on this occasion are perfectly analogous to those which have to take place on the occasion of preparing a sacrificial stake (yûpa).

267. 'In sight of everybody,' not in a solitary spot. A.

268–270. This is a digression relative to certain exceptions to the rule in pars. 257, 258. Yâ*gñ*avalkya II, 96, 99; Vish*n*u IX, 22.

268. An ordeal is ordained, when the plaintiff declares himself ready to undergo punishment. Where, however, any outrage has been committed against the royal family, an ordeal should be administered even without a declaration of this sort. A.

administered in the forenoon, the person (to be tested) having fasted for a day and a night, taken a bath, and wearing his wet dress.

269. Excepting cases of high treason, an ordeal shall not be administered, unless the plaintiff comes forward and declares himself ready to undergo punishment in case of his being defeated.

270. The king may inflict ordeals on his own servants, even without the one party declaring himself ready to undergo punishment. On the other hand, in the case of other persons accused of a crime, (he should administer ordeals) according to law (only).

* 271. After having well fastened the two scales by the hooks of the beam, he should place the man in the one scale and a stone in the other.

The essential features of the proceedings described in pars. 271–284 may be summarized as follows: 1. The person to be tested by this ordeal should be placed in the one scale, and a basket filled with stones and sand placed in the other scale, as an equivalent. 2. The basket having been made precisely equal in weight to the man with the help of goldsmiths and other persons skilled in the practice of weighing, the position of the beam should be marked on each of the two arches. 3. After that, the man should be allowed to descend from the scale. The judge should admonish him, and he should get into the scale again, after a bill recounting the charge raised against him has been fastened on his head. 4. A Brahman should address the balance with prayers. 5. The man having descended once more from the scale, the result of the second weighing should be compared with the result of the first weighing. If he has risen, i.e. if he has proved lighter than the first time, he shall be acquitted; if the scale has gone down, or if it has remained in the same place as before, he must be pronounced guilty. 6. If any part of the balance has broken during the proceeding, he has to be acquitted.

271. The term 'a stone' seems to denote an equivalent here and in the next paragraph. The sequel shows that the equivalent consists of a basket filled with stones and other objects.

* 272. He should weigh the man on the northern side, and the stone on the southern side. There (in the southern scale) he should (place) a basket and fill it up with bricks, mud, and grains of sand.

273. In the first weighing, the weight (of the man) should be ascertained with the aid of experienced men, and the arch marked at that height which corresponds to the even position of the two scales.

* 274. Goldsmiths, merchants, and skilful braziers experienced in the art of weighing, should inspect the beam of the balance.

* 275. After having first weighed the man, and having made (on the arches) a mark for the beam, in order to show the (even) position of the scales, he should cause him to descend from the balance.

* 276. After having admonished him with solemn imprecations he should cause the man to get into the scale again, after having fastened a writing on

273–275. Goldsmiths, merchants, braziers, and other persons familiar with the art of weighing, should ascertain whether the man and the equivalent are precisely equal in weight, and whether the beam of the balance is quite straight, by pouring some water (on the beam of the balance?). A. According to the Pitâmaha-smr*i*ti, the water shall be poured on the beam of the balance. If it does not trickle down from the beam, the beam may be supposed to be straight. The way in which the position of the scales and of the beam of the balance has to be marked on the two arches, may be gathered from the Yâg*ñ*avalkya-smr*i*ti, which ordains that a line shall be drawn (across the arches).

276. He should cause the man to get into the scale once more, after having reminded him of his good actions and of the preeminence of truth, having invoked the deities, and having fastened on his head a bill recounting the charge, and containing an imprecation. The whole proceeding must not take place in windy or rainy weather. A. The Vîramitrodaya and other compilations quote another text of Nârada, according to which no verdict should be given if the scales have been moved by the wind.

his head. There must be neither wind nor rainfall (at the time when this ordeal is being performed).

277. When he has ascended (the scale), a Brahman, holding the scale in his hand, should recite the following: 'Thou art called dhata (a balance), which appellation is synonymous with dharma (justice).

* 278. Thou knowest the bad and good actions of all beings. This man, being arraigned in a cause, is weighed upon thee.

279. Thou art superior to gods, demons, and mortals in point of veracity.

[Thou, Balance, hast been created by the gods in time out of mind, as a receptacle of truth.

* 280. Deign to speak truth, therefore, O propitious being, and deliver me from this perplexity. If I am an offender, take me down.

* 281. If thou knowest me to be innocent, take me upwards.] Therefore mayst thou deliver him lawfully from the perplexity in which he is involved.'

282. After having addressed him, (invoking) the guardians of the world and the gods, with these and other such speeches, he should cause the man who has been placed in the scale, to descend once more and should ascertain (the state of the matter).

* 283. If he rises, on being weighed (for the second time), he is undoubtedly innocent. If his

---

277. This quibble is based on the fact that the two words Dha*t*a and Dharma commence with the same syllable.

279–281. The words enclosed in brackets cannot be genuine. They appear to be a quotation from the Yâ*g*ñavalkya-sm*ri*ti (II, 101, 102), which has been added as a marginal gloss by a copyist, and has subsequently crept into the text. Yâ*g*ñavalkya puts this entire address in the mouth of the defendant himself, whereas all the other *Smri*ti writers put it in the mouth of a third person.

weight remains the same as before, or if he goes down, he cannot be acquitted.

* 284. Should the scales break, or the beam or the hooks split, or the strings burst, or the transverse beam split, (the judge) shall pronounce a formal declaration of his innocence.

21. The Ordeal by Fire.

* 285. I will propound, next, the excellent law regarding the (ordeal by) fire. The interval between

284. It seems strange that the accidents mentioned in this paragraph should be viewed as proofs of innocence. Vish*n*u, Kâtyâyana, and Vyâsa rule that the proceeding shall be repeated in every such case. B*ri*haspati says that these accidents shall be taken as proofs of guilt. The reading mûrtita*h* may be wrong (for puna*h* sa? 'he shall cause the proceeding to be repeated'). See Vyâsa.

285–303. Vish*n*u XI; Yâg*ñ*avalkya II, 103–107.

The essential features of the ordeal by fire are as follows: 1. Eight concentric circles of equal breadth are marked on a piece of ground. 2. An iron ball is heated repeatedly by a blacksmith. 3. The hands of the defendant are examined, and all existing sores or scars coloured with dots. 4. His hands are wrapped up in leaves, in order to protect them against the hot iron. 5. A prayer addressed to Agni, god of fire, shall be recited and written on a leaf, which is fastened on the head of the defendant. 6. The iron ball is placed in his hands, and he is made to walk slowly through all the circles successively, taking one circle with each step. On reaching the last circle he may throw the ball on the ground. 7. His hands are examined once more. If they are found to contain any fresh sores or wounds, he is guilty; if not, he is innocent. 8. If he lets the ball drop from fear, before having reached the last circle, or if the examination of his hands has yielded no definite result, the whole proceeding has to be repeated.

285. Other legislators state that each circle shall be thirty-two Angulas broad together with the space situated between it and the next circle. In par. 299 it is said that the breadth of each circle shall equal the length of the defendant's foot. This rule, according to the commentators, refers to the circle minus the intermediate space between it and the next circle, and means that a

every two circles is ordained to measure thirty-two Aṅgulas.

* 286. Thus the space covered by the eight circles will measure two hundred and fifty-six Aṅgulas.

* 287. He should place seven leaves of the holy fig-tree in the hands of the defendant, and should fasten the leaves (on his hands) with seven threads.

* 288. A professional blacksmith, who has practice in working with fire, and whose skill has been tested on previous occasions, should be caused to heat the iron in fire.

* 289, 290. An iron ball fifty Palas in weight having been repeatedly made fiery, sparkling and red-hot, a pure Brahman who reveres truth, should address it as follows, when it has been heated thrice: 'Listen to the law of Manu, which is superintended by the guardians of the world (themselves).

* 291. Thou, O fire, art the means of purification and the exalted mouth of all the gods. Thou, dwelling in the heart of all beings, knowest this affair.

* 292. Truth and falsehood proceed from thy tongue. Deign not to show thyself unworthy of the character thus attributed to thee in the Vedas and other books.

* 293. This man (the defendant) has been thus addressed by that man (the plaintiff), and has denied

---

circle shall equal the defendant's foot in breadth, where the foot is longer than sixteen Aṅgulas. Pitâmaha says that the outlines of the circles shall be marked with cow-dung.

288. 'A professional blacksmith,' not one officiating temporarily in that capacity. A.

289, 290. The Vîramitrodaya says that the iron ball shall be put into cold water, after it has been heated for the first and second times.

the charge, (declaring) "I will seize the fire, in order to show that it is all untrue."

* 294. Thus confiding in truth, this man is holding thee. Therefore, O fire, be cool for him, if he speak the truth. If, however, he should tell a lie, as a sinner, I implore thee, to burn his hands.'

* 295. This prayer having been carefully written on a leaf and recited, he should fasten the leaf on his head, and after having done so, should then give him the iron ball.

* 296. Having bathed and stepped into the space covered by the (eight) circles, he should seize the fiery ball, take his stand in one circle, and walk slowly through the seven others.

* 297. (The man) must not put it down again till he has passed through the whole of the measured ground. On reaching the eighth circle, he may drop the fiery ball.

* 298. That man who lets the ball drop from fear, or who cannot be proved to have been burnt, shall take the hot iron once more; this is a fixed rule.

* 299. Each circle should be made as broad as his foot. He must not go further than the breadth of one circle with one step, nor must he remain behind it.

300. In this way the ordeal by fire should always be performed. It is adapted for every season except summer and very cold weather.

* 301. All sores or scars on his hands should be marked with signs previously, and one should examine the hands again afterwards (and look after) the dots with which (the sores) have been marked.

---

299. Read tatpadasa*m*mitam in the text.

* 302. If it does not appear whether (either of) the two hands is burnt, he shall take and seven times crush grains of rice in his hand, with all his might.

* 303. The grains having been crushed by him, if the members of the court should declare him to be unburnt, he shall be honourably released as being innocent. If he is burnt, he shall receive due punishment.

22. The Ordeal by Water.

304. I will now proclaim the excellent law regarding the (ordeal by) water, (which may be performed at all seasons) one after the other, excepting the winter and dewy seasons.

* 305. (This ordeal may be performed) in streams

302, 303. The crushing of grains of rice serves the purpose of making visible such wounds as might have been overlooked previously. Here ends the section of the ordeal by fire. A.

305–317. Vish*n*u XII; Yâ*g*ñavalkya II, 108, 109.

The ordeal by water may be briefly described as follows: 1. This ordeal should be either performed in a tank or in a river which has no swift current. 2. Three arrows should be discharged from a bow of middling size. 3. After that, a strong man should enter the water as far as his navel. The defendant should seize him by the thigh and dive under water. 4. A swift runner should be sent after the second arrow. When he has reached the place where it has fallen, another equally swift runner should be sent back with it to the place where the defendant has entered the water. 5. The defendant is declared innocent, if he has remained under water till the arrow has been brought back. He is declared guilty, if any one of his limbs have been seen, or if he were to emerge from the water in a different spot from that where he entered it. 6. During the proceeding, a prayer is addressed to the deity of water, in which it is asserted, that fire arose from water, and that the water ordeal is superior therefore to the ordeal by fire.

305. The winter season comprises the months Agrahâya*n*a and

which have not too swift a course, in oceans, in rivers, in lakes, in ponds dug by the gods, in tanks, and in pools.

* 306. The diving shall take place after three arrows have been discharged from a bow which must not be too strong. Wise men (have declared) what its strength should be.

* 307. A strong bow is declared to be 107 (Aṅgulas) long, a moderate bow 106, and an inferior bow 105 (Aṅgulas). This is declared to be the rule regarding the bow.

* 308. A strong man should be placed like a pillar in water, reaching to his navel. The defendant should seize him by the thigh and dive under water.

Pausha. The dewy or cold season (*S*i*s*ira) comprises the months Mâgha and Phâlguna. It appears, therefore, that the ordeal by water must not be performed during the period extending from the middle of November to the middle of March, i. e. during the cold weather. This is no doubt because the low temperature of the water during the cold weather might affect the capacity of the defendant to hold out under water sufficiently long.

306. Devakhâta, 'a pond dug by the gods,' denotes a natural hollow or lake. (Böhtlingk's Dictionary.) Nandapa*nd*ita, in his Commentary of the Vish*n*u-sm*ri*ti (LXIV, 16), gives the well-known lake of Pushkara, near A*g*mîr, as an instance of a Devakhâta.

307. It seems strange that the difference in length between the bows should not amount to more than one Aṅgula or inch. The commentators take the three numerals in this paragraph to denote 105, 106, and 107 respectively, and I have translated in accordance with this interpretation. It is, however, possible to translate the three numerals by 500, 600, and 700 respectively, and to refer them to the number of Hastas (1 Hasta = 18 inches) traversed by each of the three arrows. According to another text, which is wrongly attributed to Nârada by some commentators, the arrows shall be shot at a target, which has to be placed at a distance of 150 Hastas from the marksman.

* 309. From the place where the arrows have been discharged, a young man endowed with swiftness of limb should walk as quickly as possible to the place where the middlemost arrow has fallen down.

* 310. Another man, who must be an equally swift runner, should seize the middlemost arrow and return with it quickly to the place from which the (first) man has proceeded.

311. If he who took the arrow does not see the defendant in water on arriving, because he is completely under water, the defendant must be acquitted.

* 312. Otherwise he is guilty, though only one limb of his have become visible. (He is pronounced guilty) equally, if he has moved to a different place than that where he was first immersed.

* 313. Women or children must not be subjected to the ordeal by water by persons acquainted with the law; nor sick, superannuated, or feeble men.

* 314. Cowards, those tormented by pain, and persons afflicted by a calamity should also be held exempt from this trial. Such persons perish immediately after diving, because they are declared to have hardly any breath.

* 315. Should they even have appeared before the court on account of a serious crime, he must not cause them to dive under water, nor must he subject them to the ordeal by fire, or give them poison.

* 316. 'Nothing is more capable than water and fire of showing the difference between right and wrong.

316, 317. These two paragraphs contain the prayer by which the deity of water should be addressed. A. Vish*n*u XII, 8; Yâ*gñ*avalkya II, 108.

Because fire has arisen from the waters, therefore suspected persons

* 317. Are subjected to this proof by preference, by persons thoroughly conversant with the law. Therefore deign, O venerable Lord of Waters, to effect acquittal through truth.'

23. The Ordeal by Poison.

* 318. Now I shall proclaim the excellent rule regarding the ordeal by poison: at what time, in what manner, and in what form it should be administered.

* 319. The exact quantity of the poison (to be given) having been fixed by persons conversant with the essence of law, it shall be weighed, and given to the defendant in the autumn season, when winter sets in.

320. A man acquainted with law, must not (administer this ordeal) in the afternoon, nor in the

---

318–326. The ordeal by poison consists of the swallowing of a mild poison by the defendant. He is innocent if he digests the poison without being affected by it. Vish*n*u XIII; Yâg*ñ*avalkya II, 110, 111.

319. The autumn season, *S*arad, comprises the two months of Â*s*vina and Kârttika, or from middle of September to middle of November. The winter season comprises the two months of Aprahâya*n*a and Pausha, or from middle of November to middle of January. Mitrami*s*ra, who quotes this text in the Vîramitrodaya, asserts that the term 'the winter season' must be taken in this place to include the dewy season, *S*i*s*ira, as well, i.e. the time from middle of January to middle of March.

320. Though the season of *S*arad has been referred to in par. 319, it must be reckoned among the prohibited seasons according to par. 320. A. This observation seems to be just, because the performance of this ordeal in the *S*arad season is prohibited in par. 324 as well. Vasanta, the spring season, extends from middle of March to middle of May. Grîshma, the hot season, extends from middle of May to middle of July. Varshâ, the season of the rains, extends from middle of July to middle of September.

twilight, nor at noon. It must be avoided, likewise, in the autumn, summer, spring, and rainy seasons.

* 321. Spoiled poison, shaken poison, scented and mixed poison, as well as Kâlakû*t*a and Alâbu poison, should be carefully avoided.

* 322. Poison from the *Sri*ṅga plant, which grows in the Himâlayas, of an excellent quality, having (the required) colour, flavour, and taste, and preserving its natural condition, should be given to members of the Kshatriya, Vai*s*ya, and *S*ûdra castes.

* 323. Let him give to the defendant one-eighth less than the twentieth part of a sixth part of a Pala of the poison, mixed with clarified butter.

* 324. Six Yavas should be given in the rainy season; five Yavas in the hot season; seven or eight in the winter season; in the autumn season this ordeal must not take place.

* 325. 'Thou, O poison, art the son of Brahman.

---

321. Spoiled, shaken, scented, and mixed poison should be avoided, because it has been changed from its natural state (into something different). Kâlakû*t*a and Alâbu poison should be avoided, because it is too strong. A. Kâlakû*t*a is a certain deadly poison contained in a bulbous root or tuber. According to a well-known myth, the Kâlakû*t*a poison was produced at the churning of the ocean, when it threatened to destroy the whole world, and was therefore swallowed by *S*iva. Alâbu is the bottle-gourd.

323. There are 960 Yavas to a Pala. The fraction, therefore, is as follows:—$960 \cdot \frac{1}{6} \cdot \frac{1}{20} \cdot \frac{7}{8} = 7$ Yavas. In par. 324, the author says that seven or eight Yavas of poison should be given in winter, i. e. in that season when this ordeal is ordinarily administered. Vish*n*u lays down generally that seven Yavas of poison should be given.

324. This rule shows that the prohibition which has been levelled in par. 320 against the performance of this ordeal in the rainy and summer seasons, must not be interpreted too strictly.

325. This is the prayer which should be addressed to the poison. A.

Truth and virtue are thy support. Clear this man from guilt. Become (like) Ambrosia to him, through truth.'

* 326. Let the man be kept in a shadowy place without taking food, for the whole remainder of the day. If he remains free from convulsions such as are generally caused by poison, he is declared innocent by Manu.

24. The Ordeal by Sacred Libation.

* 327. Now I shall proclaim the excellent rule regarding the ordeal by sacred libation, as it has been laid down, for all seasons indiscriminately, by learned men.

* 328. The consecrated water shall be given, early in the morning, to a virtuous man, who believes in God. He must have fasted and bathed, and wear his wet clothes.

* 329. The defendant should be made to drink three mouthfuls of water in which (an image of) the deity whom he holds sacred has been bathed and worshipped.

* 330. If he should meet himself with any calamity

---

326. Here ends the chapter of the ordeal by poison. A.

327–333. Vish*n*u XIV; Yâ*g*ñavalkya II, 112, 113.

327. The ordeal by sacred libation is performed by swallowing three mouthfuls of consecrated water in which an idol has been bathed. The defendant is declared innocent, if no misfortune befalls him within a certain period after this trial.

328. Immoral persons and infidels must not be subjected to this ordeal, because they are already deprived of the assistance of the gods in every case. A. Read pûrvâh*n*e in the text.

330. If any misfortune should happen to him, through the act of the king or through fate, it shall be taken as proof of his guilt. A. Other legislators refer in particular to illness, fire, death

within a week or a fortnight (after having undergone this ordeal), it shall be regarded as proof of his guilt.

* 331. If a great misfortune even should befall him after the lapse of a fortnight, he must not be harassed by any one, because the fixed period has elapsed.

* 332. The drinking of consecrated water should be avoided in the case of great criminals, irreligious or ungrateful men, eunuchs, low rascals, unbelievers, Vrâtyas, and slaves.

333. A righteous king, who administers the five ordeals to persons charged with a crime in the way which has been stated, acquires prosperity both in a future state and in this life.

* 334. The ordeal by water is destined for the hot season. The ordeal by poison (should be administered) in very cold weather. A Brahman should be tested by the balance, fire is reserved for the Kshatriya.

* 335. The ordeal by water should be administered to the Vais*y*a. Poison should be given to the *S*ûdra. He must not give poison to the Brahman, nor should a Kshatriya take the (hot) iron.

---

of a relation, or punishment inflicted by the king. Nor is every sort of disease to be considered as proof of guilt. It is obvious that the inclusion of a punishment inflicted by the king among the proofs of guilt tends to place the defendant at the mercy of the sovereign power.

332. All the various categories of persons that are mentioned here as unfit for the performance of this ordeal are so because they are already deprived of the assistance of the gods in every case. A. Vrâtyas, those who have not been invested with the thread.

333. The term 'persons charged with a crime' may denote both real offenders, whose offence has remained secret, and wrongly accused persons. A.

336. The (five) ordeals, ending with the sacred libation and beginning with the balance, should be administered in the case of heavy charges. One hundred and fifty (Pa*n*as) should be given (to the defendant) if he has been acquitted. One who has not been acquitted is liable to punishment.

25. The Rice Ordeal.

* 337. Now I will proclaim the rule regarding the grains of rice which have to be chewed (by the defendant). This rice ordeal should be administered in cases of larceny, but on no other occasion whatsoever. That is the law.

* 338. Let the judge, who must have cleansed himself previously, use white grains of rice, but not (the grains) of any other fruit, and let him place them in an earthen vessel in the sight of (an image of the deity of) the sun.

339. After having mixed them with water in which (an image of the sun-god) has been bathed, he shall leave them in that place for a night. At daybreak, after having prepared them three times, a worshipper of the gods shall give them himself

340. (To the defendant), who must be facing the east and must have bathed and fasted, after having proclaimed the charge himself, in order that right may be discerned from wrong.

337–342. The rice ordeal consists of chewing a number of grains of rice in the husk. If the tooth-flesh is hurt and if blood issues forth, or if the man is seen to be trembling during the proceeding, it is viewed as a proof of guilt. Otherwise he is acquitted.

339. Should the reading be tri*h* kr*i*tva*h*, '(he shall give them) thrice?'

* 341. When the defendant has chewed the grains, he shall cause him to spit them on a leaf. If a leaf of the holy fig-tree be not available, he shall take a leaf of the birch-tree (for that purpose).

* 342. Should blood issue forth, or the tooth-flesh be hurt, or the limbs shake, he must be pronounced guilty.

26. The Ordeal of the Hot Piece of Gold.

343. Now I shall give a description of the ordeal of the hot piece of gold, which has been ordained by Brahman himself for the purpose of distinguishing virtue from vice.

* 344. (The judge), after having cleansed himself, shall quickly pour clarified butter into a golden, silver, iron, or earthen vessel, and shall place the vessel on the fire.

* 345. He shall throw into it a shining coin, made of gold, silver, copper, or iron, after having washed it in water more than once.

* 346. Should (the coin) ever drop into the boiling (mixture), it would be a very dangerous thing to touch him (the fire ?). Therefore he must address the clarified butter with the following prayer:

* 347. 'Thou art the best instrument of purification, O clarified butter, and (comparable to) Am-

343–348. The ordeal of the hot piece of gold (Taptamâsha) derives its name from the gold coin (mâsha) or signet-ring (mudrikâ), which those who are tried by this ordeal are required to pick out of a vessel filled with a boiling liquid, with the thumb and forefinger. They are declared innocent, if the hand remains unhurt.

346. The reading of the first half of this paragraph is quite uncertain, and the above rendering conjectural.

brosia at a sacrifice. Burn this man at once if he is criminal, and be as cold as ice to him if he is innocent.'

* 348. If, on touching and examining the forefinger (of the defendant) it is found to be unhurt and to show no boils, he is innocent. Otherwise, he is not (innocent).

SECOND TITLE OF LAW.

Deposits.

* 1. Where a man entrusts any property of his own with another in confidence and without suspicion, it is called by the learned a Deposit, a title of law.

2. A sensible man should make a deposit with one who belongs to a respectable family, and who is virtuous, acquainted with his duties, veracious, influential, wealthy, and honourable.

3. In whatever manner a man may have delivered

---

348. Some writers refer to two further ordeals, besides the seven kinds mentioned by Nârada. One of them is the ordeal of the red-hot ploughshare, which the defendant is made to lick. The other consists of drawing lots.

II, 1. With one in whom he places no confidence, a man will not deposit a single cowry even, without the guarantee of a written receipt or of witnesses. On the other hand, he will deposit a thousand Suvar*n*as even, without a receipt or witnesses, with one in whose honesty he places implicit reliance. A.

2. A prudent man may entrust a deposit to one endowed with the seven qualities here mentioned, because he feels sure that he may recover his property at any time. A. The term mahâpaksha, 'influential,' means literally one who has many friends and relations. Identical with Manu VIII, 179.

3. Thus, e. g. a sealed deposit must be returned with the seal, a deposit made before witnesses must be restored in the presence of the same witnesses. See Jolly, translation of Book VIII of the Code of Manu. Identical with Manu VIII, 180.

any of his effects to another, in the same manner shall that article be restored to him. Delivery and receipt ought to be equal.

4. If the depositary fails to restore the deposit to the depositor as he ought, he shall be compelled to restore it by forcible means, after his guilt has been proved by ordeals or other (modes of proof).

* 5. If one article hidden in another is deposited in another man's house, without stating (what it is), it is termed an Aupanidhika deposit.

* 6. Deposits are again divided into two species, attested and unattested ones. They must be restored precisely in the same condition (as they were in at the time of their delivery). Otherwise an ordeal must take place.

* 7. The wicked man who does not return a deposit, on being asked to do so by the depositor, shall be punished by the king. If the deposit has

4. Where the depositary, actuated by interested motives, refuses to restore the deposit, and is convicted of his guilt in a court of justice, by an ordeal or by other proof, he must restore it and pay twice its value as a fine. A. Manu VIII, 190.

5. 'One article hidden in another,' such as e.g. a pearl necklace tied up with a particular sort of knot in a cloth. Such a deposit must be restored in the same condition as before, and tied with those very knots with which it was originally delivered. A. Yâ*gñ*avalkya II, 65.

6. If a deposit has been handed over to the depositary in the presence of witnesses, it must be restored before witnesses. If no witnesses were present at the time of its delivery, they may be equally dispensed with at the time when it is returned to the depositor. If it is not returned to him, the depositary must perform an ordeal or make an oath, &c. A.

7. The last clause concerns a deposit which has not been returned on demand. In that case, a calamity arising through fate or the king affects the depositary, and not the depositor. A. Manu VIII, 191; Vish*n*u V, 169–171.

been lost or destroyed, he shall make good its value.

* 8. If he derives profit from a deposit, by using it without the consent of the depositor, he shall be punished likewise, and shall restore the profit, together with interest, to the depositor.

* 9. If a deposit is lost, together with the property of the depositary, the loss shall be the depositary's. The same rule shall obtain, if the loss has been caused by fate or by the king; unless (the depositary) should have acted fraudulently.

10. The depositor being dead, if the depositary restores the deposit to his next-of-kin, of his own accord, he must not be harassed either by the king or by the relations of the depositor.

11. (The rightful owner) shall try to recover it amicably, without resorting to stratagems. Or he shall explore (the depositary's) mode of living, and cause him to restore it by friendly expostulations.

---

8. If the depositary without the knowledge of the depositor derives gain from the use of the deposit he shall be punished, and shall make over his gain, together with interest, to the depositor. A. Yâ*g*ñavalkya II, 67.

10. If, the depositor being dead, the depositary through honesty restores the deposit to his nearest relative and heir, without having been asked to do so, or without the existence of the deposit being known to the heir, he must not be harassed by the relatives of the depositor asserting, 'He has not restored all,' or by the king. A. Manu VIII, 186.

11. Nârâya*n*a, in commenting on Manu VIII, 187, observes that this rule applies to one who believes a deposit to be with another, but has not made it over himself. He shall try to recover the deposit amicably; or he shall ascertain whether the depositary has made extraordinary expenses, and may therefore be suspected to have embezzled the deposit. Other commentators explain this text in a different manner, See Professor Bühler's note on Manu VIII, 187. Nearly identical with Manu VIII, 187.

12. What has been stolen by thieves, carried away by water, or burnt by fire, need not be restored (by the depositary), unless he should have appropriated something out of it.

* 13. He who fails to restore a deposit, and he who demands what he never deposited, shall both be punished like thieves, and shall be made to pay a sum equal (in amount to the value of the deposit).

* 14. The same law applies in the case of Yâ*k*ita, Anvâhita, and other such deposits, articles made over to an artist, Nyâsa and Pratinyâsa deposits.

* 15. If a man takes charge of a wealthy boy, the law is also the same. These six cases are equal (from a legal point of view).

---

12. If, however, he is convicted, by the performance of an ordeal, of having derived some profit from the deposit, he shall restore his gains. A. Nearly identical with Manu VIII, 189.

13. Either of the two criminals here mentioned must be punished like a thief and pay the value of the deposit as a fine. A. Nearly identical with Manu VIII, 191.

14. Yâ*k*ita is what has been borrowed for use, especially clothes and ornaments, which have been borrowed on the occasion of a wedding or other festival. Anvâhita is a deposit, which has been delivered by the depositor to a third person, on condition of its being returned afterwards to the owner. 'Articles made over to an artist' are materials to be worked by an artizan, as e.g. gold delivered to a goldsmith to be made into an earring. Nyâsa is a secret deposit, which has been handed over to some one inhabitant of the house, behind the back of the house-owner. Pratinyâsa is a mutual bailment, both parties exchanging deposits with one another. Asahâya, Vi*gñ*âne*s*vara, Mitrami*s*ra, &c. Yâ*gñ*avalkya II, 67.

15. If a man takes a wealthy boy who has no guardian into his house, the property of the boy is subject to the above rules regarding deposits. A.

THIRD TITLE OF LAW.

Partnership.

* 1. Where traders or others carry on business jointly, it is called Partnership, which is a title of law.

* 2. Where several partners are jointly carrying on business for the purpose of gain, the contribution of funds towards the common stock of the association forms the basis (of their undertakings). Therefore let each contribute his proper share.

* 3. The loss, expenses, and profit of each partner are either equal to those of the other partners, or exceed them, or remain below them, according as his share is equal to theirs, or greater, or less.

* 4. The stores, the food, the charges (for tolls and the like), the loss, the freight, and the expense of keeping valuables must be duly paid for by each of the several partners, in accordance with the terms of their agreements.

* 5. (Each partner) is responsible for what has been

III, 2. Thus, e. g. a principal amounting to 1000 Drammas is invested in their common business by four partners. One contributes one-half of the principal, i. e. 500 Drammas. Another contributes one-fifth, i. e. 200 Drammas. A third contributes 200 Drammas likewise. A fourth contributes 100 Drammas. The percentage of the gain and of the charges will be in accordance with the share contributed by each partner. A.

3. Manu VIII, 211; Yâ*gñ*avalkya II, 259.

4. The expense incurred by the purchase of merchandise, for food, &c., has to be defrayed by all the partners in due shares, according to the terms originally agreed on, and the several shares contributed by them. A.

5. He who causes the loss of funds contributed by all the partners must make it good, and so must he who has infringed

lost by his want of care, or in consequence of his acting against the instructions of, or without authorization from, all the other coparceners.

* 6. Where the property of the partnership is in danger through fate, through a gang of robbers, or through the king, the tenth part of the goods shall belong to him who has preserved them through his own exertion.

* 7. Should one partner meet with an accident, his heir shall replace him; or on failure of an heir, another man, or all (the partners) if they are capable (of becoming his substitute).

* 8. In the same way, where an officiating priest has met with an accident, another (priest) shall officiate for him, and receive from him his part of the fee to the stipulated amount.

* 9. Where an officiating priest forsakes a sacri-

---

the rules of the society, or who has caused a loss by acting without authorization from his partners. A. Yâ*g*ñavalkya II, 260.

6. If any one member of the society exerts himself to guard their common property against a fire, or against a gang of robbers, or against an encroaching prince who wants to seize it, he shall receive a tenth part of it, as a reward for his trouble. A. Yâ*g*ñavalkya II, 260.

7. Should any one among the partners die, his sons or other heirs shall take his share. Failing heirs, it shall belong to any other partner, who is able to officiate for him. Or, if all are able to officiate for him, they all shall take it together. A. Yâ*g*ñavalkya II, 265.

8. If among several officiating priests one should meet with a calamity, his share of the work shall pass to another, and the stipulated fee shall also belong to his substitute. A. Manu VIII, 206.

9. If the case of an officiating priest or sacrificer who has left the other party from anger, avarice, or some other reprehensible motive, and without delinquencies on the part of the other party, be brought before the king, he shall punish him. A. Manu VIII, 389; Yâ*g*ñavalkya II, 237; Vish*n*u V, 113.

ficer, who is no offender and free from guilt, or where (a sacrificer) forsakes a faultless priest, they shall both be punished.

* 10. There are three sorts of officiating priests: one honoured by previous generations, one appointed by (the sacrificer) himself, and one who performs the functions of a priest of his own accord through friendship.

* 11. This law applies to hereditary and self-chosen priests. But it is no sin to abandon a priest officiating of his own accord.

* 12. A trader on reaching a toll-house should pay the legal duty. A prudent man must not try to evade it, (because) it is called the (king's) tax.

* 13. If he evades a toll-house, or if he buys or sells at another than the legal hour, or if he does not state the value (of his goods) correctly, he shall be fined eight times the amount which he tried to evade.

---

11. In the case of those officiating priests who have been employed by the ancestors of the sacrifices, i.e. who are hereditary in his family, and in the case of those who have been chosen by himself the punishment ordained for forsaking a priest should be inflicted. But if the sacrificer abandons one who officiates for him from friendship, and employs in his place one better qualified, or more acceptable to himself, awarding to him the stipulated fee, he is free from blame. A.

12. A duty is the king's due, and traders must not defraud the king of it. A.

13. There are three ways for evading a duty: one, if a merchant avoids a toll-house and thus escapes paying the ordinary toll; another, if he buys or sells at an unseasonable time a commodity on which he has not paid the customary duty; a third, if he does not state correctly the amount or value of his goods or chattels. A merchant, who has committed any one out of these offences, shall pay eight times the amount of the duty embezzled by him as a fine. A. Manu VIII, 400; Yâ*gñ*avalkya II, 262.

14. It is declared that a wise man should always abstain from levying a toll on that property of a learned Brahman which belongs to his household; but not (on that which he uses) for trading purposes.

15. The alms received by Brahmans, the property of stage players, and what is capable of being carried on one's back; on all that he must raise no duty.

* 16. If a travelling merchant who has come into his country should die there, the king shall preserve his goods till the heir comes forward.

* 17. On failure of an heir, he must make them over to his relatives or connexions. On failure of them, he shall keep them well guarded for a period of ten years.

* 18. When such property without an owner, and which is not claimed by an heir, has been preserved for ten years, the king may keep it for himself. Thus the sacred law will not be violated.

---

14. The term *S*rotriya, 'a learned Brahman,' applies to Brahmans generally in this place. All the chattels of a Brahman, except what belongs to the household furniture, are liable to pay duty. Likewise, if he imports and exports goods in trading, those goods have to pay duty. A. Manu VII, 133; Âpastamba II, 10, 26, 10; Vasish*th*a XIX, 23; Vish*n*u III, 26.

15. The following three descriptions of property shall be exempt from taxation: alms received by Brahmans, no matter how great their value; the property of actors, singers, and the like persons; and what may be carried on the shoulders by any one. A. Vasish*th*a XIX, 37.

18. Read adâyâda*m* in the text.

FOURTH TITLE OF LAW.

Resumption of Gift.

*1. Where a man wishes to resume what he has given, because it has been unduly given by him, it is called Resumption of Gift, a title of law.

* 2. What may be given and what not, valid gifts and invalid gifts; thus the law of gift is declared fourfold in judicial affairs.

* 3. Again, what may not be given is eightfold; what may be given is of one kind only; of valid gifts there are seven species; and sixteen sorts of invalid gifts.

* 4. An Anvâhita deposit, a Yâ*k*ita, a pledge, joint property, a deposit, a son, a wife, the whole property of one who has offspring,

* 5. And what has been promised to another man; these have been declared by the spiritual guides to be inalienable by one in the worst plight even.

* 6. What is left (of the property) after the expense of maintaining the family has been defrayed,

IV, 1. 'Unduly' means in a mode opposed to law. Mitâksharâ, Vîramitrodaya, Mayûkha, &c. Manu VIII, 214.

2. 'Valid gifts,' literally 'what is given.' 'Invalid gifts,' literally 'what is not given.'

4. For the meaning of the technical terms, Anvâhita and Yâ*k*ita, see II, 14. The prohibition of such gifts as would leave the family destitute appears to relate principally to charitable donations and religious endowments.

4–6. Yâ*gñ*avalkya II, 175.

6. That only may be given which is left after the cost of living has been defrayed for those whom the head of the family is bound to support. Any gift, on the other hand, which causes hardship to the family, is reprehensible, and not meritorious. A.

may be given. But by giving away anything besides, a householder will incur censure.

7. He who has, for three years, property sufficient to provide for those whom he is bound to maintain, or who has even more than that, shall drink the Soma juice.

* 8. The price paid for merchandise, wages, (a present offered) for an amusement, (a gift made) from affection, or from gratitude, or for sexual intercourse with a woman, and a respectful gift, are the seven kinds of valid gifts.

* 9. Invalid gifts are the following (sixteen): what

---

7. This rule applies to those cases where there is more wealth than what suffices to maintain the family. A. Manu XI, 7; Yâ*gñ*avalkya I, 124; Vasish*th*a VIII, 10; Vish*n*u LIX, 8.

8. Those gifts only are valid which have been made in one of the seven modes here mentioned. The sixteen other modes of gift are illegal. A. 'A present offered for an amusement,' i. e. what has been given to bards, eulogists, and the like persons. 'A gift made from affection,' to a daughter or other relative. Vîramitrodaya, &c. Instead of strîbhakti, 'sexual intercourse with a woman,' the MSS. of Vulg. and the quotations read strî*s*ulka, 'a nuptial gift presented to the relations of the wife.'

9–11. 1. 'Fear,' as e.g. if an honest man promises one hundred drachmas to a ruffian who addresses him, while he is passing through a forest, with the words, 'If thou givest me one hundred drachmas, thou shalt live. Otherwise, thou shalt die.' 2. 'Anger, or hatred:' if a man, actuated by jealousy, says to a Brahman, to whom his wife has offered a seat, 'All the furniture which you see in this house shall be yours.' 3. 'Sorrow:' if a man, in a heavy affliction, declares, 'I will go into the forest. My house has been given to Brahmans to-day.' 4. 'Pain:' a man distressed by a painful illness, says to a Brahman, 'I have given thee one hundred *S*uvar*n*as.' 5. 'A bribe:' a litigant says to an assessor of the court, 'I will give thee one hundred Pa*n*as if my cause is declared victorious by thee.' 6. 'In jest,' what has been laughingly given. 7. 'Under false pretences,' as e.g. under the following circumstances:—A libidinous man is enamoured of a public woman, by the name of *K*ûtama*ñg*arî ('Mango Bud'). He is deprived of her

has been given by a man under the influence of fear, anger, hatred, sorrow or pain; or as a bribe; or in jest; or fraudulently, under false pretences;

*10. Or by a child; or by a fool; or by a person not his own master; or by one distressed; or by one intoxicated; or by one insane; or in consideration of a reward, thinking 'This man will show me some service;'

*11. And so is invalid what was given from ignorance to an unworthy man thought to be worthy, or for a purpose (thought to be) virtuous.

*12. Both the donee who covets invalid gifts and accepts them from avarice, and the donor of what ought not to be given who yet gives it away, deserve punishment.

---

by a Thakur, and is bewailing his separation from her. Some one asks him whether he will make him a present of a ring, in case he should bring *K*ûtama*ñg*arî before him. He promises to give the ring and offers a surety for it. Thereupon the other exhibits a Mango bud (*K*ûtama*ñg*arî) to him, instead of the woman *K*ûtama*ñg*arî. 8. What was given by a child. 9. What was given by a fool. 10. What was given by a person not his own master. 11. What was given by one distressed, as e.g. if a man being carried away by a current of water exclaims, 'I will give one hundred Suvar*n*as to any one who saves my life.' 12. What was given by one inebriated. 13. What was given by one insane or possessed by a demon. 14. What was given through a hope of recompense, in expectation of some service to be performed by the donee. 15. What was given to an unworthy man, from ignorance, as e.g. to a *S*ûdra, whom the donor fancied to be a Brahman, because he saw him girt with the sacred thread. 16. What was given for a purpose (thought to be) virtuous, as e.g. if a devout man has made a religious endowment, and the donee employs it for gambling or libidinous purposes. A. Other jurists construe these texts somewhat differently, in order to obtain the sixteen sorts of void gifts distinguished by Nârada. Manu VIII, 212.

FIFTH TITLE OF LAW.

Breach of a Contract of Service.

* 1. If a man has promised to render service and fails to render it, it is termed Breach of a Contract of Service, a title of law.

* 2. The sages have distinguished five sorts of attendants according to law. Among these are four sorts of labourers; the slaves (are the fifth category, of which there are) fifteen species.

* 3. A student, an apprentice, a hired servant, and fourthly, an official; these must be regarded as labourers; slaves are those born in the house and the rest.

* 4. The sages have declared that the state of dependence is common to all these; but that their respective position and income depends on their particular caste and occupation.

* 5. Know that there are two sorts of occupations; pure work and impure work. Impure work is that done by slaves. Pure work is that done by labourers.

* 6. Sweeping the gateway, the privy, the road,

V, 1–4. Persons bound to obedience. A.

3. 'A student,' one studying divine science. 'A pupil,' an apprentice. Vîramitrodaya, &c.

4. Their respective position depends on their caste, and their income depends on their occupation. A.

5–7. Unclean occupations. A.

6. The term 'sweeping' has to be construed with all four nouns, the gateway and the rest. 'The privy,' i.e. a hole or other receptacle of impure substances. 'The place for rubbish,' i.e. a place where the dust and other sweepings from the house are deposited. Vîramitrodaya.

and the place for rubbish; shampooing the secret parts of the body; gathering and putting away the leavings of food, ordure, and urine,

* 7. And lastly, rubbing the master's limbs when desired; this should be regarded as impure work. All other work besides this is pure.

* 8. Till he has mastered science, let a student attend diligently on his teacher. The same conduct has to be observed by him towards his teacher's wife and son.

* 9. Let him preserve chastity and beg alms, lying on a low couch and using no ornaments. Let him go to rest after and rise before all (others who are staying at) his teacher's house.

* 10. Let him never come or stay without his teacher's bidding. His (teacher's) call he must obey without hesitation, when he is able to do so.

11. Let him read at the proper time, when his teacher is not averse to it, sitting on a lower seat than his teacher, by his side, or on a bench, and paying attention (to what he says).

12. Science, like the current of a stream, is constantly advancing towards the plain. Therefore, let one studying science be humble towards his teacher.

* 13. His teacher shall correct him, if he does not

---

8. He must obey his teacher's wife and son, as much as the teacher himself. A.

8–11. Vish*n*u XXVIII, and the references in the Notes to that Chapter.

9–15. Rules of conduct for a student. A.

12. 'The current of a stream,' meaning a river, advances into the plain, and so does science. Therefore one engaged in studying it should always be lowly and humble. A.

13–14. Gautama II, 42–44; Âpastamba I, 28, 29, 31; Manu VIII, 299, 300.

pay obedience to him, scolding him or chastising him with a rope or with a small shoot of cane.

14. (The teacher) must not strike him a heavy blow, nor (must he beat him) on a noble part or on the chest; and he must encourage him, after having chastised him. Otherwise the king shall punish him.

*15. After having completed his studies, let him give the customary present to his teacher and turn home. The conduct of a pupil has been declared.

*16. If (a young man) wishes to be initiated into the art of his own craft, with the sanction of his relations, he must go and live with a master, the duration of his apprenticeship having been fixed.

*17. The master shall teach him at his own house and feed him. He must not employ him in work of a different description, and treat him like a son.

*18. If one forsakes a master, who instructs him

13. Scolding him, i.e. abusing him. A. The Nepalese MS. has a better reading of this clause: 'Or he shall beat him without hurting him, with' &c.

14. A teacher, though angry, must not strike his pupil severely, nor on a noble part, nor on the chest. After having beaten him, he must again encourage him. If the teacher, actuated by an excess of anger, beats him too severely, the pupil shall announce it to the king, who shall punish the teacher. A.

15. Manu II, 245; Yâgñavalkya I, 51; Âpastamba I, 11, 30, 1; Gautama IX, 1; Vishnu XXVIII, 42.

16–21. Rules for an apprentice. A.

16. The teacher must make an agreement in this form, 'Let this apprentice stay with me so and so long.' Vîramitrodaya.

17. The teacher shall cause the pupil to do the work peculiar to his own profession, and no other work, and shall feed him and instruct him at his own house. He shall treat him like a son, and not like a labourer. A.

18. If a pupil forsakes his teacher, though the latter has not committed a mortal sin or other heavy crime, the teacher may compel him by forcible means to remain at his house. A.

and whose character is unexceptionable, he may be compelled by forcible means to remain (at the master's house), and he deserves corporal punishment and confinement.

*19. Though his course of instruction be completed, an apprentice must continue to reside at the house of his master, till the fixed period has expired. The profit of whatever work he may be doing there belongs to his master.

*20. When he has learnt the art of his craft within the (stipulated) period, the apprentice shall reward his master as plentifully as he can, and return home, after having taken leave of him.

21. Or, a certain fee having been agreed upon and the skill of the pupil examined, the apprentice shall take (his fee) and shall not go to live in the house of another man.

*22. Hired servants are of three kinds: highest, middlemost, and lowest. The wages due for their labour are fixed in proportion to their skill and to the value of their services.

*23. Soldiers constitute the highest class, agriculturists the middle class, and porters the lowest class. These are the three classes of hired servants.

---

19. The whole gain of that work which is done by the apprentice while staying at the house of his master after completing his course of instruction, belongs to the master, and not to the apprentice. A. Yâgñavalkya II, 184.

20. After the lapse of the stipulated period, i.e. when the time fixed for his apprenticeship has expired. A.

21. The apprentice shall receive whatever fee has been agreed upon, after his skill has been examined by the master. A. The only MS. of the earlier recension of the Nârada-smriti breaks off at this paragraph. The remainder of the present translation has been done from the more recent recension of the Nârada-smriti. See Introduction.

*24. One appointed to manage the property (of the family) and to superintend the household, must also be regarded as a labourer. He is also termed Kau*t*umbika (the general family servant).

*25. Thus have the four classes of servants doing pure work been enumerated. All the others do dirty work and are slaves, of whom there are fifteen kinds.

*26. One born at (his master's) house; one pur-

---

24. 'The property,' meaning fields or ready money, &c. 'One appointed to manage it,' i. e. one deputed to administrate it. Vîramitrodaya, p. 405.

26–28. 'One born at (his master's) house,' one born of a female slave in the house (of her master). 'One received (by gift),' one obtained by the acceptance of a gift and the like. 'One obtained by inheritance,' a slave of the father or other ancestor. 'One maintained during a general famine,' one whose life has been preserved, during a period of dearth, in order that he might do service (for his preserver). 'One pledged by his rightful owner,' one reduced to the condition of a pledge, for a loan received (by his master). 'One released from a heavy debt,' one enslaved for debt, whose debt has been paid and who has thereby become the slave (of him who paid the debt). 'One made captive in a fight,' one defeated in a combat and enslaved by the victorious party. 'One won through a wager,' one gained through the success of a cause, which was preceded by an agreement in this form, 'If I am defeated in this quarrel, I will be thy slave.' 'One who has come forward declaring, "I am thine,"' one who has promised of his own accord to become the slave of another man. 'An apostate from asceticism,' one who has forsaken the order of religious ascetics. 'One enslaved for a stipulated period,' one obtained through an agreement in this form, 'I will be thy slave for such a space of time.' 'One who has become a slave in order to get a maintenance,' one who has offered himself as a slave, on condition that food shall always be given to him. 'One enslaved on account of his connexion with a female slave:' by a female slave is meant a female house-slave; one enslaved for connexion with her is one who has married her through love, and has thus been reduced to the status of a slave. 'One self-sold' is one who has sold himself.

chased; one received (by gift); one obtained by inheritance; one maintained during a general famine; one pledged by his rightful owner;

*27. One released from a heavy debt; one made captive in a fight; one won through a wager; one who has come forward declaring, 'I am thine;' an apostate from asceticism; one enslaved for a stipulated period;

*28. One who has become a slave in order to get a maintenance; one enslaved on account of his connexion with a female slave; and one self-sold. These are the fifteen classes of slaves as declared in law.

*29. Among these, the four named first cannot be released from bondage, except by the favour of their owners. Their bondage is hereditary.

*30. Should any one out of them (however) save his master's life, when his life is in peril, he shall be released from slavery and shall take a son's share (of his master's wealth).

*31. One maintained during a famine is released from bondage if he gives a pair of oxen. It is not

---

These are the fifteen species (of slaves). Mitâksharâ, p. 268. Manu VIII, 415.

30. This rule is applicable to any of the fifteen sorts of slaves. Mitâksharâ, p. 269. Other commentators cite an encounter with a tiger as an instance of a perilous situation. The slave, in order to obtain release from slavery, must have risked his own life in rescuing his master.

31. The objection that a slave cannot give a pair of oxen, as he has no property of his own according to Nârada himself (V, 41), may be met by the argument that the dominion of slaves over affectionate gifts and the like is universally acknowledged, just as the right of a woman to dispose of Strîdhana given to her as an affectionate present. See the gloss on this text in Colebrooke's Digest, III, 1, 43.

by labour (alone) that the value of the food consumed during a famine can be repaid.

*32. One pledged (is released) when his master redeems him by discharging the debt. If, however, he causes (the pledgee) to take him in lieu of payment, he becomes equal to a purchased slave.

*33. It is by paying his debt with interest, that a debtor is released from slavery. One enslaved for a stipulated period recovers freedom on the expiration of that period.

*34. One who has come forward declaring, 'I am thine,' one made a prisoner in war, and one won through a wager, these are released on giving a substitute whose capacity for work is equal to theirs.

*35. An apostate from asceticism shall become the king's slave. He can never be emancipated, nor is there any expiation of his crime.

*36. One who has become a slave in order to get a maintenance, is released at once on giving up the said subsistence. One enslaved on account of his being connected with a female slave is released on parting with her.

*37. That wretch who, being independent, sells himself, is the vilest of slaves. He cannot be released from bondage.

*38. Those who are sold after having been captured by robbers, and those who are enslaved by forcible means, must be emancipated by the king. Their slavery is not legal.

*39. In the inverse order of the (four) castes,

---

33. Yâ*gñ*avalkya II, 182. 35. Yâ*gñ*avalkya II, 183.

36. The Mitâksharâ (p. 270) declares that sexual intercourse with a slave is prohibited. Yâ*gñ*avalkya II, 182.

38. Yâ*gñ*avalkya II, 182.

39. As a man of the highest caste may marry a wife of an

slavery is not ordained, except where a man violates the duties peculiar to his caste. Slavery (in that respect) is analogous to the condition of a wife.

*40. If one not his own master offers himself (as a slave), saying, 'I am thine,' he (to whom he has offered himself) may not dispose of him. His former master may recover him when he likes.

*41. Three persons are declared to have no proprietary right: a wife, a slave, and a son. Whatever property they acquire shall be made over to him to whom they belong.

*42. He who pleased in his mind wishes to emancipate his own slave, shall take from his (the slave's) shoulders a jar filled with water and smash it.

*43. He shall sprinkle his head with the water, which must contain whole grain and flowers, and

---

inferior caste or of his own caste, whereas a woman of the highest caste is forbidden to marry a man of inferior caste, the same rule should be observed with regard to a slave. Vîramitrodaya, p. 406. An ascetic who violates the duties of his order is liable to become the slave of his inferior in caste even. Mitâksharâ, p. 271. Yâ*gñ*avalkya II, 183.; Manu VIII, 410–414.

40. If a man, after having promised to become the slave of one man, enters the service of another man afterwards, that other man must relinquish him. 'One not his own master,' i. e. the slave of another man. Vîramitrodaya, p. 411.

41. According to the standard commentators the purport of this rule is merely to indicate the want of independence of wives, sons, and slaves in the disposal of their property. See Professor Bühler's note on Manu VIII, 416. Identical with Manu VIII, 416.

42, 43. The breaking of a water-pot which the slave is carrying on his shoulder is said to be indicative of the discontinuance of the former slave's office to carry water. The solemn smashing of a water-jar (gha*t*a-spho*t*a) forms the principal part of another ceremony of a totally different character as well, viz. of the ceremony of expulsion from caste.

having declared him a free man three times, he shall dismiss him with his face turned towards the east[1].

SIXTH TITLE OF LAW.

Non-payment of Wages.

*1. A series of rules will be stated (next) for the payment and non-payment of labourers' wages. It is termed 'Non-payment of Wages,' a title of law.

*2. A master shall regularly pay wages to the servant hired by him, whether it be at the commencement, at the middle, or at the end of his work, just as he had agreed to do.

*3. Where the amount of the wages has not been fixed, (the servant of) a trader, a herdsman, and an agricultural servant shall respectively take a tenth part of the profit (derived from the sale of merchandise), of the seed of cows, and of the grain.

*4. Their implements of work, and whatever else

[1] The Indian MSS. and some quotations insert the following paragraph here, which is omitted in the Nepalese MS. and in other quotations :—

'*44. From that time let it be said that this slave is cherished by the favour of his master. His food may be eaten, and presents accepted from him, and he shall be respected (by worthy persons).'

VI, 2. When the amount of the wages has been fixed by an agreement in this form, 'I will give thee thus much,' it shall be divided into three parts, and one part be given on three occasions, viz. at the commencement, middle, and end of the labour. This rule is applicable where the amount of the wages has been fixed. The next paragraph states the rule for those cases where the amount of the wages has not been fixed. Vîramitrodaya, p. 414.

3. The strange term 'the seed of cows' denotes cows' milk according to the commentators. Yâgñavalkya II, 194.

4. The phrase 'whatever may have been entrusted to servants for their business' is explained as referring to grain and the like

may have been entrusted to them for their business, they shall employ with due care and not neglect them wantonly.

* 5. If one fails to perform such work as he had promised to do, he shall be compelled to perform it, first paying him his wages. If he does not perform it after having taken wages, he must pay back twice the amount of his wages.

* 6. One who abandons merchandise which he had agreed to convey to its destination, shall give a sixth part of the wages. (An employer) who does not pay the wages which he had agreed to give shall forfeit those wages together with interest.

* 7. A merchant who does not take a conveyance

---

used for agriculture. It appears from the preceding paragraph that business of every sort is intended. Yâg*ñ*avalkya II, 193.

5. Manu VIII, 215; Âpastamba II, 11, 28, 2–3; Vish*n*u V, 153, 154; Yâg*ñ*avalkya II, 193.

6. The Ratnâkara refers the second half of this paragraph, like the first half, to the special case of wages or hire promised to the carrier for the transport of goods. See Colebrooke's Digest, III, 1, 92. Yâg*ñ*avalkya II, 198.

7. 'A conveyance,' a cart or the like. 'Beasts for draught or burden,' horses or others. When a man hires the conveyance, &c. of another for the purpose of transporting merchandise, and does not transport the merchandise afterwards, because he has promised to pay an excessive hire, he shall pay a fourth part of the promised hire to the owner of the conveyance. When, however, he takes the conveyance and leaves it, after having completed one half of the journey, he shall have to pay the whole of the hire. Vîramitrodaya, p. 420. Yâg*ñ*avalkya II, 198. Of vv. 6, 7, the Nepalese MS. has an entirely different version, as follows: '*6. One who abandons his work before the expiration of the term, forfeits his wages. If it is through the fault of his employer that he strikes work, he shall be rewarded for as much as has been finished by him. 7. He who leaves on the road that which he had undertaken to transport, shall give a sixth part of the (stipulated) wages. An employer who does not pay (wages) after having set the workman to work, (shall be

or beasts for draught or burden, after having hired them, shall be made to pay a fourth part of the hire; and the whole, if he leaves them half-way.

* 8. And so shall a carrier who fails to transport (the goods entrusted to him) forfeit his wages. He shall be compelled to pay twice the amount of his wages, if he raises difficulties at the time of starting.

* 9. When the merchandise has been damaged by the carrier's fault, he shall have to make good every loss, not including such losses as may have been caused by fate or by the king.

* 10. For (tending) a hundred cows, (a heifer shall be given to the herdsman) as wages every year; for (tending) two hundred (cows), a milch cow (shall be given to him annually), and he shall be allowed to milk (all the cows) every eighth day.

* 11. Those (cows) which a cowherd takes to

---

compelled to pay) the wages together with interest.' This is probably the true reading, as paragraphs 6 and 7 are quoted in this form in the Vîramitrodaya and in Colebrooke's Digest respectively.

8. According to the Mitâksharâ (p. 280), the excessive fine ordained in the second half of this paragraph shall be inflicted when a man raises obstacles on specially important occasions, such as a wedding, or the auspicious time for undertaking a journey. Yâg*n*avalkya II, 197.

9. 'Merchandise,' pearls or other commodities which are to be transported. 'Damaged,' i. e. destroyed. In the terms 'merchandise' and 'carrier,' which are successively used in this paragraph, a bull and a husbandman are included by implication. Thus it is declared in the Madanaratna. Vîramitrodaya, p. 418. What the Madanaratna means is this, that the responsibility of a husbandman for a bull used by him for the purposes of agriculture is analogous to the responsibility of a carrier for the goods he has undertaken to transport. Vish*n*u V, 155, 156; Yâg*n*avalkya II, 197.

10. Manu VIII, 231.

11. Manu VIII, 230; Yâg*n*avalkya II, 164.

pasture every day when the night is over, he shall take back again in the evening, after they have eaten (grass) and drunk (water).

*12. If such a cow meets with an accident, he shall struggle to protect her as best he may. If he is unable (to rescue her) he shall go in haste to announce it to his master.

*13. Should he neither struggle to protect (the cow), nor raise a cry, nor announce it to his master, the herdsman must make good the value of the cow (to the owner), and (must pay) a fine to the king.

*14. But the herdsman alone shall make good (the loss of an animal) which has strayed, or been destroyed by worms, or slain by dogs, or met its death (by tumbling) into a pit, if he did not duly exert himself (to prevent such accidents).

*15. So if goats or sheep are surrounded by wolves, and the herdsman does not come (to their assistance), he shall be responsible for any (animal) which a wolf may attack and kill.

---

12. He shall struggle to protect the cow, and if unable to protect her he shall raise an alarm. Ratnâkara. See Colebrooke's Digest, III, 4, 11.

13. The second half of this paragraph is read as follows in the Nepalese MS.: 'The herdsman is to blame in that case, and he shall make good the loss.'

14. Nearly identical with Manu VIII, 232. Read nash*t*am in the text. The Nepalese MS. here inserts the following paragraph, which is nearly identical with Manu VIII, 234: 'If cattle die, let him give everything to the owner: the tail, skin, the hindpart, the thigh, the bladder, tendons, and yellow concrete bile, and let him point out their particular marks.'

15. Identical with Manu VIII, 235. The Nepalese MS. adds the following paragraph, which is nearly identical with Manu VIII, 236: 'If they graze together in the forest, without being kept in order, and a wolf, suddenly jumping on one of them, kills it, the herdsman shall be free from blame in that case.'

* 16. But for (an animal) seized by robbers, though he raised a cry, the herdsman shall not be bound to pay, provided he gives notice to his master at the proper place and time.

* 17. It is according to these principles that all disputes arising with herdsmen have to be settled. In case of the (natural) death (of an animal entrusted to his care the herdsman) is free from blame, if he can produce the tail, the horns, and the rest.

* 18. If a public woman declines to receive a man after having received her fee, she shall pay twice the amount (of the fee). The same (fine shall be imposed) on a man who does not pay the (stipulated) fee, after having had connexion with a woman (of this description).

* 19. Should a man unnaturally abuse the person (of a public woman) or cause her to be approached by many, he must pay eight times the amount (of the stipulated fee), and a fine to the same amount.

* 20. If a man has built a house on the ground of a stranger and lives in it, paying rent for it, he may take with him, when he leaves the house, the thatch, the timber, the bricks, and other (building materials).

* 21. But if he has been residing on the ground

16. Identical with Manu VIII, 233.

17. The term 'the rest' may be referred, in accordance with the analogous rule of Manu, to the 'ears, hide, bladder, tendons, the yellow concrete bile, and the special proofs or marks.' Manu VIII, 234.

18. Illness, however, is considered as a legitimate reason for breaking an engagement of this sort. Vîramitrodaya, p. 422, and other commentaries.

21. The delivery of the materials, out of which the house has been constructed, to the owner of the ground, has to be regarded as a compensation for the ground having been used without authorisation from the owner.

of a stranger, without paying rent and against that man's wish, he shall by no means take with him, on leaving it, the thatch and the timber.

* 22. Hired commodities shall be restored (by the hirer), when the fixed period has expired. The hirer must make good whatever may have been spoiled or destroyed except in the case of (inevitable) accident.

SEVENTH TITLE OF LAW.

Sales Effected by Another than the Rightful Owner.

* 1. When property kept as a deposit, or the property of a stranger lost (by him) and found (by another man), or stolen articles, are sold in secret, it has to be considered as a 'Sale Effected by Another than the Rightful Owner.'

* 2. When a chattel, which had been sold by another person than the owner, has been recovered

22. This rule applies in the case of water-jars and the like having been injured or destroyed. Vîramitrodaya, p. 421. The Ratnâkara refers this paragraph to broken carriages and the like. See Colebrooke's Digest, III, 1, 104. 'Spoiled,' i. e. partially disfigured. 'Destroyed,' i. e. entirely ruined. 'Accident,' when the things have been knocked against one another. Vîramitrodaya, ibid.

VII, 1. The term 'property kept as a deposit' includes by implication a Yâkita and the other species of bailments. Vîramitrodaya, p. 374, and the other commentaries. See II. Title of Law, 14, 15.

2. The owner of a chattel, which has been sold by a stranger who has no right to it, may reclaim it from any one who happens to be possessed of it. Vîramitrodaya, p. 375; Vishnu V, 164–166; Manu VIII, 201, 202; Yâgñavalkya II, 168. In the Nepalese MS. the last clause runs as follows: 'The buyer who buys in secret is guilty of theft.'

by the owner, he may keep it. No blame attaches to a sale effected in public, but a clandestine sale is viewed in the same light as theft according to law.

* 3. If a man buys from a slave who has not been authorized (to sell) by his master, or from a rogue, or in secret, or at a very low price, or at an improper time, he is as guilty as the seller.

* 4. The purchaser must not make a secret of the way in which he came by a chattel (purchased by him). He becomes free from blame if he can point out the way in which the chattel was acquired by him. In any other case he is equally guilty with the vendor, and shall suffer the punishment of a thief.

* 5. The vendor shall restore his property to the rightful owner, and shall pay to the buyer the price for which it was sold to him; besides that he shall pay a fine to the king. Such is the rule in the case

---

3. 'One who has not been authorized (to sell) by his master,' one who has received no special permission from him (to sell the chattel). The term 'a slave' has to be interpreted in a pregnant sense, so as to include young sons and other dependent persons. Vîramitrodaya, p. 375. Vish*n*u V, 166; Yâ*gñ*avalkya II, 168.

4. It appears from the detailed provisions of B*ri*haspati, Kâtyâyana, and other Sm*ri*ti-writers on the subject of purchase and sale, that every purchase, in order to be legitimate, had to be concluded in open market, on a market day or hour; or that, at least, the purchaser was required to produce the vendor, when the purchase had not been made in open market. Yâ*gñ*avalkya II, 168. The Nepalese MS. inserts the following paragraph here: 'Any purchase or sale which has been effected by another than the rightful owner must be known to be invalid; this is a rule in lawsuits.' The quotations in the Vîramitrodaya and other works prove this verse to be genuine. Yâ*gñ*avalkya II, 170.

5. Yâ*gñ*avalkya II, 170.

of a sale effected by another than the rightful owner.

6. If any one finds a treasure, which had been deposited by a stranger, he shall take it to the king. Every treasure, found by members of any caste, belongs to the king, excepting (those treasures which have been found by) members of the Brahman caste.

7. A Brahman even, when he has found a treasure, must at once give notice to the king. If the king gives it to him he may enjoy it. If he does not give notice, he is (viewed as) a thief.

8. Of his own property also, which he had lost and found again afterwards, a man must give notice to the king. If he does so, he may keep it as his lawful property. It is not his lawful property otherwise.

EIGHTH TITLE OF LAW.

NON-DELIVERY OF A SOLD CHATTEL.

*1. When merchandise has been sold for a (certain) price and is not delivered to the purchaser, it is termed Non-delivery of a Sold Chattel, a title of law.

*2. Property in this world is of two kinds, movable and immovable. All that is termed merchandise in the laws regarding purchase and sale.

*3. The rule regarding the gift and receipt of

6–8. Gautama X, 36–38, 43–45; Vasish*th*a III, 13–14; XVI, 19, 20; Manu VIII, 30–39; Vish*n*u V, 56–64; Yâ*gñ*avalkya II, 33–35. The position of the two last paragraphs is inverted in the Nepalese MS.

VIII, 3. 'Gift' means sale. 'Receipt' means purchase. What

merchandise is declared sixfold by the learned: (what is sold) by tale, by weight, by measure, according to work, according to its beauty, and according to its splendour.

* 4. If a man sells property for a certain price, and does not hand it over to the purchaser, he shall have to pay its produce, if it is immovable, and the profits arising on it, if it is movable property.

* 5. If there has been a fall in the market value of the article in question (in the interval, the purchaser) shall receive both the article itself, and together with it the difference (in point of value). This law applies to those who are inhabitants of the same place; but to those who travel abroad, the

---

is counted before selling it is said to be sold 'by tale.' Betel-nuts may be mentioned as an instance. 'What is sold by weight,' such as gold or sandal-wood and the like substances, which are weighed on a pair of scales. 'What is sold by measure,' such as rice or the like. 'By work,' such as animals giving milk or used for draught or burden. 'According to its beauty,' something handsome, as e.g. a handsome prostitute. 'According to its splendour,' or lustre, as e.g. rubies. Vîramitrodaya, p. 437. A similar exposition is delivered in the Ratnâkara, as quoted in Colebrooke's Digest, III, 3, 3.

4. 'The profits arising on it,' such as e.g. the milk of a cow. Vîramitrodaya, p. 437. The Vivâda*k*intâma*n*i (p. 55) and the Ratnâkara, as quoted in Colebrooke's Digest (III, 3, 18), take the term kriyâphalam as a Dvandva compound, denoting 'the work, such as the carrying of burdens and the like, and the profits, such as milk and the like.' Vish*n*u V, 127; Yâ*gñ*avalkya II, 254.

5. The previous paragraph contains the rule for those cases where the value of the property has increased after its sale. The present rule refers to those cases where the value of the property has diminished after the sale. Vîramitrodaya, p. 437. Those who travel abroad, i. e. who are in the habit of visiting other countries (for trading purposes), may claim the profit which might have accrued to them from travelling abroad. Vivâda*k*intâma*n*i, pp. 55, 56. Vish*n*u V, 129; Yâ*gñ*avalkya II, 254.

profit arising from (dealing in) foreign countries shall be made over (as well).

* 6. If the article (sold) should have been injured, or destroyed by fire, or carried off, the loss shall be charged to the seller, because he did not deliver it after it had been sold by him.

* 7. When a man shows one thing, which is faultless (to the intending purchaser), and (afterwards) delivers another thing to him, which has a blemish, he shall be compelled to pay twice its value (to the purchaser), and an equal amount as a fine.

* 8. So when a man sells something to one person, and (afterwards) delivers it to another person, he shall be compelled to pay twice its value (to the purchaser), and a fine to the king.

* 9. When a purchaser does not accept an article purchased by himself, which is delivered to him (by the vendor), the vendor commits no wrong by selling it to a different person.

* 10. Thus has the rule been declared with regard

---

6. According to *G*agannâtha, this rule has reference to those cases only where the purchaser has not formally asked for the delivery of the property purchased by himself. He infers from a text of Yâ*gñ*avalkya that after a demand the loss shall fall on the vendor, even though the property was injured in one of the modes mentioned by that authority, i.e. by force majeure. See Colebrooke's Digest, III, 3, 27. It is quite doubtful, however, whether the compiler of the Nârada-sm*ri*ti had this distinction in view. Yâ*gñ*avalkya II, 256.

8, 9. Both he who shows unblemished goods, and sells blemished goods afterwards, and he who sells property to one man and afterwards sells the same property to another man, though the first sale has not been rescinded by the purchaser, shall pay twice the value of the property sold as a fine. Vîramitrodaya, p. 440. Yâ*gñ*avalkya II, 257.

9. Yâ*gñ*avalkya II, 255.

10. Consequently, where there is no agreement as to the time of

to that merchandise for which the price has been tendered. When the price has not been tendered, there is no offence to be imputed to the vendor, except in the case of a special agreement.

*11. It is for the sake of gain that merchants are in the habit of buying and selling merchandise of every sort. That gain is, in proportion to the price, either great or the reverse.

*12. Therefore shall merchants fix a just price for their merchandise, according to the locality and season, and let them refrain from dishonest dealings. Thus (by adhering to these principles) traffic becomes an honest profession.

NINTH TITLE OF LAW.

Rescission of Purchase.

*1. When a purchaser, after having purchased an article for a (certain) price, repents (of the purchase made by himself), it is termed Rescission of Purchase, a title of law.

*2. When a purchaser, after having purchased an article for a (certain) price, thinks he has made a foolish bargain, he may return it to the vendor on the same day, in an undamaged condition.

---

delivery, the vendor commits no wrong by retaining a commodity sold, on purpose to obtain payment. Thus according to the gloss in Colebrooke's Digest, III, 3, 20. The Vîramitrodaya (p. 441) has a slightly different explanation. 'Where the price for a sold chattel has not been paid, and the purchase concluded through a verbal engagement merely, there is no offence whether it be ratified or not, unless there should be an agreement in this form, "This purchase cannot be rescinded."'

*3. When the purchaser returns it on the second day (after the purchase has been made), he shall lose a thirtieth part of the price. (He shall lose) twice as much on the third day. After that time, the purchaser is bound to keep it.

*4. The (intending) purchaser shall first examine an article (before purchasing it), in order to find out its good and bad qualities. That which has been approved by the purchaser after close examination, cannot be returned to the vendor.

*5. Milch cattle may be examined for three days; animals of burden, for five days; and in the case of precious stones, pearls, and coral, the period of examination may extend over seven days.

*6. Bipeds shall be examined within half a month; a female, within twice the same (space of time); all sorts of grain, within ten days; iron and clothes, within a single day.

*7. A worn gown, which is in a ragged condition and soiled with dirt, cannot be returned to the vendor, if it was in that blemished state at the time when the purchase was effected.

*8. Wearing apparel loses the eighth part of its value on being washed for the first time; the fourth

---

IX, 3. 'He shall lose a thirtieth part,' he shall give one-thirtieth part more than the stipulated price. 'Twice as much,' i.e. a fifteenth. See Colebrooke's Digest, III, 3, 5.

5, 6. 'For three days,' including the day of purchase. The terms 'for five days,' &c., have to be interpreted in the same way. 'Milch cattle,' such as e.g. female buffaloes. 'Animals of burden,' such as e.g. young bulls. 'Bipeds,' males, i.e. male slaves. 'Twice the same space of time,' a month. 'A female,' a female slave. Vîramitrodaya, pp. 433, 434. Manu VIII, 222; Yâ*g*ñavalkya II, 177.

8, 9. When apparel has been given to a washerman to be washed by him, he is bound to make good the value of that

part (on being washed) for the second time; the third part (on being washed) for the third time; and one half (on being washed) for the fourth time.

*9. One half of the original value having been lost, a quarter (of the reduced value) shall be deducted henceforth, till the fringe is tattered and (the cloth) in rags. In the case of tattered cloth, there is no rule regarding the reduction of its value (through being washed).

* 10. There is no other way for preparing metallic apparatus of any sort than by forging it in fire according to the rules (of art). While they are being forged, (the weight of) the metals is diminished by exposure in fire.

* 11. Gold is not injured at all (by such treatment). On silver, the loss amounts to two Palas in the hundred. On tin and lead, the loss is eight Palas in the hundred.

* 12. On copper, as well as on utensils made of it, the loss should be known to be five Palas (in the hundred). As for iron, there is no fixed rule regarding the loss arising on it, because it is different in nature from the other metals.

---

which has been spoiled by him. If it has been washed a single time, he must make good its original value minus an eighth. If it has been washed twice, he must make good its original value minus a fourth. Thus if it has been washed three times, a third has to be deducted from the original value, and so forth. Vîramitrodaya, p. 372.

11, 12. The value of gold is not diminished on its being heated in fire. Therefore, as much (gold) as has been delivered to a goldsmith for making a bracelet and the like, thus much shall the goldsmith restore after having weighed it. Otherwise, he shall be compelled to restore the loss, and to pay a fine. When silver, a hundred Palas in weight, is heated in fire, the loss amounts to

13. The loss and gain arising from the preparation of cloth shall be stated (next). On yarns made of cotton or wool, the increase of value amounts to ten in the hundred.

14. (This rule has reference) to large tissue (only). In the case of (tissue of) middle size, five in the hundred (is gained). In the case of very fine tissue, the gain is said to amount to three Palas in the hundred.

15. In the case of cloth made of the hair of an animal, and of embroidered cloth, the loss amounts to one-thirtieth. In the case of silk stuff and of cloth prepared from the inner bark of trees, the gain is the same (as the loss in the preceding case). Nor is there any loss (in these cases).

*16. A merchant who is acquainted with the qualities of the merchandise (he deals in) must not

two Palas. When a hundred Palas of tin or lead is heated in fire, the loss amounts to eight Palas. In the case of copper, the loss shall be five Palas. Artizans losing more than the above amount shall be punished. Mitâksharâ, pp. 264, 265. Yâg*ñ*avalkya II, 178.

13–15. When a blanket or the like is made of coarse woollen thread, the increase must be considered to amount to ten Palas in the hundred. The same rule applies in the case of cloth and the like made of cotton thread. In the case of cloth and the like of a middling quality, i.e. which is not made of very fine thread, the increase amounts to five Palas. In the case of cloth made of very fine thread, the increase is three Palas in the hundred. All these rules apply in the case of washed cloth only. That is called 'embroidered cloth' (kârmika or karmakr*i*ta) where a circle, Svastika, or other (figure) is worked on woven cloth, with coloured yarns. 'Cloth made of the hair (of an animal)' is where hairs are joined so as to form a piece of cloth or the like. Mitâksharâ, pp. 265, 266. Manu VIII, 397; Yâg*ñ*avalkya II, 179, 180.

16. 'He must not annul a purchase,' he must not repent of it. 'He must know' before concluding a purchase, the 'loss and gain on merchandise,' such as horses or others, i.e. the diminution of

annul a purchase, after having once made it. He ought to know all about the profit and loss on merchandise, and its origin.

TENTH TITLE OF LAW.

Transgression of a Compact.

*1. The aggregate of the rules settled amongst heretics, followers of the Veda (Naigamas) and others, is called Samaya (compact, or established usage). Thus arises a title of law, termed Transgression of a Compact.

*2. Among heretics, followers of the Veda (Naigamas), guilds (of merchants), corporations (Pûgas), troops (of soldiers), assemblages (of kinsmen), and other (associations) the king must maintain the usages (settled among them), both in fortified towns and in the open country.

---

its value in one country, and the increase of its value in another country, and 'its origin,' the country where it comes from. That is the meaning. Vîramitrodaya, pp. 434, 435.

X, 1. 'Heretics,' Kshapa*n*akas (Buddhist or Jain mendicants) and others who detract from the authority of the Veda. 'Naigamas,' traders or merchants. According to the Mitâksharâ, the term Naigama refers to Pâ*s*upatas and others who uphold the authority of the Veda. The term 'and others' is used to include corporations of learned Brahmans and other (associations). Vîramitrodaya, p. 423. The term samaya, literally 'compact,' denotes local or caste usages, the violation of which forms the subject of the tenth title of law.

2. Of the term Naigama, the commentators give the same two different interpretations as in the preceding paragraph. I have referred it to 'followers of the Veda,' because it comes immediately after the term 'heretics.' The term pûga has three interpretations in this place. Some say it means 'companies of traders or others.'

*3. Whatever be their laws, their (religious) duties, (the rules regarding) their attendance, and the (particular mode of) livelihood prescribed for them, that the king shall approve of.

*4. The king shall prevent them from undertaking such acts as would be either opposed (to the wishes of the king), or contemptible in their nature, or injurious to his interests.

* 5. Mixed assemblages, unlawful wearing of arms, and mutual attacks between those persons shall not be tolerated by the king.

Others say it denotes 'associations of persons differing in caste, whose mode of subsistence is not fixed.' The Vîramitrodaya interprets it as referring to riders on elephants, horses, &c. In explanation of the terms vrâta, 'a troop of soldiers,' and ga*n*a, 'an assemblage of kinsmen,' the commentators quote the following text of Kâtyâyana: 'A multitude of united men armed with various weapons is called vrâta. An assemblage of families is called ga*n*a.' Manu VIII, 41; Yâ*gñ*avalkya II, 192, &c.

3. 'Their laws,' such as to speak the truth. 'Their (religious) duties,' such as the duty of going about begging alms when the night is over, early in the morning. 'The rules regarding their attendance,' the duty of attending, in a temple or other (public hall), for the affairs of the community, when the sound of a drum or other instrument is heard. Vîramitrodaya, p. 430. The Ratnâkara interprets the term karma, 'their (religious) duties,' by 'their proper occupation for a livelihood.' The drift of this rule, according to *G*agannâtha, is this, that the king must not act otherwise than is consistent with the usages of castes or other corporations. See Colebrooke's Digest, III, 2, 11. Yâ*gñ*avalkya II, 192, &c.

4. 'Contemptible in their nature,' essentially despicable, such as the eating of betel, which is customary among heretics and others. 'Injurious to his interests,' causing pecuniary loss, &c. 'He shall prevent them from undertaking such acts,' he shall act so that they do not undertake them. Vîramitrodaya, pp. 430, 431.

5. 'Mixed assemblages,' meetings or gatherings of persons differing in caste. 'Unlawful wearing of arms,' wearing arms without sufficient motives, such as the apprehension of a danger. See Ratnâkara, as quoted in Colebrooke's Digest, III, 2, 25.

*6. Those who cause dissension among the members of an association, shall undergo punishment of a specially severe kind; because they would prove extremely dangerous, like an (epidemic) disease, if they were allowed to go free.

*7. Whenever a criminal act, opposed to the dictates of morality, has been attempted, a king desirous of prosperity shall redress it.

ELEVENTH TITLE OF LAW.

Boundary Disputes.

*1. Whenever (a decision has to be given) in regard to landed property, whether it be a dike (or bridge), a field, a boundary, a tilled piece of ground, or a waste, it is termed a Boundary Dispute.

2. In all quarrels regarding landed property or boundaries, the decision rests with the neighbours, the inhabitants of the same town or village, the

---

6. 'An association,' a guild of merchants or other corporation. Vîramitrodaya, p. 430.

7. When an act tainted with the sin of covetousness or another crime, and opposed to the dictates of revealed and traditional law, such as e.g. the prostitution of widows or other (virtuous females) among heretics or other (sinful men), has been attempted, the king must redress it, though it may have been practised for a long time. Vîramitrodaya, p. 431.

XI, 1. The meaning is as follows: 'A dike,' an embankment for the purposes of irrigation. 'A field,' a cultivated piece of ground (under water). 'A boundary,' a landmark. 'A tilled piece of ground,' cultivated soil. 'A waste,' uncultivated ground. When a decision has to be given in a quarrel with regard to any of these, it is called a lawsuit concerning landed property, or Boundary Dispute. Vîramitrodaya, p. 451.

2. Manu VIII, 259; Yâgñavalkya II, 150.

(other) members of the same community, and the senior (inhabitants of the district),

* 3. (As also) with those living outside on the outskirts of the village and who live by the tillage of fields situated in those parts, and with herdsmen, bird-catchers, hunters, and other inhabitants of the woods.

4. These men shall determine the boundary, in accordance with the (old) landmarks, (such as) chaff of grain, coal, pot-sherds, wells, sanctuaries, trees,

5. Objects of general notoriety, such as ant-hills, artificial mounds, slopes, hills and the like, and fields, gardens, roads, and old dikes.

6. When a piece of ground has been carried off by a stream, or abandoned (by the owner), or when the boundary marks have been destroyed, (they shall fix the boundary) according to the inference to be drawn from (an inspection of) the spot, and according to the traces of possession (held by the former owner).

* 7. Should the neighbours speak falsely, when called upon to decide a question of this sort, they shall all be punished one by one by the king, each having to pay the fine of the (second or) middlemost degree.

*8. The corporation, the senior (inhabitants of

---

3. The foresters shall only be consulted in default of cultivators whose fields are adjacent to the boundaries of the village. Vîramitrodaya, p. 456. Manu VIII, 260. Yâ*g*ñavalkya II, 150.

4, 5. Manu VIII, 246–251; Yâ*g*ñavalkya II, 151.

7. Manu VIII, 263; Yâ*g*ñavalkya II, 153. The fine of the second degree consists of 500 Pa*n*as.

8. The lower degree of punishment in the case of the persons here mentioned seems to be due to the fact that they may be supposed to be interested in the suit.

the district) and the rest shall also receive punishment one by one: they shall have to pay the fine of the first degree, if they make false statements.

*9. The boundary should not be fixed by one man single-handed, though he be a reliable person. This business should be entrusted to a plurality of persons, because it is an affair of importance.

*10. Should a single man undertake to fix the boundary, (he must do so) after having kept a fast, in a collected frame of mind, wearing a garland of red flowers and a (red) cloak, having strewed earth on his head.

*11. Should there be no persons conversant (with the true state of the question) and no boundary marks, then the king himself shall fix the boundary between the two estates, as he thinks best.

12. According to this rule let all contests be decided in regard to houses, gardens, reservoirs of water, sanctuaries and the rest, as well as the space intermediate between two villages.

*13. When trees have grown on the boundary (or ridge) separating two contiguous fields, the fruits and blossoms shall be assigned to the owners of the two fields in common.

---

9. According to the Vîramitrodaya (p. 458), this prohibition in regard to the determination of the boundary by a single man, has reference to those only who are not acceptable to both parties and unacquainted with the law.

10. Manu VIII, 256; Yâg*ñ*avalkya II, 152.

11. In default of neighbours and other persons conversant with the state of the matter, and of trees and other boundary marks, the king shall fix the boundary of his own accord. He shall distribute the ground intermediate between the two villages, which has become the subject of a contest, between the two litigant parties, and fix landmarks between the two. Vîramitrodaya, p. 460. Manu VIII, 265; Yâg*ñ*avalkya II, 153.

*14. When the boughs (or offshoots) of trees grown on the field of one man should take root in the field of another man, they must be known to belong by right to the owner (of that field), because they have sprung forth in another field (than the stem of the tree).

*15. A cross-road, the sanctuary of a deity, a street, and a public road must not be obstructed by (a place for) ordure, a terrace, a pit, an aqueduct, the edge of a thatch (syandanikâ), or the like (obstructions).

16. Should any one cause such obstruction through inadvertency or by force, the king shall impose on him a fine of the highest degree.

*17. The (erection of a) dike in the middle of another man's field is not a prohibited act, as it may be productive of considerable advantage, whereas the loss is trifling. That is to be desired as (comparative) gain where there is (a slight) loss (only).

*18. There are two sorts of dikes (or water-courses), one (called kheya) which is dug into the ground, and (another called bandhya) which prevents the access of water. A kheya dike serves the purpose of irrigation, a bandhya dike serves to keep the water off.

*19. No grain is (ever produced) without water;

14. This rule seems to be intended principally for banyans and the like trees covering a large area with their offshoots. The Nepalese MS. omits vv. 13, 14, 16.

15. The term syandanikâ is variously explained as denoting either the projecting roof or the eaves of a house.

17. Yâ*gñ*avalkya II, 156.

18. Kheya means literally 'what is capable of being dug,' and bandhya 'what is capable of being stopped.' What is meant by these two terms may best be seen from the next paragraph.

but too much water tends to spoil the grain. An inundation is as injurious (to growth) as a dearth of water.

* 20. If a man were to put in repair a dike erected long ago, but decayed, without asking the permission of the owner, he shall not have (the use and) profits of it.

* 21. However, after the death of the owner or of another man sprung from the same race (who has succeeded to his property), he may repair the dike, after having been authorized to do so by the king.

* 22. By acting otherwise he will get into trouble, in the same way as the hunter (of the tale). The shafts of him are spent in vain who hits again and again one who has been hit already.

* 23. When the owner of a field is unable (to cultivate it), or dead, or gone no one knows whither, any stranger who undertakes its cultivation unchecked (by the owner or others) shall be allowed to keep the produce.

* 24. When the owner returns while the stranger

20. With the owner's permission, any man may restore a dike, &c., which has fallen into decay. Vîramitrodaya, p. 468. Yâ*g*ñavalkya II, 157. Read pravr*i*ttam in the text.

21. The authority of the king is required, because, without it, the profits of the dike would have to be enjoyed by the king himself. See Yâ*g*ñavalkya II, 157.

22. The tertium comparationis in this simile has to be sought in the vanity of the effort only. Manu (IX, 73) applies the same simile to seed, i.e. semen virile spent in vain on the field, i.e. wife of a stranger.

23. 'Unable' (to cultivate the field) through want of means. 'A field,' one which has become a desert. Vivâda*k*intâma*n*i, p. 64.

24. 'The owner,' or his son or other (descendant). 'The whole expense incurred in tilling the waste,' the cost of converting the desert into cultivated ground. Vîramitrodaya, pp. 469, 470.

is engaged in cultivating the field, (the owner) shall recover his field, after having paid (to the cultivator) the whole expense incurred in tilling the waste.

25. A deduction of an eighth part (shall be made), till seven years have elapsed. But when the eighth year arrives, (the owner) shall recover the field cultivated (by the other, as his independent property).

* 26. A tract of land (which has not been under cultivation) for a year is called Ardhakhila (half-waste). That which has not been (under cultivation) for three years is called Khila (waste). That which has not been under cultivation for five years is no better than a forest.

27. A field which has been held by three generations in succession, and a house which has been inherited from an ancestor, cannot be estranged (from its legitimate owner) by force of possession, except when the king wills it so.

* 28. When grain has been destroyed by cows or

25. It appears from an analogous text of Kâtyâyana that this rule is intended for those cases where the owner is unable to pay for the expense incurred by the cultivator. Kâtyâyana says, 'If through want of means (the owner) do not repay the expense entailed by the cultivation of the waste, the cultivator shall be allowed to keep the produce minus an eighth part. During eight years he may keep the (annual) produce (minus an eighth). After that period, it shall belong to the proprietor.'

26. These definitions are inserted here, because the previous rules according to the commentators apply to a desert or forest only, the cultivation of which causes considerable difficulty and expense.

28–42. Nârada's eleventh title of law, though called 'Boundary Disputes,' is in reality a collection of all legal rules relating to fields. Manu and those who follow him treat the subject of damage done by cattle to crops or grass as a section of the chapter on 'Disputes between master and herdsman,' which title of law is wanting in the Nârada-smriti.

28. Gautama XII, 20.

other cattle crossing a fence, the herdsman deserves punishment in that case, unless he should have done his best to keep the cattle off.

* 29. When grain has been destroyed (altogether), with the root, the owner of it may claim a corresponding quantity of grain (as damages); the herdsman shall be corporally punished; and on his master he shall impose a fine.

* 30. A cow within ten days after her calving, a full grown bull, a horse, and an elephant shall be kept off carefully. The owner of any one out of these animals is not liable to punishment (should they do mischief).

* 31. For (mischief done by) a cow he shall inflict a fine of one Mâsha; for (mischief done by) a female buffalo, two Mâshas; in the case of a goat or sheep (trespassing) with its young, the fine shall amount to half a Mâsha.

* 32. The (owners of) elephants and horses shall not have to pay any fine; for they are looked upon as protectors of (the king's) subjects. Impunity is (likewise) granted to (the owner of) a strayed cow,

29. The author of the Vîramitrodaya (p. 450) observes expressly that the term vadha denotes corporal punishment, and not execution, in this place. The other commentators agree with him. Manu VIII, 241; Yâg*ñ*avalkya II, 161; Gautama XII, 26; Vish*n*u V, 146. The Nepalese MS. omits this paragraph.

30. The reason why horses and elephants have to be kept off is given in paragraph 32. Horses and elephants were used for the purposes of war principally. Manu VIII, 242; Yâg*ñ*avalkya II, 163, &c.

31. Vish*n*u V, 140–144; Gautama XII, 22–25; Yâg*ñ*avalkya II, 159.

32, 33. Manu VIII, 242; Vish*n*u V, 150; Yâg*ñ*avalkya II, 163. The Nepalese MS. has 'a pregnant cow' for 'a strayed cow.'

of one that has recently calved, and of one unmanageable.

33. (As also to the owner of) one that has lost her way, or broken down, or stuck (in marshy ground), or (of) a bull marked with the sign of consecration. Four times (the amount of the damage done) is declared (to be the fine) in the case of (a cow) whose nostrils have been pierced and who abides in the field.

* 34. When the cattle lie down in the field (after grazing), the fine to be inflicted shall be double; when they remain (in the field for the night), it shall be four times (the ordinary amount); when they graze in the sight (of the keeper), that man shall be punished even as a thief.

* 35. When cows, straying through the fault of

---

33. The genuineness of this paragraph appears doubtful, because some of the propositions contained in it are nearly identical with the rules laid down in the paragraphs immediately preceding and following it. Besides, the language of this paragraph is obscure, and it is not given in any commentary nor in the Nepalese MS. The solemn ceremony of setting a bull at liberty and consecrating him to the gods, with a mark on each flank, is described by Vish*n*u, chapter LXXXVI, and in the G*ri*hya-sûtras. Piercing the nostrils of a barren cow is mentioned as an offence by Manu VIII, 325. It does not become clear why damage done by a cow of this sort should be a greater offence than damage done by an ordinary cow.

34. 'When they lie down in the field,' after having eaten their fill. 'When they remain,' when they spend the night in the field, after grazing. Vivâda*k*intâma*n*i, *G*agannâtha, &c. 'In the sight of the keeper:' thus according to *G*agannâtha (Colebrooke's Digest, III, 4, 46). The correctness of his interpretation is confirmed by Yâ*gñ*avalkya II, 162. According to the Vivâda*k*intâma*n*i (p. 67), the meaning is this, that the cattle are allowed to graze by the keeper, in the sight of the proprietor of the field, and in spite of the remonstrances of the latter. Vish*n*u V, 145; Yâ*gñ*avalkya II, 160, 162.

their keeper, have entered a field, no punishment shall be inflicted on the owner of the cows; the herdsman (alone) is punishable (for the damage done by them).

* 36. When (a herdsman) has been seized by the king or (devoured) by an alligator, or struck by Indra's thunderbolt, or bitten by a serpent, or fallen from a tree,

* 37. Or killed by a tiger or other (ferocious animal), or smitten by a disease of any sort, no offence can be imputed either to the herdsman or to the owner of the cattle.

* 38. When a man claims damages for grain consumed by cattle (grazing in his field), that quantity of grain must be restored to him (by the owner of the cattle), which has been consumed in the field in the estimation of the neighbours.

* 39. The cows shall be given up to their owner, and the grain to the husbandman. In the same way a fine shall be imposed on the herdsman when grain has been trodden down (by cows).

---

36. 'Seized by the king,' employed in the king's business. See Colebrooke's Digest, III, 4, 52.

37. This paragraph is omitted in the Nepalese MS.

38. Gautama XII, 26; Manu VIII, 241; Yâg*ñ*avalkya II, 161. The Nepalese MS. inserts a spurious verse here, the first half of which is identical with Manu IX, 37, and the second half identical with Nârada XI, 22.

39. The meaning of the injunction to give up the cows seems to be this, that the owner of the cows shall not at once recover them, when they have been seized by the proprietor of the field, after doing damage in the field. The Vivâda*k*intâma*n*i has a different reading of this clause: gavatra*m* gominâ deya*m*. This is explained as meaning that 'blades of corn must be made good by the owner of cattle.' Similar readings are found in other commentaries as well. Âpastamba II, 11, 28, 5.

40. When a field is situate on the borders of a village, or contiguous to a pasture ground, or adjacent to a high road, the herdsman is not reprehensible for the destruction of grain (in that field), if the field is not protected by a fence.

* 41. On (that side of) the field which faces the road a fence shall be made over which a camel cannot look, nor cattle or horses jump, and which a boar cannot break through.

* 42. A householder's house and his field are considered as the two fundaments of his existence. Therefore let not the king upset either of them; for that is the root of householders.

43. When his people are flourishing, the religious merit and the treasure of a king are sure to be in a flourishing state as well. When (the people) cease to prosper, (his merit and his treasure) are sure to abate as well. Therefore he must never lose sight of (that) cause of prosperity.

TWELFTH TITLE OF LAW.

The Mutual Duties of Husband and Wife.

* 1. That title of law in which the legal rules for women and men regarding marriage and the other

---

40. 'Pasture ground,' a meadow reserved for feeding cows or other cattle. Ratnâkara. See Colebrooke's Digest, III, 4, 27. Manu VIII, 238, 240; Vish*n*u V, 147, 148; Gautama XII, 21; Yâ*gñ*avalkya II, 162.

41. Manu VIII, 239.

42. This maxim shows that the compiler of the Nârada-sm*ri*ti wrote for an essentially agricultural people.

XII, 1. Manu IX, 1.

(mutual relations between them) are laid down is called The Mutual Duties of Husband and Wife.

2. When a woman and man are to unite (as wife and husband), the choice of the bride must take place first of all. The choice of the bride is succeeded by the (ceremony of) joining the bride and bridegroom's hands. Thus the ceremony (of marriage) is twofold.

3. Of these two parts (of the marriage ceremony) the choice of the bride is declared to lose its binding force, when a blemish is (subsequently) discovered (in either of the two parties). The Mantra (prayer), which is recited during the ceremony of joining the bride and bridegroom's hands, is the permanent token of matrimony.

4. When a Brahman, Kshatriya, Vai*s*ya, or *S*ûdra takes a wife, it is best for him to take her out of his own caste; and so is a member of her own caste the (most eligible) husband for a woman (of any caste).

5. A Brahman may marry three wives of different caste, in the direct order of the castes; and so may

---

2. The Sm*ri*ti-writers, as a rule, do not mention the act of vara*n*a, 'choice of a bride,' at all. It appears from the next paragraph that Nârada also does not place it on a par with the ceremony of marriage, which is indissoluble for life.

3. The 'choice of the bride,' or betrothal, being dissoluble on the discovery of a blemish (in either party), it follows that the act of joining the bride and bridegroom's hands, i. e. the ceremony of marriage, must be indissoluble. See, too, paragraph 28. The particular Mantras to be recited during the marriage ceremony are given in the G*ri*hya-sûtras.

4. Âpastamba II, 6, 13, 1; Vasish*th*a VIII, 1; Gautama IV, 1; Manu III, 12; Yâg*ñ*avalkya I, 55.

5, 6. It is important to note that Nârada belongs to that group of Sm*ri*ti-writers who recognise the legitimacy of marriage unions between Brahmans and *S*ûdra women. Baudhâyana I, 8, 16, 1–5;

a *S*ûdra woman take a husband of any of the three castes above her own.

6. For a Kshatriya, two wives differing (from him) in caste are permitted; for a Vai*s*ya, a single wife differing (from him) in caste. (On the other hand), a Vai*s*ya woman may take a husband of two different castes; and a Kshatriya woman may take a husband of one different caste.

7. Sagotras and Samânapravaras are ineligible for marriage up to the fifth and seventh degrees of relationship respectively, on the father's and mother's side.

*8. The man must undergo an examination with regard to his virile; when the fact of his virile has been placed beyond doubt, he shall obtain the maiden, (but not otherwise.)

*9. If his collar-bone, his knee, and his bones (in

Vasish*th*a I, 24, 25; Vish*n*u XXIV, 1–4; Manu III, 12–14; Yâ*g*ñavalkya I, 56, 57.

6. The somewhat laconic terms of the original may be paraphrased as follows: A Kshatriya may marry a Vai*s*ya and a *S*ûdra woman, besides a wife of his own caste. A Vai*s*ya may marry a *S*ûdra woman, besides a wife of his own caste. A Vai*s*ya woman may either take a Vai*s*ya husband, or she may wed a Kshatriya or a Brahman. A Kshatriya may either take a Kshatriya husband, or she may marry a Brahman.

7. A Sagotra is a relative bearing the same family name (laukika gotra). A Samânapravara is one descended from the same *Ri*shi (vaidika gotra). See Professor Bühler's notes on Gautama XVIII, 6; Âpastamba II, 5, 11, 15. Manu III, 5; Âpastamba II, 5, 11, 15–16; Gautama IV, 2–5; Vasish*th*a VIII, 1, 2; Baudhâyana II, 1, 31–38; Vish*n*u XXIV, 9, 10; Manu III, 5; Yâ*g*ñavalkya I, 53.

8. Yâ*g*ñavalkya I, 55. It should be observed, however, that the eligibility of impotent men or eunuchs for marriage is recognised in the Code of Manu (IX, 203), and that such men are very commonly married now-a-days.

9. The curious disquisition on impotency is quoted in such an

general) are strongly made; if his shoulders and his hair are (also) strongly made; if the nape of his neck is stout, and his thigh and his skin delicate; if his gait and his voice is vigorous;

*10. If his semen, when thrown into water, does not swim on the surface; and if his urine is rich and foamy: by these tokens may a potent man be known; and one impotent by the opposite characteristics.

*11. Fourteen species of impotent men are distinguished by the sages, according to the rules of science, including both the curable and incurable. The rules regarding them shall be given in order.

*12. One naturally impotent, one whose testicles have been cut out, a Pakshasha*ndh*a, one who has been deprived of his potency by a curse of his spiritual guide, or by illness, or by the wrath of a deity,

*13. One jealous, a Sevya, one whose semen is (evanescent) as air, a Mukhebhaga, one who spills

---

early compilation as Aparârka's Commentary of the Yâ*gñ*avalkya-sm*ri*ti (twelfth century), which goes far to prove its genuineness. Aparârka's gloss on this passage, scanty as it is, has proved useful in elucidating some of the difficult terms occurring in it, and in establishing the correct readings. Besides, I have been able to avail myself of some valuable remarks, kindly communicated to me by the late Dr. Haas, the well-known connoisseur of Indian medicine.

10. An analogous text is quoted from the Sm*ri*ti of Kâtyâyana. 'He is called impotent whose urine froths not and whose fæces sink in water, and whose generative organ is deficient in erection or seminal juices.' See Colebrooke's Digest, V, 5, 330.

12. 'One naturally impotent' (nisargasha*ndh*a), one born without the capacity of producing semen. Aparârka. This category seems to be synonymous with the saha*g*a of Sus*r*uta, the standard writer on medicine. Pakshasha*ndh*a, according to Aparârka, is one capable of approaching a woman once in every half-month (Paksha).

13. The jealous man, îrshyâsha*ndh*a, seems to be identical with the îrshyaka of Su*s*ruta, 'qui nisi alius cujusdam ineuntis feminam

his semen, one whose semen is devoid of strength, one timorous, and one who is potent with another woman (than his wife) only, (these are the fourteen sorts of impotent persons.)

* 14. Among these, the two first are incurable; the one called Pakshasha*nd*a should wait for a month; the (three) named after him shall have to wait for a year.

* 15. Those four, among whom, in the above enumeration, the one jealous comes first, shall be avoided by their wives just like an outcast, though they may have been enjoyed by them.

* 16. For the wife of one who spills his semen, or whose semen is devoid of strength, though they may have discharged their marital duties, another husband must be procured, after she has waited for half a year.

* 17. If a man is timorous, he fails when he is about

---

conspectu non potest.' The term sevya is obscure enough. Dr. Haas proposes to read *k*a *s*evya*sk*a or *k*a mevya*sk*a or *k*âsekya*sk*a, for *k*a sevya*sk*a. The âsekya is a species of impotent person according to Su*s*ruta. It may be, however, that the reading sevya is correct, and denotes one with whom sexual intercourse is possible. Mukhebhaga, 'is qui ore prout cunno utitur.' The revolting practice in question is repeatedly referred to e.g. by Nârada himself, VI, 19, according to the commentators, and I, 183. Dr. Haas proposes to read mushkabhagna*h*, 'one deprived of the scrotum.' It may be argued, however, that this category has already been referred to in paragraph 12, and that the reading mushkabhagna is objectionable for metrical reasons. According to Aparârka, âkshipta, the next term, means 'is cujus semen in coitu retro (aut susum) fluit;' moghabî*g*a means 'is cui semen ad propagationem aptum non est;' *s*âlîna means 'is cujus penis coitu facto collabitur;' and anyâpati, the last term, means 'is qui cum alia femina praeter uxorem potest.'

15. 'Like an outcast (patita).' Dr. Haas assigns a different meaning to the term patita, viz. 'is cujus penis collabitur;' and refers to such expressions as dhva*g*a*h* patati, 'penis collabitur,' in the Bhavaprakâ*s*a.

to approach his wife; such a feeble man shall be stirred up by bringing before him other men's wives or young maidens, &c.

* 18. If a man is potent with another woman but impotent with his own wife, his wife shall take another husband. This is a law promulgated by the Creator of the world.

19. Women have been created for the sake of propagation, the wife being the field, and the husband the giver of the seed. The field must be given to him who has seed. He who has no seed is unworthy to possess the field.

20. Let a maiden be given in marriage by her father himself, or by her brother with the father's authority, or by her paternal grandfather, or by her maternal uncle, or by her agnates or cognates.

21. In default of all these, by the mother, in case she is competent (to act as guardian); if she be wanting in competence, the distant connexions shall give a maiden in marriage.

22. If no such person be in existence, let the maiden have recourse to the king, and let her, with his permission, betake herself to a bridegroom of her own choice,

---

20, 21. The object of these rules is to prevent that any marriageable maiden should remain unmarried, which is a great point in the eyes of a Hindu legislator. Vish*n*u XXIV, 38, 39; Manu V, 151; Yâ*gñ*avalkya I, 63. The Nepalese MS. refers to the maternal instead of the paternal grandfather.

22, 23. This is the custom of Svaya*m*vara, 'self-choice (of a bridegroom),' so well known from the Indian epics. It appears from this paragraph that Nârada does not allow this custom to be practised except with certain restrictions. See, however, the next paragraph. 'Age;' Manu says (IX, 94) that a man at the age of thirty shall marry a maiden of twelve, and a man aged twenty-four, years a maiden of eight. Gautama XVIII, 20; Vasish*th*a XVII,

23. Who belongs to her own caste, and is a suitable match in point of descent, morality, age, and sacred learning. Let her discharge her religious duties in common with him, and bear children to him.

24. When a bridegroom goes abroad after having espoused a maiden, let the maiden wait till her menses have passed three times, and then choose another bridegroom.

25. Let no maiden suffer the period of maturity to come on without giving notice of it to her relations. Should they omit to give her in marriage, they would be equal to the murderers of an embryo.

26. He who does not give such a maiden in marriage commits the crime of killing an embryo as many times as her period of menstruation passes by without her having a husband.

27. Therefore a father must give his daughter in marriage once (for all), as soon as the signs of maturity become apparent. (By acting) otherwise he would commit a heavy crime. Such is the rule settled among the virtuous.

67, 68; Manu IX, 90–92; Vish*n*u XXIV, 40; Yâ*g*ñavalkya I, 64; Baudhâyana IV, 1, 14. Read anurûpa*m* in the text.

24. This is the law in the case of a woman recently married, when consummation has not yet taken place. As for the conduct enjoined to one left by her husband, when they have been married for some length of time, see paragraphs 96–101.

25. Maturity, according to a well-known versus memorialis, generally commences after completion of the tenth year. 'One aged eight years is a child; one aged nine years is a maiden; one aged ten years is a virgin; after that time she is a marriageable woman.' See Parâ*s*ara VII, 6; Sa*m*varta V, 66; Gautama XVIII, 22; Vasish*th*a XVII, 69; Vish*n*u XXIV, 41; Manu IX, 4, 93.

26. Vasish*th*a XVII, 71; Yâ*g*ñavalkya I, 64; Baudhâyana IV, 1, 13.

27. It must not be inferred from this rule that Nârada is not

28. Once is the (family) property divided, once is a maiden given in marriage, and once does a man say, 'I will give;' each of these three acts is done a single time only among the virtuous.

29. This rule applies to the five (first) marriage forms only, beginning with the Brâhma (form of marriage). In the three (others), beginning with the Âsura form, the (irrevocable) gift (of a maiden to a particular suitor) depends on the qualities (of the suitor).

30. Should a more respectable suitor, (who appears) eligible in point of religious merit, fortune, and amiability, present himself, when the nuptial gift has already been presented (to the parents by the first

---

an advocate of infant marriage, like many other Smriti-writers. Thus Daksha says, 'Let a maiden be given in marriage at the age of eight years; thus justice will not be violated.' Aṅgiras rules that a maiden must be given in marriage in her tenth year by all means. Râgamârtanda, Yama, and Parâsara declare that it is a heavy sin if she continues to reside at her father's house after having reached her twelfth year of age. Vasishtha, Gautama, Vishnu, and Manu (IX, 93) ordain to give a maiden in marriage before she attains the age of puberty.

28. This is the general rule regarding the indissolubility of the marriage tie. Divers important restrictions of this rule are stated in paragraphs 24, 29, 30, 96–101. Identical with Manu IX, 47. The Nepalese MS. inserts two paragraphs here: 'Soma springs into existence when the marks of puberty appear, and enjoys women. Their breast is a Gândharva, and Agni (the god of fire) is said to dwell in their menstrual discharge. Therefore let a father give his daughter in marriage before the marks of puberty have appeared in her, and before the menses and the breasts have been developed, and before she has been enjoyed by Soma and the rest.' The first paragraph occurs in the Pañkatantra as well. See the Petersburg Dictionary, s. v. Gândharva.

29. Other legal consequences of the choice of a particular form of marriage are stated in the law of inheritance. See XIII, 9.

30. Out of the various meanings of the term sulka, the meaning

suitor), the verbal engagement (previously made) shall be annulled.

31. Let no man calumniate a faultless maiden, neither must one calumniate a faultless suitor. When, however, there is an actual defect, it is no offence if they dissolve their mutual engagement.

32. When a man, after having made a solemn promise of giving his daughter in marriage to a certain suitor, does not deliver her afterwards, he shall be punished by the king like a thief, in case the suitor be faultless.

33. But when a man gives a maiden in marriage, who has a (secret) blemish without first making (the defect) known, the king shall visit him with punishment of the very gravest kind.

34. When a man, from hatred, declares a certain maiden to have lost her virginity, he shall pay one hundred Pa*n*as as a fine, unless he be able to give proofs of her disgrace.

* 35. When a man, after having plighted his faith to a maiden, abandons her, although she is faultless, he shall be fined and shall marry the maiden, even against his will.

36. Affliction with a chronic or hateful disease,

'nuptial gift, presented to the parents of the bride by the bridegroom,' is no doubt the only one which fits in this place, as it appears from the preceding paragraph that this rule is applicable principally to the Âsura form of marriage, i. e. marriage by purchase. Yâg*ñ*avalkya I, 65.

31. Manu VIII, 225; IX, 72; Yâg*ñ*avalkya I, 66; Vish*n*u V, 47.

32. Manu IX, 71; Yâg*ñ*avalkya I, 65.

33. Manu VIII, 224; IX, 73; Yâg*ñ*avalkya I, 66; Vish*n*u V, 45.

34. Vish*n*u V, 47; Manu VIII, 225; Yâg*ñ*avalkya I, 66.

35. Yâg*ñ*avalkya I, 66.

36. It does not become quite clear how far the last term in this

deformity, the loss of her virginity, a blemish, and proved intercourse with another man: these are declared to be the faults of a maiden.

37. Madness, loss of caste, impotency, misery, to have forsaken his relatives, and the two first faults of a maiden (in the above text): these are the faults of a suitor.

38. Eight nuptial rites have been ordained for the (four) castes, by which wedlock may be entered into. The Brâhma form is the first of these, the Prâ*g*âpatya form is the second.

39. The Ârsha, Daiva, Gândharva, and Âsura forms follow next. The Râkshasa form is no worse than the one preceding it, and the Pai*s*â*k*a is declared to be the eighth.

40. In the Brâhma form, a maiden decked with ornaments is given (to the bridegroom), after he has been invited and honourably received (by the father). When he has been addressed with the words, 'Fulfil your sacred duties together (with her),' it is termed the Prâ*g*âpatya form.

41. When (the father) receives (from the bridegroom) a dress and a bull and a cow, it is termed the Ârsha form. When she is given, before the

---

enumeration, anyagatabhâvâ, differs in import from the two terms immediately preceding it. Perhaps it denotes one pregnant, or who has had a child with another man.

37. 'To have forsaken his relatives.' It is evident that certain near relatives must be meant, as e.g. Manu says (VIII, 389) that a mother, father, wife, or son must not be forsaken.

38-43. Manu III, 20, 21, 27-34; Yâ*gñ*avalkya I, 58-61; Âpastamba II, 5, 11, 17—II, 5, 12, 2; Gautama IV, 6-13 Baudhâyana I, 20, 1-9; Vasish*th*a I, 28-35; Vish*n*u XXIV, 17-26.

40. See Professor Bühler's note on Manu III, 30, 27.

altar, to a priest, who officiates at a sacrifice, it is termed the Daiva form.

42. The union of a willing maiden with her lover is the fifth form, termed Gândharva. When a price is (asked for the bride by the father and) taken (by him), it is the form termed Âsura.

43. The Râkshasa form is declared to consist of the forcible abduction of a maiden. Sexual intercourse with a woman during her sleep or while she is unconscious (of the approach of a man) constitutes the eighth form, the basest of all.

44. Of these, the (first) four, beginning with the Brâhma form, are declared to be lawful; the Gândharva form is common (to all castes); the three forms, which come after it, are unlawful.

45. (Besides the lawful wives) seven other sorts of wives are mentioned in order, who have previously been enjoyed by another man. Among these, the Punarbhû (woman twice married) is of three kinds, and the Svairi*n*î (wanton woman) is fourfold.

*46. A maiden not deflowered, but disgraced by the act of joining the bride and bridegroom's hands, is

43. The term pramatta, translated by 'unconscious,' may either refer to a temporary or to a permanent derangement of the maiden's intellect.

44. Manu III, 23-26; Âpastamba II, 5, 12, 3; Gautama IV, 14, 15; Baudhâyana I, 20, 10-16; Vish*n*u XXIV, 27, 28.

45. The fact that Nârada treats Punarbhûs, 'remarried women,' as being only one degree superior to Svairi*n*îs, 'wanton women,' and belonging like the latter to the category of women previously enjoyed by another man, indicates the low estimation in which he holds remarried women, though remarriage is a perfectly legitimate proceeding, according to him, in certain cases. Manu V, 163; Yâg*ñ*avalkya I, 67. Read trividhâ in the text.

46. 'The act of joining the bride and bridegroom's hands,' the marriage ceremony. Vasish*th*a XVII, 20; Manu IX, 176; Vish*n*u XV, 8.

declared to be the first Punarbhû. She is required to have the marriage ceremony performed once more (when she is married for the second time).

*47. One who, after having left the husband of her youth and betaken herself to another man, returns into the house of her husband, is declared the second (Punarbhû).

*48. When a woman, on failure of brothers-in-law, is delivered by her relations to a Sapi*nd*a of the same caste, she is termed the third (Punarbhû).

*49. When a woman, no matter whether she have children or not, goes to live with another man through love, her husband being alive, she is the first Svairi*n*î (wanton woman).

*50. When a woman, after the death of her husband, rejects her brothers-in-law or other (relations) who have come to her, and unites herself with a stranger through love, she is called the second (Svairi*n*î).

*51. One who, having come from a (foreign) country, or having been purchased with money, or being oppressed with hunger or thirst, gives herself up to a man, saying, 'I am thine,'—is declared to be the third (Svairi*n*î).

*52. When a woman, after having been given in

47. Manu IX, 176; Vasish*th*a XVII, 19; Vish*n*u XV, 9.

48. This is an allusion to the custom of Niyoga or levirate, as described below, in paragraphs 80–88.

49. Yâg*ñ*avalkya I, 67.

50. The 'wanton woman' here referred to is apparently one who, after the death of her husband, declines to perform the custom of Niyoga with a brother-in-law or other relation, and goes to live with a stranger instead of it.

51. 'I am thine;' this is the formula by which a slave that is to be delivers himself to his future master. See above, V, 27.

52. The term utpannasâhasâ has been translated 'by force.'

marriage by her spiritual guides, in a manner corresponding with the usages of her country, (is afterwards married) to another by force, she is called the last Svairinî.

*53. Thus has the law been declared with regard to Punarbhû and Svairinî wives. Among them, each preceding one is inferior to the next in order, and each following one is superior to the one preceding her.

*54. The issue of those women who have been purchased for a price belongs to the begetter. But when nothing has been paid for a woman, her offspring belongs to her legitimate husband.

55. When seed is strewn on a field, without the knowledge of the owner, the giver of the seed has no share in it; the fruit belongs absolutely to the owner of the field.

56. When seed, carried off by a torrent of water or by a gust of wind, grows up in the field of a

The Mitâksharâ, p. 77, interprets it by utpannavyabhikârâ, 'through adultery,' which seems to mean that an elopement is referred to, and not a forcible abduction. In that case, however, this species of wanton women would coincide entirely with the species described in paragraph 49. Besides, it appears from what is said in paragraph 53, that the species of wanton women described in paragraph 52 must be less reprehensible than the three species described in the preceding paragraphs.

53. The Nepalese MS. has the following two paragraphs instead of 53. 'Among the four sorts of Svairinî women, the last respectively are preferable to those previously mentioned; the treatment of their offspring is optional, as regards inheritance, funeral oblations of balls of meal and water, and other concerns. To Punarbhû women, the same rule is applicable as to Svairinî women. Among them (also) each preceding one is inferior,' &c.

54. This rule shows that the purchase and sale of women must have been a very common proceeding in the times of Nârada.

56. Manu IX, 54.

stranger, the owner of that field shall obtain the produce; none of the produce shall belong to the owner of the seed.

57. When a full-grown bull begets calves with the cows of another man, while roaming in his cow-pen, the calves shall belong to him who owns the cows; in vain has the bull spent his strength.

58. When seed is sown in the field of another with the consent of the owner of that field, the offspring is considered to be the common property of the giver of the seed and the owner of the soil.

*59. Grain cannot be produced without a field, nor can it be produced without seed. Therefore offspring belongs by right to both, the father as well as the mother.

*60. Nor is (legitimate) offspring produced, when a man meets a woman at another house than her own. That is declared adultery by those conversant with (the law on) this subject, unless she have come into (the man's) house of her own accord.

*61. A man is not punishable as an adulterer for having intercourse with the wife of one who has left his wife without her fault, or of one impotent or consumptive, if the woman herself consents to it.

---

57. Manu IX, 50, &c. 58. Manu IX, 53.

60. When a woman enters the house of her paramour of her own accord to have intercourse with him, there is no offence (on his part). Vivâda*k*intâma*n*i, p. 112. The Nepalese MS. reads this paragraph differently: 'When a man has intercourse with a woman who has a protector living, at another man's house, it is termed adultery by those conversant with the subject, unless,' &c.

61. When a man has connexion with a married woman, forsaken by her husband, or whose husband is impotent or feeble, he is not punishable, in case the woman consents to it, even though he meet her at her own house. Vivâda*k*intâma*n*i, p. 112.

*62. To meet with another man's wife in an unseasonable hour or place, and to sit, converse, or dally with her, these are the three grades of adultery.

*63. When a woman and a man have meetings at the confluence of two rivers, at a Ghât, in a garden, or in a park, it is also termed adultery.

64. By the employment of go-betweens, dispatch of letters and other criminal proceedings of various kinds, adultery may be found out by the knowing.

*65. If one touches a woman in a place (where it is) improper (to touch her) or allows himself to be touched (in such a spot), all such acts, done with mutual consent, are declared to be adultery.

*66. Bestowing attentions (on a woman), sporting (with her), touching her ornaments and clothes, sitting with her on a bed, all such acts are (also) declared to be adulterous.

*67. If a man seizes a woman by the hand, by a braid of hair, or by the border of her gown, or if he calls out, 'Stop, stop,' all such acts are (also) declared to be adulterous.

68. By the sending of clothes, ornaments, garlands of flowers, drinks, food, and fragrant substances, adultery may (also) be discovered by the wise.

---

62. Manu VIII, 354; Yâg*ñ*avalkya II, 284.

63. Manu VIII, 356. The Nepalese MS. omits paragraphs 64, 65, and arranges paragraphs 66–69 differently.

65. Identical with Manu VIII, 358. 'A place (where it is) improper (to touch her).' For a different interpretation of this term, see Professor Bühler's note on Manu VIII, 358.

66. 'Bestowing attentions on a woman,' doing what is agreeable to her. Vivâda*k*intâma*n*i, p. 110. Nearly identical with Manu VIII, 357.

67. Such acts, when committed against another woman than one's own wife, constitute the offence of adultery. That is the meaning. Vivâda*k*intâma*n*i, p. 110; Yâg*ñ*avalkya II, 284.

*69. When a man, actuated by vanity, folly, or braggartism, declares himself, that he has enjoyed the love of a certain woman, that is also termed an adulterous proceeding.

70. When a man has connexion with a woman of his own caste, a fine of the highest degree (shall be inflicted on him); and the middling fine, when he has connexion with a woman of lower caste; and capital punishment, when he has connexion with a woman of superior caste.

71. (When he has connexion) with a maiden against her will, he shall have two fingers cut off. If the maiden belongs to the highest (or Brahman) caste, death and the confiscation of his entire property (shall be his punishment).

*72. When, however, he has connexion with a willing maiden, it is no offence, but he shall bestow ornaments on her, honour her (with other presents), and (lawfully) espouse her.

*73. A mother, mother's sister, mother-in-law, maternal uncle's wife, father's sister, paternal uncle's (wife), friend's (wife), pupil's wife, sister, sister's friend, daughter-in-law,

*74. Daughter, spiritual teacher's wife, Sagotra relation, one come to him for protection, a queen, a female ascetic, a nurse, an honest woman, and a female of the highest caste:

---

70. Manu VIII, 374–385; Yâ*g*ñavalkya II, 286; Vish*n*u V, 40, 41; Gautama XII, 2, 3; Baudhâyana II, 3, 52, &c.

71. Manu VIII, 366, 367; Yâ*g*ñavalkya II, 288.

72. Manu VIII, 366; Yâ*g*ñavalkya II, 288. The Nepalese MS. reads: *'When a man of the same caste has intercourse with a willing maiden.'

73–75. Manu XI, 171; Yâ*g*ñavalkya III, 231–233, &c.

*75. When a man carnally knows any one out of these (twenty) women, he is said to commit incest. For that crime, no other punishment than excision of the organ is considered (as a sufficient atonement).

* 76. When a man has sexual connexion with (small) cattle, he shall pay one hundred (Pa*n*as) as a fine; (for sexual connexion) with a cow, he shall pay the middling fine; and the same (for sexual connexion) with a low-caste woman.

* 77. Let a punishment be inflicted by the king on him who has intercourse with a woman, with whom it is forbidden to have intercourse, and let such sinners be cleared (of the moral offence committed by them) by performing a penance.

* 78. Intercourse is permitted with a wanton woman, who belongs to another than the Brahman caste, or a prostitute, or a female slave, or a female not restrained by her master (nishkâsinî), if these women belong to a lower caste than oneself; but with a woman of superior caste, intercourse is prohibited.

---

75. The fact that female ascetics (pravra*g*itâ) are reckoned by Nârada among those females whose violation is incest—literally 'an offence as heavy as the violation of a spiritual teacher's bed'—constitutes an important difference between his teaching and Manu's. Manu ordains the same punishment for the violation of female ascetics as for the violation of the wives of actors and singers and other abandoned women. See Professor Bühler's note on Manu VIII, 363. All commentators declare that this rule is applicable in the case of guarded women only. The Vivâda*k*intâma*n*i says that the term 'mother' denotes a stepmother in paragraph 73.

76. Vish*n*u V, 43, 44; Manu VIII, 385; Yâ*gñ*avalkya II, 289.

78. The two terms, svairi*n*î, 'a wanton woman,' and abrâhma*n*î, 'one not belonging to the Brahman caste,' have to be connected. 'A wanton woman,' a self-willed unchaste woman. Nishkâsinî

* 79. When, however, such a woman is the kept mistress (of another man, intercourse with her) is as criminal as (intercourse) with another man's wife. Such women, though intercourse with them is not (in general) forbidden, must not be approached, because they belong to another man.

* 80. Should the husband of a childless woman die, she must go to her brother-in-law, through desire to obtain a son, after having received the (required) authorization from her Gurus.

81. And he shall have intercourse with her, till a son be born. When a son is born, he must leave her. It would be sinful intercourse otherwise.

82–84. (He shall approach) a woman who has brought forth male issue, and who is praiseworthy, free from passion, and without amorous desire. He must have anointed his limbs with clarified butter, or with oil which has not lost its natural condition, and must turn away his face from hers, and avoid the contact of limb with limb. For this (custom is

---

means 'one who has left her family' according to the Madanaratna, and 'a female slave not restrained by her master' according to Vig*ñ*ânes*v*ara, Mâdhavâ*k*ârya, and the rest. Vîramitrodaya, p. 510. See above, V, 39.

79. Yâg*ñ*avalkya II, 290. The Nepalese MS. reads 'when they belong to another man.'

80–88. Manu IX, 59–64, 143; Yâg*ñ*avalkya I, 69; Gautama XVIII, 4–8; Âpastamba II, 10, 27, 2, 3; Vasish*th*a XVII, 55, 66; Baudhâyana II, 4, 9–10. Regarding the history of the Indian levirate, see my 'Outlines of a History of Hindu Law' (Tagore Law Lectures for 1883), pp. 153, 154.

80. The Gurus intended are, the teacher, sub-teacher, and officiating priests of the deceased husband. See Professor Bühler's note on Vasish*th*a XVII, 56. According to Vasish*th*a, the authority of both the Gurus and relatives is required. The relatives are referred to by Nârada himself, paragraphs 82–84.

practised) when the family threatens to become extinct, for the continuation of the lineage, and not from amorous desire. He must not approach a woman who is with child, or blamable, or unauthorized by her relations. Should a woman procreate a son with her brother-in-law without having been authorized thereto by her relations,

85. He is declared an illegitimate, and incapable of inheriting, by the expounders of the Veda. So when a younger brother has intercourse, without authorization, with the wife of his elder brother,

86. Or an elder brother with the wife of his younger brother, they are both declared to commit incest. After having been authorized by the Gurus, he shall approach the woman and advise her,

* 87. In the manner previously stated, (as if she were) his daughter-in-law. He becomes pure, when the ceremony for the birth of a male child is performed. (Let him approach her) once, or till she has conceived. When she is pregnant, she is even as (his daughter-in-law).

---

86. According to *G*agannâtha's reading of these texts, the appointment to raise offspring may be given by the king also, where Gurus and relations are wanting. The same clause is found in the Nepalese MS. 'He shall advise the woman' means, according to *G*agannâtha, 'he shall teach her the general illegality of receiving the caresses of other men, and the particular legality of an appointment to raise up offspring.' See Colebrooke's (*G*agannâtha's) Digest, IV, 4, 147.

87. 'His daughter-in-law;' a brother's wife is considered as similar to a daughter-in-law, according to *G*agannâtha. See loc. cit. The 'ceremony for the birth of a male child' (Pu*m*savana), which has the procreation of a son for its object, is usually performed at the time when the mother perceives the first signs of a living conception. It has to be observed that the reading of this paragraph is uncertain, and its rendering conjectural. The Nepalese MS. agrees with *G*agannâtha.

* 88. Should the man or woman behave otherwise, impelled by amorous desire, they shall be punished severely by the king. Otherwise justice would be violated.

* 89. Husband and wife must not lodge a plaint against one another with their relations, or the king, when a quarrel has arisen through passion, which has its root in jealousy or scorn.

90. When husband and wife leave one another, from mutual dislike, it is a sin, except when a woman, who is kept under supervision, commits adultery.

* 91. When a married woman commits adultery, her hair shall be shaved, she shall have to lie on a low couch, receive bad food and bad clothing, and the removal of the sweepings shall be assigned to her as her occupation.

* 92. One who wastes the entire property of her husband under the pretence that it is (her own) Strîdhana, or who procures abortion, or who makes an

---

89. The term sa*m*bandha, literally 'connexion,' has been rendered by 'a quarrel.' It can hardly be referred to friendly connexion (with another man or woman) in this place. The prohibition of lawsuits between wife and husband may be compared to the analogous prohibition, in the case of husband and wife, of suretyship, division of property, contracting of debts, and giving evidence.

91. Mitramisra, in the Vîramitrodaya, p. 520, quotes this text as proving that an adulteress even has a claim to maintenance. He interprets it as follows. When a woman has committed adultery through amorous desire, she shall be shaved and compelled to lie on a low couch, bad food and a bad dwelling shall be given to her for her maintenance; and the removal of rubbish shall be assigned to her as her occupation. Yâg*ñ*avalkya I, 70.

92. As for the constituents of Strîdhana, or separate property of a woman, see XIII, 8.

attempt on her husband's life, he shall banish from the town.

* 93. One who always shows malice to him, or who makes unkind speeches, or eats before her husband, he shall quickly expel from his house.

* 94. Let not a husband show love to a barren woman, or to one who gives birth to female children only, or whose conduct is blamable, or who constantly contradicts him; if he does (have conjugal intercourse with her), he becomes liable to censure (himself).

* 95. If a man leaves a wife who is obedient, pleasant-spoken, skilful, virtuous, and the mother of (male) issue, the king shall make him mindful of his duty by (inflicting) severe punishment (on him).

96. When a faultless maiden has been married to a man who has a blemish unknown (before his marriage), and does not repair to another man (after discovering it), she shall be enjoined to do so by her relations. If she has no relations living, she shall go (to live with another man) of her own accord.

97. When her husband is lost or dead, when he

---

93. 'He shall expel from his house.' This, according to an interpretation mentioned by *G*agannâtha, means that he shall banish her from the principal habitation, assigning to her a separate dwelling within his close. See Colebrooke's Digest, IV, 1, 63. This interpretation is hardly correct, though it is interesting as it shows the tendency of the commentators to explain away those laws under which married women were deprived of their claim to maintenance. Manu IX, 80, 81; Yâg*ñ*avalkya I, 73, &c.

96. This rule shows that a marriage is dissoluble on the discovery of a blemish, as well as a betrothal. See XII, 3.

97. 'Lost,' i.e. gone no one knows whither. This text, or an identical text of Parâ*s*ara, has been frequently appealed to by the

has become a religious ascetic, when he is impotent, and when he has been expelled from caste: these are the five cases of legal necessity, in which a woman may be justified in taking another husband.

98. Eight years shall a Brahman woman wait for the return of her absent husband; or four years, if she has no issue; after that time, she may betake herself to another man.

99. A Kshatriya woman shall wait six years; or three years, if she has no issue; a Vais*y*a woman shall wait four (years), if she has issue; any other Vais*y*a woman (i. e. one who has no issue), two years.

100. No such (definite) period is prescribed for a *S*ûdra woman, whose husband is gone on a journey. Twice the above period is ordained, when the (absent) husband is alive and tidings are received of him.

101. The above series of rules has been laid down by the Creator of the world for those cases where a man has disappeared. No offence is imputed to a woman if she goes to live with another man after (the fixed period has elapsed).

---

modern advocates of the remarriage of widows in India. Vasish*th*a XVII, 74.

98, 99. Vasish*th*a XVII, 75–80; Manu IX, 76, 77; Gautama XVIII, 15–17.

100, 101. The Nepalese MS. has three paragraphs instead of these two, as follows:—'100. No such period is ordained for a *S*ûdra woman, nor is justice violated (in her case). The utmost limit for her is a year, especially if she has no issue. 101. This term has been ordained for the wives of absent husbands who are dead. Twice the same term is ordained, when (the absent husband) is alive and tidings are received of him. 101 a. The (other) term has been ordained for those who have issue (?). Afterwards, no offence is imputed to a woman who goes to live with another man.'

102. This body of laws is applicable to the offspring of unions in the direct order of the castes; the offspring of a marriage union in the inverse order of the castes is said to be (produced by) a confusion of castes.

103. There are Anantara, Ekântara, and Dvyantara sons both in the direct and inverse order of the castes.

104. (Of this description are) the Ugra, Pâra*s*ava, and Nishâda, (who are begotten) in the direct order, as well as the Ambash*th*a, Mâgadha, and Kshatt*ri*, who spring from a Kshatriya woman.

105. One of these (latter castes) is begotten in the direct order, of the two (others) it must be known that they are (begotten) in an inverse order. The Kshatt*ri* and the rest are begotten in an

---

102. 'In the direct order of the castes,' i.e. where a man of higher marries a woman of lower caste. 'In the inverse order of the castes,' i.e. where a woman of higher marries a man of lower caste.

103–113. Manu X, 6–41; Gautama IV, 16–28; Vasish*th*a XVIII; Baudhâyana I, 16, 6–12, 17 passim; Vish*n*u XVI, 1–7; Yâ*gñ*avalkya I, 91–95.

103. An Anantara is the son of a father whose caste is only one degree higher or lower than the caste of the mother. An Ekântara is the son of a father whose caste is two degrees higher or lower than the caste of the mother. A Dvyantara is the son of a father whose caste is three degrees higher or lower than the caste of the mother. The Nepalese MS., throughout superior to the Indian MSS., reads as follows:—'103. An Ugra, Pâra*s*ava, and Nishâda are (begotten) in the direct order, and are declared to be the sons of *S*ûdra women with husbands of the (three) higher castes. 104. Of a Brahman woman are born a *K*â*nd*âla, a Sûta, and a Vaidehaka; they are declared to spring in an inverse order, from their union with husbands of different caste. 105. An Ambash*th*a, Mâgadha, and Kshatt*ri* are the sons of a Kshatriya woman. Of these, one is born in the direct, and two are born in the inverse order. 106 a. Of a Vai*s*ya woman, are born an Ambash*th*a, Yavana, and Âyogava.

inverse order, the (three) mentioned first in the direct order.

106. Sacraments, beginning with the boiling of gruel, three times seven in number (shall be performed) by them. The son (of a Brahman) with a Brahman woman is equal in caste (to his father). The son (of a Brahman) with a Kshatriya woman is an Anantara.

107. An Ambash*th*a and an Ugra are begotten in the same way by Kshatriya men and on Vai*s*ya women respectively. An Ambash*th*a is an Ekântara, the son of a Brahman with a Vai*s*ya woman.

108. In the same way, a son called Nishâda

Of these, one is born in the inverse, and two are born in the direct order. 106 b. A Sûta and the other Pratilomas (men born in the inverse order), who are begotten contrary to order, are declared to partake of the series of three times seven sacraments, beginning with the Pâka ceremony (cooking food). 106 c. The son,' &c.

106. The meaning of the first half of this paragraph is somewhat obscure. The term tri*h* sapta, 'three times seven,' has been connected with sa*m*skârâ*s*, 'sacraments.' The sacraments are peculiar to those mixed castes, which are procreated in the direct order of castes. See Manu X, 41. The 'boiling of gruel' (*k*arupâka) being mentioned as the first sacrament, it appears that the sacraments here referred to are identical with the ya*ññ*as, 'sacrifices,' of which there are twenty-one according to the usual theory. See Gautama XVIII, 18–20, and Professor Weber's paper on Vedic Sacrificial Rites, Indische Studien, X, p. 320. It is also possible to connect the clause 'three times seven' with 'them.' The number of twenty-one mixed castes procreated in a direct order is received by adding the fifteen castes springing from a further mixture between the mixed castes (Manu X, 31) to the six principal mixed castes procreated in a direct order. For vai matâ*h*, as I have conjectured, the MSS. read kosh*th*ata*h*, which might be rendered '(The twenty-one sacraments, beginning with the boiling of gruel, have to be performed by them) out of a pot.' However, the correctness of this reading is liable to considerable doubt. The Nepalese MS. reads, te sa*m*skârâ*sk*a pakâdyâs teshâ*m* tri*h* saptako ga*n*a*h*. This is perhaps the original reading. See the preceding note.

springs from the union of a Kshatriya with a *S*ûdra woman. A *S*ûdra woman obtains from a Brahman a son (called) Pâra*s*ava, who is superior (to the Nishâda).

109. Thus have the sons born in the direct order of castes been declared. The two sons called Sûta and Mâgadha as well as the Âyogava,

110. And the Kshatt*ri* and Vaidehaka are begotten in the inverse order of castes. The Sûta is declared to be an Anantara, begotten by a Kshatriya on a Brahman woman.

111. Similarly, the Mâgadha and Âyogava are the sons of Vai*s*ya and *S*ûdra fathers (and of a Brahman mother). A Brahman woman obtains of a Vai*s*ya father an Ekântara son, the Vaidehaka.

112. A Kshatriya woman (obtains of a *S*ûdra) an Ekântara son, called Kshatt*ri*. A Dvyantara son in the inverse order, the most abject of men, because he is the fruit of sinful intercourse,

113. *Kand*âla by name, is born of a *S*ûdra, when a Brahman woman forgets herself (with him). Therefore must the king take special care to prevent women from sinful intercourse with men of different caste.

THIRTEENTH TITLE OF LAW.

THE LAW OF INHERITANCE.

*1. Where a partition of the paternal property

113. The Nepalese MS. inserts the following before the clause beginning with the word 'Therefore:'—'Because confusion of the castes springs up, where the king keeps no watch over them.'

XIII, 1. The term 'sons' includes by implication grandsons and

is instituted by the sons, it is called by the learned, Partition of Property, a title of law.

* 2. The father being dead, the sons shall divide the estate as they ought; (and so shall) daughters (divide the property) of their mother (when she dies); or, failing daughters, their issue.

* 3. (The distribution of the property shall take place) when the mother has ceased to menstruate and the sisters are married, or when the father's sexual desire is extinguished and he has ceased to care for worldly interests.

* 4. Or let a father distribute his property among his sons himself, when he is stricken in years, either allotting a larger share to the eldest son, or (distributing the property in any other way) following his own inclination.

---

more remote descendants. The term 'paternal' includes property of the grandfather and more remote ancestors as well. Mandlik's Mayûkha, p. 33 (IV, 3, 1, Borrodaile). Analogous remarks are found in most other Commentaries.

2. 'Their issue' (tadanvaya*h*). According to the usual explanation, the male issue of the daughters is meant. However, there is nothing in the text to warrant an exclusion of the female issue of daughters. Manu IX, 104, 192; Yâ*gñ*avalkya II, 117; Gautama XXVIII, 1; Baudhâyana II, 3, 8.

3. According to the Mayûkha, the clause 'when the sisters are married' has to be construed with both the preceding and following clauses, the marriage of the sisters being required to precede both a division in the father's lifetime and a division in the mother's lifetime. See Mayûkha, p. 33 (translation, p. 39). The Dâyabhâga has a totally different reading of this text, which is censured in the Vîramitrodaya. Gautama XXVIII, 1.

4. The Dâyabhâga (II, 82, Colebrooke) states correctly that the unequal distribution referred to in the last clause of this text must be different from that sort of unequal distribution under which the eldest son is to receive a larger share than the rest. The Mitâksharâ school, on the other hand, recognises two different modes of

*5. Or the senior brother shall maintain all (the junior brothers), like a father, if they wish it, or even the youngest brother, if able; the well-being of a family depends on the ability (of its head).

*6. Property gained by valour, or belonging to a wife, and the gains of science, are three kinds of wealth not subject to partition; and so is a favour conferred by the father (exempt from partition).

*7. When the mother has bestowed (a portion of) her property on any (of her sons) from affection, the rule is the same in that case also; for the mother is equal to the father (as regards her competence to bestow gifts).

*8. What (was given) before the (nuptial) fire, what (was given) during the bridal procession, the husband's donation, and what was received from her brother, mother, or father, that is called the six-fold property of a woman (Strîdhana).

---

distribution only: one equal, and the other with the customary deductions in favour of the eldest son, middlemost son, &c., according to the order of seniority. The writers of this school, therefore, have endeavoured to refute the interpretation of the Dâyabhâga. See Vîramitrodaya, transl., p. 54.—Manu IX, 112 foll.; Yâ*gñ*avalkya II, 114; Âpastamba II, 6, 14; Gautama XXVIII, 2; Vish*n*u XVII, 1; Baudhâyana II, 3, 9.

5. As the management of the property and government of the family, under this rule, may devolve on the youngest brother even, it follows that the middlemost brother may get it à fortiori. This is expressly stated in the Dâyabhâga (III, 1, 15, Colebrooke). Manu IX, 108.

6. 'What was received at the time of obtaining a wife is here called the "wealth of a wife;" meaning effects obtained on account of marriage.' Dâyabhâga (VI, 1, 13, Colebrooke); Manu IX, 206; Yâ*gñ*avalkya II, 119.

8. It may be asked by whom the gifts presented before the nuptial fire and during the bridal procession, i. e. at two different stages of the marriage ceremony, must have been presented in

*9. Such property of a woman shall go to her offspring; if she have no offspring, it is declared to go to her husband (if she was married to him) according to one of the four (praiseworthy) marriage forms, beginning with the Brâhma form; (if she was married) according to one of the other forms, it shall go to her parents.

*10. When one brother maintains the family of another brother, who is engaged in studying science, he shall receive a share of the wealth gained by that study, though he be ignorant (himself).

*11. A learned man is not bound to give a share of his own (acquired) wealth against his will to an unlearned co-heir, unless it have been gained by him using the paternal estate.

*12. Two shares let the father keep for himself

---

order to be Strîdhana. As all the other gifts classed as Strîdhana are presented by relations, it may be inferred that the nuptial gifts have to come from the same quarter. Kâtyâyana declares expressly that a gift made by a stranger is not Strîdhana. Manu IX, 194; Yâ*gñ*avalkya II, 143, 144; Vish*n*u XVII, 18.

9. See XII, 38 foll. The commentators are of opinion that the Gândharva form of marriage follows the same rule as those four forms which are referred to in the first half of this text. This, however, is an artificial interpretation, which has merely been devised for the purpose of making this text agree with an analogous rule of Manu (IX, 196). Manu IX, 195–197; Yâ*gñ*avalkya II, 144, 145; Vish*n*u XVII, 19–21; Vasish*th*a XVII, 46; Baudhâyana II, 2, 3, 43. Read *k*aturshvâhu*h* in the text.

10. *S*rîk*ri*sh*n*a observes that where the support has been offered by several unlearned co-heirs, they shall all of them be made to participate in the gains of science. See Colebrooke's Dâyabhâga, VI, 1, 15, note.

11. 'The word "paternal" intends joint property.' Dâyabhâga VI, 1, 17; Manu IX, 206; Yâ*gñ*avalkya II, 119; Gautama XXVIII, 30.

12. The rule which assigns two shares to a father distributing

when distributing his property. The mother shall receive the same share as a son (when the sons divide the property) after her husband's death.

*13. To the eldest son a larger share shall be allotted, and a less share is assigned to the youngest son. The rest shall take equal shares, and so shall an unmarried sister.

*14. The same rule applies to sons of a wife (Kshetra*g*as) lawfully begotten on her. For sons of lower caste, a decrease in the shares according to the order (of their caste) is ordained, in case they are born of women legally married.

*15. When a father has distributed his property amongst his sons, that is a lawful distribution for them (and cannot be annulled), whether the share of one be less, or greater than, or equal to the shares of the rest; for the father is the lord of all.

---

his property himself, is referred to the father's self-acquired property in the Mitâksharâ school, and to ancestral property in the Bengal school. This difference of interpretation is connected with the varying views taken in the several schools of law of the extent of the patria potestas in questions of proprietary right and inheritance. See Dâyabhâga II, 35, Colebrooke; Mitâksharâ I, 5, 7, Colebrooke. Yâ*g*ñavalkya II, 123; Vish*n*u XVIII, 34.

13. The share of an unmarried daughter, according to the translation here given, would have to be equal to the shares of the middlemost brothers. According to *G*agannâtha, all that is meant by Nârada is this, that the daughter shall receive some portion of the property, the precise amount of it being left undecided. See Colebrooke's Digest, V, 1, 71.—Manu IX, 113–118; Vish*n*u XVII, 37; XVIII, 35; Baudhâyana II, 3, 9; Gautama XXVIII, 5–13; Vasish*th*a XVII, 42 foll.; Âpastamba II, 6, 14, 6–10; Yâ*g*ñavalkya II, 114, 124.

14. For the rules regarding the procreation of a Kshetra*g*a son, see XII, 80–88. Gautama XXVIII, 35–39; Vasish*th*a XVII, 47–50; Vish*n*u XVIII, 1–31; Baudhâyana II, 3, 10; Yâ*g*ñavalkya II, 125; Manu IX, 149–156.

15. The writers of the Bengal school give this text its plain

*16. A father who is diseased, or angry, or absorbed by (sinful) worldly interests, or who acts illegally, has not the power to distribute his property (as he likes).

*17. The son of a maiden, a son obtained through a pregnant bride, and one born of a woman (whose transgression was) unknown (at first and is found out subsequently): of these, the mother's husband is regarded as the father, and they are declared to be entitled to shares of his property.

*18. A maiden's son, whose father is unknown and whose mother is not legally married (to his father), shall give a funeral ball (of rice) to his maternal grandfather and inherit his property.

*19. Those sons who have been begotten by one or by many on a woman not authorized (to raise issue to her deceased husband), shall all be dis-

---

meaning, viz. that a father may distribute his property among his sons as he pleases. They add, however, that in doing so he must be guided by lawful motives, such as compassion on an incapable son, partiality for a pious son, and the like. See Dâyabhâga II, 74, 75; Colebrooke's Digest, V, 1, 32. The Mayûkha, on the other hand, declares that this rule of Nârada had legal force in the former ages of the world only. See Mandlik's Mayûkha, p. 35 (transl. p. 43). Yâ*gñ*avalkya II, 116.

16. This rule 'relates to the case where the father, through perturbation of mind occasioned by disease or the like, or through irritation against any one of his sons, or through partiality for the child of a favourite wife, makes a distribution not conformable to law.' Colebrooke's Dâyabhâga II, 83. The Mitâksharâ (I, 2, 13, 14), cutting down the privileges of the father everywhere, interprets this rule as a prohibition of any other mode of unequal distribution except that by which the customary deductions are made in favour of the eldest son, &c.

17, 18. Manu IX, 170–172; Yâ*gñ*avalkya II, 129; Vish*n*u XV, 10–17; Vasish*th*a XVII, 21–23.

19. Regarding the rule of Niyoga, or appointment of a married

inherited; they are the sons of their (respective) begetters only.

*20. They shall offer the funeral ball (of rice) to their begetter, in case their mother had been obtained for a price; if no price has been paid for her, they shall give the funeral ball to the husband (of their mother).

*21. One hostile to his father, or expelled from caste, or impotent, or guilty of a minor offence, shall not even take a share (of the inheritance), if he is a legitimate son; much less so, if he is a (Kshetra*g*a) son of the wife (only).

*22. Persons afflicted with a chronic or acute disease, or idiotic, or mad, or blind, or lame (are also incapable of inheriting). They shall be maintained by the family; but their sons shall receive their respective shares (of the inheritance).

*23. The sons of two fathers shall give the funeral

---

woman or widow to raise offspring to her husband, see XII, 80-88; Manu IX, 143.

20. See XII, 54.

21, 22. Manu IX, 201-203; Âpastamba II, 6, 14, 1, 15; Gautama XXVIII, 23, 40, 43; Vasish*th*a XVII, 52, 53; Baudhâyana II, 3, 37-40; Vish*n*u XV, 32-37; Yâ*gñ*avalkya II, 140, 141.

21. The commentators are at variance as to the precise meaning of the term 'hostile to his father.' Thus the Sarasvatîvilâsa declares it to denote one who forgets himself so far as to say, 'He is not my father.' The Dâyakramasaṅgraha says it means one who beats his father. According to *G*agannâtha and the Ratnâkara, it means 'one who attempts his father's life or commits other hostile acts against him (mâra*n*âdik*ri*t), and who fails to offer the customary funeral oblations to his father after his death.' See Colebrooke's Digest, V, 4, 320.

22. Atrophy or pulmonary consumption is instanced as a chronic, and leprosy as an acute disease, in the Ratnâkara. See Colebrooke's Digest, loc. cit.

23. 'The adoptive father,' literally 'the man who owns the

ball (of rice) and the water oblations to each of the two (fathers) singly, and shall receive one half of the property left by their natural and adoptive fathers.

*24. That portion (of the property) which belongs to a reunited coparcener is declared to be absolutely his own. So when one of the sharers has no issue it shall go to the rest (after the death) of those who are childless.

*25. If among several brothers one childless should die or become a religious ascetic, the others shall divide his property, excepting the Strîdhana.

---

mother' (Kshetrika). The 'son of two fathers' is no doubt one procreated by Niyoga on the wife of one impotent, &c. It is not equally clear why he is to obtain one half only of the property left by his two fathers, as he is elsewhere declared to succeed to both. According to the Ratnâkara, this rule 'relates to the case where the natural father has a son begotten in lawful wedlock, and the husband of the mother also has by some means (katha*m*k*it) obtained male issue by himself begotten.' See Colebrooke's Digest, V, 4, 242.—Yâ*g*ñavalkya II, 127; Manu IX, 145, 190; Baudhâyana II, 3, 18, 19.

24. For several other interpretations of this difficult text, see Colebrooke's Digest, V, 8, 433. It has to be observed, however, that the reading translated here differs from the reading translated by Colebrooke.

25, 26. The fact that the widow is invested with a claim to maintenance merely under this text, whereas the leading texts of Yâ*g*ñavalkya and Vish*n*u constitute her heir to the property of a husband who has died without leaving male issue, has caused some difficulty to the commentators. Thus Madana says that this text must be held applicable to the widow of an undivided or reunited coparcener only, who is given a mere claim to maintenance by all writers of the Mitâksharâ school. The writers of the Bengal school, on the other hand, recognise the widow's right of inheritance in the case of undivided coparceners even. It appears, however, from the order of heirs given in 49–51, that Nârada does not make the widow an heir in any case.

25. Manu IX, 212; Yâ*g*ñavalkya II, 138; Vish*n*u XVII, 17; Gautama XVIII, 21.

*26. They shall make provision for his women till they die, in case they remain faithful to the bed of their husband. Should the women not (remain chaste), they must cut off that allowance.

*27. If he has left a daughter, her father's share is destined for her maintenance. They shall maintain her up to the time of her marriage; afterwards let her husband keep her.

*28. After the death of her lord, the relations of her husband shall be the guardians of a woman who has no son. They shall have full authority to control her, to regulate her mode of life, and to maintain her.

*29. When the husband's family is extinct, or contains no male, or when it is reduced to poverty, or when no one related to it within the degree of a Sapi*nd*a is left, the father's relations shall be the guardians of a woman.

*30. It is through independence that women go

---

26. Yâ*g*ñavalkya II, 142.

27. 'They shall maintain her,' literally 'they shall give her a share.' See par. 13, where a share is allotted to an unmarried sister. The maintenance of the daughter includes, no doubt, the obligation to defray the expense of her marriage. Yâ*g*ñavalkya II, 141.

28. All the commentators declare that the right of guardianship goes in the order of proximity. 'Thus, without (her guardian's) consent, she may not give away anything to any person; nor indulge herself in matters of shape, taste, smell, and the like; and if the means of subsistence be wanting he must provide her maintenance.' *G*agannâtha. See Colebrooke's Digest, IV, 1, 13.

29. The Nepalese MS. and the commentaries insert the following text here: *'If both families are extinct, the king is declared to be the protector of a woman; he shall provide for her and punish her when she has swerved from the path of duty.'

30, 31. Vasish*th*a V, 1, 2; Baudhâyana II, 3, 44, 45; Gautama

to ruin, though born in a noble family. Therefore the Lord of creatures has assigned a dependent condition to them.

*31. The father protects her during her infancy, the husband protects her when she is grown up, and the sons (protect her) in her old age. A woman is unfit to enjoy independence.

*32. What is left (of the father's property), when the father's obligations have been discharged, and when the father's debts have been paid, shall be divided by the brothers, in order that the father may not continue a debtor.

*33. For those (brothers), for whom the initiatory ceremonies have not been duly performed by their father, they must be performed by the (other) brothers, (defraying the expense) from the paternal property.

XVIII, 1; Manu IX, 3; V, 148; Yâ*gñ*avalkya I, 85; Vish*n*u XXV, 12, 13.

30. 'They go to ruin,' i.e. they are guilty of disloyalty and other offences; thus, because they do not know what is legal for those who live exactly according to sacred ordinances, and because they cannot be instructed, they would violate the duties of their class and the like. *G*agannâtha. See Colebrooke's Digest, IV, 1, 4.

32. The term pit*r*idâyebhyo, 'when the father's obligations have been discharged,' is differently explained by different commentators. Thus Varadarâ*g*a (Burnell's Vyavahâranir*n*aya, p. 18) says it denotes the father's funeral rites and the like. A*k*yuta, as quoted in Colebrooke's Dâyabhâga I, 47, note, refers it to sums of which payment has been promised by the father. Manu VIII, 166; IX, 104; Baudhâyana II, 3, 8; Gautama XXVIII, 1; Yâ*gñ*avalkya II, 117. Read dattvar*n*a*m* in the text.

33. There appears to be some doubt as to what is meant here by the term sa*m*skâra, 'initiatory or sacramental ceremonies,' some commentators including the ceremony of marriage in that term, and others declaring the initiatory ceremonies to terminate with the investiture with the sacred thread. Yâ*gñ*avalkya II, 124.

*34. Or, no paternal wealth being left, the initiatory ceremonies must be invariably performed for their brothers by those previously initiated contributing (the required) funds from their own portions.

*35. One who, being authorized to look after the affairs of the family, charges himself with the management (of the family property), shall be supported by his brothers with (presents of) food, clothing, and vehicles.

*36. When the fact of a legal partition should be called into question, the decision of the dispute (which has arisen) among the sharers shall be founded on (the testimony of) kinsmen, the written deed recording the division of the estate, and the separate transaction of business.

*37. Among unseparated brothers, the performance of religious duties is single. When they have come to a partition, they have to perform their religious duties each for himself.

---

35. Some commentators explain this text as having reference to one who generously declines to take his share at the time of partition. His share shall be made up afterwards by the other brothers contributing severally a portion of their shares. However, there seems to be more foundation for the opinion of those commentators who interpret this text as ordaining the allotment of a preferential share or the presentation of special gifts to the manager of the family property. See Colebrooke's Digest, V, 2, 108.

36. The commentators observe that the contest here referred to does not turn on the mode but on the fact of partition. See Colebrooke's Digest, V, 6, 381. The business here referred to consists of agriculture and the like acts, according to the Mitâksharâ. Yâ*gñ*avalkya II, 149.

37. The term 'religious duties,' according to the Mitâksharâ, relates principally to the five Mahâya*gñ*as, 'great sacrifices' or 'sacraments.' Before division they are performed by one brother, generally the eldest brother, as representative of the rest. Manu IX, 111; Gautama XXVIII, 4.

*38. Giving, receiving, cattle, food, houses, fields, and servants must be regarded as separate among divided brothers, and so must cooking, religious duties, income, and expenditure (be kept separate for each of them).

*39. (The acts of) giving evidence, of becoming a surety, of giving, and of taking, may be mutually performed by divided brothers, but not by unseparated ones.

*40. If (brothers or others) should transact such matters as these publicly with their co-heirs, they may be presumed to be separate in affairs, even though no written record (of the partition) be in existence.

*41. Those brothers who for ten years continue to live separate in point of religious duties and business transactions, should be regarded as separate; that is a settled rule.

*42. When a number of persons, the descendants of one man, are separate in point of (the performance of) religious duties, business transactions, and work-

---

38. 'Giving and receiving,' without consulting each other. Purchase of 'cattle' and the like. See Colebrooke's Digest, V, 6, 380. The upshot of a long discussion of this text by *G*agannâtha is this, that none of the acts mentioned here may be regarded as conclusive evidence by itself, a great deal of collective evidence of all sorts having to be adduced in each case. See Colebrooke's Digest, V, 6, 387.

39. Yâ*gñ*avalkya II, 52.

41. The term 'brothers' is here used to denote coparceners generally. Sm*ri*ti*k*andrikâ XVI, 14. The Sarasvatîvilâsa (§ 812, Foulkes) contests the correctness of this interpretation. The Nepalese MS. does not give this paragraph, and it is elsewhere attributed to B*ri*haspati.

42, 43. 'Religious duties,' prescribed observances, such as the five great sacrifices (Mahâya*gñ*as). 'Business transactions,' such as

ing utensils, and do not consult each other about their dealings,

*43. They are quite at liberty to perform, according to pleasure, all (such transactions as) the gift or sale of their own shares. They are (in fact) masters of their own wealth.

*44. One born after partition shall receive his father's property exclusively. Or, if other sharers have reunited with the father, they shall come to a division (with the son born after partition). Such is the law.

*45. The legitimate son of the body, the son begotten on a wife (Kshetra*g*a), the son of an (appointed) daughter, the son of a maiden, the son received with the wife, the son secretly born,

*46. The son of a remarried woman, the son cast off, the adopted son, the son bought, the son made, and the son who has offered himself, are declared to be the twelve sons.

*47. Among these, six are kinsmen and heirs, and six are not heirs (but) kinsmen. Each preceding one is declared to be superior (to the one

---

trading and the like acts. 'Working utensils,' such as household furniture, the separate possession of which is indicative of partition. The meaning is that, when they are separated thus, each may give, sell, or otherwise dispose of (his share). Mayûkha, p. 51 (transl. p. 76).

44. Manu IX, 216; Yâ*gñ*avalkya II, 122; Gautama XXVIII, 29; Vish*n*u XVII, 3. This text is not found in the Nepalese MS., nor is it commonly quoted in the Digests.

45–47, 49. Manu IX, 158–184; Vish*n*u XV, 1–29; Vasish*th*a XVII, 12–39; Baudhâyana II, 2, 3, 14–32; Yâ*gñ*avalkya II, 128–132.

45, 46. Regarding the meaning of the technical terms in this text, see the corresponding portion of the Code of Manu, and the notes on them in Professor Bühler's translation.

following next), and each following one inferior (to the preceding one).

[48. Where some doubt arises in regard to a house or field, the possession of which has suffered an interruption, (the doubt) may be removed by consulting a writing, or persons who know all about the enjoyment (of the property in question by its occupant), or witnesses.]

*49. After their father's death, these (sons) shall succeed to his wealth in order. Whenever a superior son is wanting, the one next to him in rank is entitled to succession.

*50. On failure of a son, the daughter (succeeds), because she continues the lineage just like (a son); both a son and a daughter continue the lineage of their father.

*51. On failure of daughters, the Sakulyas (are to succeed) and (after them) the Bândhavas; next, a member of the same caste. In default of all, that (wealth) goes to the king,

48. This text, which comes in very awkwardly between pars. 47 and 49, is apparently spurious, as has been pointed out long ago by Professor Bühler. It is not given in the Nepalese MS.

50. *G*îmûtavâhana and other writers of the Bengal school restrict the daughter's right of succession, as declared in this text, to those daughters who are neither barren nor widowed. See Dâyabhâga IV, 2, 10. However, there is nothing in the words of the original to warrant this restriction. Âpastamba II, 6, 14, 4.

51, 52. Manu IX, 185–189; Yâ*gñ*avalkya II, 135, 136; Vasish*th*a XVII, 81–84; Vish*n*u XVII, 4–14; Âpastamba II, 6, 14, 2–5; Gautama XXVIII, 21, 41, 42.

51. The term Sakulya is apparently used to denote the agnates, and Bândhava to denote the cognates. Therefore the last term sa*g*âti cannot be referred to blood-relationship at all, and must denote connexion by membership of the same caste. It is true that the commentators explain it as denoting descent from the same *Ri*shi. See Colebrooke's Digest, V, 8, 448.

*52. Unless it should be the property of a Brahman. A king devoted to duty must allot a maintenance to his women. Thus has the law of inheritance been declared.

FOURTEENTH TITLE OF LAW.

HEINOUS OFFENCES.

*1. Whatever act is performed by force (sahas) by persons inflamed with (the pride of) strength, is called Sâhasa (a heinous offence); sahas (force) means strength in this world.

*2. Manslaughter, robbery, an indecent assault on another man's wife, and the two species of insult, such are the four kinds of Heinous Offences.

*3. It is again declared to be threefold in the law-books, viz. (heinous offences) of the first, middlemost, and highest degree. The definition of each kind shall be given as follows.

*4. Destroying, reviling, disfiguring or otherwise

52. 'His women,' i. e. the women of the deceased proprietor. Vig*ñ*ânesvara, Nîlaka*nth*a, and other commentators declare that the term strî, 'woman,' cannot denote the legitimate wives of a deceased heir, and must therefore mean his concubines. This interpretation has been called forth, no doubt, by the fact that, in the opinion of these commentators, the inheritance of one sonless belongs to the widow in the first instance, and does not go to others, where a legitimate widow is in existence.

XIV, 1. The term Sâhasa, literally 'violence,' is used to denote violent deeds or heinous offences of every sort. Manu VIII, 332; Yâg*ñ*avalkya II, 230.

2. This text is omitted in the Nepalese MS.

4. 'Destroying,' i.e. totally annihilating the fruits and other objects mentioned in this text. 'Reviling,' i.e. abusing, using bad

(injuring) fruits, roots, water and the like, or agricultural utensils, is declared to be Sâhasa of the first degree.

* 5. (Injuring) in the same way clothes, cattle, food, drink, or household utensils, is declared to be Sâhasa of the middlemost degree.

* 6. Taking human life through poison, weapons or other (means of destruction), indecent assault on another man's wife, and whatever other (offences) encompassing life (may be imagined), is called Sâhasa of the highest degree.

* 7. The punishment to be inflicted for it must be proportionate to the heaviness of the crime, (so however as) not to be less than a hundred (Pa*n*as) for Sâhasa of the first degree, whereas for Sâhasa of the middlemost degree the punishment is declared by persons acquainted with the law to be no less than five hundred (Pa*n*as).

* 8. For Sâhasa of the highest degree, a fine amounting to no less than a thousand (Pa*n*as) is ordained. (Moreover) corporal punishment, confiscation of the entire property, banishment from the town and branding, as well as amputation of that limb (with which the crime has been committed), is declared to be the punishment for Sâhasa of the highest degree.

* 9. This gradation of punishments is ordained for every (caste) indiscriminately, excepting only corporal punishment in the case of a Brahman. A Brahman must not be subjected to corporal punishment.

---

language. 'Disfiguring,' injuring so far only as to leave the form intact. Vîramitrodaya, p. 499.

8, 9. The ambiguous term vadha in these two paragraphs is

*10. Shaving his head, banishing him from the town, branding him on the forehead with a mark of the crime of which he has been convicted, and parading him on an ass, shall be his punishment.

*11. Those who have committed Sâhasa of either of the two first degrees are allowed to mix in society, after having been punished, but if a man has committed Sâhasa of the highest degree, no one is allowed to speak to him, even when he has received punishment.

*12. Theft is a special kind of it. The difference between (Sâhasa and theft) is as follows. Sâhasa is where the criminal act consists of a forcible attack, theft is where it is done by fraud.

*13. That (theft) is again declared to be threefold by the wise, according to the (value of the) articles (purloined), whether articles of small, middling, or superior value have been stolen.

*14. Earthenware, a seat, a couch, bone, wood, leather, grass, and the like, legume, grain, and prepared food, these are termed articles of small value.

*15. Clothes made of other material than silk, cattle other than cows, and metals other than gold, are (termed) articles of middling value, and so are rice and barley.

---

explained as denoting corporal punishment, and not execution, by the commentators.

9, 10. Gautama XII, 46, 47; Vish*n*u V, 2–8; Yâ*gñ*avalkya II, 270; Manu VIII, 124, 379–380.

12. 'A criminal act' (âdhi*h*), i. e. injuring another man's property; 'through a forcible attack,' i. e. violently, is called theft equivalent to Sâhasa; a criminal act done 'by fraud' is called ordinary theft. Vîramitrodaya, p. 490. Manu VIII, 332.

13. Yâ*gñ*avalkya II, 275. 14. Manu VIII, 326–329.

*16. Gold, precious stones, silk, women, men, cows, elephants, horses, and what belongs to a god, a Brahman, or a king, these are regarded as articles of superior value.

17. Taking away by any means whatsoever the property of persons asleep, or disordered in their intellect, or intoxicated, is declared to be theft by the wise.

18. Where stolen goods are found with a man, he may be presumed to be the thief. (The possession of) stolen goods may be inferred from a luxurious mode of life. Suspicion arises where a man is seen in bad company or indulges in extravagance.

*19. Those who give food or shelter to thieves seeking refuge with them, or who suffer them (to escape) though able (to arrest them), partake of their crime themselves.

*20. Those who do not come to offer assistance, when people are crying out (for help) within their hearing, or when property is being taken away, are likewise accomplices in the crime.

*21. That series of punishments, which has been ordained by the wise for the three kinds of Sâhasa, is equally applicable to theft, according as it concerns one of the three species of articles in their order.

22. When cows or other (animals) have been lost,

---

16. See the Indian law of prescription, where the property of Brahmans and kings is declared to be exempt from the ordinary rules regarding limitation. Manu VIII, 323.

18. Yâg*ñ*avalkya II, 266.

19. Those who give food or any other assistance to a thief, or who suffer a thief to escape though able to seize him, have to be punished like thieves. Vivâda*k*intâma*n*i, p. 93. Manu IX, 278; Yâg*ñ*avalkya II, 276.

20. Manu IX, 275. This text is omitted in the Nepalese MS.

or when (other) property has been taken away forcibly, experienced men shall trace it from the place where it has been taken.

23. Wherever the footmarks go to, whether it be a village, pasture ground or deserted spot (the inhabitants or owners of) that place must make good the loss, unless they can prove the footmarks to go out of that place again.

24. When the footmarks are obscured or interrupted, because (they lead to) broken ground or to a spot much frequented by other people, the nearest village or pasture ground shall be made responsible.

25. Where two persons have gone the same road, the offence, as a rule, shall be imputed to him who stood charged with other crimes before, or who associates with suspicious characters.

26. *K*a*nd*âlas, executioners, and other such persons, as well as those who are in the habit of roaming at night, shall institute a search (after the thieves) in the villages; those living outside (of inhabited places) shall search (for them) outside.

27. When the thieves are not caught, the king must make good (the loss) from his own treasury. By showing himself remiss (towards criminals), he would incur sin and would offend both against justice and his own interest.

---

23. Yâgñavalkya II, 271. 24. Yâgñavalkya II, 272.
26. Manu IX, 267.

FIFTEENTH AND SIXTEENTH TITLES OF LAW.

ABUSE AND ASSAULT.

*1. Abusive speeches, couched in offensive and violent terms, regarding the native country, caste, family, and so forth (of a man), are termed Abuse, (a title of law.)

*2. It is divided into three species, called respectively Nish*th*ura, A*s*lîla, and Tîvra. The punishment for each increases in severity according as the insult is of a more (or less) serious nature.

*3. Abuse combined with reproaches has to be regarded as Nish*th*ura; abuse couched in insulting language is A*s*lîla; charging one with an offence causing expulsion from caste is called Tîvra by the learned.

*4. Hurting the limbs of another person with a hand, foot, weapon or otherwise, or defiling him

---

XV, XVI, 1. Thus, e.g. when a man says, 'The Gau*d*as (Bengalis) are quarrelsome,' he abuses another man's native country. When a man says, 'Brahmans are very avaricious,' he abuses another man's caste. When he says, 'The Vi*s*vâmitras are a ferocious race,' he abuses another man's family. The clause 'and so forth' is added, in order to include abusive speeches levelled against learned men, artizans, or the like persons, whose learning or art has been abused. 'Violent terms,' i.e. terms which ought never to be used. Mitâksharâ, p. 285; Vîramitrodaya, p. 482.

3. 'Abuse combined with reproaches' is when e.g. a man says, 'What a fool,' or 'What a rascal.' 'Abuse couched in insulting language' is when a man says, 'I will visit your sister,' or the like. 'Charging one with a mortal sin causing expulsion from caste,' such as e.g. the drinking of spirituous liquor. See loc. cit.

with ashes or other (impure substances), is termed Assault.

* 5. There are three species of that also, as it may be either light, or of a middling sort, or heavy, according as it consists in the raising (of a hand or weapon for the purpose of striking a blow), or in an unexpected attack, or in striking a wound.

* 6. Stealing articles of small, middling, or superior value, is called the three kinds of Sâhasa; there the thorny weeds (sinners) should be extirpated.

* 7. In both kinds (of insult) five cases are distinguished, when the respective innocence or guilt of the two parties has to be established.

* 8. When two parties have been guilty of insult, and both have commenced to quarrel at the same time, they shall suffer the same punishment, in case that no difference (in their respective culpability) becomes apparent.

* 9. He who is the first to offer an insult is decidedly criminal; he who returns the insult is likewise culpable; but the one who began shall suffer the heavier punishment (of the two).

---

6. The above translation of this paragraph follows the reading of the MSS. If that reading be correct, this paragraph contains a rule relating to the subject of theft or Sâhasa. The quotations have a different reading, under which this paragraph has to be closely connected with the preceding one, and has to be referred equally to the three degrees of assault.

7. The Nepalese MS. and the commentaries insert the following paragraph here: *'When an insult has occurred between two men engaged in a violent quarrel, he who suffers the insult patiently is struck, but the offender is punishable.'

8-10. The one who has first commenced a quarrel shall receive the heavier punishment of the two. That man is liable to punishment who persists in hostility. When it is impossible to ascertain any

*10. When both parties are implicated equally, he of the two shall receive punishment who follows up his attack, whether he was (originally) the aggressor or the defendant.

*11. If a *S*vapâka, Meda, *K*a*n*d*â*la, cripple, one who gains his substance by killing (animals), an elephant-driver, one deprived of his caste for non-performance of the ceremony of initiation, a slave, or one who treats a Guru or spiritual teacher with disregard,

*12. Should offend a superior, he shall be punished by whipping him on the spot. Nor do the sages regard bodily injury done to a man of this stamp as (an offence equal to) theft.

*13. Should any such low person, abhorred by men, insult another man (his superior), that man himself shall punish him. The king has nothing to do with the penalty (to be inflicted on him).

*14. For these people are the refuse of human society, and their property is (likewise) impure. The king also is at liberty to whip them, but he must not amerce them with a fine.

15. A Kshatriya who reviles a Brahman must

---

difference in the culpability of the two parties, their punishment shall be equal. Vîramitrodaya, p. 472. Read pûrvam.

11. *S*vapâka, literally 'dog-cooking,' is the name of a particular degraded tribe, whose only office is to act as public executioners. Meda is the name of another mixed caste. *K*a*n*d*â*las are the lowest caste of all, see XII, 113. The Nepalese MS. and the commentaries read sha*n*d*h*a, 'a eunuch,' instead of Meda.

12–14. When a *S*vapâka or the like should have insulted an Ârya or member of the three higher castes, honourable men shall be entitled to punish them in person. When the (honourable men) are unable to do so, the king shall punish them; but he must not confiscate their property. Vîramitrodaya, p. 472.

15–17. Nearly identical with Manu VIII, 267–269.

pay one hundred (Pa*n*as) as a fine. A Vai*s*ya (must pay) one and a half hundred, or two hundred. A *S*ûdra deserves corporal punishment.

16. A Brahman shall be fined fifty (Pa*n*as) for calumniating a Kshatriya; in the case of a Vai*s*ya, the fine shall be half of fifty (i. e. twenty-five); in the case of a *S*ûdra, (it shall amount to) twelve (Pa*n*as).

17. When a twice-born man offends against a member of his own caste, (he shall pay) twelve (Pa*n*as as a fine). When he utters calumnies which ought never to be uttered, the fine shall be twice as high.

18. Even he who in accordance with fact (contemptuously) calls another man one-eyed, lame, or the like (names), shall be fined by the king not less than one Kârshâpa*n*a.

19. One must not tax with his offence a man who has done penance according to law, or who has received due punishment from the king. By transgressing this rule one becomes liable to punishment.

20. Two persons, a Brahman and a king, are declared to be exempt from censure and corporal punishment in this world; for these two sustain the visible world.

*21. One who calls an outcast an outcast, or a thief a thief, is equally criminal with those whom he taxes (with their offence). (If he reproaches them) without reason, he is twice as guilty as they are.

---

17. According to the commentators of Manu, the term 'calumnies which ought never to be uttered' has to be referred to insinuations against the honour of a man's mother, sisters, or other female relatives. See Professor Bühler's note on Manu VIII, 269.

18. Manu VIII, 274; Yâg*ñ*avalkya II, 204.

22. A once-born man (or *S*ûdra), who insults members of a twice-born caste with gross invectives, shall have his tongue cut out; for he is of low origin.

23. If he refers to their name or caste in terms indicating contempt, an iron rod, ten Aṅgulas long, shall be thrust red-hot into his mouth.

24. If he is insolent enough to give lessons regarding their duty to Brahmans, the king shall order hot oil to be poured into his mouth and ears.

*25. With whatever limb a man of low caste offends against a Brahman, that very limb of his shall be cut off; such shall be the atonement for his crime.

26. A low-born man, who tries to place himself on the same seat with his superior in caste, shall be branded on his hip and banished, or (the king) shall cause his backside to be gashed.

27. If through arrogance he spits (on a superior), the king shall cause both his lips to be cut off; if he makes water (on him), the penis; if he breaks wind (against him), the buttocks.

28. If he pulls (a superior) by the hair, (the king) shall unhesitatingly cause his hands to be cut off, likewise (if he seizes him) by the feet, beard, neck, or scrotum.

29. If a man breaks the skin (of his equal) or

---

22. 'He is of low origin,' because the *S*ûdra caste has been produced from Brahman's feet. Identical with Manu VIII, 270.

23. Nearly identical with Manu VIII, 271.

24. Nearly identical with Manu VIII, 272.

25. Nearly identical with Manu VIII, 279.

26, 27. Nearly identical with Manu VIII, 281, 282. In paragraph 27 the Nepalese MS. has 'the nose' instead of 'the beard.'

28. Identical with Manu VIII, 283.

29. According to the majority of the commentators of Manu,

fetches blood (from him), he shall be fined a hundred (Pa*n*as); if he cuts the flesh, six Nishkas; if he breaks a bone, he shall be banished.

*30. If a man censures a king devoted to the discharge of his duties, he shall have his tongue cut out or his entire property confiscated, as an atonement for such crime.

*31. When an evil-minded man assails a wicked king even, he shall be (fastened) on a stake and burnt in fire; (for he is) more criminal than one who has committed a hundred times the crime of killing a Brahman.

*32. A father is not liable to be punished for an offence committed by his son; nor is the owner of a horse, dog, or monkey (responsible for any damage caused by one of these animals), unless he should have set them to do it.

SEVENTEENTH TITLE OF LAW.

GAMES.

*1. Dishonest gambling with dice, small slices of leather, little staves of ivory, or other (games), and betting on birds, form (the subject of) a title of law called (Gambling with Dice and Betting on Animals).

*2. The master of the gaming-house shall arrange

this rule has reference to an equal in caste. Nearly identical with Manu VIII, 284.

XVII, 1. The translation is according to the Vîramitrodaya. The subject of bets on animals is treated at great length in the Dhammathats of Burma, which are based on the law-codes of India. 'Other games,' such as e.g. *K*aturaṅga (Shatra*ñ*g, the Indian chess). 'Birds,' such as pigeons, also bets on professional wrestlers, rams, &c. Vîramitrodaya, p. 718. Manu IX, 223.

2. 'He shall pay the stakes which have been won,' i.e. to the

the game and pay the stakes which have been won; the profit of such a conductor of games shall amount to ten per cent.

3. When the dice on being thrown fall twice in a game at dice, those acquainted with (playing at) dice allot the victory to the adversary and the defeat to the gambler.

4. When a dispute has arisen among gamblers, let (other) gamblers be appealed to; they shall act both as judges and as witnesses in a dispute of this sort.

5. No gambler shall ever enter into another gaming-house before having paid his debt; he must not disobey the master of the gaming-house, and must pay of his own accord what he owes to him.

*6. Wicked men who play with false dice shall be driven out of the gaming-house, after a wreath of dice has been hung round their necks; for that is the punishment ordained for them.

7. If a man gambles with dice, without authorization from the king, he shall not get his stake, and shall have to pay a fine.

*8. Or let the gamblers pay to the king the share

---

winning party. That portion which has to be paid to the king (see paragraph 8) may also be held to be included in this rule, as B*ri*haspati says: 'Let the master of the gaming-house collect the stakes and pay his due to the winning party and to the king.' Âpastamba II, 10, 25, 12, 13; Yâ*g*ñavalkya II, 199, 200.

3. The rendering of the first portion of this paragraph is conjectural. It might also be translated as follows: 'When the dice on being thrown fall twice repeated,' i. e. when the number is twice as high as at the preceding throw.

4. Yâ*g*ñavalkya II, 202. 6. Yâ*g*ñavalkya II, 202.

7, 8. Yâ*g*ñavalkya II, 201, 203. Paragraphs 7 and 8 are omitted in the Nepalese MS.

due to him and play in public, thus no wrong will be committed.

EIGHTEENTH TITLE OF LAW.

Miscellaneous.

*1. Under the head of Miscellaneous (Disputes) are comprised lawsuits depending on the king, (such as) transgression of the king's commandments and obedience towards his injunctions,

*2. Grants of towns, the division of the constituent elements of a state, the duties and the reverse of heretics, followers of the Veda, corporations (of merchants), and assemblages (of kinsmen).

*3. Disputes between father and son, neglect of (prescribed) penances, abstraction of gifts (made to worthy persons), the wrath of anchorites,

*4. Sinful confusion of castes, the rules regarding their means of subsistence, and (in short) whatever

---

XVIII, 1–4. The meagre contents of this title of law can hardly be said to be in keeping with the somewhat pompous announcement contained in paragraphs 1–4. On the whole, this title of Miscellanies, as defined by Nârada and Br*i*haspati, may be described as treating of public law or the law of kings (râ*g*adharma), private law being treated in the seventeen other titles of law.

1. 'Obedience towards his injunctions,' thus according to the Mitâksharâ, p. 351. The Vîramitrodaya refers the term tatkarmakara*n*am to those who, from arrogance, do such acts as are permitted to a king only, such as e. g. placing themselves on the king's throne.

2. 'Grants of towns,' i.e. to Brahmans and others. Nârada seems to be referring to the so-called Agrahâras. Regarding the seven constituent parts of a state, see Manu VII, 157; IX, 294. Naigama has been translated 'followers of the Veda,' because it comes immediately after pâsha*nd*i, 'heretics.' See, too, X, 1. It usually denotes citizens or traders.

has been omitted in the preceding (titles of law), are treated under the head of Miscellaneous.

5. The king shall be careful to protect all orders and the constituent elements of his state with the four means indicated by science.

6. When any caste should remain (behind the rest) or exceed the limits (assigned to it, the king), seeing that it has strayed from its path, shall bring it back to the path (of duty).

7. So also, when other wicked acts, opposed to the dictates of the sacred law, have been committed, the king, after having reflected (upon the matter) himself, shall inflict punishment on those who deserve it.

8. What is opposed to revealed and traditional law, or injurious to living beings, must not be practised by the king; and when it is practised (by others), he must check it.

*9. When an act contrary to justice has been undertaken by a former king from folly, he must redress that iniquitous enactment in accordance with the principles of equity.

*10. The weapons of soldiers, the tools of artizans, the ornaments of public women, the various musical or other instruments of professional (musicians, or other artists, &c.),

*11. And any implements by which artificers gain

5. 'The four means' of conciliation, division, bribery, and force. Manu VIII, 41.

6. Yâgñavalkya I, 360. The Nepalese MS. offers a variation as regards the arrangement of paragraphs 6–11.

7. Manu VII, 16; VIII, 126; Yâgñavalkya I, 367; Vasish*th*a XIX, 8; Vish*n*u III, 37.

10. For 'the tools of artizans' the Nepalese MS., in common with the Mitâksharâ, has 'the beasts of burden and the like of carriers of goods.'

their substance, must not be laid hold on by the king, even when he confiscates the entire property (of a man or woman).

12. It is not permitted to either advise or rebuke a king or Brahman, on account of their dignity and sanctity, unless they should swerve from the path (of duty).

13. That wicked man who does not act up to the laws proclaimed by the king, shall be fined and corporally punished, as offending against the king's commandments.

14. If the king were remiss in dictating punishments to (members of) any caste, when they have left the path (of duty), the created beings of this world would perish.

15. Brahmans would leave the sacerdotal caste, and Kshatriyas would forsake the Kshatriya caste. The stronger would eat up the weaker, like fish on a spit.

16. The Vaisyas would abandon their work, and the *S*ûdras eclipse all (the rest), if the kings did not visit their subjects with punishment (when they have committed an offence).

17. To show favour to the virtuous at all times and to oppress the wicked, that is declared to be the duty of kings; gain (results to them) from the oppression of their foes.

18. As fire is not polluted even though it always burns the creatures of this world, even so a king is not polluted by inflicting punishment on those who deserve it.

19. Intelligence is the glory of rulers; it becomes

14, 15. Manu VII, 20. 16. Manu VII, 21, 24.

19. For 'intelligence' the Nepalese MS. has 'a royal edict.'

manifest in their speeches; whatever sentence they may pass, whether unjust or just, settles the law between litigant parties.

20. (Law) personified as a king, roams on earth visibly, with a thousand eyes. Mortals cannot live at all if they transgress his commandments.

21. Whatever a king does is right, that is a settled rule; because the protection of the world is entrusted to him, and on account of his majesty and benignity towards living creatures.

22. As a husband though feeble must be constantly worshipped by his wives, in the same way a ruler though worthless must be (constantly) worshipped by his subjects.

23. In order that mortals, fearing the orders issued by kings, might not swerve from the path of duty, therefore royal orders are declared to arise from lawsuits.

24. It is for the establishment of order that various laws (*k*aritra) have been proclaimed by kings. A royal order is declared to overrule such laws even.

25. A ruler has purchased his subjects through (the practice of) austerities; therefore the king is their lord. For that reason, his bidding must be obeyed; their livelihood even depends on the king.

26. Kings, endowed with immense power, appear (variously) in the five different forms of Agni, Indra, Soma, Yama, and the God of Riches.

---

24. *K*aritra seems to mean 'law' or 'custom' in this place. Regarding the comparative authority of *k*aritra and râ*g*a*s*âsana, 'a royal order,' see p. 7, note. The Nepalese MS. omits 23, 24.

26. Read rûpâ*n*i in the text.

27. When a ruler is, either justly or without (sufficient) reason, ardent in wrath and burns (or torments) his subjects, he is called Agni (the god of fire).

28. When, relying on his regal power, the king attacks his foes, desirous of victory and upraising a weapon, he is termed Indra.

29. When, free from ardent wrath, he appears before his subjects with a cheerful countenance, he is denoted Soma (the Moon).

30. When the king having seated himself, full of majesty, on the throne of judgment, deals out punishment, equitable towards all creatures, he is called Vaivasvata (or Yama).

31. When a ruler gladdens with gifts petitioners, persons commanding respect, wise men, servants and others, he is called the God of Riches.

32. Therefore one must not treat him with contempt, and, particularly, not scold at him, and pay obedience to his bidding; to disobey him would bring on (instantaneous) death.

33. His duties are, the protection of his subjects, honouring the aged and wise, the trial of lawsuits, and to make (each caste) abide by the duties assigned to it.

34. Let a king be constantly intent on showing honour to the Brahmans. A field furnished with Brahmans is the root of the prosperity of the world.

35. A Brahman may command respect, and a

27. Manu IX, 310. 28. Manu IX, 304.
29. Manu IX, 309. 30. Manu IX, 307.
33. Manu VII, 35, 38; VIII, 3, &c.
34. Manu VII, 82, 83; Yâg*ñ*avalkya I, 314.
35. Manu VII, 37.

distinguished seat at the king's court. The king shall show his face in the morning before the Brahmans first of all, and shall salute them all.

36. When nine or seven persons (of different rank) meet, they shall first make room for the Brahman to pass by. (Further privileges assigned to the Brahman caste are) free access to the houses of other people, for the purpose of begging alms,

37. The right to collect fuel, flowers, water, and the like, without its being regarded as theft, and to converse with other men's wives, without being restrained (in such intercourse) by others,

38. And the right to cross rivers without paying any fare, and to be conveyed (to the other bank) before other people. When engaged in trading and using a ferry-boat, they shall have to pay no toll.

---

36. That privilege of the Brahman caste, which is referred to in the first part of this paragraph, finds its explanation in a well-known rule of the Dharma*s*âstra regarding persons for whom way must be made, on meeting them in a road. Thus it is ruled by Gautama (VI, 24) that way must be made for a man seated in a carriage, for one who is in his tenth (decade), for one requiring consideration, for a woman, for a Snâtaka, and for a king; but that a king himself must make way for a *S*rotriya (learned Brahman). This makes in all seven persons for whom way should be made. Manu (II, 138), Yâ*gñ*avalkya (I, 117), Baudhâyana (II, 6, 30), and Vish*n*u (LXIII, 51) agree in enumerating eight persons of this sort. Vasish*th*a (XIV, 57–60) mentions nine. See, too, Âpastamba II, 5, 11, 5–7.

37. Manu VIII, 339; Âpastamba I, 10, 28, 3; Gautama XII, 28; Yâ*gñ*avalkya II, 166.

38. Manu VIII, 407; Vish*n*u V, 132. The last clause is thus given in the Nepalese MS.: 'They shall have to pay no toll on being carried across a river in a ferry, unless (they should cross it) for trading purposes.'

39. A Brahman engaged in travelling, who is tired and has nothing to eat, commits no wrong by taking himself two canes of sugar or two esculent roots.

40. (No gift must be accepted) from one accused of a crime, an outcast, an enemy, an atheist, one in distress, without necessity, or after inflicting pain on the giver.

41. (Gifts shall be accepted) from industrious people on account of their wealth, and from generous people because it is proper to accept gifts from such; to accept gifts from kings is laudable; (they may be accepted) from all people excepting Brahmans.

42. Between a Brahman and a king, who are both devoted to their duty, there is no difference of any sort, when they protect mankind (acting) in accordance with the sacred law.

43. If a ruler, though severe, is mindful of his duty, correct in his conduct, and (quick to) punish the wicked, in order to protect (the virtuous), his wealth is declared to be pure.

44. When a man accepts a gift from a covetous king, who transgresses the precepts of the sacred books, he shall have to pass through the well-known twenty-one hells in succession.

45. As pure and impure waters become alike on their junction in the ocean, even so (all) property acquired by a king (becomes pure in his hands).

---

39. Gautama XII, 49, 50; Manu VIII, 341. Or 'five esculent roots,' according to the Nepalese MS.

40. Manu II, 185.

44. For a list of the twenty-one hells, see Manu IV, 88–90; Vish*n*u XLIII, 1–22. The Nepalese MS. omits this paragraph.

45. A different opinion has been enounced above, XV, 14.

46. As gold, on being thrown into blazing fire, acquires purity, even so all gains become pure in the hands of kings.

47. When any man gives any property of his to Brahmans, the king must give his consent to it; this is an eternal law.

48. Both the other customary receipts of a king and what is called the sixth of the produce of the soil, form the royal revenue, the reward (of a king) for the protection of his subjects.

49. Whatever has been bestowed on others than Brahmans may be resumed; but that which has been given to Brahmans can never be taken back again.

50. To give, to read, and to sacrifice (on his own account) are the three duties of a Brahman. To sacrifice for others, to teach, and, thirdly, to collect alms are his (three) means of subsistence.

51. Let a Brahman be devoted to his duty and take a livelihood from the king, and let him not accept gifts from persons of vile origin, if he is anxious to observe the law.

52. How should a king be inferior to a deity, as it is through his word that an offender may become innocent, and an innocent man an offender in due course?

53. Those who being acquainted with the divine nature of a king, endowed with majestic dignity as he is, accept gifts from him, do not in the least disgrace themselves (by doing so).

54. In this world, there are eight sacred objects:

---

48. Manu VII, 130–132; Gautama X, 24–27; Vasish*th*a XIX, 26, 27; Âpastamba II, 10, 26, 9; Vish*n*u III, 22–25; Baudhâyana I, 10, 18, 1.

50. Manu I, 88, &c.

a Brahman, a cow, fire, gold, clarified butter, the sun, the waters, and a king as the eighth.

55. These one must always look up to, worship and honour them personally, and turn the right side towards them, in order that one's existence may be prolonged.

APPENDIX.

THEFT[1].

1. Two kinds of robbers who steal the goods of others have to be distinguished, the one kind open, and the other kind concealed. Let a prudent king try to find them out.

*2. Open rogues are those who forge measures and weights, receivers of bribes, robbers, gamblers, public prostitutes,

*3. Those who walk in disguise, those who live by teaching the performance of auspicious ceremonies, these and such like persons are considered open rogues.

*4. Rogues acting in secret are those who roam in the wood, or lie concealed, as well as those who make a profession of stealing. They attack and rob (those who do not beware of them).

5. Those who infest a country, a village, or a house, or disturb a sacrificial act, cut-purses, and

---

[1] This section is found in the Nepalese MS. only. See Introduction. The reading of several passages is uncertain, and this circumstance, taken together with the want of a Commentary, renders my translation less reliable than could be desired.

Appendix. Theft. 1–4. Manu IX, 256–260. The technical terms have been translated in accordance with the glosses of Manu's commentators, as given in the notes to Professor Bühler's translation. In par. 4, mushyâ*m* seems to stand for mush*t*yâ*m*.

other persons of this sort have to be considered as concealed rogues also.

*6. Blameless persons with whom the stolen goods are not found must not be chastised as robbers by the king; but let him quickly punish those robbers as guilty of theft with whom the stolen goods have been found.

*7. Those (rogues) who ravage in their own country, and those who disturb sacrificial acts, he shall strip of their entire wealth and rebuke them severely.

*8. Those on whom the stolen goods have not been seized he must examine, when they have been arrested from suspicion. Their fear having been excited, they will give evidence, through anxiety, in accordance with the facts of the case.

*9. Questions shall be proposed to them antithetically with regard to place, time, region, their caste, their name, their dwelling, and their occupation, in case they happen to be workmen.

*10. When the face changes colour or the voice falters, or the features look suspicious, when they do not give evidence in public, when they make impossible statements as to place and time, when there exists a doubt as to their place of residence,

*11. When they indulge in expense for bad purposes, when they have been previously convicted of larceny, when they keep bad company, or when documents speak against them, (by all such circum-

9. 'Antithetically' (vinigrahe), or 'when they have been arrested.'

10, 11. A somewhat analogous description of the signs by which a false witness may be found out, has been given previously: I, 193-196.

stances) they may be discovered (to be thieves), not by the possession of the stolen goods alone.

*12. When a ruffian or robber becomes suspected, and (the judge) has found out circumstantial evidence (which speaks against him), he shall be caused to make an oath.

*13. Those who give food to thieves, as well as those who supply them with fire or water, or who give shelter, or show the way to them, or make their defence,

*14. Or who buy their goods, or receive (their goods), are held to be equally punishable as they, and so are those who conceal them.

15. Those who in a principality are the governors of that principality, and the neighbours called in (to watch over the safety of life and property) are (reckoned as) equal to thieves, when they stand neutral during the attack (of robbers).

*16. He on whose ground a robbery has been committed, must trace the thieves to the best of his power, or else he must make good what has been stolen, unless the footmarks can be traced from that ground (into another man's ground).

*17. When the footmarks, after leaving that ground, are lost and cannot be traced any further, the neighbours, inspectors of the road, and governors of that region shall be made responsible for the loss.

---

12. The term lesa has been rendered by 'circumstantial evidence,' because it seems to be synonymous with yuktilesa, I, 236.

13, 14. Manu IX, 271, 278.

15. Nearly identical with Manu IX, 272.

16. The term gokara, translated 'ground,' may denote the landed property or pasture ground of a whole village. See above, XIV, 22, 23.

17. See XIV, 24.

18. When a house has been plundered, the king shall cause the thief-catchers, the guards, and the inhabitants of that kingdom to make good the loss, when the thief is not caught.

19. Or, if he is a wicked man and there exists a doubt as to (whether) the robbery (was actually committed or not), the person (alleged to have been) robbed shall be caused to make an oath regarding the robbery, to clear himself (from suspicion).

20. When another person than the thief has been accused of robbery and has been declared thief, because he is unable to prove his innocence, he shall be paid twice as much (as has been stolen), after the (real) thief has been detected.

21. When a man has obtained property stolen by a thief, he must restore it in its pristine shape; if it be no longer in existence, he must make good its value, and must be made to pay a fine to the same amount.

*22. For stealing wood, cane, grass and the like, (utensils) made of clay, bamboo, utensils made of bamboo, rattan, bone, leather,

*23. Vegetables, green roots, grass or flowers, cow-milk, molasses, salt, or oil,

*24. Cooked food (and other) prepared food, spirituous liquor, flesh, and every sort of objects of small value—(for stealing any of these) a fine five times the value (of the article stolen should be paid).

*25. (For stealing) any articles sold by weight or measure or tale, the fine shall be eight times their amount, in case they are very valuable.

---

19. The senseless reading of the MS., dâpyaka teshâm, has been conjecturally altered into doshakartaisha.

22–24. Manu VIII, 326–329. 25. Manu VIII, 321.

26. Corporal punishment (or death) shall be inflicted on him who steals more than ten Kumbhas of grain; where the amount is less, he shall be made to pay eleven times as much. Thus Manu has declared.

*27. (For stealing) more than a hundred (Palas' worth) of gold, silver, or other (precious metals), or the finest clothes, or very precious gems, corporal punishment (or death shall be inflicted).

28. He who steals a man shall have to pay the highest fine; he who steals a woman (shall be stripped) of his entire wealth; and he who steals a maiden (shall suffer) corporal punishment.

*29. On him who forcibly seizes large domestic animals, the highest fine shall be inflicted; the middlemost amercement on him who takes cattle of middle size; and the smallest fine on him who steals small cattle.

30. The first (or lowest) fine to be inflicted on a guilty person shall amount to neither more nor less than twenty-four (Pa*n*as). The middlemost fine shall consist of not more than four hundred, and not less than two hundred (Pa*n*as).

31. The highest fine should be known to consist of not more than a thousand, and not less than five hundred (Pa*n*as). This is the threefold gradation of punishment, which has been proposed by the Self-Existent for robberies.

---

26. Manu VIII, 320. 27, 28. Manu VIII, 321, 323.

29. Manu VIII, 325.

30, 31. The reading of these two paragraphs is quite uncertain. The rules laid down here apparently differ considerably from the analogous rules of Manu (VIII, 158) and other legislators.

*32. (When the offence has been committed) for the first time, cut-purses shall have their (little) finger and thumb cut off. (When it has been committed) for the second time, the first fine shall be levied on them.

*33. For (stealing) cows belonging to a Brahman, for piercing (the nostrils of) a barren cow, and for stealing a female slave, (the thief) shall in every case lose half his feet.

34. With whatever limb a thief acts among men, that very (limb) shall be taken from him, this is a law enacted by Manu.

35. Let him inflict a specially heavy punishment on a specially criminal thief, or (a lighter one) on one whose offence is less heavy. But let him not (punish an habitual thief) in the same way as for the first offence.

36. Manu, the son of the Self-Existent, has declared ten places of punishment, which should be (selected) in (punishing members of the) three (lower) castes; a Brahman should remain uninjured always.

37. (Those places are) the privy parts, the belly, the tongue, the two hands, and, fifthly, the two feet; as well as the eye, the nose, the two ears, the property, and the body.

---

32. Manu IX, 277.

33. The parallel passage of Manu (VIII, 325) shows that sthûrâyâ*s* *kh*edana*m* is the correct reading. For the three different explanations of this term, which have been proposed by the commentators of Manu, see the note to Professor Bühler's translation. The translation follows the interpretation proposed by Kullûka, Govindarâ*g*a, and Râghavânanda, which appears to be preferable to the others.

34. Nearly identical with Manu VIII, 334.

36, 37. Nearly identical with Manu VIII, 124, 125.

38. After carefully considering the (nature of the) offence, the place and time, and after examining the ability (of the offender), and the motive (by which he was actuated), he shall inflict these punishments.

39. Neither for the purpose of gaining a friend (in him), nor for the acquisition of large wealth, must a wicked criminal be suffered to go free by the king. Thus Manu has declared.

40. By pardoning an offender, a king commits the same offence as by punishing an innocent man. Religious merit accrues to him from punishing (the wicked).

41. Let him not on any account kill a Brahman, though convicted of all possible crimes. He may at pleasure cause him to be banished, thus has the law been settled.

42. Let the king take his entire wealth from him or leave him a fourth part of it (only he must not take his life), remembering the law promulgated by the Creator. This is just.

43. For four offences of a Brahman, branding him is ordained (as punishment): for violating the bed of a Guru, for drinking spirituous liquor, for theft, and for hurting another Brahman.

*44. For violating the bed of a Guru, (the brand of) a female part should be made; for drinking

---

38. Manu VIII, 126. 39. Manu VIII, 347.

40. Nearly identical with Manu IX, 249.

41. Manu VIII, 380.

42. The third Pâda of this paragraph has been conjecturally altered, as it cannot be made out in the MS.

43. Manu IX, 236.

44, 45. Manu IX, 237. The last Pâda in paragraph 44 cannot be made out in the MS.

spirituous liquor, (the brand of) a liquor sign is ordained; for theft, he shall make (the brand of) a dog's foot (on his forehead).

45. The slayer of a Brahman shall have (the brand of) a headless man stamped on his forehead, and it is forbidden to speak to him. This is a law enacted by Manu.

46. A thief must approach the king with flying hair, running, and proclaiming his theft (with the words): 'Thus have I acted. Chastise me.'

47. By so doing he is cleared from guilt, because he has confessed his deed; the king, thereupon, shall touch him (with a club), or dismiss him, if he is innocent.

48. Those men who have received a punishment from the king for an offence committed by them, proceed to heaven, free from sin, as (if they were) virtuous men who had acted well.

49. Whether he be punished or released, the thief is freed from his crime; if, however, the king does not punish him, the crime committed by the thief falls on (the king) himself.

50. Self-possessed men are corrected by their Guru; wicked men are corrected (or punished) by the king; but those who have sinned in secret are corrected by Yama, the son of Vivasvat.

51. The crime of a *S*ûdra in theft is eightfold (that of a man of the lowest caste); of a Vai*s*ya, sixteenfold; and of a Kshatriya, thirty-twofold.

---

46. Nearly identical with Manu VIII, 314.
48. Identical with Manu VIII, 318.
49. Nearly identical with Manu VIII, 316.
51. Nearly identical with Manu VIII, 337.

52. Of a Brahman, sixty-fourfold; thus the son of the Self-Existent has declared. Knowledge makes a difference also. For knowing persons, (the punishment) is specially severe.

*53. Punishment is pronounced to be twofold: corporal punishment and fines. Corporal punishment is again declared to be of ten sorts; fines are (also) of more than one kind.

*54. Fines begin with a Kâka*n*î, and the highest amount of a fine is one's entire property. Corporal punishment begins with confinement and ends with capital punishment.

*55. 'Fines beginning with a Kâka*n*î' are declared to amount to no less than one Mâsha. Those are called 'fines amounting to no less than a Mâsha' which amount to one Kârshâpa*n*a at most.

*56. 'Fines beginning with no less than a Kârshâpa*n*a' are those amounting to no less than four Kârshâpa*n*as; or which begin with two, and end with eight (Kârshâpa*n*as); or which begin with three, and end with twelve (Kârshâpa*n*as).

*57. A Kârshâpa*n*a is a silver coin in the southern country; in the east, it is an equivalent for (a certain number of) Pa*n*as, and is equal to twenty Pa*n*as.

---

52. Manu VIII, 338.

53. Manu VIII, 129. See too, above, paragraphs 36, 37.

54. Kâka*n*î or Kâki*n*î is the name of a small coin. See par. 58.

53-56. This passage is quoted in the Sm*ri*ti*k*andrikâ, with several different readings. One of them, in par. 55, deserves special notice. For mâshâvara*h* smata*h* (read sm*ri*ta*h*), the Sm*ri*ti*k*. reads mâshapara*h* sm*ri*ta*h*, 'are declared to amount to no more than one Mâsha.' This is probably the correct reading.

57. According to Manu (VIII, 136), the Kârshâpa*n*a is a copper coin. The reading of the second half of this paragraph is quite uncertain.

*58. A Mâsha should be known to be the twentieth part of a Kârshâpa*n*a. A Kâka*n*î is the fourth part of a Mâsha or Pala.

59. By that appellation which is in general use in the region of the Punjaub, the value of a Kârshâpa*n*a is not circumscribed here.

*60. A Kârshâpa*n*a has to be taken as equal to an A*nd*ikâ; four of these are a Dhânaka; twelve of the latter are a Suvar*n*a, which is called Dînâra otherwise.

61. Let the king practise the duties of his office, and (follow) the rule of inflicting punishment, faithful to the tenets (of the sacred law). Let him destroy accordingly, as governor, the evil-doers, after having traced them by the application of cunning stratagems and arrested them.

---

59. The term iha, 'here,' may be either referred to the place of residence of the author of the Nârada-sm*ri*ti, or it may mean 'in this work.'

60. An A*nd*ikâ is elsewhere reckoned at four Yavas. In the Vîramitrodaya and other works, this text is attributed to B*ri*haspati. The coin called Dînâra is the Roman denarius.

QUOTATIONS FROM NÂRADA.

I. Judicial Procedure.

1, 2. He is called a (Prâdvivâka or) chief judge who—fully acquainted with the eighteen titles (of law) and with the eight thousand subdivisions thereof, skilled in logic and other branches of science, and thoroughly versed in revealed and traditional lore—investigates the law relative to the case in hand by putting questions (prât) and passing a decision (vivekayati) according to what was heard or understood by him.

3. Let not a king actuated by arrogance or avarice promote litigation among persons not engaged in a controversy.

4. The king shall examine judicial quarrels between two litigant parties in a proper way, acting on principles of equity and discarding both love and hatred.

5. (In disputes) among merchants, artizans, or the like persons, and in (disputes concerning) persons subsisting by agriculture or as dyers, it is impossible for outsiders to pass a sentence; and the passing of

---

I, 1, 2. Smritik. ashtâdasapadâbhigñas tadbhedâshtasahasravit । ânvîkshikyâdikusalah srutismritiparâyanah ॥ vivâdasamsritam dharmam prikkhati prât srutam matam । vivekayati yas tasmât prâdvivâkas tu sa smritah ॥

3. Vîram. p. 48.

4. Vy. *K*. râgâ dharmasahâyas tu dvayor vivadamânayoh samyak kâryâny aveksheta râgadveshavivargitah ॥

5. Vy. *K*.; May. p. 6 ('Vyâsa').

the sentence must, therefore, be entrusted to persons acquainted with such matters (in a cause of this sort).

6. A lawsuit cannot be instituted mutually between a teacher and his pupil, or between father and son, or man and wife, or master and servant.

7. A plaint is declared (inadmissible) likewise by the learned in law, when it has been raised by one against many, or by women, or by menials.

8. He shall be admitted as plaintiff whose grievance is the greater, or whose affair is the more important of the two, and not he who was the first to go to law.

9. Half of the (ordinary) punishment is declared for him who either confesses his deed, after having committed an illicit act of violence, or says of his own accord, 'It is true.'

10. When (an assessor of the court) has recognised the royal mind to swerve from the path of duty, he must not pronounce an opinion which is agreeable to the king. (It is only by declaring what is just that) he becomes free from sin.

11. Transgression of (the king's) commands, killing a female, mixture of castes, illicit intercourse with another man's wife, robbery, pregnancy caused by another man than the husband,

---

6. Vy. *K.*; Vîram. p. 46 ('B*ri*haspati').

7. Vy. *K.*; Vîram. p. 47. 8. Vîram. p. 60.

9. Sm*ri*ti*k*. ayukta*m* sâhasa*m* k*ri*tvâ pratyâpatti*m* vra*g*et tu ya*h* ।
brûyât svaya*m* vâ sad iti tasya *k*ârthadama*h* sm*ri*ta*h* ॥

10. Vîram. p. 15. 'He must not pronounce an opinion which is agreeable to the king,' i. e. he must not endeavour to please him by what he declares, but must deliver an equitable opinion. By acting thus, he becomes free from sin. Vîram.

11, 12. Vîram. p. 50.

12. Abuse, insulting language, assault, and procuring abortion, are the ten (principal) crimes.

13. He who arrests (his adversary) by illegal means, such as by stopping his speech (through gagging the mouth), or by preventing him from breathing, and the like practices, is liable to punishment; but one who breaks (such arrest) is not (punishable).

14. When a lawsuit has been judged without any previous examination of witnesses (or other evidence), or when it has been decided in an improper manner, or when it has been judged by unauthorized persons, the trial has to be renewed.

15. Whatever property, whether movable or immovable, has been kept (under the care of the judge, after having become the subject of a dispute), must be handed over afterwards to the victorious party together with the interest (accruing on it) and with a document (attesting his victory).

II. The Plaint.

1. The defects of a plaint have been declared as follows. (It is defective, if it) relates to the property of a stranger; if it is without an object; if it does not state any quantity; if the mode of acquisition is not referred to in it; if too little or too much is written in it; and if it is unmeaning.

---

13. May. p. 2. See above, pp. 12–19. This text shows very clearly what is meant by the technical term 'arrest' (âsedha).

14. Vy. *K*. asâkshika*m* tu yad d*r*ish*t*a*m* vimârge*n*a *k*a tîritam ı asa*m*matamatair d*r*ish*t*a*m* punardar*s*anam arhati ıı

15. Sm*r*iti*k*. madhye yat sthâpita*m* dravya*m* *k*ala*m* vâ yadi vâ sthiram ı pa*sk*ât tat sodaya*m* dâpya*m* *g*ayine pattrasa*m*yutam ıı

II, 1–8. Vîram. pp. 65, 66.

2. That plaint is declared by the wise to 'relate to the property of a stranger' in which joint property is referred to in a claim raised by one man alone who has no right to it, or without authorization from the other joint proprietors.

3. A plaint is said to be 'without an object' when a man, actuated by hatred or anger, taxes another with the murder of a Brahman (or some other deadly sin) and revokes his own charge afterwards on being required to prove it.

4. That plaint 'does not state any quantity' in which no figure is given with regard to a certain quantity, writing, measure, field, house, or other (object).

5. That plaint 'contains no reference to the mode of acquisition' which does not say whether (the property in dispute) has been acquired by learning, or gained as profit (or interest), or purchased, or obtained by inheritance.

6. 'Too little' is said to be written in that plaint in which the year, month, fortnight, lunar day, and day of the week is not referred to.

7. 'Too much' may be said to be written in that plaint in which (the plaintiff) after having caused the plaint to be written goes on to mention the witnesses at once, without waiting for the answer (of the defendant) to be delivered.

8. That plaint is declared to be 'unmeaning'

2. That plaint is meant in which a stranger or one not authorized by his partners claims the property of a fellowship. Vîram.

3. That plaint is said to be without an object which is dropped afterwards by the claimant himself. Vîram.

7. 'Witnesses,' or evidence generally. Vîram.

8. There is another reading, ubhaya*m* pûrva*m*, under which the

which is rendered unclear by the mode of writing (exhibited in it), though the claimant's previous statements be (duly) entered in it.

9. Let him avoid, as a mere semblance of a declaration, (a plaint the tenour of) which is unnatural, not connected with an injury, senseless, purposeless, incapable of being proved, or at variance (with possibility, or with justice).

10. That suit which is prohibited by the king, or opposed to the interests of the citizens, or of the whole kingdom, or of the constituent elements of the state,

11. As well as (those suits) which are opposed to the interests of a town or village, or of eminent persons: all such suits are declared to be inadmissible.

12. A plaint in which several different subjects are mixed up together can have no effect.

---

claimant is stated to have proffered both the accusation and the answer. Vîram.

9. Vy. *K.*; M. Macn. I, 4, 10 (uncertain). 'Unnatural,' such as e.g. That person has taken my rabbit's horn and refuses to restore it. 'Not connected with an injury,' as, That man is doing his business in his own house by the light of a lamp which is burning in mine. 'Senseless' (a number of syllables strung together), without any intelligible meaning, as, e.g. ka*k*a*t*apam or *g*a*d*adagavam. 'Purposeless,' as, This man, Dedavatta, is warbling a melodious song before my house. 'Incapable of being proved,' as, Devadatta mocks me by a frown. Such an assertion as this is incapable of being proved, because it does not admit of proof. Owing to the transient nature of the act, witnesses are not available, much less can documentary evidence be resorted to; nor would it be proper to perform an ordeal, on account of the trifling nature of the charge. 'At variance' (with possibility), as, A dumb man has cursed me. Or, 'at variance' with the interests of a town or kingdom. M.

10, 11. Vy. *K.*; M. Macn. I, 4, 11 and May. p. 10 (uncertain).

12. V. T.; M. Macn. I, 4, 12, &c. (uncertain). Each subject shall

13. That plaint is declared to be inadmissible in which the order (of the words) is inverted, or the arrangement confused, or scattered what belongs together, or which is meaningless, or relative to bygone times, or unapproved.

14. The order (of the words) is said to be inverted in that plaint the meaning of which is rendered unclear by the omission (of certain words) in their proper place, and which is not accepted (in consequence).

15. When the original claim is forsaken and replaced by a different proposition, the plaint is declared to be meaningless, and the previous claim is not carried.

16. When a claim is raised in regard to certain property long after the expiration of the proper time, the plaint is said to relate to bygone times, though evidence be forthcoming.

17. That suit in which the claim relates to one thing, and the judicial investigation to another, is declared to be unapproved, because the trial is inconsistent.

18. When the plaintiff in his written claim con-

---

be examined in its turn, not all subjects at the same time. A plaint referring to many distinct articles or to several different accusations is not faulty under this rule. M.

13–20. Vîram. pp. 67, 68.

13, 14. 'The order is inverted,' i. e. several syllables are inverted in position in the written charge. Vîram., Smr*i*tik*.

13. 'The arrangement is confused,' when the natural order of the sentence is interrupted and the sense vitiated in consequence. Vîram., Smr*i*tik.

13. 'Scattered what belongs together,' i.e. the several parts of a proposition are not put together. Ibid.

17. 'Because the trial is inconsistent,' because the different parts of the suit do not agree. Smr*i*tik*.

founds the charge with the evidence, such a claim also cannot take effect, because the proper order of propositions is violated in it.

19. That plaint should be utterly rejected in which two claims are entered at once, one reasonable, and the other unreasonable.

20. Should a man make mutually conflicting statements in a plaint, his claim cannot succeed because of its being vitiated by inconsistent assertions.

21. When a man though capable (of proving his claim) omits to prove it for twenty or ten years, after the plaint has been lodged by him, his declaration becomes futile (in consequence).

22. (The plaintiff) may amend the plaint while the answer has not been delivered. When the plaint has been answered, the corrections must cease.

III. The Answer.

1. When a plaint of this description has been tendered by the plaintiff, the defendant shall deliver an answer corresponding to such plaint.

2. That is called a (true) answer by those acquainted with the subject, which meets the plaint, and is concise, clear, consistent, and easily intelligible without an explanation.

3. If a man's courage fails him when he is about to make a statement in a lawsuit, a delay must be

21. Smr*i*tik. upekshâ yatra sâdhyasya vi*m*s*a*ti*m* da*s*a vâ samâ*h* | *s*aktenâpi k*ri*te vâde tasya paksho m*ri*shâ bhavet ||

22. Vîram. p. 20.

III, 1. Smr*i*tik.; Raghunandana, pp. 12, 16 ('B*ri*haspati').

2. M. Macn. I, 5, 3 (uncertain); V. T., &c.

3. Smr*i*tik. matir notsahate yasya vivâde vaktum i*kkh*ata*h* | dâtavya eva kâla*h* syâd arthipratyarthinor api ||

granted to him (by the judge), whether he be plaintiff or defendant.

4. When the defendant contradicts the charge, such an answer is termed a denial in a cause.

5. When, the plaint having been reduced to writing by the plaintiff, the defendant admits it but adduces some special circumstance, it is called a (retort in the form) pratyavaskandana (special plea).

6. That (answer) is no (true) answer which is dubious, not to the point, too narrow, too extensive, or meeting one part only of the plaint.

7. An answer which treats of a different subject, or which is incomplete, or couched in obscure language, or confused, not intelligible without an explanation, or unreasonable, will never enable (the defendant) to gain his cause.

---

4. Raghunandana, p. 17; M. Macn. I, 5, 7, &c. ('Kâtyâyana').

5. M. Macn. I, 5, 9.

6, 7. V. T.; M. Macn. I, 5, 11. 'Dubious,' as when (the plaintiff) having declared: This man has received a hundred Suvar*n*as from me, (the defendant replies): Yes, I have received a hundred Suvar*n*as or a hundred Mâshas. 'Not to the point,' as when a debtor being sued for a hundred Suvar*n*as, replies that he has received a hundred Pa*n*as. 'Too narrow,' as when (a debtor) being sued for a hundred Suvar*n*as, replies that he has received five. 'Too extensive,' as when (a debtor) being sued for a hundred Suvar*n*as, replies that he has received two hundred. 'Meeting one part only of the plaint,' as when (a debtor) being sued for gold, clothes, and other objects, replies that he has received gold but nothing else. 'Which treats of a different subject,' as when an action for debt is answered by referring to a different title of law, e.g. when a man being sued for a debt of a hundred Suvar*n*as, replies, He (the plaintiff) has struck me. 'Incomplete,' not containing any reference to the particulars of country, place, and so on, as when the plaint states a certain field situated in the central country (Madhyade*s*a) near Benares, towards the east of it, to have been seized by the defendant, and the defendant replies merely, 'I

8. In the case of a denial, the burden of proof rests with the plaintiff; in the case of a special plea, (it rests) with the defendant.

9. Let (the plaintiff) make an answer which corresponds to (the contents of) the plaint. If he does not (make an answer), the king shall cause him to make one, by employing (any of) the (four) methods of conciliation, division, and the rest, till the matter has been cleared up.

10. When, in the case of a denial (on the part of the defendant) the plaintiff himself admits such (denial) as correct, it has to be considered as a confession, and one half of the (ordinary) fine shall be inflicted on the plaintiff.

11. In the case of a denial, the burden of proof rests with the plaintiff; in the case of a special plea,

---

have taken it.' 'Couched in obscure terms,' as when in a suit for a hundred Suvar*n*as the defendant exclaims, 'Am I the only person indebted to this man?' implying by his speech that the chief judge, or assessors, or plaintiff, is indebted to another man. 'Confused,' inconsistent, as when in an action for a hundred Suvar*n*as the defendant declares, 'Yes; I have received that sum, but I do not owe it.' 'Not intelligible without an explanation,' owing to the use of wrong inflections, compounds, or constructions, or to the employment of a foreign language. 'Unreasonable,' contrary to common sense, as when the plaint runs as follows: The defendant has received a hundred Suvar*n*as from me, repayable with interest, and has paid the interest only, and not the principal; and the defendant replies: 'Yes; I have paid the interest, but have not received the principal.' M.

8. M. Macn. I, 5, 14 (uncertain); May. p. 11.

9. Smr*i*ti*k*. yathârtham uttara*m* dadyân na *k*et tad dâpayen n*ri*pa*h* । sâmabhedâdibhir mârgair yâvat so*x*rtha*h* samuddhr*i*ta*h* ॥ Bribery and force are the two remaining methods.

10. Smr*i*ti*k*. nihnave tu yadâ vâdî svaya*m* tat pratipadyate । *gñ*eyâ sampratipattis tu tasyârdho vinaya*h* smr*i*ta*h* ॥

11. M. Macn. II, 6, 5.

it rests with the defendant; but in a plea of former judgment, all that is required in the shape of proof is to produce the previous decree.

12. The defendant is at liberty to delay his answer for three days, or for five days even.

IV. Writings and Possession.

1. A writing (or document) should be signed by witnesses, the (natural) order of ideas and syllables should not be interrupted, local customs and general rules should be observed in it, and it should be complete in every respect.

2. A document signed by the king with his own hand, or sealed with his own seal, is declared to be a royal document, and is (considered as equal to) an attested document in all affairs.

3. A document suspected (to have a blemish) is valid, unless the debtor should have clearly indicated its blemish; and so (is the validity of) a document which is more than twenty years old (established by mere lapse of time).

4. In the beginning, gift is a cause (of ownership);

---

12. Vy. *K*. pratyarthî labhate kâla*m* tryaha*m* pa*ñk*âham eva vâ ı

IV, 1. Sm*ri*ti*k*. lekhya*m* tu sâkshimat kârya*m* aviluptakramâksharam ı de*s*â*k*ârasthitiyuta*m* samagra*m* sarvavastushu ıı

2. Sm*ri*ti*k*.; Vîram. p. 195 ('Vasish*th*a').

3. Sm*ri*ti*k*.; Vîram. p. 200 ('Kâtyâyana'). The validity of a document having been called into doubt, because it either has a blemish or has been vitiated by the lapse of a considerable time, it becomes valid through proof by ordeal. This is the meaning, mere lapse of time being insufficient to produce validity. Sm*ri*ti*k*. This interpretation can hardly be correct, as ordeals are not referred to in this text.

4. M. Macn. III, 6, 5. In the case of the first man (possessor)

in the middle, possession with a title; but continued and hereditary possession by itself is also a good cause (of ownership).

5. There are six modes of acquiring wealth: by obtaining (property), what is declared to have been given or earned, (acquisition through) valour, (in the shape of) a marriage portion, and through inheritance from relations or others.

6. Having listened to the answer, (the plaintiff) at the trial shall produce a document as evidence, or he shall prove possession continued for a long time, and corroborated by (the statements of) the neighbours, or by (other) evidence.

7. Supposing a religious student were to perform some vow extending over a period of thirty-six years, or a man (engaged in trade or traffic) were to reside abroad for a long time in the pursuit of wealth:

---

possession proved by witnesses is superior to, or more decisive than, possession, excepting hereditary possession. Such hereditary possession, again, is superior in the case of the fourth in descent to a title proved by documents. In the case of an intermediate claimant (as e.g. the second or third in descent) a title coupled with possession of short duration even is more decisive than a title entirely destitute of possession. M.

5. Smr*i*ti*k*. labdha*m* dânakriyâprokta*m* *s*aurya*m* vaivâhika*m* tathâ ı bândhavâdipra*g*â*g*âta*m* sha*d*vidhas tu dhanâgama*h* ıı 'Obtaining,' by birth, paternal or other (inherited) wealth; or, obtaining property by finding it, as in the case of treasure-trove. Smr*i*ti*k*.

6. Smr*i*ti*k*. *s*rutvottara*m* kriyâpade lekhya*m* sâdhanam uddi*s*et ı sâmantalaksha*n*opetâ bhuktir vâ *k*irakâlikî. 'The term sâdhanam a fortiori denotes witnesses in this place. Therefore the meaning is as follows. In a dispute regarding a house, field, or other (immovable property), the claimant must adduce a document or witnesses, or he must plead possession.' Smr*i*ti*k*.

7–10. Smr*i*ti*k*. brahma*k*ârî *k*aret ki*m**k*id vrata*m* sha*t*tri*m**s*adâbdika*m* ı arthârthî *k*ânyavishaye dîrghakâla*m* vasen nara*h* ıı samâ-

8. If, then, the student after having completed his period of studentship (and returned from his preceptor) were to look after his property, possession (by a stranger) continued for fifty years would be capable of depriving him of his property.

9. Twelve years for (the study of) each Veda is the period ordained for those engaged in the pursuit of religious knowledge; for those engaged in the acquisition of mechanical (or manual) skill, the period (of apprenticeship) is declared to last till they have acquired their art.

10. What has been possessed against their wish by their friends or relations, and what has been possessed by persons offending against the king, is not lost by the lapse of (a long) time.

V. Witnesses.

1. (By false evidence concerning land, a witness kills everything; beware, then, of giving false evidence concerning land.) In the case of (false evidence concerning) water, the consequence is said to be the same as for land, and so it is in the case of carnal connexion with a female, as well as (in the

vr*i*tto vratî kuryât svadhanânveshan*am* tata*h* ı pa*ñk*â*s*adâbdiko bhogas taddhanasyâpahâraka*h* ıı prativeda*m* dvâda*s*âbda*h* kâlo vidyârthinâ*m* sm*ri*ta*h* ı *s*ilpavidyârthinâ*m* *k*aiva graha*n*ânta*h* prakîrtita*h* ıı suh*ri*dbhir bandhubhi*s* *k*aishâ*m* yat syâd bhuktam ava*s*yatâm ı n*ri*pâparâdhikâ*m* *k*aiva na tat kâlena hîyate ıı See Manu III, 1.

V, 1-3. Vîram. p. 171. See Nârada I, 17, 209 (above, p. 92), the text immediately preceding these texts in the Vîramitrodaya. 1, 3=Manu VIII, 100, 101. All these texts, up to 10, form part of the exhortation to be addressed to the witnesses by the judge. In 2, I have substituted tathâ*s*vavat, the reading of the *Tod*arânanda, for tathâpnuyât.

case of false evidence) concerning gems produced in water, and everything consisting of stone.

2. In the case of honey or clarified butter (the consequence) is the same as (when false evidence has been given) with regard to small cattle. He incurs the same guilt as in the case of a horse (by giving false evidence) regarding a vehicle. The case of silver, clothes, grain, or the Veda is equal to the case of a cow.

3. Having considered all these evil consequences attending a false declaration, (a witness) must declare openly everything as (he has) heard or seen (it).

4. Kubera, Âditya, Varu*n*a, *S*akra (Indra), the son of Vivasvant (Yama), and the (other) guardian deities of the world are constantly looking on with divine eyes.

5. Let (the judge) ask a Brahman for his testimony by saying, 'Speak;' a Kshatriya by saying, 'Speak the truth;' a Vai*s*ya, by referring to his kine, grain, and gold; but a *S*ûdra (by conjuring him) by all possible wicked deeds.

6. Whatever places (of torment) are assigned (in a future state) to the murderers of Brahmans, or to the slayers of women and children, and to him who betrays a friend, or shows ingratitude, those very places shall be thy home (after death) if thou speakest falsely.

7. All meritorious deeds which thou, O good man, hast done since thy birth, would go to the dogs, if thou shouldst speak falsely.

---

4. Sm*ri*ti*k*. kuberâdityavaru*n*a*s*akravaivasvatâdaya*h* । pa*s*yanti lokapâlâ*s* *k*a nitya*m* divyena *k*akshushâ ॥

5–9. Vy. *K*. Identical with Manu VIII, 88–92.

8. Although, O virtuous man, thou thinkest of thyself, 'I am alone,' yet that says who sees the evil and the good ever resides in thy heart.

9. If thou art not at variance with the god Yama, the son of Vivasvant, who resides in thy heart, thou needest not go to the Ganges or to (the country of) the Kurus.

10. Perjured witnesses, as well as those who rob others of their property, and wicked kings, shall have to reside (hereafter) in a very dreadful hell for the time of a kalpa.

11. When (a calamity such as) an illness, or fire, or the death of a relative, happens to a witness within seven days after his evidence has been taken, he shall be made to pay the debt and a fine.

12. Learned Brahmans and other such persons (are incompetent witnesses) under a text of law; thieves and the like persons, on account of their notorious perversity; (the deposition of the witnesses is worthless) owing to mutual contradiction when the witnesses make mutually conflicting statements at the trial of a cause.

13. 'One who gives evidence of his own accord' is a witness who comes to make a deposition of his own accord, without being appointed (a witness). Such a man is termed a spy in the law-books, and he is not worthy to become a witness.

---

10. Smri*t*ik. atîvanarake kalpa*m* vaseyu*h* kû*t*asâkshi*nah* ׀ paravittaharâ ye *k*a râ*g*ânas *k*âpyadhârmikâ*h* ׀׀ A kalpa is a fabulous period of time, the duration of which is reckoned in various ways.

11. *Tod.* Identical with Manu VIII, 108.

12–14. Vîram. p. 151. 12, 13a, and 14 occur in the Minor Nârada as well (p. 34), where they come immediately after a text which is identical with Nârada I, 12, 157 (above, p. 82).

14. 'One rendered incompetent by intervening decease' is a witness (who comes) after the death of the claimant, unless he should have been instructed (by the claimant) on his deathbed.

VI. Ordeals.

1. Let (the defendant) touch the heads of his sons, wife, or friends; or else the (ordeal by) sacred libation (may be performed), whatever the nature of the charge may be.

2. It is on the claimant that the duty of declaring his readiness to take on himself the penalty (to be awarded to the losing party) devolves in every case. Or the ordeal may be performed by either party at pleasure, the other party consenting to give the penalty (to be awarded in case of defeat).

3. To persons suspected by the king, or denounced (as criminals) by (intercourse with) robbers, or intent on their own justification, an ordeal must be administered without binding (an opponent) to give the penalty.

4. (The performance of) an ordeal is ordained in

VI, 1. Vîram. p. 226; M. Macn. X, 1, 5 (uncertain).

2. Vîram. p. 228.

3. V. T.; M. Macn. X, 1, 5 a (uncertain). The Mitâksharâ explains the term *s*ira*h* or *s*îrsha, which has been translated by 'penalty' in this paragraph and in the preceding text, as denoting the head, i.e. the fourth or principal division of a lawsuit, which involves defeat or success, and results in the awarding of a punishment or fine to the losing party. It appears more probable, however, that *s*iras, 'head,' is an equivalent for 'life,' the accuser having to declare his readiness to risk his life, i.e. a heavy punishment, in case of defeat.

4. Sm*ri*tik. kâra*n*e mahati prokta*m* divya*m* vâdârthinâ*m* n*ri*nâm | *s*irovartî yadâ na syât tadâ divya*m* na dîyate || This is apparently the

important cases, when people are engaged in a controversy; an ordeal must not be administered when there is no one ready to take the punishment on himself.

5. Justice is based on truth, and litigation (depends) on witnesses. When a case admits of divine test, human evidence (the testimony of witnesses) or documents must not be resorted to.

6. The (ordeal by) sacred libation has been declared by the wise to be applicable to all (castes), and poison (to all castes), excepting the Brahman (caste). (Either the balance is reserved for Brahmans), or the balance may be administered to (members of) every caste.

7. The (ordeal by) sacred libation may be administered in every case. The (ordeal by) balance is admissible in every season.

8. Eunuchs, distressed or feeble persons, the severely afflicted, infants, old men, women, and the blind should be tested by the balance always.

9. (The ordeal by) poison is not destined for

---

correct reading of the text translated above, Nârada I, 19, 257 (pp. 101, 102).

5. M. Macn. X, 1, 7. In actions for debt and the like, though witnesses possessing the required qualifications (such as veracity, &c.) should have been adduced by the plaintiff, an ordeal may be administered, if the defendant proposes an ordeal and promises to give the fine or other penalty to be inflicted in case of his being defeated, because witnesses are subject to the fault of partiality, whereas an ordeal shows the true state of the case, as no fault can be found with it, and is an emblem of justice. M.

6. Vîram. p. 235. This text comes after Nârada I, 24, 335 (above, p. 117).

7. May. p. 18 (text).

8, 9. Vîram. p. 235. In the third Pâda of 8, I read bâlav*ri*ddhâstriyo*-*ndhâ*ms**k*a with Sm*ri*tik. for bâlav*ri*ddhâturân strî*s* *k*a

women, nor is (the ordeal by) water fit to be administered to them; it is through (the ordeals by) balance, sacred libation, and others that (the judge) must explore the true state of their minds.

10. Let (the judge) test strong men by fire, water, or poison, and let him test infants, old or distressed men by the balance.

11. Let (the judge) avoid (the ordeal by) fire in the case of lepers, (the ordeal by) water in the case of the asthmatic, and (the ordeal by) poison in the case of bilious or phlegmatic persons.

12. In the season of the rains, let the (ordeal by) fire be administered; also in the cold and chilly seasons. In the summer season, the (ordeal by) water is the proper (kind of ordeal). Poison (is destined) for the cold weather.

13. The chilly, cold, and rainy seasons are declared to be (the proper seasons) for the (ordeal by) fire; the autumn and summer seasons, for the (ordeal by) water; the (ordeal by) poison, (is fit) for the cold and chilly seasons.

14. The months of *K*aitra (March–April), Mârga*s*îrsha (November–December), and Vai*s*âkha (April–

(Vîram., *Tod.*), as the term âtura occurs twice under the latter reading.

9. M. Macn. X, 1, 12 (uncertain); Nepalese Nârada.

10, 11. Minor Nârada I, 5, 116, 118 (p. 46). For the Sanskrit, see Nârada-smr*i*ti, p. 112, note. Nearly identical with a text usually attributed to Pitâmaha, Vîram. p. 237.

12. Vîram. pp. 239, 240. Nearly identical with Nârada I, 19, 254 (p. 101) and Minor Nârada I, 5, 113, 114 (p. 46).

13, 14 a. V. T.; M. Macn. X, 1, 10 (uncertain). These two texts are elsewhere attributed to Pitâmaha, and it is certainly difficult to reconcile them with 12.

14 b. Vîram. p. 240. In the quotations, this text comes after

May) are proper months for all (ordeals), and not adverse to any kind of ordeal. (Ordeals must) never (be administered) in the afternoon, nor in the twilight, nor at noon.

15. Ordeals administered at an improper place, or at an unsuitable time, or performed at a distance from human habitations, constitute a deviation from the proper course of a lawsuit, this is certain.

16. The chief judge must superintend the whole of the proceedings at an ordeal, fasting and obeying the king's instructions in the same way as an Adhvaryu (priest officiates) at a sacrifice.

17. The chief judge, who must be a Brahman, thoroughly versed in the Vedas and Vedâṅgas, instructed in sacred learning and of religious conduct, tranquil-minded, unambitious,

18. Fond of veracity, pure, able, delighting in the welfare of all sentient beings, having kept a fast, clad in his moist garments (after a bath), having cleansed his teeth, should worship all deities according to rule.

19. With red perfumes and garlands, as well as

Nârada I, 19, 259 (above, p. 102). 'The prohibition to administer an ordeal at noon has reference to ordeals other than the ordeal by water.' Vîram.

15. Vîram. p. 241; May. p. 18 (text). I read bahirvâsak*ri*tâni in the second Pâda (bahirvâdik*ri*tâni, May.), and vyabhi*k*âra*m* sadartheshu in the third Pâda (vyabhi*k*âre sadartheshu, Vîram.). 'At a distance from human habitations,' in solitude. Vîram.

16. M. Macn. X, 1, 8 a; 'Pitâmaha,' elsewhere.

17, 18. Vîram. p. 245; M. Macn. X, 2, 18 ('Pitâmaha'). I read kuryâd in 18, as in Mitâksharâ, Vivâdatâ*nd*ava, &c. (k*ri*tvâ, Vîram.). These texts, although generally quoted in the section on the ordeal by balance, seem to contain a rule applicable to every ordeal.

19. M. Macn. X, 2, 17, &c. This text is supposed to apply to

with curds, cakes of flour, fried grain and other (offerings), he should first worship the balance, and then show honour to the others.

20. The balance and the other ordeals ordained by the sages should be administered by the king by consent of the claimant, but not otherwise.

21. When they are performed otherwise (the claimant not giving his consent), he incurs the same guilt as a thief.

22. I will state next the excellent rule regarding the (ordeal by) balance, as the king and the chief judge should administer that ordeal to a man (arraigned in a cause).

23. The two posts supporting the beam of the balance should measure four Hastas above ground, their (entire) length should be six Hastas.

24. The king should cause a wooden beam of the balance to be made, which must be four Hastas long,

---

a judge who is about to administer the ordeal by balance to one arraigned in a cause. The term 'the others' is said to relate to Indra and the other deities.

20, 21. Minor Nârada I, 5, 112, 113 (pp. 45, 46). The second half occurs in the Nepalese Nârada as well, where the chapter on the ordeal by balance commences with it. For the Sanskrit, see Nârada-smr*i*ti, loc. cit.

22. Minor Nârada I, 5, 119 (p. 46). ata*h* para*m* pravakshyâmi dha*t*asya vidhim uttamam | râ*g*â *k*a prâ*d*vivâka*s* *k*a yathâ ta*m* kârayen naram ||

23. Nepalese Nârada. *k*aturhastau tulâpâdâv u*kkh*raye*n*a prakîrtitau | sha*ddh*asta*m* tu tayor bhavet pramâ*n*a*m* parimâ*n*ata*h* || The Minor Nârada has the following text instead of this: dha*t*asya pâdâv (pâdâd) ûrdhva*m* tu *k*aturhastau prakîrtitau | pa*ñk*ahastâ tulâ kâryâ dvihastâ *k*ârgalâ smr*i*tâ || Under this reading, the beam of the balance would have to be five Hastas long, whereas the following text (24) states its length at four Hastas.

24–26. Minor Nârada I, 5, 121, 122 (p. 47 and Addenda, pp. xxxii, xxxiii). kârayeta *k*aturhastâ*m* samâ*m* laksha*n*alakshitâm |

polished, furnished with the required characteristics, and having the two scales suspended by both extremities.

25. After having caused two posts to be erected, on even ground, which must be placed from north to south, and must be arranged both in one line, he shall cause the beam of the balance to be fastened across (the transverse beam which connects) them.

26. With an iron cord let a virtuous man surround the beam in the middle and fasten it in an east-western direction, after having carefully connected it (with the transverse beam).

27. The (appointed) examiners have to take care always that the two perpendiculars of the balance should be equal in length. Water must be poured out on (the beam of) the balance by skilled persons.

28. If the water does not trickle down (from the balance), the balance may be considered as being level.

29. With red perfumes and garlands, as well as with curds, cakes of flour, fried grain and other (offerings, the judge) should first worship the balance, and then show honour to the others.

---

tulâ*m* kâsh*th*amayî*m* râ*g*â *s*ikyaprântâvalambinîm || dakshi*n*ottara-sa*m*sthânâv ubhâv ekatrasa*m*yatau | stambhau k*ri*tvâ same de*s*e tayo*h* sa*m*sthâpayet tulâm || âyasena tu pâ*s*ena madhye sa*m*g*ri*hya dharmavit | yo*g*ayet tâ*m* susa*m*yuktâ*m* tulâ*m* prâgaparâyatâm ||

27, 28. May. p. 20 (text); M. Macn. X, 2, 6 (uncertain). These two texts are elsewhere attributed to Pitâmaha, and this is probably the correct view, as the fastening of the two perpendiculars by the two arches in which the balance moves up and down is described in another text of Pitâmaha.

29. M. Macn. X, 2, 17. 'The injunction contained in this text concerns a judge who is about to administer the ordeal by balance to one arraigned in a cause. The others,' i.e. Indra and the other deities. Vîram. p. 251. See 19.

30. (The person accused being about to be placed in the scale for the second time, the judge should address the balance as follows): 'Thou, O Balance, hast been created by Brahman, to test the wicked. On account of the syllable dha thou art the image of Dharma (Justice), on account of the syllable *t*a, thou

31. Being used for balancing (dh*ri*ta, in this ordeal) discoverest the vicious. Therefore thou art called dha*t*a (balance).'

32. If (the person) remains level (sama), he is considered to be in a middling position (samatâ). If he comes down, he loses his cause. He who goes down is not innocent; he is innocent who goes up.

33. He who remains level is also not acquitted. These are the three possible cases in the (ordeal by) balance. Thus has been declared the never-failing acquittal (obtainable) through the test by balance.

34. When (the scales fixed) at the two extremities of the beam have been moved, when the mark which had been made has come off, when (the balance) is going up and down, being agitated by wind,

35. Or when (the man appointed to hold it) lets it

30, 31. Vîram. p. 251; M. Macn. X, 2, 23 (uncertain).

32, 33. Nepalese Nârada. samena samatâm eti hîyamânas tu hîyate | adhogatir na *s*udhyeta *s*udhyetordhvagatis tathâ || samo*pi na (hi MS.) vi*s*uddha*h* syâd ity eshâ trividhâ tulâ | eshoditâ tulâkalpe (tulâkalpa*h* MS.) *s*uddhir avyabhikâri*n*î || 32b, 33a are attributed to Vyâsa in the Vivâdatâ*nd*ava. The reading na for hi has been taken from the same compilation. It appears from Nârada I, 20, 283 (above, pp. 107, 108) that an equal result of the first and second weighing was not considered as a proof of innocence. According to others, such a result proves the person balanced to be guilty in some degree; or the proceeding has to be repeated.

34, 35. Vîram. p. 254; Sm*ri*tik.; V. T. I read with Sm*ri*tik.

go all of a sudden: (in all these cases) the matter in dispute must not be decided either way.

36. Now then I will proclaim the excellent rule regarding the (ordeal by) fire, as it has been declared (by the sages). The intermediate space between two circles is ordained to measure thirty-two Aṅgulas.

37. The seven circles are thus declared by persons thoroughly conversant with the art of computation to cover a space of two hundred and twenty-four Aṅgulas.

38. Let the peculiar signs be marked which he has on both hands, both visible and invisible ones, whether caused by a scar or not caused by a scar.

39. After having first marked in this way the hands of the person accused, he should offer clarified butter in fire according to rule, as a propitiatory rite, reciting Mantras (at the same time).

---

tulâ*s*irobhyâm udbhrânta*m* vi*k*ala*m* nyastalaksha*n*am । yadi vâyupra*n*unno vâ dhâvaty ûrdhvam adho*s*pi vâ ॥ nirmukta*h* sahasâ vâpi tadâ naikatara*m* vraget ॥ 'The mark,' i. e. 'the water or whatever else has been used to mark the even position of the scales' (Sm*r*ti*k*., Vîram.), or 'the bill recounting the charge which has been fixed on the head of the person balanced' (V. T.).

36. Vîram. p. 256.

37. Nepalese Nârada; Minor Nârada I, 6, 3 (p. 49). I read: saptabhir ma*nd*alair evam aṅgulânâ*m* *s*atadvayam । sa*k*aturvi*ms*ati prokta*m* sa*m*khyâtattvârthadar*s*ibhi*h* ॥ The quotations agree with Nârada I, 21, 286 in referring to eight, instead of seven, circles.

38. Vîram. p. 259. The marking of the hands serves the purpose of marking the difference between the previously extant sores and those eventually caused by the hot iron ball.

39–45. Sm*r*ti*k*. k*r*tvaivam abhi*s*astasya prathama*m* hastalaksha*n*am । *s*ântyartha*m* *g*uhuyân mantrair gh*r*tam agnau yathâvidhi ॥ tarpiteshv atha deveshu lokapâleshu *k*aiva hi । âdityâbhimukho bhûtvâ ima*m* mantram udîrayet ॥ tvam agne sarvadevânâm antas *k*arasi pâvaka*h* । havya*m* vahasi devânâm anta*h**s*ânti*m* praya*kkh*asi ॥ pra*kkh*anâni manushyâ*n*â*m* pâpâni suk*r*tâni *k*a । tvam eva

40. The gods and the guardian deities of the world having been hospitably entertained, let (the person accused) utter the following prayer, facing the sun.

41. 'Thou, O fire, dwellest in the interior of all deities as a flame. Thou conveyest burnt-oblations to the gods, and givest peace of mind.

42. 'Thou, O God, knowest the secret offences and merits of men. Thou, O deity, knowest whatever mortals do not comprehend.

43. 'Arraigned in a cause, I am about to be tested by fire. Therefore deign to deliver me lawfully from the perplexity in which I am involved.'

44. The man (about to be examined) having made this speech, facing the east, with firmness, his joined hands should be covered with seven equal leaves of the holy fig-tree,

45. And both hands should be tied with seven strings of light-coloured thread.

46. (Then the man) should take a smooth ball of red-hot iron, fifty Palas in weight, in both hands, and step gradually across the seven circles.

47. When a man has carefully stepped through

---

deva *g*ânîshe na vidur yâni mânushâ*h* ‖ vyavahârâbhi*s*asto*'*ya*m* vahnau tish*th*âmi sa*ms*aye ׀ tasmân mâ*m* sa*ms*ayârû*dh*a*m* dharmatas trâtum arhasi ‖ evam uktavatas tasya prâṅmukhasya tu dhîmata*h* ׀ pattrair a*ñg*alim âpûrya a*s*vatthai*h* saptabhi*h* samai*h* ‖ vesh*t*ayîta sitair hastau saptabhi*h* sûtratantubhi*h* ‖ For similar prayers, which are put in the mouth of the judge however, see Nârada I, 21, 290–294 (above, pp. 109, 110); Minor Nârada I, 6, 10, 11 (p. 41).

45. M. Macn. X, 3, 2.

46. Minor Nârada I, 6, 6, 7 (p. 49). hutâ*s*ataptalohasya pa*ñk*â*s*atpalika*m* samam ׀ hastâbhyâ*m* pi*nd*am âdâya ma*nd*alâni *s*anair vra*g*et ‖

47. Nepalese Nârada. tîrtvânena vidhânena ma*nd*alâni samâhita*h* ׀

the (seven) circles in this way, without having burnt himself in the least, he is acquitted.

48. When he has dropped the ball, his hands should be inspected. If the marks have retained their previous appearance, he should examine (the hands) elsewhere as well.

49. When a bloodshot round stain or any other sore caused by fire is seen, the man has to be considered as guilty, because truth and virtue are not found in him.

50. I will proclaim next the excellent rule regarding the (ordeal by) water. Let a king who is desirous of establishing perfect truth refrain from administering (this ordeal) in winter.

51. With perfumes, garlands, sweet-smelling substances, honey, milk, clarified butter, and the like, let (the judge) perform the worship of Varu*n*a (the deity of water) first of all.

52. Let (the judge) cause this ordeal to be per-

---

adagdha*h* sarvathâ yas tu sa vi*s*uddho bhaven nara*h* ‖ Nearly identical with Minor Nârada I, 6, 7a, 8b.

48, 49. *Tod.*; Sm*r*iti*k*.; Vîram. p. 264 ('Kâlikâpurâ*n*a'). 48b according to the Nepalese Nârada. tasyaiva muktapi*nd*asya kuryât karanirîksha*n*am | pûrvarûpeshu *k*ihneshu tato*-*nyatrâpi lakshayet ‖ ma*nd*ala*m* raktasa*m*kâ*s*a*m* ya*k* *k*ânyad vâgnisa*m*bhavam | so*-*vi*s*uddhas tu vi*g*ñeyo*-*satyadharmavyavasthita*h* ‖ 'If a boil or other (tumour) caused by fire should be discovered on the palms of his hands, he has to be considered as guilty. If nothing of the kind is discovered, he is innocent.' Sm*r*iti*k*., Vîram.

50–79. The ordeals by water and poison are omitted in the Sm*r*iti*k*andrikâ, 'because they are obsolete now-a-days.'

50. Nepalese Nârada. ata*h* para*m* pravakshyâmi toyasya vidhim uttamam | hemante var*g*ayed râ*g*â ya i*kk*he*k* *kh*uddhim uttamâm ‖

51. M. Macn. X, 4, 3 (uncertain); Vîram. p. 269.

52. Minor Nârada I, 7, 2 (p. 50). sva*kk*he *g*ale su*s*îtale *g*alau*k*a*h*pañkavar*g*ite | vipule nâtigâ*dh*e *k*a kuryâd divyasya nir*n*ayam ‖

formed in transparent and very cool water, which does not contain aquatic animals or mud, and is abundant and not too shallow.

53. Let (a man) go near the bank of the water (in which the accused is to be immersed) and erect an arch as high as the ear (of the person) on the edge (of that water), on level and purified ground.

54. A strong bow should be known to have seven hundred; one not particularly strong, six hundred; a weak bow, five hundred. Thus has the rule regarding the bow been declared.

55. From a bow of a middling quality let a skilful (archer) discharge three arrows, after having made a target one hundred and fifty Hastas distant.

56. (The archer) is blameable if the arrows discharged by him fall short of or go beyond the target. (The person accused) obtains acquittal if his body continues immersed in water after the middling arrow has been (discharged and) brought back.

---

53. M. Macn. X, 4, 13.

54. Nepalese Nârada. krûra*m* dhanu*h* sapta*s*ata*m* nâtikrûra*m* tu sha*t*satam । manda*m* pa*ñk*a*s*ata*m* *gñ*eyam esha prokto dhanurvidhi*h* ॥ Nearly identical with Minor Nârada I, 7, 4 (p. 50); Nârada I, 22, 307 (above, p. 112); Vîram. p. 268, &c. The translation of this text is based on the interpretation given in *Tod.* 'That bow which bends sufficiently to admit of discharging an arrow from it, when a weight of seven hundred Palas is fastened by the string, is said to have seven hundred. The terms "six hundred" and "five hundred" have to be understood in the same way.' See too, above, p. 112, 307 note.

55, 56a. M. Macn. X, 4, 15. The rule regarding the distance of the target, which renders the arrows entirely superfluous, seems to belong to a more recent period than the other rules. See Prof. Stenzler's Essay on Indian Ordeals.

56b. *Tod.* ânîte madhyame vâ*n*e magnânga*h* *s*u*k*itâm iyât ।

57. Among fifty runners, those two who are the quickest runners should be appointed to fetch the arrow.

58. Let a strong man, who may be a Brahman, Kshatriya or Vai*s*ya, and must be free from affection and hatred, be placed in water reaching his navel, (standing erect) like a pillar.

59. (The accused), thoroughly controlled in mind, shall seize the thighs of that man under water, and stand in it composed all the time till the (runner) appointed to fetch (the arrow) has returned.

60. Then let men strictly devoted to veracity and virtue, acquainted with the application of legal rules, and free from affection and hatred, see that everything is fair.

61. An intelligent, pious-minded man should descend into the water and duly address (the deity of water) with the following auspicious texts.

61 b. The sacred prayer (runs as follows). 'Om, adoration to Justice.

62. 'Thou, O lord of waters, who art so pleasantly

---

57. M. Macn. X, 4, 12. 58. Vîram. p. 269.

59. Nepalese Nârada. toyam adho manushyasya g*ri*hîtvorû susa*m*yata*h* ı tâvat tish*th*eta niyato yâvat prâpta*h* samâpakî ıı

60. Minor Nârada I, 7, 8 (p. 51). dharmasthâna*m* tata*h* kuryu*h* satyadharmaparâya*n*â*h* ı dharma*s*âstravidhâna*g*ñâ râgadveshavivar*g*itâ*h* ıı

61. Nepalese Nârada. avatîrya *g*ale vidvân snâta*h* prayatamânasa*h* ı *s*râvayeta yathânyâyam ebhir mantrapadai*h* *s*ubhai*h* ıı The correctness of this reading seems doubtful. According to the other authorities, the prayer is to be recited by the judge or by the accused.

61 b. Nepalese Nârada. dharmamantra*h* ı o*m* namo dharmâya ı

62. Nepalese Nârada. yonis tvam asi (yatas tvam asti MS.) bhûtâna*m* *g*ale*s*a sukha*s*îtala ı trâyasvaina*m* nara*m* pâpât pa*s*yasi tva*m* *s*ubhâ*s*ubham ıı

cool, art the source of (all) beings. Save this man from guilt, thou knowest both good and evil.

63. 'Thou art the first of the gods and the great comforter of the world. Thou, O water, dwellest in the interior of all beings, like a witness.

64. 'Thou, O deity, alone knowest what mortals do not understand. This man, being arraigned in a cause, is going to dive in thee. Therefore deign to deliver him lawfully from this perplexity.'

65. Then (the accused) should submerge all his limbs in water so as to become invisible.

66. A prudent man should leave the water, after having seen the arrow brought back, and should approach the king and all the assessors of the court, after saluting them reverentially.

67. Though only his ear, eye, mouth or nose should become visible while he is in water, he cannot be acquitted. If he remains invisible, he obtains acquittal.

63a occurs in the Minor Nârada and Nepalese Nârada (Minor Nârada I, 7, 15 a). âdidevo*si devânâm (bhûtânâ*m* Nep. Nâr.) lokasyâpyâyana*m* mahat । After this, the Nepalese Nârada has two texts, which are identical with Nârada I, 22, 316, 317.

63b. Minor Nârada I, 7, 16 a. tvam ambha*h* sarvabhûtânâm anta*s* *k*arasi sâkshivat । Identical with Vish*n*u XII, 7 a.

64 a, b. Minor Nârada I, 7, 16 b, 17 a. tvam eva deva *g*ânîshe na vidur yâni mânavâ*h* । vyavahârâbhi*s*asto*ya*m* mânushas tvayi ma*gg*ati ॥ Nearly identical with Vish*n*u XII, 7 b, 8 a.

64 c. Minor Nârada I, 7, 17 b. tad ena*m* sa*m*s*ayâd asmâd dharmatas trâtum arhasi । Identical with Vish*n*u XII, 8 b.

65. Nepalese Nârada. tato nima*gg*et salile sarvâ*n*y aṅgâny adar*s*anât ॥

66. Nepalese Nârada. prâpta*m* tu sâyaka*m* d*r*ish*t*vâ *g*alâd uttîrya buddhimân । pra*n*ipatya n*r*ipa*m* ga*kkh*et sarvâ*m*s *k*aiva sabhâsada*h* ॥

67. Minor Nârada I, 7, 12. kar*n*âkshimukhanâsânâ*m* yasya toye vyavasthitam । d*r*i*s*yate na vi*s*uddha*h* syâd ad*r*i*s*ya*h* *s*uddhim âpnuyât ॥

68. Now then I will proclaim the excellent rule regarding the (ordeal by) poison, (stating) how the king should give poison, the best means of purification for a man.

69. Let him give the poison in the presence of (images of) the deities and Brahmans, after having kept a fast and worshipped Mahe*s*vara with incense, offerings, and sacred texts.

70. (The judge) should give the poison with fixed attention, facing the north or the east, in the presence of Brahmans, (while the accused) is facing the south.

71. Let seven Yavas be given, as a test of innocence, without doubt, of poison from the *Sri*ṅga tree or Vatsanâbha (poison) or Hima*g*a poison.

72. In the morning and in a cool place let the poison be given to all persons, after it has been finely ground, and mixed with clarified butter thirty times the quantity.

73. He must not give poison to infants, disabled or superannuated persons, or to those who have committed a very light offence only, or to a madman, to one severely afflicted, to a cripple, or to ascetics.

74. If the person (examined) undergoes no change

---

68. Minor Nârada I, 8, 1 (p. 52). ata*h* para*m* pravakshyâmi vishasya vidhim uttamam | yathâ dadyâd visha*m* râ*g*â *s*odhana*m* parama*m* n*ri*n*â*m ||

69. M. Macn. X, 5, 4. 70. M. Macn. X, 5, 6.

71. *Tod.*; Vîram. p. 273 ('Pitâmaha'). Hima*g*a poison is no doubt the poison elsewhere called Haimavata, 'coming from the Himalayas.'

72. Vîram. p. 275; M. Macn. X, 5, 13 ('Kâtyâyana').

73. Nepalese Nârada. na bâlâturav*ri*ddheshu naiva svalpâparâdhishu | nonmattârte tathâ vyaṅge na *k*a dadyât tapasvishu ||

74. M. Macn. X, 5, 16.

of appearance during the time occupied by clapping the hands five hundred times, he is acquitted, and should be cured (by giving him antidotes of poison).

75. 'On account of thy poisonous and dangerous nature thou art hard on all persons. Thou art appointed to show the difference between good and evil like a witness.

76. 'Thou, O deity, knowest the sacred ordinances and the conduct of men, both good and evil actions, (in short) whatever men do not comprehend.

77. 'This man being arraigned in a cause, wishes to obtain acquittal. Therefore deign to deliver him lawfully from this perplexity.'

78. This prayer should be pronounced according to rule, while the poison is being swallowed (by the person).

79. The king having known the man to be innocent should honourably dismiss him, and proclaim him (innocent) with a loud voice. Thus has the law been laid down.

80. (Let the ordeal by sacred libation be administered) to one who consents to it and puts faith (in

---

75. Minor Nârada I, 8, 7. vishatvâd vishamatvâ*k* *k*a krûra*m* tva*m* sarvadehinâm । *s*ubhâ*s*ubhavivekârtha*m* niyukto hyasi sâkshivat ॥ The first half is identical with Vish*n*u XIII, 6a.

76. Minor Nârada I, 8, 8. dharmâ*n*i *k*arita*m* pu*m*sâm a*s*ubhâni *s*ubhâni *k*a । tvam eva deva *g*ânîshe na vidur yâni mânavâ*h* ॥

76 b is identical with Vish*n*u XIII, 6 b.

77. Identical with Vish*n*u XIII, 7.

78. Nepalese Nârada. iti mantra*m* pa*th*et tatra vidhinâ vishabhaksha*n*e (vibhaksha*n*e MS.).

79. *Tod.* ta*m* vi*s*uddham iti *g*ñâtvâ râ*g*â satk*ri*tya mo*k*ayet । u*kk*ai*h* prakâ*s*aye*k* *k*ainam esha dharmo vyavasthita*h* ॥

80. Vîram. p. 278, where this text is preceded by two texts identical with Nârada I, 24, 327, 328 (above, p. 116).

religion) in the presence of the deities and Brahmans.

81. Having called near the person accused, (the judge) should place him inside the circle and cause him to swallow three handsful of water, after having caused him to face the sun.

82. After having worshipped that deity (to which the accused is devoted, the judge) should wash (the image of that deity) with water, proclaim his crime, and cause him to swallow the three handsful of water.

83. When some one drinks consecrated water of his own accord, after having been charged with a crime, and does not confess his guilt, actuated by avarice, such a wicked man will become a leper (in a future birth).

84. When a man tells a lie knowingly and intentionally, after having drunk consecrated water, he is born as a poor, sick, or foolish person in seven (successive) existences.

85. When a man administers the (ordeal by) sacred libation by force to procure some advantage to himself, it will destroy himself, nor will his affairs prosper.

86. When a man has been convicted (by this

---

81. M. Macn. X, 6, 8 (uncertain); V. T. The circle has to be made with cowdung. M.

82. Vîram. p. 279.

83. Vîram. p. 279; Sm*ri*ti*k*. I read, with the latter work, ya*h* ka*s**k*id dûshito nara*h*, 'after having been charged with a crime,' instead of na kva*k*id dûshito nara*h*, 'without having been charged with a crime' (Vîram.).

84, 85. Ibid.

86. Minor Nârada I, 9, 5. vibhâvita*m* sa dâpya*h* syâd dhaninâ tu svaya*m* dhanam | *rin*â*k* *k*a dvigu*n*a*m* da*nd*a*m* râ*g*â dharme*n*a dâpayet ||

ordeal) he may be compelled by his creditor himself to repay the debt proved against him, and the king may exact from him with justice a fine amounting to twice as much as the debt.

VII. Miscellaneous Laws.

1. (Because fathers desire offspring, to be released from debt by their sons), therefore should a son begotten (by his father) give up his own property and assiduously redeem his father from debt, lest he should go to hell.

2. The interest is unlimited on thread, cotton, substances from which spirits may be extracted, tin, lead, weapons of all sorts, skins, copper, iron,

3. And all other articles of this kind, as well as bricks. This has been declared by Manu Pragâpati.

4. On oil of every sort, on intoxicating drinks, on honey, on butter, on sugar, and on salt, the interest shall cease when it reaches eight times the original amount.

5. The debts of sick, mad, overaged, or long absent persons: such debts should be discharged by their sons even while such persons are alive.

6. A wife, a daughter-in-law, a grandson's wife, and the presents bestowed on a wife (which constitute her separate property): if a man takes any of these, he shall be made to pay the debts (of such

VII, 1. Vîram. p. 340; Minor Nârada I, 3, 5. See Nârada-smriti, p. 47, note.

2–4. Minor Nârada I, 4, 34, 35. See Nârada-smriti, p. 77, note.

5. Minor Nârada I, 3, 15. See Nârada-smriti, p. 50, note.

6, 7. Minor Nârada I, 3, 22, 23. See Nârada-smriti, pp. 53, 54, note.

women); and so shall he who lives on the landed property (of a stranger).

7. It is on the wife that the performance of religious acts depends in all (four) castes, one after the other. He who takes the wife of a man, takes his property (and debts) as well.

8. Females are not entitled to bestow gifts, or to sell property. It is only while she is living together (with her family), that a woman may enjoy (the family property).

9. It is by permission (of the owner) only that a female slave, cattle, or an estate may be enjoyed (by a stranger). He who enjoys that which had not been given up to him (by the owner), must pay for the (illegitimate) enjoyment of what he had been enjoying.

10. When a man forcibly enjoys property, such as a house, field, cow or the like, without authorization (from the owner), he deserves the same punishment as a thief.

11. He who uses a bull, or a milch-cow, or a boat, or a female slave, without authorization (from the owner), shall pay four Pa*n*as (as a fine).

---

8. Minor Nârada I, 3, 28. See Nârada-smr*i*ti, p. 56, note.

9–15. Smr*i*ti*k*. uddish*t*am eva bhoktavya*m* strî pa*s*ur vasudhâpi vâ । anarpita*m* tu yo bhuṅkte bhuktabhoga*m* pradâpayet ॥ anuddish*t*am tu yad dravya*m* vâsakshetragavâdikam । svabalenaiva bhu*ñ*gânas *k*oravad da*nd*am arhati ॥ ana*d*vâha*m* tathâ dhenu*m* nâva*m* dâsî*m* tathaiva *k*a । anuddish*t*a*m* tu bhu*ñg*âno dadyât pa*n*a*k*atush*t*ayam ॥ dâsî naukâ tathâ dhuryo bandhaka*m* nopabhu*g*yate । upabhoktâ tu tad dravya*m* pa*n*air eva vi*s*odhayet ॥ divase dvipa*n*a*m* dâsî*m* dhenum ash*t*apa*n*a*m* tathâ । trayoda*s*am ana*d*vâham a*s*va*m* bhûmi*m* *k*a sho*d*a*s*a ॥ naukâm a*s*va*m* *k*a dhenu*m* *k*a lâṅgala*m* kârmikasya *k*a । balâtkâre*n*a yo bhuṅkte dâpya*s* *k*âsh*t*agu*n*a*m* dine ॥ ulûkhale pa*n*ârdha*m* tu musalasya pa*n*advayam । *s*ûrpasya *k*a pa*n*ârdha*m* tu *g*aiminir munir abravît ॥

12. A female slave, a boat, a beast of burden, and a pledge is not lost (to the owner) by adverse possession. The possessor is bound to give a compensation in money for his enjoyment of them.

13. (Let him give) two Pa*n*as a day for the use of a female slave; eight Pa*n*as for the use of a milch-cow; thirteen for the use of a bull; sixteen for the use of a horse or of an estate.

14. He who forcibly enjoys a boat, a horse, a milch-cow, or the plough of an agriculturist, shall be made to pay eight times (their value) each day.

15. (For the use) of a mortar, half a Pa*n*a; for the use of a pestle, two Pa*n*as; for the use of a winnowing basket, half a Pa*n*a. Thus has the sage *G*aimini declared.

16. A deposit which has been entrusted to a friend, is called a deposit based on confidence.

17. Should a man, after entering the order of religious ascetics, violate the duties of his order, the king should cause him to be branded with a dog's foot and banish him quickly (from his realm).

18. These two persons are (as contemptible as) *K*a*nd*âlas for their acts, and should be kept entirely apart from the world: one who has forsaken the order of religious ascetics, and one who has entered an order prohibited in law.

19. He is called Guru (a teacher) who instructs his pupil, duly addressing him in Prâk*ri*t or Sa*m*sk*ri*t, or employing a local or other dialect.

16, 17. Vîram. pp. 406, 407.

18. Sm*ri*ti*k*. dvâv eva karma*k*a*nd*âlau loke dûrabahishk*ri*tau | pravra*g*yopaniv*ri*tta*s* *k*a v*ri*thâ pravra*g*ita*s* *k*a ya*h* ||

19. Vîram. p. 72.

20. When a quarrel has arisen between prostitutes and the lovers frequenting their house, the principal prostitutes and the lovers shall decide the dispute in common.

21. If other persons (than the neighbours) should give false evidence in a dispute concerning land, such low persons shall be condemned to pay the first fine each in his turn.

22. A boundary is declared to be of five sorts, as it may be either marked by signs (such as trees), or by water (of a river), or by articles deposited underground, or subject to no quarrel (being determined by consent of both parties), or fixed by royal command.

23. After having traced those (robbers) with the aid of able spies acquainted with their habits, he shall avoid frightening them, and shall cause them to be arrested by officials secretly set upon them.

24. It is not from the air, from the sky, from the sea, or from other (such parts) that robbers will come; therefore one should act thus.

25. (The king) shall endeavour to inveigle (thieves and robbers) through cunning spies who are anxious to catch thieves. Other skilful and reliable persons also, artful talkers and former thieves, shall (be appointed to) detect the thieves.

26. By giving them wealth and valuable presents,

20. Viv. p. 102; Col. Dig. III, 1, 98; Ratn. p. 167.

21. Vîram. p. 459; Ratn. p. 212. 'Other persons,' i.e. hunters, foresters, and so forth. This text comes in between Nârada XI, 7 and 8.

22. Ratn. p. 214; Vîram. p. 452. 23. Ratn. p. 292.

24. Ratn. p. 335. This text should come in immediately after Nârada XIV, 25.

25–29. Ratn. p. 337. Read *k*auryâpade*s*ai*s* *k*a in 26.

by causing them to attend at public shows and festivals, and by pretending intended robberies, they shall cause (the thieves) to assemble together.

27. Those who fail to make their appearance on such occasions, though skilful spies have been set on them, shall be arrested together with their sons, kinsmen, and relatives.

28. He shall then arrest the thieves after having convicted and enticed them (to make their appearance), and shall inflict capital punishment on them in various ways, after having proclaimed (their deeds) everywhere.

29. Innocent persons also are seen to mingle with thieves (occasionally); let not the king inflict punishments indiscriminately on such.

BR*I*HASPATI.

INTRODUCTION

TO THE

FRAGMENTS OF B*R*I*HASPATI.

THE fragments of B*ri*haspati are among the most precious relics of the early legal literature of India. Apart from their intrinsic value and interest, as containing a very full exposition of the whole range of the Hindu law, their close connexion with the Code of Manu gives them a special claim to consideration, and renders them a valuable link in the chain of evidence[1] by which the date of the most authoritative code of ancient India has been approximately determined[2].

Importance of B*ri*haspati.

The connexion between the Manu and B*ri*haspati Sm*ri*tis appears first from the way in which B*ri*haspati refers to, and quotes from, the Code of Manu. In the chapter on Gambling and Betting, B*ri*haspati says (XXVI, 1), 'Gambling has been prohibited by Manu, because it destroys truth, honesty, and wealth. It has been permitted by others, when conducted so as to allow the king a share (of every stake).' The observation that Manu disagrees with the other legislators as to the permissibility of gambling is perfectly just. See Manu IX, 221–228; Yâ*gñ*avalkya II, 199–203; Âpastamba II, 25, 12, 13; Nârada XVII, 1–8; Kâtyâyana XXV, 1. B*ri*haspati goes on to say (XXVI, 2) that 'Gambling shall take place under the superintendence of keepers of gaming-houses, for the purpose of discovering thieves.' This rule agrees almost literally with Yâ*gñ*avalkya II, 203, and the fact that B*ri*haspati does not refer to Yâ*gñ*avalkya by name, although he names Manu, can only be accounted for by his very particular veneration for the latter, as the fountain-head of Sacred Law.—On the

He refers to Manu.

[1] Bühler, The Laws of Manu (Sacred Books of the East, vol. xxv), pp. cviii–cx.

[2] What follows up to p. 275 has been reprinted, with modifications and additions, from a paper on 'Manu and B*ri*haspati,' in the first volume of the Vienna Zeitschrift f. d. Kunde d. Morgenlandes, pp. 275–280.

subject of weights or coins, B*ri*haspati says (X, 10), 'The quantities beginning with a floating particle of dust and ending with a Kârshâpa*n*a have been declared by Manu.' The statements of Manu which are thus referred to by B*ri*haspati may be found, Manu VIII, 132–137.—In speaking of the Niyoga or appointment of a widow to raise offspring to her deceased husband, B*ri*haspati says (XXIV, 12), 'The Niyoga has been declared by Manu, and again prohibited by the same; on account of the successive deterioration of the (four) ages of the world, it must not take place (in the present or Kali age).' This text shows that the conflicting statements of Manu (IX, 57–68) with regard to the Niyoga, which have been the matter of so much comment among European philologists, had already struck his follower B*ri*haspati, and were ingeniously explained by him, in accordance with the practice of his own times.—In the chapter on Inheritance (XXV, 33), B*ri*haspati observes that out of the thirteen sons declared by Manu, a legitimate son of the body (aurasa) and an appointed daughter (putrikâ) are the only ones that represent real issue. It is true that Manu (IX, 158, 180) speaks emphatically of twelve sons only, but the appointed daughter or her son is not among these, and he advocates in strong terms the rights of an appointed daughter's son (IX, 127–140), and cuts down very much the rights of all the other substitutes for a son (IX, 180, 181). This shows that B*ri*haspati's rules on this head are perfectly in keeping with the teaching of Manu.—In the chapter on Sale without Ownership (XIII, 1) he refers to Manu (VIII, 197) by the name of Bh*ri*gu.

Indirect references.

Secondly, in a number of other instances, the Code of Manu, though not appealed to by name, is nevertheless distinctly referred to by B*ri*haspati. Thus, in the chapter on Inheritance (XXV, 79), he observes that 'those by whom clothes and so forth have been declared impartible have not decided properly.' The well-known versus memorialis concerning impartible property, the contents of which are further discussed in the sequel by B*ri*haspati, occurs both in the Code of Manu (IX, 219) and in the Vish*n*u-sm*ri*ti ; and it may be presumed either that the authors of these two works are the authorities referred to by B*ri*haspati, or that Manu is referred to in the pluralis majestatis, as is often the case with teachers. The reason why Manu is not referred to by name may be sought in the fact that B*ri*haspati does not care to openly avow his dissent from so eminent an authority.—In the chapter on Debts, B*ri*haspati remarks (XI, 4) that interest is divided into four species by some, into five by others, and by others again into six sorts. Four sorts of interest are mentioned by Manu, VIII, 153.—In the chapter on Inheritance (XXV, 35), he declares that an appointed daughter or her son has been pronounced equal to a legitimate son of the body. The rights of an appointed daughter, as shown before, are laid great stress upon by Manu, and he actually states that an (appointed) daughter is equal to a son (IX, 130).

Comments on Manu.

Thirdly, B*ri*haspati, even when not expressly referring to Manu, presupposes throughout an acquaintance with his Code, and a very large portion of his Sm*ri*ti is devoted to the interpretation of technical terms or to the elucidation or amplification of the somewhat laconic enunciations of Manu. Thus, for example, in the chapter on Debts (XI, 5–11), he explains, comments on, and amplifies the four sorts of interest mentioned by Manu (VIII, 153). In the same chapter (XI, 55–58) he interprets the curious terms used by Manu (VIII, 49) to denote the various modes of recovering an outstanding debt. In the chapter on Sale without Ownership (XIII, 2), he explains the technical term asvâmin, 'another person than the owner,' which had been first used by Manu. From the general maxim of Manu (VIII, 2, 11) that the allotment of shares among partners in any undertaking shall be arranged in the same way as for a company of officiating priests, B*ri*haspati (XIV, 20–32) has developed a series of elaborate rules regarding partnership in tillage, workmanship, trade, musical performances, and robbery. In the same way, the threefold law of breach of promised obedience, non-payment of wages, and disputes between the owner of cattle and his servants has been developed by Br*i*haspati (XVI, 1, 2) from Manu's two titles of non-payment of wages and disputes between master and servant. An analogous course of development may be observed in the chapters on Ordeals, Resumption of Gift, and Violation of Agreements, as compared to the scanty provisions of Manu (VIII, 114–116, 212–214, 218–221) on the same subjects. In the chapter on Boundary Disputes, Manu's technical term maula, 'an original inhabitant of a place,' is interpreted by Br*i*haspati (XIX, 12). It would be easy to multiply examples. One more analogy between the Manu and Br*i*haspati Smr*i*tis seems to be specially deserving of notice. Both agree in arranging the whole field of legal controversies under eighteen heads, and it appears from the introductory verses to several chapters (XII, 1; XIII, 1; XV, 1; XVI, 1; XVII, 1, &c.) that Br*i*haspati was anxious to discuss the eighteen titles of law in the same order as Manu. Nevertheless, he applies an interesting new principle of division to the eighteen titles of law by distinguishing fourteen titles relating to civil law, and four titles relating to criminal law (II, 3–9), and introduces a number of subdivisions (II, 2, 10; XVI, 1–3; XXII, 1, 2).

F o u r t h l y, Br*i*haspati declares emphatically that any Smr*i*ti text opposed to the teaching of Manu has no validity (XXVII, 4).

Result.

Under these circumstances the tradition preserved in the Skanda-purâ*n*a that there are four versions of the Code of Manu, by Bh*r*igu, Nârada, Br*i*haspati, and Añgiras, acquires a peculiar significance. Taking the version attributed to Bh*r*igu to be identical with the Code of Manu, the s o i - d i s a n t composition of Bh*r*igu, it is impossible to doubt its connexion with the Nârada[1] and Br*i*haspati Smr*i*tis. It is but natural to find, therefore, that Nârada and Br*i*haspati agree very closely i n t e r s e, as e.g. in adding a title called 'Miscellaneous' to Manu's eighteen titles of law (Br*i*haspati XXVII, 1), in enumerating and describing three sorts of proof, eleven or twelve kinds of witnesses, eight or ten 'members of a lawsuit,' four parts of a judicial proceeding, four sorts of answer in a suit,

[1] See above, Introduction to Nârada.

various 'defects of a plaint,' three kinds of officiating priests, four species of gifts, four divisions of violence (sâhasa), five modes of recovery of a debt, &c. Many other analogies between the two works may be gathered from a mere cursory comparison of their contents; they agree particularly in the use of many technical terms. One of these, the designation of a gold coin by the Roman or Greek term dînâra, i.e. denarius (X, 15), is an important test for the date of both works, and compels us to refer the earlier date of the composition of B*ri*haspati's law-book to the first century A.D., the period to which belong the earliest Indian coins corresponding in weight to the gold denarius of the Romans[1]. As regards the lower limit, one might feel inclined to assign an earlier date to B*ri*haspati than to Nârada, on the ground of his being a faithful follower of Manu in a far higher degree than is Nârada, who differs from Manu on such important points as the names and order of several titles of law, the legitimacy of the Niyoga, &c.[2] Nevertheless, the enlightened views of B*ri*haspati on the subject of women's rights[3], and the advanced character of his teaching generally, render it probable that his learned composition belongs to a somewhat more recent period than the Nârada-sm*ri*ti.

The fact that B*ri*haspati was considered an inspired writer by the very earliest commentators of law-books, such as e.g. by Medhâtithi (ninth century), proves him to have preceded those commentators by several centuries. An analogous result may be obtained by comparing the laws of B*ri*haspati with the corresponding portions of the Burmese Dhammathats, the Buddhist Indian originals of which, according to Dr. Forchhammer, were composed in the seventh, eighth, and ninth centuries. The coincidences between B*ri*haspati and the Dhammathats are both numerous and striking[4]. It may be added that

The Dhammathats.

[1] West and Bühler, Digest of the Hindu Law, I, p. 48; Jolly, Tagore Lect. p. 56.

[2] See above, Introduction to Nârada.

[3] Jolly, Tagore Lectures, pp. 193, 241.

[4] Several coincidences between B*ri*haspati and the Wagaru, the earliest law-book of Burma, have been collected by Dr. Forchhammer, Jardine Prize Essay, pp. 55, 57, 58. For other examples, see Dr. Forchhammer's edition of th Wagaru, pp. 12 (gifts), 36 (twelve witnesses), &c.

the judicial proceeding described in the well-known drama M*ri*kk*h*aka*t*ika corresponds to the rules laid down by B*ri*haspati, as has been shown elsewhere. For all these reasons, the composition of the B*ri*haspati-sm*ri*ti cannot be referred to a later period than the sixth or seventh century A.D.

Religious texts.

Hitherto, those texts of B*ri*haspati have been entirely left aside which relate to other parts of the sacred law than Civil and Criminal Law and Procedure. Hemâdri's *K*aturvarga*k*intâma*n*i, Devâ*nd*abha*tt*a's Sm*ri*ti*k*andrikâ, and most other standard Dharmanibandhas contain a number of texts of B*ri*haspati on Dâna, Vrata, Prâya*s*kitta, and all other parts of the religious law. However, an examination of these texts has yielded no definite result, and they are not sufficiently numerous by far to admit of reconstructing the purely religious portion of the ancient B*ri*haspati-sm*ri*ti from them. Nor is it at all improbable that the legal texts of B*ri*haspati may have formed an independent work from the outset, just like the Nârada-sm*ri*ti, or like the Burmese Dhammathats, in which forensic law was treated by itself, without any admixture of religious elements.

Arrangement.

The legal texts attributed to B*ri*haspati are so numerous as to make up in their entirety a law-book which contains a full exposition of forensic law, hardly inferior in size to the Nârada-sm*ri*ti. The principles on which the texts have been collected and arranged are the same as in the case of the Quotations from Nârada. The preservation of the introductory texts to several titles of law, and the occurrence of many long series of consecutive texts of B*ri*haspati in the Dharmanibandhas, facilitate considerably the task of arrangement, though the original position of many texts in B*ri*haspati's Dharma*s*âstra must needs remain doubtful. For the chapter on Inheritance the following other works have been used, besides those consulted for the Quotations from Nârada: G. Sarkar's translation of the Vîramitrodaya on Inheritance (V.); Dr. Burnell's Mâdhavîya and Varadarâ*g*a; Professor Bühler's edition of the U*gg*valâ of Haradatta; Haradatta's Gautamîyâ Mitâksharâ (MS.); Nandapa*nd*ita's Vai*g*ayantî (MS.).

B*RI*HASPATI.

I. Constitution of a Court of Justice.

1. In former ages men were strictly virtuous and devoid of mischievous propensities. Now that avarice and malice have taken possession of them, judicial proceedings have been established.

2. A judicial assembly is declared to be of four sorts: stationary, not stationary, furnished with (the king's) signet-ring, and directed (by the king). The judges are of as many sorts.

3. A stationary (court meets) in a town or village; one not stationary is called movable; one furnished with (the king's) signet-ring is superintended by the chief judge; one directed (by the king) is held in the king's presence.

4. The king, his chosen representative (the chief judge), the judges, the law (Sm*ri*ti), the accountant and scribe, gold, fire, water, and the king's own officer are ten members of legal procedure.

5. A court of justice is composed of these ten members; and a judicial assembly of this sort, in which the king examines causes attentively, is comparable to an act of religion.

I, 1. Vîram. p. 5. 2–10. Sm*ri*ti*k*.

2, 3. Aparârka. pratish*th*itâpratish*th*itâ mudritâ *s*âsitâ tathâ । *k*aturvidhâ sabhâ proktâ sabhyâ*s* *k*aiva tathâvidhâ*h* ॥ pratish*th*itâ pure grâme *k*alâ nâmâpratish*th*itâ । mudritâdhyakshasa*m*yutâ râga-yuktâ *k*a *s*âsitâ ॥ The Sm*ri*ti*k*andrikâ reads *s*âstritâ, 'governed by the science of law,' for *s*âsitâ, 'directed.'

4–10. Vîram. pp. 41, 42.

6. The office of these ten (members) is separately declared for each. The chief judge decides causes; the king inflicts punishments; the judges investigate the merits of the case.

7. The law furnishes the decree, whether victory or defeat; gold and fire serve the purpose of administering ordeals; water is required for persons suffering from thirst or hunger.

8. The accountant should compute the sum (in dispute); the scribe should record the proceedings; the king's own officer should compel the attendance of the defendant, assessors, and witnesses.

9. And he should constantly keep both the plaintiff and defendant in custody, if they have given no sureties. Of these members (of a court of justice) the king is the head; the chief judge is the mouth;

10. The judges are both arms; the law is both hands; the accountant and the scribe are the legs; gold, fire, and water are the eyes and the heart; and the king's own officer is the feet.

11. That judicial assembly is equal (in sanctity) to a sacrificial meeting in which there sit seven or five or three Brahmans, who are acquainted with the world, with (the contents of) the Veda, and with law.

12. In a controversy he examines the (plaint in) question and the answer; he speaks gently at first

---

11. M. Macn. I, 1, 11.

12. Vîram. p. 37. If the reading be correct, a double etymology of the term prâ*d*vivâka, 'a judge,' is propounded in this text: (1) he who asks or examines (p*rikkh*ati) and afterwards decides (vadati); (2) he who speaks gently at first (prâg vadati). There is another reading, pravadati for prâg vadati, under which the former etymology is the only one propounded in this text. It is beyond doubt the true etymology.

(prâg vadati). Therefore he is called Prâ*d*vivâka (judge).

13. Men qualified by the performance of devotional acts, strictly veracious and virtuous, void of wrath and covetousness, and familiar with (legal) lore, should be appointed by the ruler as judges (or assessors of the court).

14. Two persons thoroughly familiar with grammar and vocabulary, skilled in (the art of) computation, honest, and acquainted with various modes of writing, should be appointed by the king as accountant and scribe (respectively).

15. A veracious man, who pays obedience to the judges, should be appointed (by the king) as his own officer, to summon and to keep in custody the witnesses, plaintiff, and defendant.

16. The king should sit facing the east; the judges, facing the north; the accountant, facing the west; and the scribe, facing the south.

17. The king should cause gold, fire, water, and codes of the sacred law to be placed in the midst of them, also (other) holy and auspicious things.

18. In the middle of his fortress, he should build a house, with water and trees adjacent to it, apart (from other buildings), and let him use as court of justice (a room situated) on the eastern side of it, properly constituted and facing the east,

19. Furnished with garlands and with a throne,

---

13. Aparârka. sâdhukarmakriyâyuktâ*h* satyadharmaparâya*n*â*h* ı akrodhalobhâ*h* *s*âstra*gñ*â*h* sabhyâ*h* kâryâ mahîbhu*g*â ıı

14, 15. Vîram. p. 42. 15, 16. May. p. 4 (Mandlik).

17. Sm*ri*ti*k*. hira*n*yam agnim udaka*m* dharma*s*âstrâ*n*i *k*aiva hi ı tanmadhye sthâpayed râ*g*â pu*n*yâni *k*a hitâni *k*a ıı

18, 19. Vîram. p. 10. The epithet laksha*n*yâ*m*, 'properly con-

supplied with grain, (decorated) with jewels, adorned with statues, pictures, and images of deities, and (provided) with fire and water.

20. Let the king try causes, attended by three judges, after having entered the excellent judicial assembly, in a sitting or standing posture.

21. The king having risen early in the morning and performed ablutions according to rule, and having shown due honour to Gurus (persons entitled to respect), astronomers, physicians, deities, Brahmans, and domestic priests,

22. And having saluted the Gurus and the rest, should enter the court-room, decorated with flowers, ornaments, and (fine) clothes, with a cheerful countenance.

23. Having entered the judicial assembly in the forenoon, together with the seniors, ministers, and attendants, he should try causes and should listen to (the expositions of) the Purâ*n*as, codes of law, and rules of polity.

24. Let the king or a member of a twice-born caste officiating as chief judge try causes, acting on principles of equity, and abiding by the opinion of the judges, and by the doctrine of the sacred law.

---

stituted,' means 'constructed according to the rules of architecture.' Vîram.

20. Smr*i*ti*k*. râ*g*â kâryâ*n*i sa*m*pa*s*yet sabhyair eva tribhir v*ri*ta*h* \| sabhâ*m* eva pravi*s*yâgryâm âsîna*h* sthita eva vâ \|\| Nearly identical with Manu VIII, 10.

21, 22. Smr*i*ti*k*. prâtar utthâya n*ri*pati*h* *s*au*k*a*m* k*ri*tvâ vidhânata*h* \| gurû*ñ* *g*yotirvido vaidyân devân viprân purohitân \|\| yathârham etân sa*m*pû*g*ya sapushpâbhara*n*âmbara*h* \| abhivâdya *k*a gurvâdîn sumukha*h* pravi*s*et sabhâm \|\|

23. May. p. 5.

24. Smr*i*ti*k*. râ*g*â kâryâ*n*i sa*m*pa*s*yet prâ*d*vivâko*x*thavâ dvi*g*a*h* \| nyâyâ*ñg*âny agrata*h* k*ri*tvâ sabhya*s*âstramate sthita*h* \|\|

25. For persons roaming the forest, a court should be held in the forest; for warriors, in the camp; and for merchants, in the caravan.

26. Cultivators, artizans (such as carpenters or others), artists, money-lenders, companies (of tradesmen), dancers, persons wearing the token of a religious order (such as Pâ*s*upatas), and robbers should adjust their disputes according to the rules of their own profession.

27. (The king) should cause the disputes of ascetics and of persons versed in sorcery and witchcraft to be settled by persons familiar with the three Vedas only, and not (decide them) himself, for fear of rousing their resentment.

28. Relatives, companies (of artizans), assemblies (of co-habitants) and other persons duly authorized by the king, should decide lawsuits among men, excepting causes concerning violent crimes (sâhasa).

29. (Meetings of) kindred, companies (of artizans), assemblies (of co-habitants), and chief judges, are declared to be resorts for the passing of a sentence, to whom he whose cause has been previously tried may appeal in succession.

30. When a cause has not been (duly) investigated by (meetings of) kindred, it should be decided after due deliberation by companies (of artizans); when it has not been (duly) examined by companies (of artizans, it should be decided) by assemblies (of co-habitants); and when it has not been (sufficiently) made out by such assemblies, (it should be tried) by appointed (judges).

25. May. p. 4. 26, 27. Vîram. p. 30.
28–32. Vîram. p. 40.

31. Judges are superior in authority to (meetings of) kindred and the rest; the chief judge is placed above them; and the king is superior to all, because he passes just sentences.

32. The insight of princes surpasses by far the understandings (of other persons), in the decision of the highest, lowest, and middling controversies.

33. They who are ignorant of the customs of the country, unbelievers, despisers of the sacred books, insane, irate, avaricious, or troubled (by pain or illness) should not be consulted in the decision of a cause.

34. A Brahman is the root of the tree of justice; the sovereign prince is its stem and branches; the ministers are its leaves and blossoms; just government is its fruit.

35. Renown and wealth are the sap of its fruit; a dignified station, invincibility, esteem among men, and an eternal residence in paradise is enjoying its fruit.

36. Having recognised these advantages in (the pursuit of) justice, a king should be equitable towards litigants, and should pass a just sentence, discarding avarice and other (evil propensities).

II. General Rules of Procedure.

1. This legal procedure is declared, however, to be divided into a number of branches. Hear, now,

33. Smritik. desâkârânabhigñâ ye nâstikâh sâstravargitâh । unmattakruddhalubdhârtâ na prashtavyâ vinirnaye ॥

34–36. Vîram. p. 14. Read bhogo*tha grahapûganam in 35; vivâdinâm । tyaktvâ lobhâdikam râgâ dharmyam in 36.

II, 1, 2. Vîram. p. 292.

its various divisions which may become the causes of lawsuits.

2. I will proclaim in due order, according to truth, (the titles of law) beginning with the recovery of a debt and ending with (the title of) gambling with dice and betting on animals, as well as the subdivisions of the titles of law.

3. When a master pays wages to the labourers hired by him, for the purpose of doing work, and the labourers do not work, a lawsuit will arise in consequence.

4. When any man injures (another), or when he refuses to give what he ought to give: such are the two principal motives for going to law. Their subdivisions are manifold.

5. Lawsuits are of two kinds, according as they originate in (demands regarding) wealth or in injuries. Lawsuits originating in wealth are (divided again) into fourteen sorts; those originating in injuries are of four sorts.

6. Lending money at interest; deposits (and treasure-trove); (the title) called invalid gifts; concerns of a partnership; non-payment of wages; disobedience; disputes concerning land; sale without ownership;

7. Revocation of sale and purchase; breach of

3, 4. Smr*i*ti*k*. praya*kkh*e*k* *k*ed bhr*i*ti*m* svâmî bhr*i*tyânâ*m* karma kurvatâm | na kurvanti *k*a bhr*i*tyâ*s* *k*et tatra vâda*h* pravartate || hi*m*sâ*m* yo kurute ka*s**k*id deya*m* vâ na praya*kkh*ati | dve hi sthâne vivâdasya tayor bahutarâ gati*h* ||

5–9. Smr*i*ti*k*. dvipâdo vyavahâra*h* syâd dhanahi*m*sâsamudbhava*h* | dvisaptako-rthamûlas tu hi*m*sâmula*s* *k*aturvidha*h* || kusîdanidhyadeyâkhya*m* sa*m*bhûyotthânam eva *k*a | bhr*i*tyadânam a*s*u*s*rûshâ bhûvâdo-svâmivikraya*h* || krayavikrayânu*s*aya*h* samayâtikra-

agreements; the law between wife and husband; theft; the law of inheritance; and gambling with dice.

8. These are the fourteen titles of law that originate in (demands regarding) wealth. There are again various subdivisions of them, owing to the diversity of lawsuits.

9. The two kinds of insult; violence; and criminal connexion with the wife of another man: these have been declared by Brihaspati to be the four titles of law originating in injury.

10. Each of them embraces again several different kinds, according as they are of a superior, middling, or of the lowest description. Thus are those four subdivided each in its turn.

11. Those who understand the eighteen titles of law, as proclaimed in the law-books, to be at the root of all lawsuits, are intelligent men indeed.

12. No sentence should be passed merely according to the letter of the law. If a decision is arrived at without considering the circumstances of the case, violation of justice will be the result.

13. The issue of a lawsuit may convert a thief into an honest man, and an honourable man into an

mas tathâ । strîpuṃsayogaḥ steyaṃ ka dâyabhâgo-kshadevanam ॥ evam arthasamutthâni padâni tu katurdasa । punar eva prabhinnâni kriyâbhedâd anekadhâ ॥ pârushye dve sâhasas ka parastrîsaṃgrahas tathâ । hiṃsodbhavapadâny evaṃ katvâry âha brihaspatiḥ ॥

10, 11. Smritik. hînamadhyottamatvena prabhinnâni prithak prithak । visesha eshâṃ nirdishtas katurnâm apy anukramât ॥ padâny ashtâdasaitâni dharmasâstroditâni tu । mûlaṃ sarvavivâdânâṃ ye vidus te parîkshakâḥ ॥

12–14. Vîram. p. 18. See Nârada I, 1, 42, 71 (above, pp. 16, 23). For the story of Mândavya, who was falsely charged with theft, see ibid. p. 16, note.

offender. Mâ*nd*avya acquired the reputation of a thief in consequence of a decision passed without considering the circumstances of the case.

14. Dishonest men may seem honest, and honest men dishonest, so that wrong notions may be easily created; therefore sentences should be passed after due consideration of the circumstances only.

15. By killing an aggressor, a man does not commit sin by any means. He who takes the life of one approaching with intent to murder him is no offender.

16. If one abused returns the abuse, or if one struck strikes again, and kills the assailant, such a man commits no offence.

17. He who refrains from killing an aggressor who abuses him aloud, and is ready to murder him, (because the aggressor) is a virtuous man (otherwise) and practices regularly the recitation of the Veda, obtains the same reward as for performing a horse-sacrifice.

18. The judgment in a doubtful matter is declared to be of four sorts, according as it is based on moral law, or on the issue of the case, or on custom, or on an edict from the king.

19. Each of these has been declared to be twofold by the sages, owing to the diversity of legal affairs.

20. When the matter in dispute has been decided according to equity, after due deliberation, and

---

15. Vîram. p. 24. 16. Raghunandana, p. 9.

17. Vîram. p. 25.

18. Vîram. p. 8. See Nârada I, 1, 11 (above, p. 7).

19–24. Vîram. pp. 118, 119. I read, with Smr*i*tik., divyair vâ *s*odhita*h* in 21; pramâ*n*anis*k*ito in 22; and pramâ*n*arahitâ in 24.

20, 21. The first kind is when the truth has been duly ascer-

thoroughly examined by means of oaths (or ordeals), it should be known to be a judgment based on moral law.

21. When the defendant admits the accusation, or furnishes clear evidence of his innocence through performing an ordeal, it should be known to be another sort of a decision based on moral law.

22. A sentence founded on an examination of the evidence is termed (a decision based on) the issue of the case. When (the defendant) tells a lie, or makes no answer, it is also termed (a decision based on the issue of the case).

23. When a sentence is passed according to the inference (to be drawn from circumstantial evidence), it is termed (a decision based on) custom. When it is passed according to local usages, it is termed another sort (of a decision based on custom) by the learned in law.

24. A decision based on an edict from the king is ordained, first, for those cases in which no evidence is forthcoming. When the law-books or the judges are at variance with one another, the second sort (of this species of decisions) is said to be applicable.

25. When a sentence is passed exclusively according to the letter of the law, it should be con-

---

tained and a sentence passed accordingly. The second kind is when no examination of the facts takes place, the question being settled either through a confession on the part of the defendant, or through the performance of an ordeal. Smritikandrikâ.

22. The evidence here referred to can be human evidence only, i.e. the deposition of witnesses, documents, or possession, divine test being referred to in the two preceding texts. Smritik.

23. 'Inference,' such as when a man is caught with a firebrand in his hand. Smritik. See Nârada I, 18, 172–175 (above, pp. 85, 86).

25–27. Vîram. pp. 120, 121.

sidered as (a decision based on) the issue of the case. Moral law is overruled by it.

26. When a decision is passed in accordance with local custom, logic, or the opinion of the traders (living in that town), the issue of the case is overruled by it.

27. Where the king, disregarding established usage, passes a sentence (according to his own inclination), it is (called) an edict from the king, and local custom is overruled by it.

28. The time-honoured institutions of each country, caste, and family should be preserved intact; otherwise the people would rise in rebellion; the subjects would become disaffected towards their rulers; and the army and treasure would be destroyed.

29. The maternal uncle's daughter is taken in marriage among the twice-born inhabitants of the South. In the central country (Madhyade*s*a), they become labourers or artizans, and eat cows.

30. The inhabitants of the East are fish-eaters, and their women engage in promiscuous intercourse. In the North the women take intoxicating drinks, and in their courses have intercourse with men.

31. The people of Kha*s*a marry the widow of a brother who has died. These men are not subject to the performance of a penance or to punishment on account of any such offence.

32. Thus has legal procedure with its manifold

28–31. Vîram. p. 29; May. p. 5. I read pûrve for sarve in 30, with Mayûkha, Kalpataru, and other compilations. Baudhâyana I, 2, 1–7.

32. Sm*ri*ti*k*. eva*m* *k*ânekadhâ prokto vyavahâro manîshibhi*h* । tasyâ nir*n*ayak*ri*d râ*g*â brâhma*n*as *k*a bahu*s*ruta*h* ॥

ramifications been represented by the sages. The sentence in a legal controversy has to be passed by the king or by a Brahman thoroughly versed in the Veda.

33. Against whomsoever an accusation has been raised, whether founded on fact or on suspicion, let the king summon that man either through (a letter signed with) his seal or through an attendant.

34. For one timorous, or idiotic, or mad, or over-aged, and for women, boys, and sick persons, a kinsman or appointed agent should proffer the plaint or answer (as their representative).

35. When a man who has a family and relations does not appear before the court through pride after having been summoned, (the king or judge) should inflict on him punishment corresponding to the nature of the accusation.

36. (The plaintiff) is not permitted to put under restraint a person engaged in study; nor one about to marry; nor one sick; nor one afflicted by sorrow; nor one insane; nor an infant; nor one intoxicated; nor a very old man; nor one charged with a crime; nor one engaged in the king's service; nor one performing a vow;

37. Nor a soldier at the time of battle; nor a husbandman at the time of harvest; nor one in a perilous situation; nor a (respectable) woman; nor one not his own master.

38. A king thus obeying the dictates of law in passing sentences, acquires widespread renown in

---

33. Vîram. p. 52.
34. Vîram. p. 53.
35. May. p. 8.
36, 37. Vîram. p. 56.
38. Vîram. p. 125.

this world and becomes an associate of great Indra (after death).

39. He who effects a perfect cure, by the application of surgical instruments smeared with the ointment of law, of persons blinded by ignorance, and whose eyes are veiled with a mist of doubt,

40. Obtains fame and royal favours in this world and a residence in heaven. Therefore should a decision be passed for those who are blinded by doubt.

41. An officiating priest and one entrusted with the trial of causes are declared to be equal. In a sacrifice, the sacrificer acquires religious merit; in a lawsuit, (the parties obtain) defeat or victory.

42. He who, divesting himself of avarice, hatred, and other (evil propensities), passes sentences according to the dictates of law, obtains the same reward as for the performance of a sacrifice.

III. The Plaint.

1. The part called the declaration; the part called the answer; the part called the trial; and the part called the deliberation of the judges regarding the onus probandi: these are the four parts of a judicial proceeding.

2. The plaint is called the (first) part; the answer is the second part; the trial is the third part; and the judgment is the fourth part.

39, 40. Raghunandana, p. 3. I read svargati*m* for sadgati*m*, with Sm*ri*ti*k*.

41. Raghunandana, p. 7.

42. Sm*ri*ti*k*. lobhadveshâdika*m* tyaktvâ *ya*h kuryât kâryanir*n*ayam | *s*âstroditena vidhinâ tasya *yag*ñaphala*m* bhavet ||

III, 1, 2. Vîram. pp. 59, 60.

3. In the case of a denial, (a judicial proceeding) consists of four parts; likewise, in the case of a special plea; the same rule applies to a plea of former judgment; but in the case of a confession, it has two parts only.

4. When plaintiff and defendant come together, each claiming to be first, their declarations should be received in the order of their castes, or after considering their respective grievances.

5. Those acquainted with (the true nature of) a plaint declare that to be a (proper) plaint, which is free from the defects of a declaration, susceptible of proof, provided with good arguments, precise, and reasonable,

6. Brief in words, rich in contents, unambiguous, free from confusion, devoid of improper arguments, and capable of meeting opposite arguments;

7. When a plaint of this description has been proffered by the plaintiff, the defendant should tender an answer conformable to such plaint.

---

3. Vîram. p. 59.

4. Vîram. p. 60. 'When Brahmans and others have entered the judicial assembly simultaneously, the four parts of a judicial proceeding should be instituted in the order of their castes, the Brahman's cause being tried first of all by the king, then the Kshatriya's, and so on, in the order (of their castes). If the comparative importance or heaviness of the respective grievances of each party differs, the order in which the causes are tried is not made to depend either on the relative priority of each declaration, or on the respective caste of the parties. If they are all of equal caste, the relative priority of the declarations is taken into account. If the declarations have been simultaneous, and if the litigants are equal in caste, and their grievances are also equal, the order is made to depend on the choice of the judge and of the assessors of the court.' Vîram.

5-7. Raghunandana, p. 12.

8. The above and other qualities (of a plaint) having been duly considered, a plaint (containing them) may be regarded as a proper plaint; one not answering this description is a mere semblance of a plaint.

9. That (plaint) which (mentions an act that) has never been done by anybody is called impossible; one referring to a slight offence, or to a trifling sum, is called unmeaning; one in which neither a demand nor a grievance is referred to, should be known to be purposeless.

10. (Or) that plaint is unmeaning which does not concern one of the (fourteen) titles of law relating to the lending of money at interest and so forth; and that plaint is purposeless which does not concern one of the (four) titles of law relating to insult and so forth.

11. (When a claimant declares): This man is bound to give me a bow made of the horn of a hare, the wise declare such a plaint to be unreasonable and unsusceptible of proof.

12. When the interests of a town or kingdom are violated by bringing a certain plaint before a chief judge or before the king, it is termed a plaint contrary (to equity).

13. When a man, (whether) acting as plaintiff (or as defendant), is forsaken by his strength on being about to make a statement in a suit, it is proper

8. Smr*i*ti*k*. evamâdi gu*n*ân samyag âlokya *k*a munis*k*itam ı pakshah kritah samâdeyah pakshâbhâsas tv ato-nyathâ ıı

9. Vîram. p. 66.

10. Vîram. p. 67. Regarding the titles of law, see Br*i*haspati, II, 5–9.

11, 12. Vîram. p. 67.

13. Raghunandana, p. 11.

that a delay should be granted to him, according to circumstances and according to his ability.

14. Let him remove superfluous statements and amplify incomplete ones, and let him write down (everything) on the floor, till the (whole) matter has been definitely stated.

15. The plaintiff is at liberty to alter his declaration, when it is defective or redundant, till the defendant has tendered his answer in the presence of the judges.

16. When the plaintiff through timorousness does not dare to speak, it devolves on the judges to amend his declaration, according to the circumstances of the case.

17. A charge founded on suspicion, (one founded on) fact, a petition regarding the recovery of a debt, and claiming a fresh trial of a cause previously tried: thus a plaint is represented as fourfold.

18. The plaint is fourfold, and so is the answer; the judgment is declared to be of four kinds also; by some it is represented as being of eight sorts.

19. Suspicion is explained to mean doubt; fact is (said to be) an insight into the real nature of a matter; a petition regarding the recovery of a debt is (plea of) error; a fresh trial is the repetition of a previous trial.

IV. The Answer.

1. When the plaint has been well defined, a clear exposition given of what is claimed and what not, and the meaning of the plaint fully established, (the

14. Vîram. p. 70. 15. Raghunandana, p. 14.
16–19. Vîram. p. 71. IV, 1. Vîram. p. 72.

judge) shall then cause the answer to be written (by the defendant).

2. If the defendant does not make an answer fully meeting the contents of the plaint, he shall be compelled to pay by gentle remonstrances, and the other (two) methods (to be indicated directly).

3. Kindly speeches are gentle remonstrances; intimidation is pointing out dangers; force consists of depriving one of his property, or striking, or binding him.

4. When a man makes no answer, though both (mild and harsh methods) have been adopted against him, he is defeated, and liable to punishment after the lapse of a week.

5. When the defendant asks for a delay through (natural) timidity, or terror, or because his memory has been deranged, the delay shall be granted to him.

6. He should be allowed (a delay extending to) one day, or three days, or five days, or seven days, or a fortnight, or a month, or three seasons (equalling six months), or a year, according to his ability.

7. The insane and intoxicated, those abandoned by their relatives or friends, those charged with a heavy crime, idiots, persons cast off from society, and infants, should be considered unable to deliver an answer.

8. One should not cause to be written an answer

2–4. Vîram. p. 74. 5, 6. Vîram. p. 138.

7. *Tod.* unmattamattanirdhûtâ mahâpâtakadûshitâ*h* | ga*d*âpaviddhabâlâ*s* *k*a vig*ñ*eyâs te niruttarâ*h* || Such persons should appoint an agent to deliver the answer in their place. *Tod.*

8. Sm*ri*ti*k*. prastutânya*m* *k*a madhyastha*m* nyûnâdhikam asa*m*gatam | avyâpyasâra*m* sa*m*digdha*m* pratipaksha*m* na lekhayet ||

which wanders from the subject, or which is not to the point, too confined or too extensive, or not in conformity with the plaint, or not thorough enough, or absurd, or ambiguous.

9. If (the defendant) confesses, he shall state his confession; in the case of a denial, he shall cause (his denial) to be written; and so (should he record) his special plea in an answer by special plea, and his previous victory in an answer by previous victory.

10. A denial called forth by fear (of punishment) is contemptible in the eyes of men familiar with law; a true confession is declared to be meritorious.

11. In a plea by victory in a former trial, a true statement is praised by the virtuous; a false one is sinful and causes the defeat of the defendant.

V. The Trial.

1. When litigants are quarrelling in a court of justice, the judges, after examining the answer, shall adjudge the burden of proof to either of the two parties.

2. The judges having heard both the plaint and the answer, and determined to which party the burden of proof shall be adjudged, that person shall substantiate the whole of his declaration by documents or other proofs.

3. The plaintiff shall prove his declaration, and

9–11. *Tod.* tathye tathya*m* prayu*ñg*îta mithyâyâ*m k*âpi lekhayet । kâra*n*a*m* kâra*n*opete prâg*g*aye tu *g*aya*m* tathâ ॥ bhayad*ri*sh*t*odbhavâ mithyâ garhitâ *s*âstravedibhi*h* । satyâ sa*m*pratipattis tu dharmyâ sâ parikîrtitâ ॥ prâṅnyâyakara*n*e tathya*m* *s*lâghya*m* sadbhir udâh*ri*tam । viparîtam adharmya*m* syât pratyarthî hânim âpnuyât ॥

V, 1–3. Vîram. pp. 92, 93.

the defendant his special plea; victory in a previous trial shall be proved by a document recording that victory.

4. When people try to excite fear, or to cause dissension, or terror (among the judges or witnesses), or to throw (other) obstacles in their way, such litigants lose their suit.

5. One who absconds after receiving the summons; one who remains silent; one convicted (of a crime) by the (depositions of) witnesses; and one who admits the correctness of the charge: such are the four losers of their suit.

6. One who absconds loses the suit after three fortnights; one who remains silent, after a week; and one convicted by the witnesses, or confessing his crime, all at once.

7. He who announces witnesses and does not produce them afterwards, within thirty days or three fortnights, suffers defeat in consequence.

8. When a person has promised to appear at a trial or for the performance of an ordeal, and does not make his appearance, it must not be viewed as fraud.

9. If an obstacle caused by fate or the king should intervene during that time, he does not lose his cause through the mere non-observance of the fixed period.

10. Those (litigants) who make a private arrangement with one another, when the plaint and the

---

4. Vîram. p. 99.

5. Vîram. p. 102. 6, 7. Vîram. p. 102.

8. Vîram. p. 103. I read k*ri*tvopasthânanis*k*ayam | with Sm*ri*ti*k*andrikâ.

9. Vîram. p. 103. 10. Vîram. p. 103.

answer have been delivered, and the judgment is about to be given, shall be compelled to pay twice the amount (in dispute) as a fine.

11. When the plaint and the answer have been reduced to writing, and the trial has commenced, the two parties may be welded together like two pieces of red-hot iron.

12. While both parties are in suspense there regarding the (approaching declarations of the) witnesses and judges, those litigants are clever who arrive at a mutual understanding while the uncertainty lasts.

13. When the evidence is equally strong on both sides, and law and custom divided, in such a case a mutual reconciliation between the two parties through royal order is recommended.

14. Gain of religious merit and wealth, and renown accrues to the ruler from an equitable decision; the witnesses and assessors are exempt from censure, and enmity ceases,

15. When an unfavourable or a favourable decree, punishment or praise, renown or infamy has been obtained; whereas (continued) strife among men leads to sin.

16. Therefore should an intelligent (prince) enact that which has been propounded by dutiful and equitable associations, corporations, and chief judges, (in an impartial spirit) devoid of malice and avarice.

11–16. Vîram. p. 104. Read dvayo*h* sa*m*taptayo*h* in 11, with Sm*ri*ti*k*andrikâ.

12. The translation follows the gloss of the Kalpataru, as quoted in the Vîramitrodaya. The Ratnâkara (ibid.) translates the first half as follows: 'When the witnesses and judges are at variance with one another.'

17. Evidence is declared to be twofold, human and divine. Each of these is again divided into a number of branches by sages declaring the essence of things.

18. Human evidence is threefold, as it consists of witnesses, writings, and inference. Witnesses are of twelve sorts; writings are declared to be tenfold; inference is twofold; divine test is ninefold.

19. In the case of an answer of the first or third kinds, divine and human proof should be employed; but in the case of an answer of the fourth kind, an attested document recording the success of either party should be produced.

20. In the cases of a plea of former judgment and of a special plea, the defendant shall prove the contents of his answer; but in the case of a denial, the plaintiff shall prove the contents of the plaint.

VI. The Judgment.

1. He is said to have gained his cause in this world who has proved his claim, and has been honourably dismissed by the chief judge and the other judges, and received a document recording his victory.

2. Punishment corresponding to the nature of the offence shall be ordained there (in the decree).

17, 18. Vîram. p. 110.

19. Sm*ri*ti*k*. prathame vâ t*ri*tîye vâ pramâ*n*a*m* daivamânusham I uttare syâ*k* *k*aturthe tu sasâkshi *g*ayapattrakam II An answer of the first kind is a denial; an answer of the third kind is a confession; an answer of the fourth kind is a plea of former judgment.

20. Sm*ri*ti*k*. prâṅnyâye pratyavaskande pratyarthî sâdhayet svakam I uttarârtha*m* prati*gñ*ârtham arthî mithyottare puna*h* II

VI, 1. Raghunandana, p. 60. 2. Vîram. p. 124.

3. Whatever has been transacted in a suit, the plaint, answer, and so forth, as well as the gist of the trial, should be noted completely in the document recording the success (of the claimant or defendant).

4. When the king gives the victorious party a document recording the plaint, answer, and trial, and closing with the sentence, it is called a document recording the success (of either party).

5. When a man does not feel satisfied with a decision passed by meetings of kindred or other (resorts for the redress of wrongs), the king should revise the decision declared by them, and institute a fresh trial, if it should prove unjust.

6. After having considered the matter in common with many Brahmans well versed in science, he should punish the wicked men, who were acting as judges in the former trial, together with the victorious party.

7. One appointed by his master to look after his expenses and to superintend (transactions regarding) tillage, loans, and trade, is called a manager.

8. Whatever has been transacted by him is valid, whether relating to receipt, non-receipt, expenses or income, and whether it may have been transacted at home or abroad. The master must not annul such transactions as these.

3, 4. Raghunandana, p. 60. I read pûrvottarakriyâyukta*m* in 4.

5, 6. Vîram. p. 123.

7, 8. Vîram. p. 127. Read in 7, k*ri*shikusîdavâ*n*igye. These two texts relate to the subject of valid and invalid transactions, which is generally discussed along with the rules of judicial procedure, and with the onus probandi and judgment in particular. They might also have been inserted in the chapter on Master and Servant.

VII. Witnesses.

1. A subscribing witness, one caused to be written, a secret witness, one who has been reminded, a member of the family, a messenger, a spontaneous witness, an indirect witness, a stranger who has accidentally witnessed the deed,

2. The king, a chief judge, and the (people of the) village: thus have the twelve kinds of witnesses been declared. I am going to declare precisely in order their respective characteristics.

3. He is called a subscribing witness who enters in a deed his own as well as his father's caste, name, and so forth, and his place of residence.

4. He is termed one caused to be written, who has been distinctly entered in the deed, together with the details of the agreement, by the plaintiff when writing a contract of loan or another (contract).

5. He is called a secret witness who is made to listen to the speeches of the debtor, standing concealed behind a wall, (and relates them) just as they were spoken, (when the debtor tries to deny them.)

6. He is called one reminded who, after having been appointed and invited to be present at a transaction concerning a loan, deposit, purchase, or the like, is repeatedly reminded of it.

7. He is designed as a family witness who is appointed by both parties to witness a deed of partition, gift, or sale, being connected and on good

---

VII, 1, 2a. May. p. 23. 2b–15. Vîram. pp. 144, 145.

3. I read *g*âtinâmâdi, with Sm*ri*ti*k*andrikâ.

6. I read krayâdike, with Sm*ri*ti*k*andrikâ.

terms with both parties, and acquainted with (the rules of) duty.

8. He is denominated a messenger who is a respectable man, esteemed and appointed by both parties, and has come near to listen to the speeches of the plaintiff and defendant.

9. He is a spontaneous witness who declares that he has witnessed the transaction, after having approached the court of his own accord, while a cause is being heard.

10. That witness who communicates what he has heard to another man, at a time when he is about to go abroad, or lying on his deathbed, should be considered as an indirect witness.

11. He also is called an indirect witness who repeats, from his own hearing or from hearsay, the previous statements of actual witnesses.

12. He is called a secret witness to whom an affair has been entrusted or communicated by both parties, or who happens to witness the transaction.

13. The king in person having heard the speeches of plaintiff and defendant, may act as witness if both should quarrel with one another.

14. If after the decision of a suit a fresh trial should take place, the chief judge, together with the assessors, may act as a witness there, but not in any other case.

15. The (people of the) village may no doubt give testimony, even without a special appointment, as to what has been anywhere spoiled or damaged in the boundary line.

---

11. The reading bhâshatâm in the Vîramitrodaya is a misprint for bhâshate.

16. There should be nine, seven, five, four, or three witnesses; or two only, if they are learned Brahmans, are proper (to be examined); but let him never examine a single witness.

17. Of subscribing and secret witnesses, there should be two (of each sort); of spontaneous, reminded, family witnesses, and indirect witnesses, there should be three, four, or five (of each sort).

18. A single witness even may furnish valid proof, if he is a messenger, an accountant, one who has accidentally witnessed the transaction, or a king, or chief judge.

19. (A witness) should be exhorted by judges acquainted with law, by speeches extolling veracity and denouncing falsehood.

20. Whatever religious merit has been acquired by thee from the time of thy birth to the time of thy death, all that will be lost by thy telling a falsehood.

21. An iniquitous judge, a false witness, and the slayer of a Brahman are pronounced to be criminal in an equal degree; nor is a killer of an embryo or a destroyer of wealth considered as a greater sinner than they are.

22. Knowing this, a witness should give evidence according to truth.

16–18. May. p. 23. The 'accountant' is a species of 'messenger.' Vîramitrodaya. Regarding the 'witness who has accidentally witnessed the transaction,' see VII, 12.

19–22. *Tod.* satyapra*s*a*m*sâva*k*anair an*ri*tasyâpavâdanai*h* | sabhyai*h* sa bodhanîyas tu dharma*s*âstrapravedibhi*h* || â *g*anmata*s* *k*â mara*n*ât suk*ri*ta*m* yadupâr*g*itam | tat sarva*m* nâ*s*am âyâti an*ri*tasyâbhi*s*a*m*sanât || kû*t*asabhya*h* kû*t*asâkshî brahmahâ *k*a samâ*h* sm*ri*tâ*h* | bhrû*n*ahâ vittahâ *k*aishâ*m* nâdhika*h* samudâh*ri*ta*h* || eva*m* viditvâ tat sâkshî yathâbhûta*m* vadet tata*h* ||

23. After putting off his shoes and his turban, he should stretch out his right hand, and declare the truth, after taking in his hands gold, cow-dung, or blades of sacred grass.

24. When witnesses summoned (in a suit) are faulty, the opponent may expose them. But a litigant trying to cast a blemish on faultless witnesses is liable to pay a fine to the same amount (as the property in dispute).

25. Whatever faults there may be in a document or in witnesses, they should be exposed at the time of the trial; those cannot be used as valid objections which are declared afterwards.

26. He whose documents or witnesses are objected to in a suit, cannot gain his cause till he has removed the objections raised against it.

27. I will now state, according to the rules of science, which men may be appointed as witnesses, and which others should be avoided as being low wretches.

28. Those may be witnesses who are in the habit of performing religious ceremonies taught in the Vedas and Smritis, free from covetousness and malice, of respectable parentage, irreproachable, and zealous in performing austerities, practising liberality, and exhibiting sympathy (with all living creatures).

29. The mother's father, the father's brother, the

---

23. Vîram. p. 172.

24. May. p. 25. I read arthî, for arthe, with Vîram.

25. May. p. 26. 26. May. p. 27.

27. Smritik. prash*t*avyâ*h* sâkshi*n*o ye tu var*g*yâ*s* *k*aiva narâdhama*h* । tân aha*m* kathayishyâmi sâ*m*prata*m* *s*âstra*k*oditân ॥ *s*rautasmârtakriyâyuktâ lobhadveshavivar*g*itâ*h* । kulînâ*h* sâkshi*n*o *s*nindyâs tapodânadayânvitâ*h* ॥

29. May. p. 25.

wife's brother and maternal uncle, a brother, a friend, and a son-in-law are inadmissible witnesses in all disputes.

30. Persons addicted to adultery or to drinking, gamblers, those who calumniate everybody, the insane, the suffering, violent persons, and unbelievers cannot act as witnesses.

31. If a witness being summoned does not make his appearance, without being ill, he should be made to pay the debt and a fine, after the lapse of three fortnights.

32. Where the contents of the plaint have been fully corroborated by the witnesses, it is (valid) testimony; in every other case (the plaintiff) will not succeed with his claim.

33. When nothing less (than what has been declared in the plaint) is stated with regard to place, time, age, caste, number, matter, and quantity, the cause should be considered to have been proved.

34. Let him preserve, even by telling a lie, a Brahman who has once sinned through error and is in peril of his life and oppressed by rogues or other (enemies).

35. In a conflict between witnesses, (the testimony of) the majority should be received; when the number is equal (on both sides, the testimony of)

30. Vîram. p. 160.

31. Smr*i*ti*k*. âhûto yas tu nâga*kkh*et sâkshî rogavivargita*h* ı *rin*am dama*m* *k*a dâpya*h* syât tripakshât paratas tu sa*h* ıı

32. Smr*i*ti*k*. yatrâ*s*eshâ*h* prati*gñ*ârthâ*h* sâkshibhi*h* prativar*n*itâ*h* ı sâkshya*m* syâd anyathâ tu ta*m* sâdhyârtha*m* na samâpnuyât ıı

33. May. p. 29.

34. Smr*i*ti*k*. sakr*i*t pramâdâparâdhivipra*m* vyâpadi pî*d*itam ı *s*a*t*â-dibhir vadhyamâna*m* rakshed uktvânr*i*tâny api ıı

35. *Tod.* sâkshidvaidhe prabhûtâs tu grâhyâ*h* sâmye gu*n*âdhikâ*h* ı gu*n*idvaidhe kriyâyuktâs tatsâmye smr*i*timattarâ*h* ıı

the more virtuous ones; when the virtuous (witnesses) are divided, (the testimony of) those specially eminent for the performance of acts of religion; when they are divided, (the testimony of) those endowed with a superior memory.

VIII. Documents.

1. The rule regarding the number of witnesses and their respective characteristics has been thus communicated to you; now I will state in order the laws regarding documents.

2. Within a sixmonth's time even, doubts will arise among men (regarding a transaction). Therefore the letters occurring in a writing were invented of yore by the Creator.

3. Writings are declared to be of three kinds, those written by the king, those written in a particular place, and those written (by a person) with his own hand. Their subdivisions again are numerous.

4. Writings proceeding from (ordinary) people are sevenfold, (viz.) a deed of partition, of gift, of purchase, of mortgage, of agreement, of bondage, of debt, and other (such deeds). The king's edicts are of three sorts.

VIII, 1. Vîram. p. 188.

2. Vîram. p. 188. Hiouen-Thsang (I, 71), the celebrated Chinese pilgrim, reports the Indian tradition that letters were invented by the deity Fan (Brahman). See Führer, Lehre von den Schriften in Brihaspati's Dharmasâstra, p. 27; Nârada I, 5, 70 (above, p. 58).

3. May. p. 16. The term 'written in a particular place' seems to relate to documents written by a professional scribe and attested by subscribing witnesses. See Nârada I, 10, 135 (above, p. 75).

4. May. p. 17. The term âdi, 'and other (such deeds),' is explained to denote deeds of purification, or of reconciliation, or regarding a boundary, or the rules of a corporation.

5. Where brothers being divided in interests according to their own wish, make a deed of division among themselves, it is called a partition-deed.

6. When a person having made a grant of landed property, records it in a deed as being endurable as long as the moon and sun are in existence, and which must never be cut down or taken away, it is termed a deed of gift.

7. When a person having purchased a house, field or other (property), causes a document to be executed containing an exact statement of the proper price paid for it, it is called a deed of purchase.

8. When a person having pledged movable or immovable property, executes a deed stating whether (the property pledged) is to be preserved, or used, it is termed a mortgage-deed.

9. When (the people of) a village or province execute a deed of mutual agreement, (the purpose of) which is not opposed to the interests of the king, and in accordance with sacred law, it is designed as a deed of agreement.

10. That document which a person destitute of clothes and food executes in a wilderness stating, 'I will do your work,' is termed a deed of bondage.

11. That contract of debt which a man having borrowed money at interest executes himself or causes to be written (by another), is called a bond of debt by the wise.

12. Having given a tract of land or the like, the

5–11. May. p. 16.

12–18. Vîram. p. 192. For specimens of royal grants precisely corresponding to the rules laid down here, see e.g. Dr. Burnell's Elements of South Indian Palaeography, pp. 87 foll.

king should cause a formal grant to be executed on a copper-plate or a piece of cloth, stating the place, the ancestors (of the king), and other particulars,

13. And the names of (the king's) mother and father, and of the king himself, (and containing the statement that) 'This grant has been made by me to-day to N. N., the son of N. N., who belongs to the Vedic school N. N.

14. As being endurable while the moon and sun last, and as descending by right of inheritance to the son, grandson, and more remote descendants, and as a gift which must never be cut down or taken away, and is entirely exempt from diminution (by the allotment of shares to the king's attendants, and so forth),

15. Conveying paradise on the giver and preserver, and hell on the taker, for a period of sixty thousand years, as the recompense for giving and taking (the land).'

16. (Thus the king should declare in the grant), the Secretaries for peace and war signing the grant with the remark, 'I know this.'

17. (The grant) should be provided with (the king's) own seal, and with a precise statement of the year, month and so forth, of the value (of the donation), and of the magistrate. Such a document issued by the king is called a royal edict.

18. When the king, satisfied with the faithful services, valour or other (laudable qualities) of a person, bestows landed or other property on him, it

---

13. All commentators explain that the name of the particular Veda, such as e. g. the Rig-veda, or the Ka*th*a branch of the Yagur-veda, should be given which the donee is studying.

is (called) a writing containing a mark of royal favour.

19. That which establishes a claim, recording the four parts of a judicial proceeding and bearing the royal seal, is termed a document of success (or decree).

20. Clever forgers acquainted with place and time will make a writing similar (to the original document). Such (writings) should be examined with great care.

21. Women, infants, the suffering, and persons unacquainted with the art of writing, are deceived by their own relations fabricating documents signed with their names. Such (forgery) may be found out by means of internal evidence and legitimate titles.

22. A document executed by a madman, an idiot, an infant, one who has absconded through fear of the king, a bashful person, or one tormented by fear, is not invalidated (by an impossibility to produce its author).

23. (But, as a rule) a document executed by a dying person, an enemy, one oppressed with fear, a suffering person, a woman, one intoxicated, distressed by a calamity, at night, by fraud, or by force, does not hold good.

24. Where even a single witness entered in a deed is infamous and reproached (by the public voice), or where its writer is held in such estimation, it is called a false document.

---

19. Sm*ri*ti*k*., quoted by Burnell, Elements of South Indian Palaeography, p. 100.

20, 21. Vîram. p. 197.

22. Vîram. p. 198. The translation follows the gloss in the Vîramitrodaya.

23, 24. May. p. 20.

25. A writing being spoiled by fire, or executed a long time ago, or soiled with dirt, or intended for a very short period only, or containing (a number of) mutilated or effaced syllables, is reckoned as a false document.

26. Let a man show (a document) on every occasion to (meetings of) families, associations (of traders), assemblies (of cohabitants), and other (bodies of persons), and read it out to them, and remind them of it, in order to establish its validity.

27. The acquirer (of landed or other property) should establish the written title (under which he is holding it); his son should establish the fact of possession only. If (the father) has been impeached in a court of justice, the son also should be required to prove the written title.

28. When a loan (recorded in a bond) is not expressly claimed from a debtor who has means enough (to discharge it) and is at hand, the bond loses its validity, as the debt is presumed to have been paid (in that case).

29. A writing which has neither been seen nor read out for thirty years, should not be recognised as valid, even though the (subscribing) witnesses be living.

30. When a man does not produce the bond and omits to ask his debtor (to restore the loan), after

---

25. Aparârka and Smr*i*tik., quoted by Führer, No. 29.

26. Vîram. p. 200. 27. Vîram. p. 199.

28–30. Aparârka, quoted by Führer, loc. cit., Nos. 33–35; Smr*i*tik. ('Kâtyâyana'); *Tod.* In 28, I read *s*uddhar*n*asaṅkayâ, for *s*uddha*m* nâ*s*aṅkayâ, with *Tod*arânanda.

30. The interest on a loan, according to the Indian Law of Debt, ceases on its becoming equal to the principal.

his loan has ceased to yield interest, the bond becomes suspected.

31. A document is certainly not overruled either by witnesses or by an oath (or ordeal), but its validity is diminished by neglect, if it is neither shown nor read.

IX. Possession.

1. This set of rules regarding witnesses and documents has been propounded. The law concerning the acquisition of immovable property and possession will be proclaimed next.

2. Immovable property may be acquired in seven different ways, viz. by learning, by purchase, by mortgaging, by valour, with a wife (as her dowry), by inheritance (from an ancestor), and by succession to the property of a kinsman who has no issue.

3. In the case of property acquired by one of these seven methods, viz. inheritance from a father (or other ancestor), acquisition (in the shape of a dowry), purchase, hypothecation, succession, valour, or learned knowledge, possession coupled with a legitimate title constitutes proprietary right.

4. That possession which is hereditary, or founded on a royal order, or coupled with purchase, hypothecation or a legitimate title: possession of this kind constitutes proprietary right.

---

31. Smritik. and Aparârka, quoted by Führer, No. 38.

IX, 1-7. Vîram. pp. 203, 204.

1. The Vîramitrodaya argues that, although immovable property is principally referred to, the same law applies a fortiori to movable property.

5. Immovable property obtained by a division (of the estate among co-heirs), or by purchase, or inherited from a father (or other ancestor), or presented by the king, is acknowledged as one's lawful property; it is lost by forbearance in the case of adverse possession.

6. He who is holding possession (of an estate) after having merely taken it, occupying it without meeting with resistance, becomes its legitimate owner thus; and it is lost (to the owner) by such forbearance.

7. He whose possession has been continuous from the time of occupation, and has never been interrupted for a period of thirty years, cannot be deprived of such property.

8. That property which is publicly given by co-heirs or others to a stranger who is enjoying it, cannot be recovered afterwards by him (who is its legitimate owner).

9. He who does not raise a protest when a stranger is giving away (his) landed property in his sight, cannot again recover that estate, even though he be possessed of a written title to it.

10. Possession held by three generations produces ownership for strangers, no doubt, when they are related to one another in the degree of a Sapi*nd*a; it does not stand good in the case of Sakulyas.

11. A house, field, commodity or other property having been held by another person than the owner,

5, 6. Col. Dig. V, 6, 384. 8, 9. Vîram. p. 209.

10–12. Col. Dig. V, 7, 396.

10–14. Vîram. p. 221. Sapi*nd*aship in this rule includes four generations; the term Sakulya is used to denote more remote relations.

is not lost (to the owner) by mere force of possession, if the possessor stands to him in the relation of a friend, relative, or kinsman.

12. Such wealth as is possessed by a son-in-law, a learned Brahman, or by the king or his ministers, does not become legitimate property for them after the lapse of a very long period even.

13. Forcible means must not be resorted to by the present occupant or his son, in maintaining possession of the property of an infant, or of a learned Brahman, or of that which has been legitimately inherited from a father,

14. Nor (in maintaining possession) of cattle, a woman, a slave, or other (property). This is a legal rule.

15. If a doubt should arise in regard to a house or field, of which its occupant has not held possession uninterruptedly, he should undertake to prove (his enjoyment of it) by means of documents, (the depositions of) persons knowing him as possessor, and witnesses.

16. Those are witnesses in a contest of this kind who know the name, the boundary, the title (of acquisition), the quantity, the time, the quarter of the sky, and the reason why possession has been interrupted.

17. By such means should a question regarding occupation and possession be decided in a contest concerning landed property; but in a cause in which

15–17. Vîram. p. 222.

16. Read nâmâghâ*t*âgama*m*. 'The title,' the cause of ownership, such as gift. 'The quantity,' of land. 'The quarter of the sky,' a description of the region in which a certain estate is situated. 'The time,' at which the estate was acquired. *Tod*arânanda.

no (human) evidence is forthcoming, divine test should be resorted to.

18. When a village, field, or garden is referred to in one and the same grant, they are (considered to be) possessed of all of them, though possession be held of part of them only. (On the other hand) that title has no force which is not accompanied by a slight measure of possession even.

19. Not to possess landed property, not to show a document in the proper time, and not to remind witnesses (of their deposition): this is the way to lose one's property.

20. Therefore evidence should be preserved carefully; if this be done, lawsuits whether relating to immovable or to movable property are sure to succeed.

21. Female slaves can never be acquired by possession, without a written title; nor (does possession create ownership) in the case of property belonging to a king, or to a learned Brahman, or to an idiot, or infant.

22. It is not by mere force of possession that land becomes a man's property; a legitimate title also having been proved, it is converted into property by both (possession and title), but not otherwise.

---

18. Vîram. pp. 221, 222; Col. Dig. V, 6, 383.

19, 20. *Tod.* bhûmer abhuktir lekhyasya yathâkâlam adar*s*anam । asmâra*n*am sâkshi*n*âm *k*a svârthahânikarâ*n*i *k*a ॥ tasmâd yatnena kartavya*m* pramâ*n*aparipâlanam । tena kâryâ*n*i sidhyanti sthâvarâ*n*i *k*arâ*n*i *k*a ॥

21. Sm*ri*ti*k*. na strî*n*âm upabhoga*h* syâd vinâ lekhya*m* katha*m*-*k*ana । râga*s*rotriyavitte *k*a *g*a*d*abâladhane tathâ ॥

22. Sm*ri*ti*k*. bhuktikevalayâ naiva bhûmi*h* siddhim avâpnuyât । âgamenâpi *s*uddhena dvâbhyâ*m* sidhyati nânyathâ ॥

23. Should even the father, grandfather, and great-grandfather of a man be alive, land having been possessed by him for thirty years, without intervention of strangers,

24. It should be considered as possession extending over one generation; possession continued for twice that period (is called possession) extending over two generations; possession continued for three times that period (is called possession) extending over three generations. (Possession continued) longer than that even, is (called) possession of long standing.

25. When the present occupant is impeached, a document or witness is (considered as) decisive. When he is no longer in existence, possession alone is decisive for his sons.

26. When possession extending over three generations has descended to the fourth generation, it becomes legitimate possession, and a title must never be inquired for.

27. When possession undisturbed (by others) has been held by three generations (in succession), it is not necessary to produce a title; possession is decisive in that case.

28. In suits regarding immovable property, (pos-

23, 24. Sm*ri*ti*k*. pitâ pitâmaho yasya *g*îve*k* *k*a prapitâmaha*h* ı tri*m*sat samâ yâ tu bhuktâ bhûmir avyâhatâ parai*h* ıı bhukti*h* sâ paurushî *gñ*eyâ dvigu*n*â *k*a dvipaurushî ı tripaurushî *k*a trigu*n*â parata*h* syâ*k* *k*irantanî ıı

25. Sm*ri*ti*k*. yatrâhartâbhiyukta*h* syâl lekhya*m* sâkshî tadâ guru*h* ı tadabhâve tu putrâ*n*â*m* bhuktir ekâ garîyasî ıı

26. Sm*ri*ti*k*. bhuktis tripurushî yâ *k*a *k*aturthe sampravartitâ ı tad bhogasthiratâ*m* yâti na p*rikkh*ed âgama*m* kva*k*it ıı

27. Sm*ri*ti*k*. anishedhena yad bhukta*m* purushais tribhir eva tu ı tatra naivâgama*h* kâryo bhuktis tatra garîyasî ıı

28. Sm*ri*ti*k*. sthâvareshu vivâdeshu kramât tripurushî *k*a yâ ı svatântraiva hi sâ *gñ*eyâ pramâ*n*a*m* sâdhyanir*n*aye ıı

session) held by three generations in succession, should be considered as valid, and makes evidence in the decision of a cause.

29. He whose possession has passed through three lives, and is duly substantiated by a written title, cannot be deprived of it; such possession is equal to the gift of the Veda.

30. He whose possession has passed through three lives and has been inherited from his ancestors, cannot be deprived of it, unless a previous grant should be in existence (in which the same property has been granted to a different person by the king).

31. That possession is valid in law which is uninterrupted and of long standing; interrupted possession even is (recognised as valid), if it has been substantiated by an ancestor.

32. A witness prevails over inference; a writing prevails over witnesses; undisturbed possession which has passed through three lives prevails over both.

33. When an event (forming the subject of a plaint) has occurred long ago, and no witnesses are forthcoming, he should examine indirect witnesses, or he should administer oaths, or should try artifice.

---

29. Sm*ri*ti*k*. yasya tripurushâ bhukti*h* samyag lekhyasamanvitâ । eva*m*vidhâ brahmadeyâ hartu*m* tasya na *s*akyate ॥ The 'gift of the Veda,' i. e. instruction is mentioned as an instance of an inalienable gift.

30. Sm*ri*ti*k*. yasya tripurushâ bhukti*h* pâra*m*paryakramâgatâ । na sâ *k*âlayitu*m* *s*akyâ pûrvakâ*k* *kh*âsanâd *ri*te ॥

31. Sm*ri*ti*k*. bhuktir balavatî *s*âstre-py avi*kkh*innâ *k*irantanî । vi*kkh*innâpi hi sâ *gñ*eyâ yâ tu pûrvaprasâdhitâ ॥ 'If it has been substantiated by an ancestor,' i. e. if a previous possessor has adduced a legitimate title.

32. Raghunandana, p. 49. 33. Vîram. p. 223.

X. Ordeals.

1. A forger of gems, pearl, or coral, one withholding a deposit, a ruffian, and an adulterer, shall be tested by oaths or ordeals in every case.

2. In charges relating to a heavy crime or to the appropriation of a deposit, the king should try the cause by ordeals, even though there be witnesses.

3. When a thing has happened long ago or in secret, or when the witnesses have disappeared long ago, or are perjured all of them, the trial should be conducted by having recourse to an ordeal.

4. The balance, fire, water, poison, and, fifthly, sacred libation; sixthly, grains of rice; seventhly, a hot piece of gold, are declared (to be ordeals).

5. The ploughshare is mentioned as the eighth kind, the ordeal by Dharma (and Adharma) as the ninth. All these ordeals have been ordained by the Self-existent (Brahman).

6. Truth, a vehicle, weapons, cows, seeds, and gold, venerable gods or Brahmans, the heads of sons or wives:

7. By these have oaths been ordained, which are easy to perform and proper for trifling occasions.

8. When a quarrel between two litigants has arisen regarding a debt or other charge, that ordeal

---

X, 1–3. Vîram. p. 114.

4. M. Macn. X, 1, 2 (uncertain); Vîram. p. 225.

5. Vîram. p. 225. For a description of the ordeal by Dharma and Adharma, see the laws of Pitâmaha.

6, 7. Vîram. p. 226. See Manu VIII, 114; Nârada I, 19, 248 (above, p. 100).

8. *Tod.* *ri*n*âdishu tu kâryeshu visa*m*vâde parasparam । divya*m* sa*m*khyânvita*m* deya*m* purushâpekshayâ tathâ ॥

must be administered which corresponds to the amount (of the sum in dispute) and to the (character or strength of the) individual (to be examined).

9. (The ordeal by) poison should be administered when (property worth) a thousand (Panas) has been stolen; (the ordeal by) fire, when a quarter less than that (or 750, has been stolen).

10. When the charge concerns four hundred, the hot piece of gold should be administered. (When it concerns) three hundred, the grains of rice should be given; and the sacred libation, (when it concerns) half of that.

11. When a hundred has been stolen or falsely denied, purgation by Dharma should be administered. Thieves of cows should be subjected by preference to the (ordeal by the) ploughshare by the judges.

12. These figures are applicable in the case of low persons; for persons of a middling kind, double is ordained; and for persons of the highest rank, the amount has to be fixed four times as high by persons entrusted with judicial affairs.

13. The quantities (of various coins or weights), beginning with a floating particle of dust and ending with a Kârshâpana, have been declared by Manu. They are applicable both to ordeals and to fines.

14. A Nishka is four Suvarnas. A Pana of

9–12. Vîram. p. 230. I read, with Smritik., katuhsatâbhiyoge in 10, and sabhyaih phâlam prayatnatah in 11.

11. Dharma, 'test of right and wrong,' is the ordeal which consists of drawing lots or slips of white and black paper.

12. 'Eminent persons,' through their birth, qualities, or virtue. The same interpretation applies to the two other terms. Vîram.

13. Vîram. p. 233. See Manu VIII, 131–138.

14, 15. Viram. p. 234. I read kândikâ for kândrikâ in 11, with Vîramitrodaya.

copper is a Kârshika (having the weight of one Karsha). A coin made of a Karsha of copper has to be known as a Kârshika Pa*n*a.

15. It is also called an A*nd*ikâ. Four such are a Dhânaka. Twelve of the latter are a Suvar*n*a. That is also called a Dînâra (denarius).

16. (The testimony of) witnesses is apt to become invalid, whether it be through affection, anger, or avarice. An ordeal properly administered never loses its validity.

17. When a doubt arises with regard to a document or oral evidence, and when ratiocination also fails, purgation through ordeal (is the proper test).

18. Let an ordeal be administered according to the established rule by persons acquainted with the rule of ordeals. If it is administered against the rule, it is ineffective as a means of proving what ought to be proved.

19. If one who has been subjected to the ordeal by balance goes down on being weighed (for the second time), he shall be held guilty. If he remains level, he shall be balanced once more. If he rises, he gains his cause.

20. Should the scale break, or the balance, or beam, or iron hooks split, or the strings burst, or the transverse beam split, he would have to be declared guilty.

---

15. Nearly identical with Nârada, Appendix, 62 (p. 232).

16. Vîram. p. 242.

17. Smri*t*i*k*. likhite sâkshivâde *k*a sa*m*deho yatra *g*âyate I anumâne *k*a sa*m*bhrânte tatra daiva*m* vi*s*odhanam II

18. *Tod*. yathoktavidhinâ deya*m* divya*m* divyavi*s*âradai*h* I ayathoktapradatta*m* tu na satya*m* sâdhyasâdhane II

19. Vîram. p. 253. 20. Vîram. p. 254.

21. (In the ordeal by water) he should immerse the individual in water and discharge three arrows.

22. He is acquitted (in the ordeal by poison) who has digested poison, which has been given to him according to rule, without the application of spells or antidotes. Otherwise he should be punished and compelled to pay the sum in dispute.

23. To whatsoever deity the accused happens to be devoted, let (the judge) bathe the weapon of that deity in water, and give him to drink three handfuls of it.

24. He to whom no calamity happens, within a week or a fortnight, (either to himself or) to his son, wife or property, is innocent beyond doubt.

25. Let a man chew grains of rice after having kept a fast and purified himself, at a time when the sun is not visible. He is acquitted if what he spits out is pure; but if it be mixed with blood, he must be (held) guilty.

26. Let (the person) take a hot piece of gold out of (a mixture of) well-heated oil and butter.

27. He whose fingers' ends do not tremble, and who does not become blistered, is acquitted according to law, as has been declared by Pitâmaha.

28. Iron twelve Palas in weight should be formed into what is called a ploughshare. It should be eight Aṅgulas long by four Aṅgulas broad.

---

21. Vîram. p. 271. 22. Vîram. p. 276.

23. Vîram. p. 280. 24. Vîram. p. 281.

25. Vîram. p. 282. The *Tod*arânanda attributes to B*ri*haspati another text identical with Nârada I, 25, 342 (above, p. 119).

26. Vîram. p. 283.

27. Vîram. p. 284. The same text occurs in the Nepalese Nârada.

28, 29. Vîram. p. 285. Some texts relating to this kind of

29. (The ploughshare) having been made red-hot in fire, a thief should be made to lick at it once with his tongue. If he is not burnt, he obtains acquittal. Otherwise he loses his cause.

30. (Images of) Dharma and Adharma, one black and the other white, should be painted on two leaves. Then they should be invoked with prayers producing life or others, and with the Gâyatrî or other Sâmans,

31. And should be worshipped with perfumes and with white and black flowers, sprinkled with the five products of a cow, and enclosed in balls made of earth afterwards.

32. After having been made equal in size, they should be placed unobserved in a fresh jar. Then the person should take one ball out of the vessel at the bidding (of the judge).

33. If he takes out Dharma, he is acquitted, and should be honoured by the (appointed) examiners.

XI. The Law of Debt.

1. A creditor should never lend money without having first secured a pledge of adequate value, or a

ordeal are found in the Nepalese Nârada as well, but they are very incorrectly given in the MS. 'The judge, after having placed a ploughshare of the size stated in the text into a fire kindled for that purpose, should perform the whole general rite of ordeals, beginning with the invocation addressed to Dharma and ending with the fixing of a writing on the head of the person. Then, after addressing the fire with the text previously quoted (of Pitâmaha), "Thou, O Agni," &c., and after causing the person to address the fire with the text previously quoted, "Thou, O Agni, (livest) in all beings" (Yâ*gñ*avalkya II, 104), he should cause the person to lick (at the ploughshare).' Vîram., Sm*ri*ti*k*.

30–33. Vîram. p. 286. 'Prayers producing life,' such as e.g. Rig-veda X, 57, 1; Vîram.

XI, 1. May. p. 102; Col. Dig. I, 1, 11. The commentators agree

deposit, or a trustworthy surety; nor without a bond written (by the debtor himself) or attested (by subscribing witnesses).

2. That (loan) is termed kusîda (a loan on interest) which is exacted by persons apprehending no sin (from the act), from a mean (kutsita) or wretched (sîdat) man, after having been increased to four or eight times the original amount (through the interest accruing on it).

3. An eightieth part (of the principal) accrues as interest on it (every month); and it is certainly doubled by such interest within a third of a year less than seven years (that is to say, within six years and eight months).

4. Interest is declared (by some) to be of four

in explaining the term âdhi, 'a pledge,' as denoting a pledge to be used, such as e.g. a cow to be used with her milk, or landed property pledged together with its produce. The term bandha, 'a deposit,' is supposed to denote a pledge which must not be used; according to the Mayûkha, however, it means a pledge which is not actually delivered to the creditor, the debtor merely promising not to alienate it. 'A pledge of adequate value' is one corresponding in value to the principal together with the interest. Vîram. p. 293. The term sâkshimat, 'attested,' is referred to a debt contracted orally before witnesses, both by Colebrooke (Dig. I, 1, 11) and Mandlik (May. loc. cit.). This, however, is opposed to the gloss of the Vîramitrodaya.

2. May. p. 102; Col. Dig. I, 1, 3. It is hardly necessary to point out that the etymology here proposed of the term kusîda, 'a loan on interest,' is entirely fanciful. It is really derived from ku and sîda, and denotes 'that which adheres closely, and cannot easily be got rid of.' The commentators explain the clause 'apprehending no sin' to imply that it is sinful otherwise to accept a gift from an unworthy person.

3. Smr*i*ti*k*.; Col. Dig. I, 2, 26. a*s*îtibhâgo vardheta lâbhe dvigu*n*atâm iyât | prayukta*m* saptabhir varshais tribhâgonair na sa*m*-*s*aya*h* ||

4–8. Vîram. pp. 294, 295; Col. Dig. I, 2, 35.

sorts; by others, it is stated to be fivefold; and by others again, it is said to be of six kinds. Learn their (various) qualities.

5. Kâyikâ (bodily interest); kâlikâ (periodical interest); *k*akravr*i*ddhi (compound interest); kâritâ (stipulated interest); *s*ikhâvr*i*ddhi (hair-interest); and bhogalâbha (interest by enjoyment): such are the six kinds of interest.

6. Kâyikâ interest is connected with bodily labour; kâlikâ is due every month; *k*akravr*i*ddhi is interest on interest; kâritâ is interest promised by the borrower.

7, 8. When interest is received every day, it is termed *s*ikhâvr*i*ddhi (hair-interest, because it grows every day). Because it grows constantly like hair, and does not cease growing except on the loss of the head, that is to say, on payment of the principal, therefore it is called hair-interest. The use of a (mortgaged) house, or the produce of a field, is termed bhogalâbha (interest by enjoyment).

9. That kâritâ (stipulated) interest has to be paid always, which has been stipulated by the debtor himself, over and above (the ordinary rate of interest), and has been promised in times of distress.

10. When (such special) interest has been stipulated in any other manner, it must not be paid by any means.

11. Hair-interest, bodily interest, and interest by

6. 'Bodily labour,' when the milk of a pledged cow or the strength of a pledged animal for draught or burden is used by the creditor, being, as it were, the interest on his loan. Vîram.

9, 10. Vîram. p. 295; Col. Dig. I, 2, 37 ('Kâtyâyana').

10. 'In any other manner,' i.e. by the creditor. Vîram.

11. Vîram. p. 301; Col. Dig. I, 2, 35.

enjoyment shall be taken by the creditor so long as the principal remains unpaid.

12. But the use of a pledge after twice the principal has been realised from it, compound interest, and the exaction of the principal and interest (together as principal) is usury and reprehensible.

13. On gold (and other precious metals), the interest may make (the debt) double; on clothes and base metals (such as tin or lead), treble; on grain, it is allowed to rise to four times the original amount, and so on edible plants (or fruit), beasts of burden, and wool.

14. It is allowed to make (the debt) quintuple, on pot-herbs; sextuple, on seeds and sugar-cane; and it may make (the debt) octuple, on salt, oil, and spirituous liquor.

15. Likewise, on sugar and honey, if the loan be of old standing.

16. On grass, wood, bricks, thread, substances from which spirits may be extracted, leaves, bones, leather, weapons, flowers, and fruits, no interest is ordained.

17. A pledge is termed bandha, and is declared to

---

12. Viv. p. 12; Col. Dig. loc. cit.

13–16. Vîram. pp. 298, 300; Viv. pp. 17, 18; May. p. 104; Çol. Dig. I, 2, 63, 67, 69.

13. The Vîramitrodaya reads *k*armâsthivarma*n*âm, 'leather, bones, and armour.'

16. The commentators observe that no interest should be exacted, unless there be a special agreement to the purpose. There is, however, another reading (v*ri*ddhis tu na nivartate), under which the purport of this rule becomes quite different, viz. that there is absolutely no limit regarding the interest on the articles mentioned in it. This version is in harmony with the corresponding regulations of other legislators.

17. Col. Dig. I, 3, 80; May. p. 105; Vîram. p. 305.

be of four sorts; movable or immovable; to be kept only or to be used; to be released at any time, or limited as to time; stated in writing, or stipulated (orally) before witnesses.

18. Should the creditor, actuated by avarice, use a pledge before interest has ceased to accrue on the loan (on becoming equal to the principal), or before the fixed period has expired, such use shall be stopped.

19. The pledge has to be kept carefully, like a deposit; interest is forfeited in case of its being damaged.

20. A pledge having been used and rendered worthless (by such use), the principal (itself) is lost; if a very valuable pledge be spoiled, he must satisfy the pledger.

21. If a pledge be destroyed by a fatal accident or by an act of the king, the debtor shall be caused either to deliver another pledge or to pay the debt.

22. When the debtor restores the principal and asks for his pledge, it must be restored to him; otherwise the creditor is liable to punishment.

18, 19. Col. Dig. I, 3, 92; Vîram. p. 306.

20. Col. Dig. I, 3, 86; Vîram. p. 309; May. p. 105.

21. Col. Dig. I, 3, 93; May. p. 105; Vîram. p. 309. This text has been translated according to the Vîramitrodaya. Under the reading of the other compilations, payment of the debt together with interest is enjoined. 'A king,' i.e. a ruler who offends against the dictates of religion. Vîram.

22. Col. Dig. I, 3, 103; Vîram. p. 319. The rule that the principal only needs to be restored concerns a pledge for use. In the case of a pledge for custody, interest has to be paid besides the principal. Vîram.

23. When a field or other (immovable property) has been enjoyed, and more than the principal realised by it, then the debtor shall recover his pledge, if the principal and interest has been actually got out of it (by the creditor).

24. (This law applies) when the debtor delivers a field to the creditor, with the following stipulation, 'This (field) shall be enjoyed by you, when interest has ceased (on becoming equal to the principal), that is certain. When the principal has been realised together with the interest, you shall restore (the field) to me.'

25. When the time (for payment) has passed and interest has ceased (on becoming equal to the principal), the creditor shall be owner of the pledge; but, till ten days have elapsed, the debtor is entitled to redeem it.

26. Notice having been given to the debtor's family, a pledge to be kept (only) may be used, after the principal has been doubled; and so may a pledge for a fixed period, on the expiration of that term.

27. When the principal has been doubled, or the stipulated period expired in the case of a pledge delivered for a certain time only, the creditor

23. Col. Dig. I, 3, 108; May. p. 107.

23, 24. Vîram. p. 320. Under a stipulation of this sort, the mortgagee shall recover his pledge, as soon as the creditor has fully realised his demand out of the mortgage, no matter whether he has contributed little or much himself towards its realisation. Vîram. The Ratnâkara (p. 29) inserts the following text after 24, 'This lawful rule has been proclaimed with regard to loans on interest and so forth.'

25. Col. Dig. I, 3, 115; Vîram. p. 316.

26. Vîram. p. 316; Col. Dig. I, 3, 119 ('Smriti').

27, 28. Vîram. p. 315. 'During that interval,' i. e. before the ten days have elapsed. Vîram. These two texts are elsewhere

becomes owner of the pledge, after having waited for a fortnight.

28. If the debtor should pay the debt during that interval, he may recover his pledge (even then).

29. When the amount of the debt has been doubled (by the interest accruing on it), and the debtor is either dead or no longer present, (the creditor) may take his chattel and sell it before witnesses.

30. Or, its value having been estimated in an assembly, he may keep it for ten days; after which, having realised a sufficient sum to cover his demand, he should relinquish the balance.

31. When a man neither enjoys a pledge, nor obtains it (from the debtor), nor points it out (to others), his written contract (concerning the pledge) is invalid, (just like) a document when the (subscribing) witnesses and debtor are dead.

32. When a house or field has been mortgaged for use and the period (fixed for such use) has not expired, the debtor cannot recover his property, nor can the creditor (recover) his loan.

33. When the (stipulated) period has elapsed, both

---

attributed to Vyâsa. This is probably the correct view, as it is difficult to reconcile these texts either with the preceding or with the following ones.

29. May. p. 106.

29, 30. Vîram. p. 316; Col. Dig. I, 3, 121. 'The chattel,' i.e. the pledged commodity. 'A sufficient sum to cover his demand,' i.e. twice as much as the principal. Vîram. The balance should be handed over to the relatives of the debtor or to the king. Colebrooke's Digest has another text after these two, in which it is stated that the precise amount of the debt should be ascertained by persons skilled in computation.

31. Col. Dig. I, 3, 126; Smritik.; Ratn. p. 35.

32, 33. Viv. p. 25; Col. Dig. I, 3, 105, 118. In ordinary cases,

parties are at liberty to do so. But, even before (the stipulated period) has elapsed, they may make an arrangement by mutual consent.

34. Where one field has been mortgaged to two creditors at the same time, it shall belong to that mortgagee who was the first to obtain possession of it.

35. If both have possessed it for an equal time, it shall be held in common (or shared equally) by them. The same rule is ordained in the case of a gift or a sale.

36. Which course should be adopted in cases of a competition between three different acts, the identical property having been sold, mortgaged, and given away on one and the same day?

37. The three parties should divide that lawful property of theirs among themselves in proportionate shares, the two first in the ratio of their respective claims, whereas the donee ought to obtain a full third.

38. The pledgee can never be compelled to restore the pledge against his will, before the whole amount due to him has been paid, nor must (the pledge be obtained from him) by deceit or by (the mode called) *K*arita.

---

the recovery of the loan, attended by the restoration of the pledge to the pledger, takes place after the lapse of the stipulated period. By mutual consent, however, it may take place before that time.

34. The term 'a field' includes by implication any pledge for use. Vîram. p. 312. Other commentators add that possession must have been obtained without forcible means. Col. Dig. I, 3, 132.

35. Smr*i*tik.; Col. Dig. I, 3, 133; Ratn. p. 37.

36, 37. Vîram. p. 314 ('Vasish*th*a'); V. T.

38. Ratn. p. 27; Col. Dig. I, 3, 102. Regarding the mode called *K*arita or Â*k*arita, see below, XI, 58.

39. For appearance, for confidence, for payment, and for delivering the assets of the debtor: it is for these four different purposes that sureties have been ordained by the sages in the system (of law).

40. The first says, 'I will produce (that man);' the second (says), 'He is a respectable man;' the third (says), 'I will pay the debt;' the fourth (says), 'I will deliver his assets.'

41. If the debtors fail in their engagements, the two first (sureties themselves, but not their sons) must pay the sum lent at the appointed time; both the two last (sureties), and in default of them their sons (are liable for the debt), when the debtors break their promise (to pay the debt).

42. The creditor should allow time for the surety to search for a debtor who has absconded; a fortnight, a month, a month and a half, according to (the distance of) the place (where he is supposed to be hiding himself).

43. (Sureties) must not be excessively harassed; they should be made to pay the debt by instalments;

---

39. Col. Dig. I, 4, 142; Vîram. p. 321; Viv. p. 27. The author of the last-mentioned work reads *rin*e dravyârpa*n*e for *rin*idravyârpa*n*e, which reading he refers to as the traditional one, and defines the fourth kind of surety to be one who vouches for the return of articles lent for use, such as ornaments for a festivity.

40. May. p. 107. The first surety promises to produce a debtor, who is likely to abscond; the second vouches for the debtor's honesty, declaring that he is a virtuous man, who will not deceive the creditor; the third promises to pay the debt himself together with the interest, if the debtor should fail to pay it; the fourth promises to deliver his movable property, such as household furniture, in the same case.

41. May. p. 107.

42, 43. Vîram. pp. 323, 328; Col. Dig. I, 4, 148; Ratn. p. 45.

they must not be attacked when the debtor is present: such is the law regarding sureties.

44. When (a surety), being harassed, pays a proved debt which he has vouched for, (the debtor) shall pay him twice as much, after the lapse of a month and a half.

45. Should foolish (sureties) in good faith pay the debt, though not required to do so, or on being required to pay a different debt, how and from whom can they recover that sum?

46. By whom, to whom, and how, should, or should not, be paid a loan which has been received from the hands of another man in the shape of a loan on interest, will now be declared.

47. A loan shall be restored on demand, if no time has been fixed (for its restoration); or on the expiration of the time (if a definite period has been fixed); or when interest ceases (on becoming equal to the principal). If the father is no longer alive, (the debt must be paid) by his sons.

48. The father's debt must be paid first of all, and after that, a man's own debt; but a debt contracted by the paternal grandfather must always be paid before these two even.

49. The father's debt, on being proved, must be paid by the sons as if it were their own; the grandfather's debt must be paid (by his son's sons) without

44. Vîram. p. 328.

45. Ratn. p. 46; Col. Dig. I, 4, 163.

46. Ratn. p. 47; Col. Dig. I, 5, 166.

47. Ratn. p. 47; Col. Dig. I, 5, 166; Viv. p. 32.

48. Ratn. p. 47; Col. Dig. I, 5, 167; May. p. 112.

49. May. p. 112; Col. Dig. I, 5, 167. 'As if it were their own,' i.e. with interest. Ratn.

interest; but the son of a grandson need not pay it at all.

50. When a debt has been incurred, for the benefit of the household, by an uncle, brother, son, wife, slave, pupil, or dependant, it must be paid by the head of the family.

51. Sons shall not be made to pay (a debt incurred by their father) for spirituous liquor, for losses at play, for idle gifts, for promises made under the influence of love or wrath, or for suretyship, nor the balance of a fine or toll (liquidated in part by their father).

52. The liability for the debts devolves on the successor to the estate, when the son is involved in calamity; or on the taker of the widow, in default of a successor to the estate.

53. Debts contracted by the wives of distillers of spirituous liquor, hunters, washermen, herdsmen, barbers or the like persons, shall be paid by their protector; they were contracted for the affairs of their husbands.

54. When (a debtor) has acknowledged a debt, it may be recovered from him by the expedients of friendly expostulation and the rest, by moral suasion,

---

50. Ratn. p. 54; Col. Dig. I, 5, 189; Viv. p. 39.

51. Ratn. p. 57; Col. Dig. I, 5, 201; May. p. 113. Regarding promises made under the influence of love or wrath, see Kâtyâyana X, 53, 54.

52. Ratn. p. 64; Col. Dig. I, 5, 174; May. p. 114; Viv. p. 37.

53. Vîram. p. 354 ('Kâtyâyana'); Col. Dig. I, 5, 217; Ratn. p. 60. 'Protector' means husband. Ratn. 'Barbers,' nâpita, are referred to according to the reading of the Ratnâkara. The Vîramitrodaya reads nâvika, 'sailors,' which reading is mentioned as a varia lectio in the Ratnâkara. Colebrooke has 'shepherds.'

54. Col. Dig. I, 6, 244; May. p. 109.

by artful management, by compulsion, and by confinement at his house.

55. When a debtor is caused to pay by the advice of friends or kinsmen, by friendly remonstrances, by constant following, or by (the creditor) starving himself to death, it is termed moral suasion.

56. When a creditor, with a crafty design, borrows anything from his debtor, for his own use, or withholds an Anvâhita deposit or the like, and thus enforces payment of the debt, it is termed artful management.

57. When a debtor is fettered and conducted into (the creditor's) own house, where he is compelled to pay the debt by beating or other (forcible) means, it is called compulsion.

58. When a debtor is made to pay by confining his wife, son or cattle, and by watching at his door, it is termed Â*k*arita (the customary mode).

59. An indigent debtor may be taken to his own house by the creditor and compelled to do work there, such as distilling spirits and the like; but a Brahman must be made to pay gradually.

---

55. Col. Dig. I, 6, 236; May. p. 109; Ratn. p. 67; Viv. p. 43. The term prâya or prâyopave*s*ana corresponds without doubt to the modern custom of Dhar*n*a, or 'fasting upon' a debtor, when the creditor places himself before the debtor's house and threatens to starve himself to death, unless the debt be paid. It is true that some commentators interpret prâya by 'importunate demands' (prârthanâbâhulya or prârthanâ).

56. Col. Dig. I, 6, 238; May. p. 109, &c. 'With a crafty design,' as e. g. when valuable ornaments are borrowed from the debtor, on the pretence of using them at a festivity. 'An Anvâhita deposit' is an article deposited for delivery to another person. Vîram. p. 333.

57. Col. Dig. I, 6, 240. 58. Col. Dig. I, 6, 239.

59. Ratn. p. 71; Col. Dig. I, 6, 246.

60. When the time fixed (for payment) has elapsed, and the interest has ceased (on becoming equal to the principal), the debtor may either recover his loan or cause a new bond to be written in the form of compound interest.

61. As compound interest is taken on the doubled principal, so does the use of a pledge (become a new principal), the debt together with the interest being considered as the (new) principal.

62. This rule concerns an acknowledged (debt); but (a debtor) denying (his liability) shall be compelled to pay, on the debt being proved in a (judicial) assembly by a document or by witnesses.

63. (A debtor) claiming judicial investigation in a doubtful case, shall never be put under restraint (by the creditor). He who puts under restraint one not liable to such treatment, shall be fined according to law.

64. A debtor who makes a declaration in this form, 'What may be found to be justly due, that I will pay,' is termed 'one claiming judicial investigation.'

65. When there is a difference of opinion between the two parties regarding the nature (of the loan), or the number or the like, or the (amount of) interest,

---

60. May. p. 110; Col. Dig. I, 6, 255. The new bond is to be one in which the interest is calculated on the interest added to the principal, i. e. on the doubled principal.

61. Ratn. p. 72; Col. Dig. I, 6, 259. The comparison here proposed relates to the case when a pledge for use has been accidentally destroyed, and a new bond is executed, in which the interest is calculated on the principal together with the lost usufruct.

62. Ratn. p. 75; May. p. 110; Col. Dig. I, 6, 160.

63. May. p. 110; Col. Dig. I, 6, 161.

63–65. Ratn. p. 25. 64. May. p. 110; Col. Dig. I, 6, 162.

65. Col. Dig. I, 6, 163. 'The nature of the loan,' whether it be gold or silver, &c.; 'or the like,' such as the pledge given, &c. Ratn.

or whether the sum be due or not, it is termed a doubtful case.

66. Should a man, after recovering his debt by moral suasion or one of the other modes, fail to receipt it on the bond, or to give a deed of acquittance, it shall yield interest (to the debtor).

XII. Deposits.

1. The Law of Debt, beginning with the delivery of a loan and ending with its recovery, has been declared. Hear, now, the complete set of rules concerning Deposits.

2. When any chattel is deposited in the house of another man, through fear of the king, robbers, or other dangers, or for the purpose of deceiving one's heirs, it is called a Nyâsa deposit.

3. When a chattel enclosed in a cover and marked with a seal (is deposited) without describing its nature or quantity, and without showing it, it is termed an Aupanidhika deposit.

4. Let a man make a deposit, after duly considering the place, house, master of the house, the power, means, qualities, veracity, and kindred (of the depositary).

5. (A deposit) is declared to be of two sorts:

66. Ratn. p. 80; Col. Dig. I, 6, 288. The term *vriddhi*, 'interest,' is interpreted 'forfeiture' by a certain number of commentators. This erroneous interpretation has been adopted by Colebrooke. Sir W. Jones has the correct translation.

XII, 1. Ratn. p. 83; Col. Dig. II, 1, 1.

2. Ratn. p. 83; Col. Dig. II, 1, 6; Vîram. p. 361.

3. Ratn. p. 83; Col. Dig. II, 1, 7 (with several different readings).

4. Ratn. p. 85; Col. Dig. II, 1, 14.

5–8. Ratn. pp. 85, 86; Col. Dig. II, 1, 19.

attested, or deposited in private; it must be guarded with the same care as a son; for it would be destroyed by neglect.

6. The merit of one who preserves a deposit or one who places himself under his protection, is equal to the merit of one who gives (articles made of) gold, or of base metal, or clothes.

7. The sin of those who consume or spoil (by negligence) a bailed chattel is as great as (the sin) of a woman who injures her husband, or of a man who kills his son or his friend.

8. It is the best course not to accept a deposit; but to destroy it (after having received it) is disgraceful; after having taken it, a man should keep it carefully and restore it when it has been asked for even once only.

9. A deposit must be returned to the very man who bailed it, in the very manner in which it was bailed; it must not be delivered to the successor of that man.

10. When a deposit is destroyed, together with the goods of the depositary, by the act of fate or of the king, (the depositary) is not to blame.

11. If the depositary should suffer the deposit to be destroyed by his want of care or indifference, or should refuse to restore it on being asked for it, he shall be made to pay (the value of) it with interest.

6, 9. May. p. 115. 7, 8. Col. Dig. II, 1, 19.

9. Col. Dig. II, 1, 18; Viv. p. 51; Ratn. p. 87.

10. Ratn. p. 88; Col. Dig. II, 1, 23; Vîram. p. 362; May. p. 116.

11. Ratn. p. 90; Col. Dig. II, 1, 34; May. p. 116; Viv. p. 53. The commentators take bheda, 'want of care,' to mean separation of the deposit from the depositary's own property, and bestowing less care on it than on the effects of the depositary.

12. Should any (depositary) procure advantage for himself by an article deposited (with him), he shall be fined by the king, and compelled to pay its value together with interest.

13. He who, after receiving a deposit, denies the fact, and is convicted by (the evidence of) witnesses or ordeal, shall be compelled to give up the deposit and to pay an equal amount as a fine.

14. When a dispute arises with regard to a deposit privately made, the performance of an ordeal is ordained for both parties, to establish the facts of the case.

15. The same set of rules applies in the case of a bailment for delivery (to a third person), a loan for use, an article delivered to an artist (such as gold delivered to a goldsmith to be worked by him into an earring), a pledge, and a person offering himself for protection.

XIII. Sale without Ownership.

1. Immediately after deposits, sale by another person than the owner has been declared by Bh*ri*gu; listen attentively, I will expound that subject thoroughly.

---

12. Ratn. p. 91; Col. Dig. II, 1, 31. The commentators observe that the use here referred to must have been made without the consent of the owner.

13. Ratn. p. 93; Col. Dig. II, 1, 45.

14. Ratn. p. 95; Vîram. p. 366. The term 'both parties' is used in order to imply that the ordeal may be performed either by the alleged depositor or depositary. Vîram.

15. May. p. 116; Ratn. p. 96; Viv. p. 54.

14, 15. Col. Dig. II, 1, 12.

XIII, 1. Ratn. p. 101; Col. Dig. II, 2, 1.

2. An open deposit, a bailment for delivery (Anvâhita), a Nyâsa (sealed) deposit, stolen property, a pledge, or what has been borrowed for use: when any one of these articles has been sold in secret by a man, he is declared a person different from the owner (asvâmin).

3. When the vendor has been produced and has been cast in the suit, (the judge) shall cause him to pay the price and a fine to the buyer and king respectively, and to restore the property to the owner.

4. When the former owner comes forward and makes good his claim to the thing bought, the vendor shall be produced (by the purchaser); by doing so, the purchaser may clear himself.

5. That greedy man who covets another man's property, without having any claim to it, shall be compelled to pay twice the value (of the property claimed) as a fine, if he is unable to prove his claim.

6. When there is no evidence in a suit, the king shall consider the character of the parties and pass a decree himself, according to the equal, greater, or less (credibility of the parties).

7. When a purchase has been made before an assembly of merchants, the king's officers being aware of it (also), but from a vendor whose habitation is unknown; or when the purchaser has deceased:

8. The owner may recover his own property by

2. Ratn. p. 101; Col. Dig. II, 2, 2; Vîram. p. 374.
3. Ratn. p. 102; Col. Dig. II, 2, 30; Viv. p. 57.
4. Ratn. p. 101; Col. Dig. II, 2, 33; Vîram. p. 379.
5. Ratn. p. 106; Col. Dig. II, 2, 46.
6. Ratn. p. 108; Col. Dig. II, 2, 52.
7–9. Ratn. p. 109; Col. Dig. II, 2, 53, 54.

paying half the price (tendered), the custom in that case being that one half of the value is lost to each of the two.

9. A purchase from an unknown (vendor) is one fault (in that case); want of care in keeping it is another; these two faults are viewed by the wise as legitimate grounds of loss to each party.

10. When a man purchases (a commodity) at a fair price, and (the purchase) has been previously announced to the king, there is no wrong about it; but he who makes a fraudulent purchase is a thief.

11. That should be known as a fraudulent purchase which is made at an unreasonably low price, in the interior of a house, outside of the village, at night, in secret, or from a dishonest person.

XIV. Concerns of a Partnership.

1. Trade or other occupations should not be carried on by prudent men jointly with incompetent or lazy persons, or with such as are afflicted by an illness, ill-fated, or destitute.

2. A man should carry on business jointly with persons of noble parentage, clever, active, intelligent, familiar with coins, skilled in revenue and expenditure, honest, and enterprising.

3. As an equal, smaller, or larger share (of the

10, 11. Viv. p. 60; Vîram. p. 375; Col. Dig. II, 2, 57. In 10, Colebrooke has 'delivered by the owner in the presence of credible persons.' I have translated the reading of the Vîramitrodaya, 'previously announced to the king.' In 11, the clause 'in secret' is omitted in the Vîramitrodaya.

XIV, 1, 2. Ratn. p. 111; Col. Dig. II, 3, 2; Vîram. pp. 383, 384.

3. Ratn. p. 112; Col. Dig. II, 3, 5.

joint stock) has been contributed by a partner, in the same proportion shall he defray charges, perform labour, and obtain profit.

4. Of those who lend (jointly) gold, grain, liquids and condiments, or the like, the gain shall be equal to their respective shares (of the joint expenditure), whether equal, more, or less.

5. Whatever property one partner may give (or lend), authorized by many, or whatever contract he may cause to be executed, all that is (considered as having been) done by all.

6. They are themselves pronounced to be arbitrators and witnesses for one another in doubtful cases, and when a fraudulent act has been discovered, unless a (previous) feud should exist between them.

7. When any one among them is found out to have practised deceit in a purchase or sale, he must be cleared by an oath (or ordeal); such is the rule in all disputes (of this sort).

8. When a loss or diminution has occurred through fate or the king, it is ordained that it should be borne by all (partners) in proportion to their respective shares.

9. When (a single partner acting) without the assent (of the other partners) or against their express instructions injures (their joint property)

4. Ratn. p. 123; Col. Dig. II, 3, 45.

5–7. Ratn. pp. 123, 113; Col. Dig. II, 3, 45, 9, 10; May. p. 121; Vîram. p. 385.

8. Ratn. p. 113; Col. Dig. II, 3, 11. 'A loss,' destruction of the principal; 'diminution,' loss of profits. Ratn.

9. Ratn. p. 113; Col. Dig. II, 3, 12; Viv. p. 61; Vîram. p. 385.

through his negligence, he must by himself give a compensation to all his partners.

10. That (partner), on the other hand, who by his own efforts preserves (the common stock) from a danger apprehended through fate or the king, shall be allowed a tenth part of it (as a reward), the remainder being distributed among the other (partners), according to their shares (in the stock).

11. Should any such partner in trade happen to die through want of proper care, his goods must be shown (and delivered) to officers appointed by the king.

12. And when any one comes forward claiming that man's property as heir (to the deceased partner), he shall prove his right to it by (the evidence of) other men, and then let him take it.

13. The king shall take a sixth, a ninth, and a twelfth part respectively from the property of a *S*ûdra, Vai*s*ya, and Kshatriya; and a twentieth from the property of a Brahman.

14. But after the lapse of three years, if no owner should come forward by any means, the king shall take that property; the wealth of a Brahman he shall bestow on (other) Brahmans.

15. So among (several) persons jointly performing a ceremony, if any one should meet with an accident, his (part of) the ceremony shall be performed by a kinsman of his, or by all his associates (in work).

---

10. Ratn. p. 114; Col. Dig. II, 3, 15; Viv. p. 61; Vîram. p. 386.

11, 12. Ratn. p. 116; Col. Dig. II, 3, 21; Viv. p. 63.

13, 14. Ratn. p. 116; Col. Dig. II, 3, 22; Viv. p. 64.

15. Ratn. p. 117; Col. Dig. II, 3, 29; Viv. p. 65. 'A ceremony,' such as a sacrifice.

16. They (the officiating priests) are pronounced to be threefold: coming (of their own accord), hereditary in the family, and appointed by (the sacrificer) himself; their business should be performed by them accordingly.

17. To a kinsman, relative, or friend one may lend money with a pledge (only); a loan to others must be guaranteed by a surety, or there must be a written contract or witnesses.

18. Gold or silver may be lent according to one's own choice; liquids and condiments, and grain, for a specified period only; it is by local custom that both the loan and its recovery should be regulated.

19. That, however, which has been lent by several persons in common, must be recovered by them jointly; any (such lender) who fails to demand (the loan together with his partners) shall forfeit interest.

20. The law regarding loans has been declared before, (therefore) it is referred to in an abridged form only in the present chapter. Listen to the legal rules regarding cultivators of the soil and other (associates in work), which are declared as follows.

21. Tillage should be undertaken by a sensible

---

16. Ratn. p. 120; Col. Dig. II, 3, 44. The analogous text of Nârada shows that officiating priests are the persons intended by this rule.

17–26. Ratn. pp. 123, 124; Col. Dig. II, 3, 47–51.

18. In a loan of gold, a definite period for its return need not be specified; but for liquids, &c. the stipulation of a fixed term is necessary. Ratn.

20. 'Declared before,' i. e. in Chapter XI. All the rules declared in that chapter are equally applicable to loans made by an association.

man jointly with those who are his equals in point of cattle, workmen, seeds, and the like, as well as implements of husbandry.

22. They should refrain anxiously from cultivating an enclosed pasture-ground, land adjacent to a town, or to the king's highway, barren soil, and ground infested by mice.

23. That man will enjoy produce who sows fertile land, which has many holes and is wet, capable of irrigation, surrounded by fields on all sides, and cultivated in due season.

24. A sensible cultivator must not admit cattle which is lean, very old, tiny, diseased, apt to run away, blind of one eye, or lame.

25. When by the deficiency of one (partner) as to cattle or seeds a loss happens in (the produce of) the field, it must be made good by him to all the husbandmen.

26. This primeval set of rules has been declared for cultivators of the soil.

27. One able to work up gold, silver, thread, wood, stone, or leather, and acquainted with the articles to be manufactured (with such materials), is called *S*ilpin (an artizan or artist) by the wise.

28. When goldsmiths or other (artists) practise their art jointly, they shall share the profits in due proportion, corresponding to the nature of their work.

27, 28. Ratn. p. 124; Col. Dig. II, 3, 52; Viv. p. 70; Vîram. p. 396. Some compilations exhibit the readings kupya, 'base metals,' for rûpya, 'silver;' pattra, 'leaves,' for sûtra, 'thread;' tattatkalâbhi*gñah*, 'acquainted with the minute particles of these materials,' for *k*a phalâbhi*gñah*, 'and acquainted with the articles to be manufactured.'

29. The headman among a number of workmen jointly building a house or temple, or digging a pool or making articles of leather, is entitled to a double share (of the remuneration).

30. The same rule has been declared by virtuous men for musicians; he who knows how to beat the time shall take a share and a half, but the singers shall take equal shares.

31. When anything has been brought from a hostile country by freebooters, with the permission of their lord, they shall give a sixth part to the king and share (the remainder) in due proportion.

32. Four shares shall be awarded to their chief; he who is (specially) valiant shall receive three shares; one (particularly) able shall take two; and the remaining associates shall share alike.

XV. Resumption of Gifts.

1. The system of rules relative to Concerns of a Partnership has been fully declared thus; the rules regarding what may, or may not, be given, valid, and invalid gifts, will be declared (next).

---

29. Ratn. p. 125; Col. Dig. II, 3, 54; May. p. 121; Viv. p. 70; Vîram. p. 390. The last two works read vâpi for vâpî, and under this reading the clause 'or digging a pool' would have to be omitted. The Mayûkha reads dhârmika, 'sacred articles,' for *k*ârmika, 'articles made of leather.'

30. Ratn. p. 125; Col. Dig. II, 3, 55; Viv. p. 71; Vîram. p. 391; May. p. 121.

31, 32. Ratn. p. 125; Col. Dig. II, 3, 56; Viv. p. 71; Vîram. p. 391. 'Their chief,' i. e. one who exerts mind and body. Ratn., Viv.

XV, 1. Ratn. p. 127; Col. Dig. II, 4, 1; Vîram. p. 392.

2. That which may not be given is declared to be of eight sorts, joint property, a son, a wife, a pledge, one's entire wealth, a deposit, what has been borrowed for use, and what has been promised to another.

3. What remains after defraying (the necessary expenses for) the food and clothing of his family, may be given by a man; otherwise (by giving more than that), the religious merit (supposed to be acquired by the giver) though tasting like honey at first, will change into poison in the end.

4. When any field (or house) is given away, belonging to a number of houses or fields acquired in one of the seven modes of (lawful) acquisition, it is ordained to be viewed as a valid gift, whether it have been inherited from the father or acquired by the donor himself.

5. Self-acquired property may be given away at pleasure (by its owner); a pledge may be disposed of according to the rules of mortgage; in the case of property received as a marriage portion, or inherited from an ancestor, the bestowal of the whole is not admitted.

6. When, however, a marriage gift, or inherited property, or what has been obtained by valour, is

---

2. Ratn. p. 127; Col. Dig. II, 4, 5; Viv. p. 72; Vîram. p. 392.

3. Ratn. p. 129; Viv. p. 75; Col. Dig. II, 4, 18.

4, 5. Viv. p. 76. The seven modes of acquisition are, according to Manu (X, 115), inheritance, finding, purchase, conquest, lending at interest, doing work, and the acceptance of gifts from virtuous men. The prohibition to give away the whole, in 5, relates to property acquired by valour as well, according to the Ratnâkara. The clause translated by 'bestowal of the whole' may also mean, 'every gift,' i.e. a gift not sanctioned by the persons referred to in 6.

4–7. Ratn. p. 130; Col. Dig. II, 4, 18.

given with the assent of the wife, kinsmen, or supreme ruler, the gift acquires validity.

7. Co-heirs (or joint-tenants), whether divided in interests or not, have an equal claim to the immovable wealth; a single (parcener) has no power to give, mortgage, or sell the whole (wealth).

8. The following eight sorts of gifts are recognised as valid by persons acquainted with the law of gift, viz. wages, (what was given) for the pleasure (of hearing bards, or the like), the price of merchandise, the fee paid for (or to) a damsel, (and what was given) to a benefactor (as a return for his kindness), through reverence, kindness, or affection.

9. What has been given by one angry, or resenting an injury, or through inadvertence, or by one distressed, by a minor, a madman, one terrified, intoxicated, overaged, cast out from society, idiotic, or afflicted with grief or an illness,

10. Or what is given in jest; all such gifts are declared to be void gifts.

11. When anything has been given through desire of a reward, or to an unworthy man mistaken for a worthy person, or for an immoral purpose, the owner may resume the gift.

XVI. Master and Servant.

1. What may not be given and kindred subjects have been declared; the law of servants shall be propounded next. (There) the title of Breach of Promised Obedience is treated first.

---

8. Ratn. p. 133; Col. Dig. II, 4, 49; Viv. p. 81.

9, 10. Ratn. p. 136; Viv. p. 83; Col. Dig. II, 4, 62.

11. Ratn. p. 136; Viv. p. 83; Col. Dig. II, 4, 62.

XVI, 1, 2. Ratn. p. 139; Col. Dig. III, 1, 1; Viv. p. 84.

2. The titles of non-payment of wages, and then (of disputes) between the owner (of cattle) and his servants are to follow in due order. Such are the three divisions of (the law of) servants.

3. They are pronounced to be of many sorts, according to their particular caste and occupation; and fourfold, according as they serve for science, human knowledge (or skill), love, or gain.

4. Each of these is again divided (into several species), according to the difference of occupation.

5. Science is declared to be a knowledge of (one of) the three Vedas, called Rig-veda, Sâma-veda, and Ya*g*ur-veda; for the purpose of acquiring such knowledge, he should pay obedience to a spiritual teacher, as ordained in law.

6. Arts (consisting of) work in gold, base metals, and the like, and the art of dancing and the rest are termed human knowledge; he who studies them should do work at his teacher's house.

7. He who has intercourse with another man's female slave, should be considered as a slave for the sake of his paramour; he must do work for her master, like another hired servant.

8. The servant for gain (or pay) is declared to be of many sorts, another is the servant for a share (of the gain). Of all, a low, a middle, and a high sort is distinguished.

9. A servant engaged for a day, a month, half a month, a sixmonth, two months, or a year, must do

3, 4. Ratn. p. 140; Col. Dig. III, 1, 4; Viv. p. 84.

5. Ratn. p. 140; Col. Dig. III, 1, 8; Viv. p. 86.

6. Ratn. p. 141; Col. Dig. III, 1, 16; Viv. p. 86.

7. Viv. p. 87; Col. Dig. III, 1, 32.

8–11. Ratn. pp. 142, 143; Col. Dig. III, 1, 24.

the work which he promised to do, and receives the stipulated fee.

10. The warrior is the highest of these; the cultivator of the soil is the middlemost; the porter is declared to be the lowest, and so is (a servant) employed in household work.

11. A servant for a share of the gain is declared to be twofold, either serving a husbandman or an owner of cattle; he shall receive, no doubt, a share of the grain produced, or of the milk.

12. A third or a fifth (of the produce) shall be awarded to the cultivator of the soil as his share.

13. Let that cultivator to whom food and clothing is given take a fifth of the crop; and let him who serves in consideration of the profit (alone) take a third part of the grain produced.

14. Should a hired servant fail in the performance of ever so small a part of his master's work, he forfeits his wages, and may be sued in court for his offence.

15. When a servant does not perform his work after having received his wages, though able (to do work), he shall be compelled to pay twice as much (as his wages) as a fine (to the king), and (shall restore) the wages (to his master).

16. He who has promised (to do work) and does not perform it, shall be compelled to do so by forcible means even; and if, through obstinacy, such a servant should still not do it as engaged for, he shall be fined

12, 13. Ratn. pp. 157, 158; Col. Dig. III, 1, 66, 67.

14, 15. Ratn. p. 159; Col. Dig. III, 1, 71.

16. Ratn. p. 160; Col. Dig. III, 1, 75. There is another reading, translated by Colebrooke, under which the fine is to amount to two hundred Pa*n*as, instead of eight K*r*ish*n*alas.

eight Krishnalas, and his wages shall not be paid to him.

17. When a servant, commissioned by his master, does any improper act (such as theft) for the benefit of his master, the latter shall be held responsible for it.

18. When a master does not pay wages for the labour stipulated after the work has been performed, he shall be compelled by the king to pay it, and a proportionate fine besides.

19. (A man) hired for attendance on milch cows of another shall receive the whole milk every eighth day.

20. (A cowherd) shall save cattle from danger of reptiles, robbers, and tigers, and from caverns or pits; let him try his best to protect them, call out for help, or give notice to his master.

XVII. Violation of Agreements.

1. Thus has been declared the law concerning the mutual relations between master and servant; learn now concisely the performance of agreements.

2. Brahmans imbued with a knowledge of the Veda and of sacred lore, learned divines, and persons keeping a sacrificial fire, (the king) should worship, establish them there (in his kingdom), and provide a maintenance for them.

17. Ratn. p. 162; Col. Dig. III, 1, 84; Viv. p. 100.

18. Ratn. p. 165; Col. Dig. III, 1, 93; Viv. p. 100.

19. Viv. p. 105; Ratn. p. 170; Col. Dig. III, 4, 4.

20. Ratn. p. 172; Viv. p. 106; Col. Dig. III, 4, 10.

XVII, 1–10. Ratn. pp. 177–179; Col. Dig. III, 2, 2, 6.

2–9. Vîram. pp. 423–427. The readings given in the Vîramitrodaya have been translated everywhere, except in 2, where the Ratnâkara has been followed.

3. Let him bestow on them houses and landed property, exempt from taxation, declaring in a written grant that the revenue is remitted.

4. They shall perform for the citizens constant, special, and voluntary rites, as well as expiatory and auspicious ones, and pass a decision in doubtful cases.

5. A compact formed among villagers, companies (of artizans), and associations is (called) an agreement; such (an agreement) must be observed both in times of distress and for acts of piety.

6. When a danger is apprehended from robbers or thieves, it is (considered as) distress common to all; in such a case, (the danger) must be repelled by all, not by one man alone whoever he may be.

7. Mutual confidence having first been established by means of (the ordeal by) sacred libation, by a stipulation in writing, or by umpires, they shall then set about their work.

8. Enemies, dissolute, bashful, indolent, timid, avaricious, overaged or very young persons must not be chosen as intendants of affairs.

9. Honest persons, acquainted with the Vedas and with duty, able, self-controlled, sprung from noble families, and skilled in every business, shall be appointed as heads (of an association).

10. Two, three, or five persons shall be appointed as advisers of the association; their advice shall be taken by the villagers, companies (of artizans), corporations (of cohabitants), and other (fellowships).

11. When a stipulation has been entered in a

11–14. Ratn. p. 181; Col. Dig. III, 2, 14; Vîram. p. 425. For kulâyana*m* in 13, the Vîramitrodaya reads kulâyandairodhas *k*a and

document as follows, 'The construction of a house of assembly, of a shed for (accommodating travellers with) water, a temple, a pool, or a garden,

12. Relief to helpless or poor people, the performance of sacrificial acts, a common path, or defence, shall be undertaken by us in proportionate shares:' that is a lawful agreement.

13. (Such an agreement) must be kept by all. He who fails (in his agreement), though able (to perform it), shall be punished by confiscation of his entire property, and by banishment from the town.

14. And for that man, whoever he may be, who falls out (with his associates), or neglects (his work), a fine is ordained amounting to six Nishkas of four Suvar*n*as each.

15. He who injures the joint stock, or insults a Brahman acquainted with the three Vedas, or breaks the mutual agreement, shall be banished from the town.

16. An acrimonious or malicious man, and one who causes dissension or does violent acts, or who is inimically disposed towards that company, association, or the king, shall be banished instantly from the town.

17. The heads of families, companies (of artizans) and associations, whether inhabiting a town or a stronghold, shall censure and reprimand offenders, and forsake them.

---

interprets it by 'the maintenance of a family, including its preservation in times of distress.'

15. Ratn. p. 183; Col. Dig. III, 2, 19.

16. Ratn. p. 184; Col. Dig. III, 2, 20; Vîram. p. 430.

17. Ratn. p. 184; Col. Dig. III, 2, 21; Vîram. p. 429; Viv. p. 110.

18. Whatever is done by those (heads of an association), whether harsh or kind towards other people, must be approved of by the king as well; for they are declared to be the appointed managers (of affairs).

19. Should they agree, actuated by hatred, on injuring a single member of the fellowship, the king must restrain them; and they shall be punished, if they persist in their conduct.

20. When a dispute arises between the chiefs and the societies, the king shall decide it, and shall bring them back to their duty.

21. Those (companions in trade) who conspire to cheat the king of the share due to him (of their profits), shall be compelled to pay eight times as much, and shall be punished if they take to flight.

22. Whatever is obtained then by a man, shall belong to all in common; whether it have been obtained a sixmonth or a month ago, it shall be divided in due proportion.

23. (Or) it shall be bestowed on the idiotic, the aged, the blind, to women or children, to afflicted or diseased persons, to persons having issue, or the like (worthy persons). This is an eternal law.

24. Whatever is obtained or preserved by the members of a fellowship, or spent on behalf of the

18. Ratn. p. 184; Col. Dig. III, 2, 22; Vîram. p. 429.

19. Ratn. p. 184; Col. Dig. III, 2, 23; Vîram. p. 429.

20. Ratn. p. 184; Col. Dig. III, 2, 24.

21. Ratn. p. 185; Col. Dig. III, 2, 27; Viv. p. 110.

22. Ratn. p. 186; Col. Dig. III, 2, 30; Viv. p. 116. The commentators observe that gifts obtained from a king are meant.

23, 24. Ratn. pp. 186, 187; Col. Dig. III, 2, 31; Vîram. p. 432. For prakalpitam in 24, 'what is spent,' the last two works read *ri*na*m*k*ri*tam, 'what is borrowed.'

society, or acquired through the king's favour, is common to all (members of the society).

XVIII. Rescission of Purchase and Sale.

1. This set of rules concerning the law of agreements has been briefly stated; disputes arising from purchase and sale shall be treated next.

2. Two sorts of property are distinguished, immovable and movable; when a purchase is concluded, the term 'vendible property' (pa*n*ya) is applied to both.

3. The purchaser shall examine a chattel himself and show it to others; when, after examining and approving it, he has accepted it, he is not at liberty to return it again.

4. The foolish man who sells an article, though acquainted with its blemish, shall have to pay twice its value (to the vendee), and (a fine of) the same amount (to the king).

5. What has been sold by one intoxicated or insane, or at a very low price, or under the impulse of fear, or by one not his own master, or by an idiot, shall be relinquished (by the purchaser, or it) may be recovered (from the purchaser) by forcible means.

6. Within that period, if a blemish should be

XVIII, 1, 2. Ratn. p. 189; Col. Dig. III, 3, 1.

3. Vîram. p. 433; Col. Dig. III, 3, 11; Ratn. p. 198; Viv. p. 117.

4. Vîram. p. 441; Ratn. p. 192; Col. Dig. III, 3, 31; Viv. p. 114.

5. Vîram. p. 441; Ratn. p. 193; Col. Dig. III, 3, 37. Thus, according to some commentators; others construe the clause 'at a very low price' with each part of the sentence.

6. Viv. p. 116; Col. Dig. III, 3, 14; May. p. 131. 'Within that period,' i. e. the period allowed for examination.

discovered anywhere in the commodity purchased, it shall be returned to the vendor, and the purchaser shall recover the price.

XIX. Boundary Disputes.

1. This rule regarding rescission of purchase and sale has been declared. Hear the laws concerning boundaries of villages, fields, houses, and so forth.

2. The determination of boundaries should be settled at the time of foundation, and it should be marked by visible and invisible signs, so as to dispel doubt.

3. Wells, tanks, pools, large trees, gardens, temples, mounds, channels, the course of a river, reeds, shrubs, or piles of stones:

4. By such visible signs as these a boundary line should always be caused to be marked; also, by other (marks) deposited underground which the earth is not likely to destroy.

5. Dry cowdung, bones, chaff, charcoal, stones, potsherds, sand, bricks, cows' tails, cotton seeds, and ashes:

6. After having placed these substances in vessels, one should deposit them underground at the extremities of the boundary. After that, one should take care to point them out to youths and infants.

7. These (youths and infants) should again show them to their own children, after having grown old;

XIX, 1. Ratn. p. 201.

2. Ratn. p. 202. 'Invisible signs' are substances deposited underground.

3, 4. Viv. p. 120; Ratn. p. 203; Vîram. p. 452.

5, 6. Ratn. p. 204; May. p. 134; Vîram. pp. 452, 453.

7. Ratn. p. 204.

by knowledge thus passing from one generation to the other, doubts regarding boundaries may be obviated.

8. In disputes regarding a house or field, the decision belongs to the neighbours, as well as to the inhabitants of that town or village, or to members of the same society, and to the elders (of that district).

9. (Likewise, to) husbandmen, artizans, servants, cowherds, hunters, gleaners, diggers of roots, fishermen, kinsmen, mischief-makers, and robbers.

10. After having been adjured by imprecations befitting their station, they shall determine the boundary, and shall indicate the marks deposited underground, as evidence. Such is the law.

11. In default of witnesses and signs, even a single man, agreeable to both parties, may fix the boundary, wearing a red garland of flowers and a red cloak, putting earth on his head, adhering to truth, and having kept a fast.

12. Neighbours born in that district, though they be living abroad, are termed natives of the place; they should be consulted in the decision of a suit.

13. What they should declare in a doubtful case, as honest men and impartial to both parties, shall be held decisive; thus justice will not be violated.

14. Those are witnesses in a suit of this kind who know the title of acquisition, the size, the duration of the enjoyment, the name, and the characteristics of the land in question.

8, 9. Ratn. p. 209. 10. Ratn. p. 210; Vîram. p. 457.
11. Vîram. p. 458; Ratn. p. 211; Viv. p. 122; May. p. 134.
12, 13. Ratn. p. 213. 14. Vîram. p. 453.

15. The same rule holds good in all suits concerning immovable property. If their statements do not agree, they shall be made to pay the highest fine.

16. Supposing a piece of land to have been taken from a village belonging to one man, and given to another man, either by a large river or by the king, what should be decided in that case?

17. The land abandoned by a river or granted by the king belongs to him who receives it. Otherwise, there would be no acquisition through fate or the king among men.

18. Loss and gain and life among men depend on the act of fate and of the king; therefore, in all affairs, what is effected by them must not be rescinded.

19. When a river has been fixed as the boundary line between two villages, it shall never be removed, on account of loss or gain arising (from that river to either village). He who removes it, is liable to punishment.

20. The encroachment (of a river) on one side produces an increase of land elsewhere in banks of rivers; that (increase) must not be taken from him (who gets it).

21. When land is carried away by the swift course

15. Vîram. p. 457; Smr*i*tik.

16–23. Ratn. pp. 216, 217; Viv. pp. 123, 124; Vîram. pp. 461, 462. The second half of 19 is read as follows in the Vîramitrodaya, '(The river) effects gain or loss, according as people are lucky or unlucky.' This reading may have crept in from 16. For taulyâ, I read *k*âlyâ, with Vîram.

21. Such a tilled piece of land shall be made over to the previous owner till the harvest is over. When the harvest is over, the previous rule (20) holds good. Vîram.

of a river overflowing a tilled piece of ground, the previous owner shall recover it.

22. When land is taken from one man by a king actuated by anger or avarice, or using a fraudulent pretext, and bestowed on a different person as a mark of his favour, such a gift is not considered as valid.

23. When (however) land is taken from a person enjoying it without a legitimate title of ownership, and given to a worthier person, (the latter) must not be deprived of it.

24. A house, pool, shop or the like having been used by a man since the time of its foundation, must not be taken from him, nor diminished or altered.

25. A window, a watercourse, a peg projecting from a wall (used to hang things upon), a shed (erected in a courtyard), a square of four buildings, and a channel for the exit of water (after a rainfall), must not be blocked up, when previously constructed.

26. A privy, a fireplace, a pit, or a receptacle for leavings of food and other (rubbish), must never be made very close to the house of another man.

27. A passage by which men and animals go to and fro unprevented is called Samsarana, and must not be obstructed by any one.

28. He who purposely crowds such a place (by carts and the like), or makes a pit, or plants trees, or voids excrements, shall pay a Mâshaka as a fine.

---

23. I read vai dattâ, with Vîram., for vâdeyâ or vâdattâ (Ratn., Viv.).

24. Viv. p. 124; Vîram. p. 463; Ratn. p. 219.

25. Viv. p. 124; Vîram. p. 465; Ratn. p. 219.

26. Viv. p. 125; Vîram. p. 464; Ratn. p. 219; May. p. 135.

27. May. p. 136; Viv. p. 125; Ratn. p. 220; Vîram. p. 464.

28. Vîram. p. 465; May. p. 136.

29. When a man has leased ground, he shall sow and watch it, and reap the harvest in due season. If he fails to do so, he shall be compelled to make good the average value of the crop to the owner.

XX. Defamation.

1. Injury (pârushya) is declared to be of two kinds, harsh speeches and beating; each of these two kinds is again divided into three species, and the punishment is pronounced to be threefold.

2. Abuse of the first (or lowest) degree means offensive language against, or defamation of, a country, village, family, or the like, without (mentioning) an (individual ignominious) act.

3. Referring (in terms of contempt) to a man's sister or mother, or charging him with a minor sin, is termed abuse of a middling sort by the learned in law.

4. Charging a man with taking forbidden food or drinks, or taxing him with a mortal sin, or maliciously exposing his weakest points, is termed abuse of the highest degree.

5. When two persons abuse each other, their punishment shall be equal, if they are equals in caste; if one is inferior to the other, his punishment shall be double; for a superior, half (of the ordinary punishment) is ordained.

---

29. Viv. p. 129; Ratn. p. 229.

XX, 1. Ratn. p. 243; Viv. p. 138. The former work reads 'two species.'

2–4. Ratn. pp. 243, 244; Viv. p. 138; May. p. 137; Vîram. p. 483. 'Terms of contempt' in 3 means filthy speeches, such as 'I shall visit your sister or mother.'

5. Ratn. p. 245; Vîram. p. 484.

6. When persons equal in caste and qualities abuse one another, the punishment ordained for them in the system of law is thirteen Pa*n*as and a half.

7. For a Brahman abusing a Kshatriya, the fine shall be half of a hundred (fifty Pa*n*as); for abusing a Vai*s*ya, half of fifty (twenty-five Pa*n*as); for abusing a *S*ûdra, twelve and a half.

8. This punishment has been declared for (abusing) a virtuous *S*ûdra who has committed no wrong; no offence is imputable to a Brahman for abusing (a *S*ûdra) devoid of virtue.

9. A Vai*s*ya shall be fined a hundred (Pa*n*as) for reviling a Kshatriya; a Kshatriya reviling a Vai*s*ya shall have to pay half of that amount as a fine.

10. In the case of a Kshatriya reviling a *S*ûdra, the fine shall be twenty Pa*n*as; in the case of a Vai*s*ya, the double amount is declared to be the proper fine by persons learned in law.

11. A *S*ûdra shall be compelled to pay the first fine for abusing a Vai*s*ya; the middling fine (for abusing) a Kshatriya; and the highest fine (for abusing) a Brahman.

12. (A *S*ûdra) teaching the precepts of religion, or uttering the words of the Veda, or insulting a Brahman, shall be punished by cutting out his tongue.

13. (A man) reviling a sister or other (relation) of

---

6. Ratn. p. 247; Vîram. p. 483.

7–11. Ratn. pp. 251, 252; Vîram. p. 485.

7. May. p. 138.

12. May. p. 138; Vîram. p. 486; Viv. p. 141; Ratn. p. 252.

13. Ratn. p. 250; Vîram. p. 485. The latter work reads viprâdika*m*, 'a Brahman or other person,' for svasrâdikam, 'a sister or other relative.'

another person shall give a fine amounting to fifty Pa*n*as.

14. He who reviles a person's native country or other (belongings of his), shall be fined twelve Pa*n*as and a half. He who through arrogance imputes an offence to him, shall be compelled to pay the first fine.

15. This gradation of fines has been declared by me, subject to modification by the sages, in conformity with the (particular caste or qualities of a) man, so as either to remain as declared, or to be reduced or raised.

XXI. Assault.

1. Injuring (a man) with a hand, stone, club, or (throwing at him) ashes, or mud, or dust, or (attacking him with) a weapon, is termed assault.

2. Throwing ashes or the like (at a man), or striking him with a hand or the like, is (termed) an assault of the first degree; the fine to be inflicted in that case shall amount to a Mâsha.

3. This fine is ordained for (an assault on) equals in caste; (for assaults) on another man's wife or on a superior, it shall be twofold or threefold, according to the sages, according to the rank (of the person injured).

4. He who having been abused returns the abuse, or having been beaten returns the blow, or strikes an offender down, commits no wrong.

14, 15. Vîram. p. 488; Ratn. p. 257.
XXI, 1. Ratn. p. 259.
2, 3. Ratn. p. 261; Viv. p. 144.
4. May. p. 139; Vîram. p. 472; Viv. p. 153; Ratn. p. 276.

5. When a person throws gravel, stones, or pieces of wood at another, the first (or lowest) fine shall be inflicted on him. When they mutually strike one another with a hand or foot, it shall amount to ten or twenty Panas respectively.

6. The second fine shall be imposed when two persons in anger use weapons against one another; when a wound has been inflicted, the punishment shall be fixed by experts, corresponding to the severity of the hurt.

7. For injuring (a person) with bricks, stones, or a wooden club, (the fine shall be) two Mâshas; the double fine shall be inflicted, according to the sages, when blood flows.

8. For tearing the skin, the first (or lowest) fine (shall be inflicted); for tearing the flesh, the second fine; for breaking a bone, the highest fine; for killing, capital punishment.

9. For breaking the ear, nose, or hand (of a person), or injuring his teeth, or feet, the second fine shall be inflicted; and double of that, for entirely cutting off (any of those limbs).

10. He who injures a limb, or divides it, or cuts it off, shall be compelled to pay the expense of curing it; and (he who forcibly took an article in a quarrel, shall restore) his plunder.

11. When a man has been beaten in a solitary place, or when no wound is seen, the offender shall

5. Ratn. p. 263; Viv. p. 145; Vîram. p. 473.
6, 7. Vîram. p. 474; Viv. p. 147; Ratn. p. 264.
8, 9. Viv. p. 148.
10. Viv. p. 153; Ratn. p. 270; Vîram. p. 477.
11, 12. Ratn. p. 273.

be found out by circumstantial evidence or by an oath or ordeal.

12. When he has been struck in the interior of a house, or in a wood, or at night, and blood becomes visible, one shall not examine witnesses.

13. When two persons strike simultaneously, the punishment shall be equal for both; the first aggressor and he who is a habitual mischief-maker shall be compelled to pay a larger fine.

14. When a low person offends a man in high position by harsh words or the like, that man must not be persecuted by the king if he beats his aggressor.

15. Persons begotten in the inverse order of castes, and members of the lowest caste, are called the refuse of society; should they insult a Brahman, they shall be corporally punished, and shall never be amerced in a fine.

16. He who employs at an improper time, for drawing or carrying, tired, or hungry, or thirsty animals, shall be compelled to atone for it in the same way as a cow-killer, or to pay the first fine.

XXII. Robbery and Violence.

1. Homicide, theft, assault on another man's wife, and the two kinds of injury (abuse and assault) are the four species of violence (Sâhasa).

2. Thieves are declared to be of two kinds, open and concealed. These are subdivided a thousand-

13. Ratn. p. 275. 14. Ratn. p. 276.
15. Ratn. p. 277. 16. Ratn. p. 280.
XXII, 1. May. p. 145.
2–4. Ratn. p. 289; Vîram. p. 491.

fold, according to their skill, ability, and mode of cheating.

3. (Fraudulent) traders, quacks, gamblers, (corruptible) judges, those who accept bribes, cheats, persons (pretending) to know how to interpret evil omens, or to practise propitiatory rites, low artists, forgers,

4. (Hired servants) refusing to do their work, (roguish) umpires, perjured witnesses, and, lastly, jugglers: these are termed open thieves.

5. Housebreakers, highwaymen, robbers of bipeds or quadrupeds, thieves of clothes and the like, and stealers of grain, should be considered secret thieves.

6. (Thieves or robbers) having been found out by the king's attendants by their associating (with thieves) or by marks of their criminality, or by their being possessed of stolen goods, shall be compelled to restore their plunder, and shall be visited with punishments ordained in law.

7. A merchant who conceals the blemish of an article which he is selling, or mixes bad and good articles together, or sells (old articles) after repairing them, shall be compelled to give the double quantity (to the purchaser) and to pay a fine equal (in amount) to the value of the article.

8. A physician who, though unacquainted with drugs and spells, or ignorant of the nature of a disease, yet takes money from the sick, shall be punished like a thief.

9. Gamblers playing with false dice, prostitutes,

---

5. Ratn. p. 292. 6. Viv. p. 157; Ratn. p. 293.

7–15. Ratn. pp. 297, 306–311, 314; May. p. 142; Vîram. p. 492; Viv. pp. 159–165. The readings of the Ratnâkara have been followed throughout, in preference to those found in the other works.

those who appropriate what belongs to the king, and those who cheat an association, are pronounced to be impostors, and punishable as such.

10. Judges passing an unjust sentence, those who live by taking bribes, and those who disappoint confidence (placed in them): all such persons shall be banished.

11. Those who, without knowing the science of stars, or portents, expound them to the people from avarice, shall be punished by all means.

12. Those who show themselves in public wearing a staff, a skin, and the like (insignia of a religious order), and injure mankind by deceiving them, shall be corporally punished by the king's officers.

13. Those who by artificially getting up articles of small value cause them to appear very valuable, and deceive women or children (by doing so), shall be punished in proportion to their gain.

14. Those who make false gold or factitious gems or coral shall be compelled to restore their price to the purchaser, and to pay the double amount to the king as a fine.

15. Arbitrators who cheat either party from partiality, avarice or some other motive, and witnesses who give false evidence, shall be compelled to pay twice the amount (in dispute) as a fine.

16. Those who procure gain by means of spells or medicines (shall be compelled to give up) their gain; those who practise incantations with roots shall be banished by the ruler of the land.

17. Housebreakers shall be compelled to relinquish their plunder and be impaled on a stake after-

10. Ratn. p. 315.

17. Ratn. p. 317; May. p. 143; Vîram. p. 494; Viv. p. 166.

wards, and highwaymen shall be bound and hanged by the neck from a tree.

18. Those who have kidnapped a man shall be burned by the king with a fire kept up with straw; the stealer of a woman (shall be placed) on a bed of hot iron, or burned with a fire kept up with straw.

19. Stealers of grain shall be compelled to give ten times as much (to the owner), and the double amount as a fine; a cow-stealer shall have his nose cut off, and shall be plunged into water, after having been fettered.

20. When a man takes grass, wood, flowers, or fruit without asking permission to do so, he deserves to have a hand cut off.

21. On him who steals more than ten kumbhas of grain, corporal punishment (or execution) shall be inflicted; (for stealing) less than that, a man shall be fined eleven times the quantity stolen, and shall restore his property to the owner.

22. When a religious man and diligent reader of the Veda has committed theft, he shall be kept in prison for a long time, and shall be caused to perform a penance after having been compelled to restore the stolen goods to the owner.

23. Hear now (the law regarding) theft coupled with violence, which springs from either wrath or avarice.

---

18. Ratn. p. 317; Viv. p. 166.

19. Ratn. p. 322; Vîram. p. 494; May. p. 143.

20. Ratn. p. 329; Viv. p. 174. 21. Viv. p. 169.

22. Ratn. p. 331; Viv. p. 176. Under the version found in the latter work, the punishment does not take place when the Brahman performs a penance.

23. Vîram. p. 503.

24. It is declared to be threefold, as it may be (theft or violence) of the lowest, second, or highest kind; the punishment in each case should also be of the lowest, middling, or highest sort, according to the (nature of the) article (stolen or injured).

25. He who destroys or takes implements of husbandry, an embankment, flowers, roots, or fruit, shall be fined a hundred (Pa*n*as) or more, according (to the nature of his offence).

26. So one injuring or stealing cattle, clothes, food, drinks, or household utensils, shall be compelled to pay a fine of not less than two hundred (Pa*n*as), like a thief.

27. In the case of women, men, gold, gems, the property of a deity or Brahman, silk, and (other) precious things, the fine shall be equal to the value (of the article stolen).

28. Or the double amount shall be inflicted by the king as a fine; or the thief shall be executed, to prevent a repetition (of the offence).

29. Violence is declared to be of five sorts, and of these, manslaughter is declared to be the worst; those who have perpetrated it, shall not be amerced in a fine, they shall be put to death by all means.

30. Both notorious murderers and secret assassins shall be put to death by the king by various modes of execution, after their property has been duly seized.

31. When several persons in a passion beat a single individual (and kill him), the responsibility

24–28. Ratn. p. 350; May. p. 147.
29, 30. Ratn. p. 371; Viv. p. 192.
30. May. p. 145; Vîram. p. 501.
31–33. Ratn. p. 373; Viv. p. 194.

for his death shall be charged to him who strikes the fatal blow.

32. He who struck the fatal blow shall have to atone for his offence as directed; the first aggressor and the associates shall be punished half as much.

33. The decision should be given after carefully ascertaining by signs the less or greater severity of a wound, the seat of vital power, the strength (of the murdered individual), and the repetition (of the blows or cuts).

34. Where the corpse is found, but the murderer cannot be discovered, the king shall trace him by drawing an inference from previous enmities of his.

35. His immediate neighbours, and their neighbours, as well as his friends, enemies, and relatives, shall be questioned by the king's officers, employing towards them the (four) expedients of conciliation and so forth.

36. The (guilty) person may be found out from his keeping bad company, from signs (of the crime committed), and from the possession of stolen property. Thus has been declared the method of discovering murderers and robbers.

37. He who has been arrested on suspicion and does not confess his guilt, shall clear himself (from suspicion) by ordeal; this rule holds good for causes of every sort.

38. He who has been cleared of guilt by ordeal shall be released; he who has been convicted shall be put to death. By punishment (of the wicked)

34–36. Ratn. p. 377; Viv. p. 197 (the better version).

35. The three other expedients are, bribery, intimidation, and violence.

37, 38. Ratn. pp. 377, 378; Viv. p. 198.

and release (of the virtuous), the renown and religious merit of a king is increased.

XXIII. Adultery.

1. The two kinds of injury (abuse and assault) and the three kinds of violence have been declared. Learn the threefold (offence of) adultery, which is productive of sin.

2. The two first kinds of it are connected with violence and deception respectively, the third kind springs from sensual desire; the last is again of three sorts, being of the first, second, or highest degree.

3. When a man has intercourse with a woman in secret against her will, when she is asleep, or disordered in her intellect, or does not notice his approach, it is (termed) forcible enjoyment of a woman.

4. When he conducts her into his house under false pretences, and after giving her intoxicating drugs, has intercourse with her, it is considered fraudulent enjoyment of a woman.

5. When a man exchanges looks with a woman or sends her messages, and has intercourse with her impelled by sensuality, it has to be considered as (adulterous intercourse) springing from sensual desire.

6. Winking (at a woman), smiling (at her), sending her messengers, and touching her ornaments or clothes, is termed an adulterous act of the first (or lowest) degree.

7. Sending perfumes, garlands, fruit, spirituous liquor, food, or clothes, and conversing with her in

XXIII, 1–5. Vîram. pp. 504, 505; Ratn. pp. 378, 379.
6–8. Vîram. p. 505; Ratn. pp. 379, 380; Viv. p. 200.

secret, is considered an adulterous act of the second degree.

8. Sitting on the same bed, dallying, and kissing or embracing each other, is defined as an adulterous act of the highest degree by persons acquainted with law.

9. For these three gradations of adultery, the first, middling, and highest fines shall be inflicted respectively; the fine shall be even higher than that, in the case of a very rich man.

10. (The king) shall confiscate the whole wealth of him who violates an unwilling woman, and having caused his penis and scrotum to be cut off, shall cause him to be paraded on an ass.

11. When a man enjoys a woman by fraud, his punishment shall be confiscation of his entire wealth, and he shall afterwards be branded with the mark of a female part and banished from the town.

12. The highest fine (shall be inflicted for connexion) with a woman of equal caste; half of that (for connexion) with a woman of inferior caste; but a man who has connexion with a woman of higher caste than his own, shall be put to death.

13. When a woman has been enjoyed against her

---

9. Ratn. p. 384; Vîram. p. 506; Viv. p. 202; May. p. 149. The Mayûkha as printed reads this text differently, but one MS. of it agrees with the other compilations.

10. Ratn. p. 388; Viv. p. 212; May. p. 148.

11, 12. Ratn. p. 389; Viv. p. 213; May. p. 149. The reading of the Mayûkha seems to be wrong. This rule (12) is declared to apply to those cases where force or deception has not been used. Ratn., Viv.

11. Vîram. p. 506.

13, 14. Ratn. p. 400. For the K*rikkh*ra (Prâgâpatya) and Parâka penances, see Manu XI, 212, 216.

will, she shall be kept in the house well guarded, smeared (with ashes), lying on a low couch, and receiving a bare maintenance only.

14. To atone for her sin, she shall be caused to perform the K*rikkh*ra or Parâka penance, in case she had intercourse with her equal in caste; but if she has been enjoyed by a man of inferior caste, she shall be abandoned and put to death.

15. When a woman comes to a man's house and excites his concupiscence by touching him or the like acts, she shall be punished; half of her punishment shall be inflicted on the man.

16. Her nose, lips, and ears having been cut off, she shall be paraded in the streets and plunged into water; or she shall be torn to pieces by dogs in a public place frequented by many persons.

XXIV. Duties of Man and Wife.

1. The whole set of commandments concerning adultery has thus been stated; listen to me proclaiming the conduct prescribed for man and wife.

2. A woman must be restrained from slight transgressions even by her relations; by night and by day she must be watched by her mother-in-law and other wives belonging to the family.

3. A father who does not give his daughter in

15. Vîram. p. 513; Viv. p. 217.

16. Viv. p. 217.

XXIV, 1. Ratn. p. 409; Col. Dig. IV, 1, 1.

2. Ratn. p. 411; Col. Dig. IV, 1, 12.

3. Ratn. p. 412; Col. Dig. IV, 1, 15; Viv. p. 220. Regarding the time favourable for procreation, see Manu III, 46.

marriage in proper time (before she has reached maturity), a husband who has not connexion with his wife at the time favourable for procreation, and a son who does not support his mother: all such deserve contempt and shall be punished as ordained in law.

4. Employing (a woman) in the receipt and expenditure (of wealth), in the preparation of food, in the preservation of domestic utensils, in purification, and in the care of the (sacred household) fire, is declared to be the (best) way of guarding women.

5. Let not a woman reside in another man's house, separated from her father, husband, or sons; by (giving way to) malicious propensities, particularly, she is sure to lose her reputation.

6. Rising before (the others), paying reverence to the elders of the family, preparing food and condiments, and using a low seat and bed: thus have the duties of women been declared.

7. Drinking (spirituous liquor), rambling abroad, sleeping by day, and neglect of her daily duties, are faults disgracing a woman.

8. That wife is declared to be devoted to her husband who is afflicted when he is afflicted, pleased when he is happy, squalid and languid when he is absent, and who dies when he dies.

9. While her husband is absent, a woman must avoid decorating herself, as well as dancing, singing,

---

4. Ratn. p. 416; Col. Dig. IV, 1, 31; Vîram. p. 419.
5. Ratn. p. 427.
6. Ratn. p. 428; Col. Dig. IV, 2, 90.
7. Ratn. p. 431; Col. Dig. IV, 2, 100.
8. Ratn. p. 436; Col. Dig. IV, 2, 107. See 11.
9. Ratn. p. 439; Col. Dig. IV, 2, 118.

looking on at public spectacles or festivals, and using meat or intoxicating drinks.

10. A wife practising religious austerities, fasting and preserving her chastity, self-controlled and liberal always, goes to heaven even though she have no son.

11. A wife is considered half the body (of her husband), equally sharing the result of his good or wicked deeds; whether she ascends the pile after him, or chooses to survive him leading a virtuous life, she promotes the welfare of her husband.

12. The Niyoga (appointment of a widow to raise offspring to her deceased lord) has been declared by Manu, and again prohibited by the same; on account of the successive deterioration of the (four) ages of the world, it must not be practised by mortals (in the present age) according to law.

13. In the ages K*ri*ta, Tretâ, and Dvâpara, men were imbued with devotion and sacred knowledge; in the (present or) Kali age, a decrease of its power has been ordained for the human race.

14. The various sons who were appointed by ancient sages cannot be adopted now by men of the present age, as they are destitute of power.

XXV. The Law of Inheritance.

1. After the death of both parents, division of the property among brothers has been ordained (to take

10. Ratn. p. 443; Col. Dig. IV, 3, 138.

11. Ratn. p. 442; Col. Dig. IV, 3, 132. It appears from these texts that B*ri*haspati advocates the custom of Satî (self-immolation of the widow) as an optional rite only, in common with Vish*n*u and other Indian legislators and jurists.

12–14. Ratn. pp. 449, 450; Col. Dig. V, 4, 279 and IV, 4, 157. See Manu I, 81–86; IX, 56–70.

XXV, 1. Col. Dig. V, 2, 99, 115; D. II, 1; May. p. 39; V. p. 46;

place). It may take place even in their lifetime, if the mother be past child-bearing.

2. Houses and landed property inherited from an ancestor shall be shared equally by the father and sons; but the sons cannot claim a share of their father's own property without the consent of the father.

3. Of property acquired by the grandfather, whether immovable or movable, father and son are declared to be entitled to equal shares.

4. Those (sons) for whom their shares have been arranged by the father, whether equal, less, or greater, must be compelled to abide by such arrangement. Otherwise (if they try to alter the arrangement), they shall be punished.

5. When a partition is made during (the father's) life, the father shall reserve a couple of shares for himself.

6. The worship of the Manes, gods, and Brahmans by those residing (together) and cooking their food (in one house) is single. But when they divide the

---

Ratn. p. 462. The author of the Dâyabhâga and other writers of the Bengal school hold that this rule applies to ancestral wealth only, and that, moreover, the consent of the father is required in every division of his property during his lifetime. In the other schools of law, this text is given its plain meaning.

2. Col. Dig. V, 2, 94 ('Vyâsa'); May. p. 39. The Mayûkha deduces from this text the doctrine, generally held by the followers of the Mitâksharâ, that partition of property inherited from a grandfather or more remote ancestor may be instituted by sons even against their father's wish.

3. Col. Dig. V, 2, 93; D. II, 50; V. p. 66; May. p. 43.

4. Col. Dig. V, 1, 31; D. II, 75; V. p. 56; Ratn. p. 468.

5. Col. Dig. V, 2, 97; D. II, 46; Ratn. p. 465.

6. V. pp. 53, 257; Ratn. p. 459; Viv. p. 227; Col. Dig. V, 6, 388.

property, (the worship) takes place separately in each house.

7. Partition among coparceners is declared to be of two kinds; one is with attention to priority of birth, the other consists of the allotment of equal shares.

8. All sons of the twice-born, begotten on women equal in caste (to their husbands), shall take equal shares, after giving a preferential share to the eldest.

9. He who is the first by birth, sacred knowledge, or good qualities, shall take a couple of shares out of the partible wealth, and the rest shall take equal shares; but he stands to them in the relation of a father, as it were.

10. When they divide their father's heritage, all the sons shall share alike; but he who is distinguished by sacred knowledge and virtue, shall obtain a greater share (than the rest).

11. They are parents in the true sense of the term who have a son whose fame is spread in the world for sacred knowledge, cleverness, valour, wealth, and for knowledge, liberality, and pious acts.

12. In property belonging to the grandfather which had been taken away and has been (afterwards) recovered by the father through his own

---

7. Col. Dig. V, 1, 30; D. II, 80.
8. Col. Dig. V, 1, 53; D. II, 42.
9. Col. Dig. V, 1, 45; D. II, 42; V. p. 67; Viv. p. 235.
10. Col. Dig. V, 1, 67; V, 3, 116.
11. Col. Dig. V, 3, 116; Ratn. p. 484.
12, 13. Col. Dig. V, 2, 90; D. VI, 2, 34; V. p. 126; May. p. 40; Ratn. p. 461. Some compilations read bhâga*m*, 'withhold it from partition,' for bhoga*m*, 'consume it.'

ability, as well as in property acquired by sacred knowledge, valour in arms, &c., the father's ownership has been declared.

13. He may make a gift out of that property, or even consume it, at his will. But in his default, his sons are pronounced to be equal sharers.

14. Whatever has been acquired by all together, in that property they all have equal shares. Their sons, whether unequal or equal (in number), are declared (to be) heirs of the shares of their (respective) fathers.

15. When there are many sons sprung from one father, equal in caste and number, but born of different mothers, a legal division (of the property) may be effected by adjusting the shares according to the mothers.

16. (When there are several brothers) equal in caste, but varying in number (of sons begotten with each wife), a division according to males is ordained.

17. When step-brothers born of different mothers or uterine brothers have come to a division with their father, afterborn brothers shall take their father's share.

18. A son born before (partition) has no claim to the paternal wealth; nor (can) a brother's wealth (be claimed by) one born after partition.

19. Whatever has been acquired, with his own

14. Ratn. p. 481; Aparârka.

15. Col. Dig. V, 1, 62; D. III, 1, 12; May. p. 46; V. p. 76; Ratn. p. 975.

16. Col. Dig. V, 1, 63; May. p. 46; V. p. 76.

17, 18. Col. Dig. V, 2, 100; D. VII, 5; V. p. 93; Ratn. p. 538.

18. M. I, 6, 4; V. p. 219.

19. M. I, 6, 6; Col. Dig. V, 7, 392.

effort, by a father who has come to a partition with his sons, all that belongs to the son born after partition. Those born before it are declared to have no right.

20. In regard to the property as well as regards debts, gifts, pledges, and purchases, they are independent of each other, excepting impurity (caused by a death) and offerings consisting of water libations.

21. Should there be younger brothers, whose initiation has not been performed, they must be initiated by the other brothers (the expense being defrayed) out of the family property (inherited) from the father.

22. Whether partition has or has not been made, whenever an heir comes forward, he shall receive a share of such wealth as he can prove to be the joint property (of the family).

23. Whether it be a debt, or a document, or house, or field, which has been inherited from the paternal grandfather, he shall take his proper share of it, when he returns after a protracted absence even.

24. When a man has gone abroad, leaving the joint estate of his family, his share must undoubtedly be given to his descendant who has returned from abroad.

25. Whether he be the third or the fifth or even the seventh in descent, he shall receive the share belonging to him by right of succession, his

---

19, 20. Ratn. p. 539; May. p. 47; D. VII, 6; V. pp. 93, 219.
21. Col. Dig. V, 3, 132; May. p. 48; V. p. 86; Viv. p. 277.
22–26. Col. Dig. V, 7, 394; D. VIII, 1–3; Ratn. p. 540.
24–26. Viv. p. 241.
25. May. p. 46.

birth and family name having been ascertained (first).

26. He whom indigenous inhabitants and neighbours know to be the (legal) owner, to the descendants of that man must the land be surrendered by his kinsmen, when they make their appearance.

27. Let Brahmans, Kshatriyas, Vai*s*yas, and *S*ûdras, begotten in order by a Brahman, take four, three, two shares, and one share, in succession.

28. Let those begotten by a Kshatriya (take) three shares, two shares, and one share (respectively). Let those begotten by a Vai*s*ya take two shares and one share.

29. The son by a Kshatriya wife, if elder by birth and endowed with superior qualities, shall take an equal share with the Brahman (son); and so shall a son by a Vai*s*ya wife (share equally) with a Kshatriya son.

30. Land obtained by acceptance of a gift must never be given to the son of a Kshatriya woman or other (wife inferior in caste to her husband). Though their father may have given it to them, the son by a Brahman wife shall take it after the death (of the father).

31. An obedient and excellent son of a man having no other male issue, shall receive a maintenance (though he be born) of a *S*ûdra woman; let the Sapi*nd*as take the remainder.

---

27. U*gg*valâ, p. 79; Varadarâ*g*a, p. 19.

28. Varadarâ*g*a, p. 19.

29. Col. Dig. V, 3, 156; D. IX, 15; V. p. 98.

30. Col. Dig. V, 3, 161; D. IX, 19; M. I, 4, 36, I, 8, 8; May. p. 46; V. p. 99; Viv. p. 272.

31. Col. Dig. V, 3, 168; D. IX, 28; Viv. p. 274; May. p. 47.

32. A son begotten with a *S*ûdra woman by a twice-born man is not entitled to a share of the landed property; one begotten with a woman of equal caste shall take all. Thus has the law been settled.

33. Of the thirteen sons mentioned in succession by Manu, the legitimate son of the body (Aurasa) and the appointed daughter (Putrikâ) continue the family.

34. As in default of ghee, oil is admitted by the virtuous as a substitute (at sacrifices), so are the eleven sons (admitted as substitutes), in default of a legitimate son of the body and of an appointed daughter.

35. No one but a legitimate son of the body is declared to be heir of his father's wealth. An appointed daughter is said to be equal to him. All the others are stated to have a claim to maintenance (only).

36. Because a son (Putra) saves his father from the hell called Put by the very sight of his face, therefore should a man be anxious to beget a son.

37. Both a son's son and the son of an appointed daughter cause a man to attain heaven. Both are pronounced to be equal as regards their right of inheritance and the duty of offering funeral balls of meal (Pi*nd*as).

---

32. Col. Dig. V, 3, 164; V. p. 99; Ratn. p. 534. The Ratnâkara after this text inserts two other texts on the right of a Nishâda son, which are elsewhere attributed to Devala.

33, 34. V. p. 120. See Manu IX, 126, 158–160.

35. Col. Dig. V, 4, 215; Viv. p. 285; V. p. 121.

36. Col. Dig. V, 4, 304. punnâmno narakât putra*h* pitara*m* trâyate yata*h* | mukhasa*m*dar*s*anenâpi tadutpattau yateta sa*h* ||

37. Col. Dig. V, 4, 304; Uggvalâ, p. 80.

38. Gautama has declared that a daughter is appointed after performing a sacrifice to Agni and Pragâpati; others have said that she is an appointed daughter (Putrikâ) who was merely supposed to be one (before her birth) by a man having no male issue.

39. The other sons, beginning with the son begotten on a wife (Kshetraga), shall (respectively) take a fifth, a sixth, and a seventh part.

40. The son given, the son cast off, the son bought, the son made (or adopted), the son by a Sûdra wife: these, when pure by caste and irreproachable as to their conduct, are considered sons of middle rank.

41. The son begotten on a wife (Kshetraga) is despised by the virtuous; and so are the son begotten on a woman twice married, the son of an unmarried damsel, the son received with the wife, and the son secretly born.

42. Though born of a wife of the same caste, a son destitute of good qualities is unworthy to obtain the paternal wealth; it shall go to those learned (kinsmen) who offer the funeral ball of meal (Pinda) for the father.

43. A son redeems his father from the highest

38. Col. Dig. V, 4, 225; Ratn. p. 562. See Gautama XXVIII, 18.

39. Col. Dig. V, 4, 246; Ratn. p. 545; V. p. 125. The Vîramitrodaya reads samabhâginah for sapta bhâginah, 'The other five or six sons beginning with the wife's son are equal sharers.' Regarding the wife's son (Kshetraga), see Manu IX, 167; Brihaspati XXIV, 12–14.

40, 41. Col. Dig. V, 4, 202; V. p. 128; Ratn. p. 552.

42, 43. May. p. 101.

42–45. Col. Dig. V, 4, 264; V, 319; D. V, 4; V. p. 256; Viv. p. 242.

and lowest debts; consequently there is no use of him who acts otherwise.

44. What can be done with a cow which neither gives milk nor is (ever) pregnant? What is the good of a son being born who is neither learned nor virtuous?

45. A son who is destitute of learning, valour, and wealth, void of devotion and insight, and unobservant of good custom, such a son is declared to be no better than urine and fæces.

46. In the revealed texts (of the Veda), in the traditional law (of the Smritis), and in popular usage, the wife is declared to be half the body (of her husband), equally sharing the outcome of good and evil acts.

47. Of him whose wife is not dead, half his body survives. How should any one else take the property, while half (his) body lives?

48. Although kinsmen (Sakulyas), although his father and mother, although uterine brothers be living, the wife of him who dies without leaving male issue shall succeed to his share.

49. A wife deceased before (her husband) takes away his consecrated fire (Agnihotra); but if the husband dies before the wife, she takes his property, if she has been faithful to him. This is an eternal law.

50. After having received all the movable and immovable property, the gold, base metals and grain, liquids and wearing apparel, she shall cause

46. See XXIV, 11.
46–52. Col. Dig. V, 8, 399; V. 8, 416; D. XI, 1, 2; Ratn. p. 589.
46–49. V. pp. 141, 142. 47. M. II, 1, 6.
48–52. Viv. pp. 289, 290.

his monthly, sixmonthly, and annual *S*râddhas to be performed.

51. Let her propitiate with funeral oblations and pious liberality her husband's paternal uncles, Gurus, daughter's sons, sister's sons, and maternal uncles; also aged or helpless persons, guests, and women (belonging to the family).

52. Should agnates (Sapi*nd*as) or cognates (Bândhavas) or enemies injure the property, let the king inflict on them the punishment destined for a thief.

53. The husband being separated (in interests from his former coparceners), his wife shall take after his death a pledge and whatever else is recognised as property, excepting the immovable wealth.

54. A wife, though preserving her character and though partition have been made, is unworthy to obtain immovable property. Food or a portion of the arable land shall be given to her at will (for her support).

55. The wife is declared to succeed to her husband's property, and in her default, the daughter.

56. A daughter, like a son, springs from each member of a man; how then should any other mortal inherit the father's property while she lives?

57. Equal in caste (to her father) and married to a man of the same caste as her own, virtuous, habitually submissive, she shall inherit her father's property, whether she may have been (expressly) appointed or not.

53, 54. May. p. 77; V. pp. 134, 135, 173.
55, 56. M. II, 2, 2; Smr*i*tik. (K. Iyer's translation) XI, 2, 113.
56–58. Col. Dig. V, 4, 224; D. XI, 2, 8, 17; V. pp. 176, 180, 183; Viv. pp. 292–294. 56, 57. Ratn. p. 591.

58. As her father's wealth becomes her property, though kinsmen be in existence, even so her son becomes the owner of his mother's and maternal grandfather's wealth.

59. In default of them, uterine brothers or brother's sons, agnates (Sakulyas) and cognates (Bândhavas), pupils, or learned Brahmans are entitled to the inheritance.

60. When a man dies leaving no issue, nor wife, nor brother, nor father, nor mother, all his Sapi*nd*as shall divide his property in due shares.

61. Half the entire wealth, however, shall first be set apart for the benefit of the deceased (owner) and carefully assigned for his monthly, sixmonthly, and annual *S*râddhas.

62. When there are several relatives, agnates (Sakulyas), and cognates (Bândhavas), whosoever of them is the nearest shall take the wealth of him who died leaving no issue.

63. When a man dies without leaving either wife or male issue, the mother has to be considered as her son's heiress, or a brother (may succeed) if she consents to it.

64. But on his death the mother shall take a son's share. The mothers shall share equally with the sons, the maidens shall take fourth-part shares.

---

59. Col. Dig. V, 8, 422; D. XI, 2, 26. 'In default of them,' i. e. of a daughter or daughter's son.

59–62. Col. Dig. V, 8, 437; Ratn. p. 595.

60. V. p. 216. 61. D. XI, 6, 13.

62. V. p. 194; May. p. 81.

63. Col. Dig. V, 8, 423; V. p. 191; Viv. p. 293; D. XI, 3, 2.

64. Col. Dig. V, 2, 85; V. pp. 81, 84, &c. 'On his death,' i.e. on the father's death. For tanayâ*m*sasamâ*m*sinî, 'shall take a son's share,' the Vîramitrodaya reads tanayâ vâ samâ*m*sinî, 'or the

65, 66. To a father the funeral ball (Pi*nd*a) and water oblation shall be offered by his son; in default of a son, the widow (succeeds); in her default, a uterine brother; in default of him, the co-heirs (dâyâdâ*h*); afterwards, the property goes to the daughter's son.

67. Should a Kshatriya, Vai*s*ya, or *S*ûdra die without leaving male issue, or wife, or brother, their property shall be taken (as escheat) by the king, for he is the lord of all.

68. Except in the case of a Brahman; but a king bent on the practice of virtue must allot a maintenance to his women. Thus has the law of inheritance been declared.

69. For her food (he must assign) a Prastha of rice every afternoon, together with fuel, and one dress purchased for three Pa*n*as must be given to her every three months.

70. What is left after setting apart property suffi-

---

daughter shall take an equal share.' Vâ*k*aspatimi*s*ra, Kamalâkara, Nandapa*nd*ita, and other commentators explain the term mâtara*h*, 'mothers,' as denoting step-mothers who have no issue, whereas in the first clause the term 'mother' (*g*ananî), according to them, denotes a woman who has male issue. It seems more natural, however, to interpret the term 'mother' in the same way in both clauses. Vish*n*u (XVIII, 34, 35) has the analogous precept that mothers and maiden daughters shall receive shares corresponding to the shares of sons. Vish*n*u's rule relates to a division of property among sons differing in caste, and the present text of B*ri*haspati seems to apply to the same case.

65, 66. Aparârka; Sm*ri*ti*k*. XI, 4, 19 (Iyer). These texts are quoted in some works only, and it is certainly difficult to reconcile them with the other texts of B*ri*haspati on inheritance.

67. Col. Dig. V, 8, 446; D. XI, 1, 49; May. p. 83; Viv. p. 298.

68–71. Nandapa*nd*ita's Vai*g*ayantî; U*gg*valâ, p. 82; Gautamîyâ Mitâksharâ. The reading in 71 is uncertain.

cient for the expense of her dress, food, and for the washerman, shall be made over to the co-heirs.

71. (The widow) shall recite the Dhûmâvasânika prayer in the evening, bathe frequently, and pay no regard to dwelling, food, or clothing after her husband's death.

72. He who (having been divided) is again living, through affection, together with his father or brother, or with his uncle even, is said to be reunited with them.

73. When brothers formerly divided are again living together through affection and arrange a second division, the right of primogeniture does not accrue in that case.

74. When any one (brother) should die or anyhow renounce worldly interests, his share is not lost; it is allotted to his uterine brother.

75. If there be a sister, she is entitled to a share of his property. This is the law regarding (the wealth of) one destitute of issue, and who has no wife or father.

76. When two (coparceners) have again established together, they shall mutually inherit their property.

77. If among reunited coparceners any one should acquire property through learning, valour, or other (independent effort of his own), a double share must be given to him; the rest shall take equal shares.

78. Whatever has been given by the paternal

---

72. Col. Dig. V, 8, 430; M. II, 9, 3; May. p. 84; V. pp. 40, 162, 205; Viv. p. 300; D. XI, 1, 30, XII, 3; Ratn. p. 605.

73–75. Col. Dig. V, 8, 407; Viv. p. 302; V. p. 159.

76. May. p. 88; Viv. p. 305; Ratn. p. 602.

77. Col. Dig. V, 8, 460; V. p. 205; May. p. 85; Viv. p. 302.

78. May. p. 69; Smritik. (Iyer) VII, 23.

grandfather, the father, or the mother, (all that) shall not be taken from him (who possesses it); (he may keep), likewise, property acquired by valour and the wealth of his wife.

79. Those by whom clothes and the like articles have been declared indivisible have not decided properly. The wealth of the rich depends on clothes and ornaments.

80. (Such wealth) when withheld from partition will yield no profit; but neither can it be allotted to a single (coparcener). Therefore it has to be divided with some skill; or else it would be useless.

81. Clothes and ornaments are divided by (distributing the proceeds after) selling them; a written bond (concerning a debt, is divided) after recovering the sum lent; prepared food (is divided) by an exchange for (an equal amount of) unprepared food.

82. The water of a well or pool shall be drawn and used according to need. A single female (slave) shall be (successively) set to work at their houses (by the several sharers) according to their shares (of the inheritance).

83. If there are many of them, they shall be divided equally. The same rule applies to male slaves as well. Property obtained for a pious purpose shall be divided in equal shares.

84. Fields and embankments shall be divided according to their several shares. A common (road or) pasture-ground shall be always used by the coheirs in due proportion to their several shares.

79–84. Col. Dig. V, 5, 366; May. pp. 71, 72; Smritik. (Iyer) VII, 41–43, &c. The arrangement of these texts varies in the several works.

80 b, 82. D. I, 10; V, 3.

85. The clothes, ornaments, bed, and the like, as well as the vehicle and the like, appertaining to the father, shall be given to the person who partakes of his funeral repast, after honouring him with fragrant drugs and flowers.

86. Such property, whether immovable or other, as has been given to women by their father-in-law, can never be taken away from them by the co-heirs.

87. Strîdhana goes to the children, and the daughter if not betrothed has a share in it. If she is married, she shall receive an honorary trifle only.

88. The mother's sister, the wife of a maternal uncle, a paternal uncle's wife, a father's sister, a mother-in-law, and an elder brother's wife are declared to be equal to a mother.

89. If they have no legitimate son of the body, nor (other) son, nor daughter's son, nor their son, their sister's son, &c. shall inherit their property.

90. A heinous crime, (a claim regarding) immovable property, a deposit, and a previous partition among co-heirs, have to be ascertained by circumstantial evidence, in default of documents and witnesses.

91. A family feud, mutual malice, or the discovery of stolen goods, may be evidence of a heinous crime; possession of the land may be proof of property; and separate property is an argument of partition.

85. M. I, 4, 17; May. p. 70; V. p. 250.

86. V. p. 174; Smr*i*ti*k*. XI, 1, 44.

87. Col. Dig. V, 9, 487; D. IV, 2, 3; Viv. p. 267; V. p. 229. The two first works read, 'she does not take her mother's wealth' for 'she shall receive an honorary trifle only.'

88, 89. Col. Dig. V, 9, 513; D. VI, 3, 31; May. p. 98; V. p. 243.

90–92. Col. Dig. V, 6, 389; D. XIV, 8.

90, 92. V. p. 261.

92. Those who keep their income, expenditure, and mortgages distinct, and engage in mutual transactions in money-lending and traffic, are undoubtedly separate.

93. Whether kinsmen are united or separate, they are all alike as regards immovable property, as no one of them has power in any case to give, mortgage, or sell it.

94, 95. Whatever share is enjoyed by each, must not be changed from him. If he should subsequently contest a distribution, which was made with his own consent, he shall be compelled by the king to content himself with his share, and shall be punished if he should persist in contention.

96. When the loan or mortgaging of joint property is concealed with a fraudulent purpose, the king shall recover it from the cheat by artifice, but not use violence to extort it from him.

97. Cheats, robbers of wealth, crafty and covetous men, shall be reclaimed by friendly expostulation, by the loss of their own property, or by stratagem.

98. Household utensils, beasts of burden and the like, milch cattle, ornaments, and workmen have to be divided on being discovered. When property is (supposed to be) hidden, proof by sacred libation is ordained.

---

92. May. p. 75; Viv. p. 313; Ratn. p. 608.

93. M. I, 1, 30; May. p. 76; V. pp. 87, 158; D. II, 27 ('Vyâsa'). For 'kinsmen' some works read 'coparceners' or 'co-heirs' (dâyâdâ*h*). The general meaning remains the same.

94, 95. Col. Dig. V, 6, 378; May. p. 76; V. pp. 258, 259.

96, 97. Col. Dig. V, 6, 379; Ratn. p. 526.

98. Sm*ri*ti*k*. (Iyer) VI, 11.

99. When there are many uterine brothers sprung from one (father), and a son is born even to one of them only, they all are declared to have male offspring (through that son).

100. The same rule is declared for a plurality of wives of one (husband); if one of them has male issue, that (son) shall present the funeral ball of meal to them all.

101. (For one leaving no male issue), a brother, or brother's son, or a Sapi*nd*a, or a pupil, should first perform the ceremony of uniting him with the Sapi*nd*as (to be worshipped at a *S*râddha offering), and then offer him the funeral ceremonies customary on joyful occasions.

XXVI. Gambling and Betting.

1. Gambling has been prohibited by Manu, because it destroys truth, honesty, and wealth. It has been permitted by other (legislators) when conducted so as to allow the king a share (of every stake).

2. It shall take place under the superintendence of keepers of gaming-houses, as it serves the purpose of discovering thieves. The same rule has to be observed in bets on prize-fights with animals.

3. When birds, rams, deer or other (animals) are caused to fight against one another, after a wager has been laid, it is called betting on animals (samâhvaya).

99, 100. Ratn. p. 583; Varadarâ*g*a, p. 27.
101. Ratn. p. 600; Col. Dig. V, 8, 454.
XXVI, 1, 2. Viv. p. 318; Vîram. pp. 721, 722. See Manu IX, 224.
3. Viv. p. 317; Ratn. p. 610.

4. When any one is defeated in a prize-fight between two animals, the wager which has been laid shall be paid by the owner of the (defeated) animal.

5. A wager (or game) shall be made in public; false gamblers shall be banished.

6. When there is a point at issue between the two parties (in a game or wager, other) gamblers shall examine (and decide) the matter; if they are enemies (of either party), the king shall decide the dispute.

7. One defeated in a secret game; or ignorant of the rules; or (defeated) by the use of false dice, or by deceit, though acquainted with the game, shall be released; and one who has lost his entire wealth in a game shall not be compelled to give the whole of it.

8. The keeper of the gaming-house shall receive the stakes and pay the victorious gambler and the king; he shall also act as witness in a dispute, assisted by three other gamblers.

9. Those wicked men who use false dice in a game, or rob the king of his due, or cheat by making false computations, are declared to be gamblers deserving punishment.

XXVII. Miscellaneous (Prakîrnaka).

1. This (aggregate of rules concerning) lawsuits instituted by litigants has been briefly declared; I will declare (next the law concerning) Miscellaneous Causes instituted by the king (in person).

4, 5. Viv. p. 318; Vîram. p. 720. 6. Vîram. p. 720.
7–9. Ratn. pp. 614–617.
XXVII, 1. Vîram. p. 722; Ratn. p. 621.

2. In the case of a conflict between two Smritis (texts of law), equity should be resorted to; when the law-books are inapplicable, that course should be followed which is indicated by a consideration of the circumstances of the case.

3. (However) the first rank (among legislators) belongs to Manu, because he has embodied the essence of the Veda in his work; that Smriti (or text of law) which is opposed to the tenor of the laws of Manu is not approved.

4. When he has discovered a man to be an offender, (the king) should inflict (one of the various sorts of punishment) on him, (gentle) admonition, (harsh) reproof or corporal chastisement, or one of the four gradations of fines.

5. (Let him inflict) a (gentle) admonition, when the offence is very light; (harsh) reproof, for a crime in the first degree; a fine, for a crime in the (second or) middlemost degree; and arrest, in the case of high-treason.

6. Banishment also may be resorted to by (a king) desirous of promoting his own welfare in order to meet opposition, and all (the various) sorts (of punishment) should be united in the case of one who has committed a mortal sin.

7. (The king) should punish elders, domestic priests, and persons commanding respect, with (gentle) admonition only; other litigants he should amerce in a fine, when they are found to be guilty;

---

2. Vîram. p. 119.

3. Col. Dig. V, 5, 333. vedârthopanibaddhatvât prâdhânyam tu manoh smritam | manvarthaviparîtâ yâ na sâ smritih prasasyate ||

4–7. Ratn. p. 629.

and on the perpetrators of a heavy crime he should inflict corporal punishment.

8. (Gentle) admonition and (harsh) reproof are declared to be the privilege of the Brahman (appointed as chief judge); but both fines and corporal punishment may be inflicted by the king only.

9. Both hands, both feet, the male organ, the eye, the tongue, both ears, the nose, the neck, one half of the feet, the thumb and index, the forehead, the lips, the hindpart, and the hips:

10. These fourteen places of punishment have been indicated. For a Brahman, branding him on the forehead is ordained as the only kind of punishment.

11. A Brahman, though a mortal sinner, shall not suffer capital punishment; the king shall banish him, and cause him to be branded and shaved.

12. That man who deserves capital punishment shall be compelled to pay one hundred Suvar*n*as; one deserving to have a limb cut off, half as much; and one deserving to have the thumb and index (cut off), half of that.

13. The eighteen titles of law have been explained, together with the particulars of plaint and answer. Learn now (the law regarding) the relative validity of transactions.

14. That transaction which has been prior in time (to another) shall be upheld. If it is departed from, that is (called) an alteration of a transaction.

15. If a creditor or debtor revokes a previous

---

8. Ratn. p. 630. 9, 10. Ratn. p. 631. 11. Ratn. p. 634. 12. Ratn. p. 656. 13–18. Ratn. pp. 618–620.

agreement and makes another contract of the same description, (in which a) greater or less (amount is stated), it is termed an alteration of a transaction.

16. When (a debtor) having received a loan at the rate of two per cent. (in the month) promises to pay five per cent., that subsequent agreement is valid.

17. Between two successive transactions, the first is (rendered) void (by the second); a subsequent agreement prevails over the one preceding it in time.

18. When a man first makes a deposit and converts it into a pledge afterwards, after receiving money (for it), or sells it, the second transaction prevails over the first.

[19. Forbidden practices are found among the Southerners in the present day, (such as) matches with a maternal uncle's daughter, in spite of the prohibited degree of relationship on the mother's side (causing such unions to be illegal).

20. The highly reprehensible custom of a brother living with his deceased brother's wife, and the delivery of a marriageable damsel to a family is found in other countries.

21. What is more, matches with a mother occur among the Pârasîkas. The inhabitants of some countries do not allow the presentation of fresh gifts (of food) at a *S*râddha offering to those Brahmans who have been fed at a *S*râddha held on the eleventh

---

19–24. These texts will be published elsewhere. They have been taken from the Sa*m*skâra Kâ*nd*a of the Sm*ri*ti*k*andrikâ, where they are quoted from an uncertain author. 20 has been printed, as a text of B*ri*haspati, in Professor Bühler's Uggvalâ, p. 101. The term 'Pârasîkas' denotes the Persians, or perhaps the Parsis of India.

day (after the decease of a person) or at some other *S*râddha.

22. Others, after lending grain, take twice as much back in the autumn season and occupy the embanked land, after having received twice the amount lent,

23. Though the principal has been repaid. This is reprehensible also. Such forbidden practices (the king) should check (when they are resorted to) through folly.

24. Such customs as are not opposed to the laws of particular countries and castes or other (corporations), every king should establish in accordance with the sacred law, after consulting the law-books.]

25. Thus let the king every day examine, in common with learned Brahmans, both the suits proffered by litigants and those instituted by the king (himself).

26. When the safety of many may be effected by destroying a single offender, his execution is productive of religious merit (even).

---

25. Ratn. p. 618.

26. Smr*i*tik. ekasmin yatra nidhana*m* prâpite dush*t*a*k*âri*n*i ı bahûnâ*m* bhavati kshemas tasya pu*n*yaprado vadha*h* ıı

ADDENDA.

P. 231, Appendix v. 56. This difficult text, together with an additional text, is quoted in a somewhat different, but equally faulty form, in the recently published last fasciculus of the Vivâdaratnâkara in the Bibliotheca Indica. I propose to render the two texts as follows: 'Fines beginning with a Kârshâpa*n*a may amount to four Kârshâpa*n*as at most (in heavy cases); there are others beginning with two and rising to eight, or beginning with three and rising to twelve Kârshâpa*n*as. All those (fines) which have been declared to begin with one Kârshâpa*n*a may be raised to the fourfold amount; the same rule applies to the other fines as well, excepting the highest fine (which consists of 2500 Pa*n*as).'

P. 369, *after* v. 14, *add* '15. A wife should be honoured by her husband with (presents of) clothes, ornaments, and food; and at a festival (she should receive similar presents) from her father and brothers, her parents-in-law, and other relations.'

P. 369, *after* note on vv. 12–14, *add* 15. Smr*i*ti*k*. bhartrâ patnî samabhyar*k*yâ vastrâla*m*kârabhoganai*h* । utsave tu pit*ri*bhrât*ris*va-*s*urâdyai*s* *k*a bandhubhi*h* ॥

CONSONANTS.	MISSIONARY ALPHABET. I Class.	II Class.	III Class.	Sanskrit.	Zend.	Pehlevi.	Persian.	Arabic.	Hebrew.	Chinese.
Gutturales.										
1 Tenuis	k	...	...	क	𐬐	[illegible]	ك	ك	כּ	k
2 „ aspirata	kh	...	...	ख	𐬑	[illegible]	...	...	כ	kh
3 Media	g	...	...	ग	𐬔	[illegible]	گ	...	גּ	...
4 „ aspirata	gh	...	...	घ	𐬖	[illegible]	...	...	ג	...
5 Gutturo-labialis	q	...	...	...	...	...	ق	ق	ק	...
6 Nasalis	ṅ (ng)	...	...	ङ	𐬢 (ng) 𐬣 (N)	...	...	...	...	...
7 Spiritus asper	h	...	...	ह	𐬵 (𐬓𐬎 *hv*)	[illegible]	ه	ه	ה	h, hs
8 „ lenis	’	...	...	...	...	...	ا	ا	א	...
9 „ asper faucalis	‘h	...	...	...	...	...	ح	ح	ח	...
10 „ lenis faucalis	’h	...	...	...	...	...	ع	ع	ע	...
11 „ asper fricatus	...	*‘h*	...	...	...	...	خ	خ	ח	...
12 „ lenis fricatus	...	*’h*	...	...	...	...	...	...	...	...
Gutturales modificatae (palatales, &c.)										
13 Tenuis	...	*k*	...	च	𐬗	[illegible]	چ	...	...	*k*
14 „ aspirata	...	*kh*	...	छ	...	...	...	...	...	*kh*
15 Media	...	*g*	...	ज	𐬘	[illegible]	ج	ج	...	...
16 „ aspirata	...	*gh*	...	झ	...	...	غ	غ	...	...
17 „ Nasalis	ñ	...	...	ञ	...	...	...	...	...	...

CONSONANTS (*continued*).	MISSIONARY ALPHABET. I Class.	II Class.	III Class.	Sanskrit.	Zend.	Pehlevi.	Persian.	Arabic.	Hebrew.	Chinese.
18 Semivocalis	y	...	....	य	[illegible]; [illegible] init.	[illegible]	ي	ي	י	y
19 Spiritus asper	...	($\acute{y}$)	....	...	....	...	...	...	...	...
20 „ lenis	...	($\grave{y}$)	....	...	....	...	...	...	...	...
21 „ asper assibilatus	...	*s*	....	श	[illegible]	[illegible]	ش	ش	...	...
22 „ lenis assibilatus	...	*z*	....	...	[illegible]	[illegible]	ژ	...	...	*z*
Dentales.										
23 Tenuis	t	...	....	त	[illegible]	[illegible]	ت	ت	תּ	t
24 „ aspirata	th	...	....	थ	[illegible]	...	...	...	ת	th
25 „ assibilata	...	...	TH	...	....	...	ث	ث	...	...
26 Media	d	...	....	द	[illegible]	[illegible]	د	د	דּ	...
27 „ aspirata	dh	...	....	ध	[illegible]	...	...	...	ד	...
28 „ assibilata	...	...	DH	...	....	...	ذ	ذ	...	...
29 Nasalis	n	...	....	न	[illegible]	[illegible]	ن	ن	נ	n
30 Semivocalis	l	...	....	ल	....	[illegible]	ل	ل	ל	l
31 „ mollis 1	...	*l*	....	ळ	....	...	...	...	...	...
32 „ mollis 2	...	...	L	...	....	...	...	...	...	...
33 Spiritus asper 1	s	...	....	स	[illegible]	[illegible]	س (ث)	س	שׂ	s
34 „ asper 2	...	...	s (ʃ)	...	....	...	...	...	ס	...
35 „ lenis	z	...	....	...	[illegible]	[illegible]	ز (ذ)	ز	ז	z
36 „ asperrimus 1	...	...	z (ʒ)	...	....	...	ص	ص	צ	ʒ, ʒh

Dentales modificatae (linguales, &c.)										
38 Tenuis	...	*t*	....	ट	....	...	ط	ط	ט	...
39 „ aspirata	...	*th*	....	ठ	....	...	ظ	ظ	...	...
40 Media	...	*d*	....	ड	𐬜	[illegible]	...	...	...	...
41 „ aspirata	...	*dh*	....	ढ	....	...	...	ض	...	...
42 Nasalis	...	*n*	....	ण	𐬣	...	...	...	...	...
43 Semivocalis	r	...	....	र	𐬭	[illegible]	ر	ر	ר	...
44 „ fricata	...	*r*	....	...	....	...	...	...	...	*r*
45 „ diacritica	...	...	R	...	....	...	...	...	...	...
46 Spiritus asper	sh	...	....	ष	𐬴	[illegible]	...	...	...	sh
47 „ lenis	zh	...	....	...	....	...	...	...	...	...
Labiales.										
48 Tenuis	p	...	....	प	𐬞	[illegible]	پ	...	פּ	p
49 „ aspirata	ph	...	....	फ	....	...	...	...	פ	ph
50 Media	b	...	....	ब	𐬠	[illegible]	ب	ب	בּ	...
51 „ aspirata	bh	...	....	भ	....	...	...	...	ב	...
52 Tenuissima	...	*p*	....	...	....	...	...	...	...	...
53 Nasalis	m	...	....	म	𐬨	[illegible]	م	م	מ	m
54 Semivocalis	w	...	....	...	𐬎	...	...	...	...	w
55 „ aspirata	hw	...	....	...	....	...	...	...	...	...
56 Spiritus asper	f	...	....	...	𐬟	[illegible]	ف	ف	...	f
57 „ lenis	v	...	....	व	»	[illegible]	و	و	ו	...
58 Anusvâra	...	*m*	....	अं	[illegible] ã	...	...	...	...	...
59 Visarga	...	*h*	....	अः	....	...	...	...	...	...

VOWELS.	Missionary Alphabet. I Class.	II Class.	III Class.	Sanskrit.	Zend.	Pehlevi.	Persian.	Arabic.	Hebrew.	Chinese.
1 Neutralis	0	...	....	...	....	...	...	...	ֳ	ă
2 Laryngo-palatalis	ĕ	...	....	...	....	...	...	...	...	...
3 „ labialis	ŏ	...	....	...	....	ا fin.	...	...	...	...
4 Gutturalis brevis	a	...	....	अ	𐬀	𐬀 init.	َ	َ	ַ	a
5 „ longa	â	(*a*)	....	आ	𐬁	𐬀	َا	َا	ָ	â
6 Palatalis brevis	i	...	....	इ	𐬌	...	ِ	ِ	ִ	i
7 „ longa	î	(*i*)	....	ई	𐬍	و	ِي	ِي	ִי	î
8 Dentalis brevis	*li*	...	....	ऌ	....	...	...	...	...	...
9 „ longa	*lî*	...	....	ॡ	....	...	...	...	...	...
10 Lingualis brevis	*ri*	...	....	ऋ	....	...	...	...	...	...
11 „ longa	*rî*	...	....	ॠ	....	...	...	...	...	...
12 Labialis brevis	u	...	....	उ	𐬎	...	ُ	ُ	ֻ	u
13 „ longa	û	(*u*)	....	ऊ	𐬏	ا	ُو	ُو	וּ	û
14 Gutturo-palatalis brevis	e	...	....	...	𐬈 (e) 𐬆 (*e*)	...	...	...	ֶ	e
15 „ longa	ê (ai)	(*e*)	....	ए	𐬉, 𐬇	و	...	...	ֵ	ê
16 Diphthongus gutturo-palatalis	âi	(*ai*)	....	ऐ	....	...	َيْ	َيْ	...	âi
17 „ „	ei (ĕi)	...	....	...	....	...	...	...	...	ei, êi
18 „ „	oi (ŏu)	...	....	...	....	...	...	...	...	...
19 Gutturo-labialis brevis	o	...	....	...	𐬊	...	...	...	ָ	o
20 „ longa	ô (au)	(*o*)	....	ओ	𐬋	ا	...	...	וֹ	...
21 Diphthongus gutturo-labialis	âu	(*au*)	....	औ	𐬃𐬎 (*au*)	...	َوْ	َوْ	...	âu
22 „ „	eu (ĕu)	...	....	...	....	...	...	...	...	...
23 „ „	ou (ŏu)	...	....	...	....	...	...	...	...	...
24 Gutturalis fracta	ä	...	....	...	....	...	...	...	...	...
25 Palatalis fracta	ï	...	....	...	....	...	...	...	...	...
26 Labialis fracta	ü	...	....	...	....	...	...	...	...	ü

SACRED BOOKS OF THE EAST

TRANSLATED BY

VARIOUS ORIENTAL SCHOLARS

AND EDITED BY

F. MAX MÜLLER

*** *This Series is published with the sanction and co-operation of the Secretary of State for India in Council.*

REPORT presented to the ACADÉMIE DES INSCRIPTIONS, May 11, 1883, by M. ERNEST RENAN.

'M. Renan présente trois nouveaux volumes de la grande collection des "Livres sacrés de l'Orient" (Sacred Books of the East), que dirige à Oxford, avec une si vaste érudition et une critique si sûre, le savant associé de l'Académie des Inscriptions, M. Max Müller. . . . La première série de ce beau recueil, composée de 24 volumes, est presque achevée. M. Max Müller se propose d'en publier une seconde, dont l'intérêt historique et religieux ne sera pas moindre. M. Max Müller a su se procurer la collaboration des savans les plus éminens d'Europe et d'Asie. L'Université d'Oxford, que cette grande publication honore au plus haut degré, doit tenir à continuer dans les plus larges proportions une œuvre aussi philosophiquement conçue que savamment exécutée.'

EXTRACT from the QUARTERLY REVIEW.

'We rejoice to notice that a second series of these translations has been announced and has actually begun to appear. The stones, at least, out of which a stately edifice may hereafter arise, are here being brought together. Prof. Max Müller has deserved well of scientific history. Not a few minds owe to his enticing words their first attraction to this branch of study. But no work of his, not even the great edition of the Rig-Veda, can compare in importance or in usefulness with this English translation of the Sacred Books of the East, which has been devised by his foresight, successfully brought so far by his persuasive and organising power, and will, we trust, by the assistance of the distinguished scholars he has gathered round him, be carried in due time to a happy completion.'

Professor E. HARDY, Inaugural Lecture in the University of Freiburg, 1887.

'Die allgemeine vergleichende Religionswissenschaft datirt von jenem grossartigen, in seiner Art einzig dastehenden Unternehmen, zu welchem auf Anregung Max Müllers im Jahre 1874 auf dem internationalen Orientalistencongress in London der Grundstein gelegt worden war, die Übersetzung der heiligen Bücher des Ostens' (*the Sacred Books of the East*).

Oxford

AT THE CLARENDON PRESS

LONDON: HENRY FROWDE

OXFORD UNIVERSITY PRESS WAREHOUSE, AMEN CORNER, E.C.

FIRST SERIES.

VOL. I. The Upanishads.

Translated by F. MAX MÜLLER. Part I. The *Kh*ândogya-upanishad, The Talavakâra-upanishad, The Aitareya-âra*n*yaka, The Kaushîtaki-brâhma*n*a-upanishad, and The Vâ*g*asaneyi-sa*m*hitâ-upanishad. 8vo., cloth, 10*s*. 6*d*.

The Upanishads contain the philosophy of the Veda. They have become the foundation of the later Vedânta doctrines, and indirectly of Buddhism. Schopenhauer, speaking of the Upanishads, says: 'In the whole world there is no study so beneficial and so elevating as that of the Upanishads. It has been the solace of my life, it will be the solace of my death.'

[See also Vol. XV.]

VOL. II. The Sacred Laws of the Âryas,

As taught in the Schools of Âpastamba, Gautama, Vâsish*th*a, and Baudhâyana. Translated by GEORG BÜHLER. Part I. Âpastamba and Gautama. 8vo., cloth, 10*s*. 6*d*.

The Sacred Laws of the Âryas contain the original treatises on which the Laws of Manu and other lawgivers were founded.

[See also Vol. XIV.]

VOL. III. The Sacred Books of China.

The Texts of Confucianism. Translated by JAMES LEGGE. Part I. The Shû King, The Religious Portions of the Shih King, and The Hsiâo King. 8vo., cloth, 12*s*. 6*d*.

Confucius was a collector of ancient traditions, not the founder of a new religion. As he lived in the sixth and fifth centuries B.C. his works are of unique interest for the study of Ethology.

[See also Vols. XVI, XXVII, and XXVIII.]

VOL. IV. The Zend-Avesta.

Translated by JAMES DARMESTETER. Part I. The Vendîdâd. 8vo., cloth, 10*s*. 6*d*.

The Zend-Avesta contains the relics of what was the religion of Cyrus, Darius, and Xerxes, and, but for the battle of Marathon, might have become the religion of Europe. It forms to the present day the sacred book of the Parsis, the so-called fire-worshippers. Two more volumes will complete the translation of all that is left us of Zoroaster's religion.

[See also Vols. XXIII and XXXI.]

VOL. V. Pahlavi Texts.

Translated by E. W. WEST. Part I. The Bundahis, Bahman Yast, and Shâyast lâ-shâyast. 8vo., cloth, 12*s*. 6*d*.

The Pahlavi Texts comprise the theological literature of the revival of Zoroaster's religion, beginning with the Sassanian dynasty. They are important for a study of Gnosticism.

VOLS. VI AND IX. The Qur'ân.

Parts I and II. Translated by E. H. PALMER. 8vo., cloth, 21*s*.

This translation, carried out according to his own peculiar views of the origin of the Qur'ân, was the last great work of E. H. Palmer, before he was murdered in Egypt.

VOL. VII. The Institutes of Vish*n*u.

Translated by JULIUS JOLLY. 8vo., cloth, 10*s*. 6*d*.

A collection of legal aphorisms, closely connected with one of the oldest Vedic schools, the Kathas, *but considerably added to in later time. Of importance for a critical study of the Laws of Manu.*

VOL. VIII. The Bhagavadgîtâ, with The Sanatsugâtîya, and The Anugîtâ.

Translated by KÂSHINÂTH TRIMBAK TELANG. 8vo., cloth, 10*s*. 6*d*.

The earliest philosophical and religious poem of India. It has been paraphrased in Arnold's 'Song Celestial.'

VOL. X. The Dhammapada,

Translated from Pâli by F. MAX MÜLLER; and

The Sutta-Nipâta,

Translated from Pâli by V. FAUSBÖLL; being Canonical Books of the Buddhists. 8vo., cloth, 10*s*. 6*d*.

The Dhammapada contains the quintessence of Buddhist morality The Sutta-Nipâta gives the authentic teaching of Buddha on some of the fundamental principles of religion.

VOL. XI. Buddhist Suttas.

Translated from Pâli by T. W. RHYS DAVIDS. 1. The Mahâparinibbâna Suttanta; 2. The Dhamma-*k*akka-ppavattana Sutta. 3. The Tevigga Suttanta; 4. The Âkaṅkheyya Sutta; 5. The *K*etokhila Sutta; 6. The Mahâ-sudassana Suttanta; 7. The Sabbâsava Sutta. 8vo., cloth, 10*s*. 6*d*.

A collection of the most important religious, moral, and philosophical discourses taken from the sacred canon of the Buddhists.

VOL. XII. The *S*atapatha-Brâhma*n*a, according to the Text of the Mâdhyandina School.

Translated by JULIUS EGGELING. Part I. Books I and II. 8vo., cloth, 12*s*. 6*d*.

A minute account of the sacrificial ceremonies of the Vedic age. It contains the earliest account of the Deluge in India.

[See also Vol. XXVI.]

VOL. XIII. Vinaya Texts.

Translated from the Pâli by T. W. RHYS DAVIDS and HERMANN OLDENBERG. Part I. The Pâtimokkha. The Mahâvagga, I–IV. 8vo., cloth, 10*s*. 6*d*.

The Vinaya Texts give for the first time a translation of the moral code of the Buddhist religion as settled in the third century B.C.

[See also Vols. XVII and XX.]

VOL. XIV. The Sacred Laws of the Âryas,

As taught in the Schools of Âpastamba, Gautama, Vâsish*th*a, and Baudhâyana. Translated by GEORG BÜHLER. Part II. Vasish*th*a and Baudhâyana. 8vo., cloth, 10*s*. 6*d*.

VOL. XV. The Upanishads.

Translated by F. MAX MÜLLER. Part II. The Ka*th*a-upanishad, The Mu*nd*aka-upanishad, The Taittirîyaka-upanishad, The B*ri*hadâra*n*yaka-upanishad, The *S*vetâ*s*vatara-upanishad, The Pra*s*ñ*a*-upanishad, and The Maitrâya*n*a-brâhma*n*a-upanishad. 8vo., cloth, 10*s*. 6*d*.

VOL. XVI. The Sacred Books of China.

The Texts of Confucianism. Translated by JAMES LEGGE. Part II. The Yî King. 8vo., cloth, 10*s*. 6*d*.

VOL. XVII. Vinaya Texts.

Translated from the Pâli by T. W. RHYS DAVIDS and HERMANN OLDENBERG. Part II. The Mahâvagga, V–X. The *K*ullavagga, I–III. 8vo., cloth, 10*s*. 6*d*.

VOL. XVIII. Pahlavi Texts.

Translated by E. W. WEST. Part II. The Dâ*d*istân-î Dînîk and The Epistles of Mânû*s*k*î*har. 8vo., cloth, 12*s.* 6*d.*

VOL. XIX. The Fo-sho-hing-tsan-king.

A Life of Buddha by A*s*vaghosha Bodhisattva, translated from Sanskrit into Chinese by Dharmaraksha, A.D. 420, and from Chinese into English by SAMUEL BEAL. 8vo., cloth, 10*s.* 6*d.*

This life of Buddha was translated from Sanskrit into Chinese, A.D. 420. It contains many legends, some of which show a certain similarity to the Evangelium infantiae, etc.

VOL. XX. Vinaya Texts.

Translated from the Pâli by T. W. RHYS DAVIDS and HERMANN OLDENBERG. Part III. The *K*ullavagga, IV–XII. 8vo., cloth, 10*s.* 6*d.*

VOL. XXI. The Saddharma-pu*nd*arîka; or, The Lotus of the True Law.

Translated by H. KERN. 8vo., cloth, 12*s.* 6*d.*

'The Lotus of the true Law,' a canonical book of the Northern Buddhists, translated from Sanskrit. There is a Chinese translation of this book which was finished as early as the year 286 A.D.

VOL. XXII. *G*aina-Sûtras.

Translated from Prâkrit by HERMANN JACOBI. Part I. The Â*k*ârâṅga-Sûtra and The Kalpa-Sûtra. 8vo., cloth, 10*s.* 6*d.*

The religion of the Gainas was founded by a contemporary of Buddha. It still counts numerous adherents in India, while there are no Buddhists left in India proper.

VOL. XXIII. The Zend-Avesta.

Translated by JAMES DARMESTETER. Part II. The Sîrôzahs, Ya*s*ts, and Nyâyi*s*. 8vo., cloth, 10*s.* 6*d.*

VOL. XXIV. Pahlavi Texts.

Translated by E. W. WEST. Part III. Dînâ-î Maînôg-î Khira*d*, *S*ikand-gûmânîk Vigâr, and Sad Dar. 8vo., cloth, 10*s.* 6*d.*

SECOND SERIES.

VOL. XXV. Manu.

Translated by GEORG BÜHLER. 8vo., cloth, *21s.*

This translation is founded on that of Sir William Jones, which has been carefully revised and corrected with the help of seven native Commentaries. An Appendix contains all the quotations from Manu which are found in the Hindu Law-books, translated for the use of the Law Courts in India. Another Appendix gives a synopsis of parallel passages from the six Dharma-sûtras, the other Sm*ri*tis, the Upanishads, the Mahâbhârata, etc.

VOL. XXVI. The *S*atapatha-Brâhma*n*a.

Translated by JULIUS EGGELING. Part II. Books III and IV. 8vo., cloth, *12s. 6d.*

VOLS. XXVII AND XXVIII. The Sacred Books of China.

The Texts of Confucianism. Translated by JAMES LEGGE. Parts III and IV. The Lî *K*î, or Collection of Treatises on the Rules of Propriety, or Ceremonial Usages. 8vo., cloth, *12s. 6d.* each.

VOL. XXIX. The G*ri*hya-Sûtras, Rules of Vedic Domestic Ceremonies.

Part I. *S*âṅkhâyana, Â*s*valâyana, Pâraskara, Khâdira. Translated by HERMANN OLDENBERG. 8vo., cloth, *12s. 6d.*

These rules of Domestic Ceremonies describe the home life of the ancient Âryas with a completeness and accuracy unmatched in any other literature. Some of these rules have been incorporated in the ancient Law-books.

VOL. XXX. The G*ri*hya-Sûtras. Part II. [*In the Press.*]

VOL. XXXI. The Zend-Avesta.

Part III. The Yasna, Visparad, Âfrînagân, Gâhs, and Miscellaneous Fragments. Translated by L. H. MILLS. 8vo. cloth, *12s. 6d.*

VOL. XXXII. Vedic Hymns.

Translated by F. MAX MÜLLER. Part I. [*In the Press.*]

VOL. XXXIII. The Minor Law-books.

Translated by JULIUS JOLLY. Part I. Nârada, B*ri*haspati. 8vo. cloth, *10s. 6d.*

VOL. XXXIV. The Vedânta-Sûtras, with *S*ankara's Commentary.

Translated by G. THIBAUT. [*Immediately.*]

VOL. XXXV. Milinda. Translated by T. W. RHYS DAVIDS. [*In the Press.*]

VOL. XXXIX. The Sacred Books of China.

Tâo Teh King. Translated by JAMES LEGGE. [*In the Press.*]

VOL. XL. The Contents of the Nasks, as stated in the Eighth and Ninth Books of the Dînka*rd.* Translated by E. W. WEST.

***** The Second Series will consist of Twenty-four Volumes in all.**

SOME ORIENTAL WORKS

RECENTLY PUBLISHED BY THE CLARENDON PRESS.

A Catalogue of the Chinese Translation of the Buddhist Tripi*t*aka, *the Sacred Canon of the Buddhists in China and Japan.*

Compiled by order of the Secretary of State for India by BUNYIU NANJIO, Priest of the Temple, Eastern Hongwanzi, Japan; Member of the Royal Asiatic Society. 4to., 32*s.* 6*d.*

'An immense service rendered to Oriental scholarship.'—*Saturday Review.*

Record of Buddhistic Kingdoms; being an Account by the Chinese Monk FÂ-HIEN of his Travels in India and Ceylon (A.D. 399–414) in search of the Buddhist Books of Discipline. Translated and annotated, with a Corean recension of the Chinese Text, by JAMES LEGGE, M.A., LL.D. Crown 4to., boards, 10*s.* 6*d.*

Catalogue of the Hebrew Manuscripts in the Bodleian Library and in the College Libraries of Oxford.

Compiled by AD. NEUBAUER, M.A. *With* 40 *Facsimiles.* cloth, 5*l.* 5*s.*

Also separately:

The Catalogue. 3*l.* 13*s.* 6*d.*
The Facsimiles. 2*l.* 12*s.* 6*d.*

Anecdota Oxoniensia.

ARYAN SERIES.

Buddhist Texts from Japan. I. Vagrakkhedikâ; *The Diamond-Cutter.*

Edited by F. MAX MÜLLER, M.A. Small 4to., 3*s.* 6*d.*

One of the most famous metaphysical treatises of the Mahâyâna Buddhists.

Buddhist Texts from Japan. II. Sukhâvatî-Vyûha: *Description of Sukhâvatî, the Land of Bliss.*

Edited by F. MAX MÜLLER, M.A., and BUNYIU NANJIO. With two Appendices: (1) Text and Translation of Sanghavarman's Chinese Version of the Poetical Portions of the Sukhâvatî-Vyûha; (2) Sanskrit Text of the Smaller Sukhâvatî-Vyûha. Small 4to., 7*s.* 6*d.*

The *editio princeps* of the Sacred Book of one of the largest and most influential sects of Buddhism, numbering more than ten millions of followers in Japan alone.

Buddhist Texts from Japan. III. *The Ancient Palm-Leaves containing the* Pragñâ-Pâramitâ-H*ri*daya-Sûtra *and the* Ush*n*îsha-Vigaya-Dhâra*n*î.

Edited by F. MAX MÜLLER, M.A., and BUNYIU NANJIO, M.A. With an Appendix by G. BÜHLER, C.I.E. With many Plates. Small 4to., 10*s.*

Contains facsimiles of the oldest Sanskrit MS. at present known.

Dharma-Sa*m*graha, *an Ancient Collection of Buddhist Technical Terms.*

Prepared for publication by KENJIU KASAWARA, a Buddhist Priest from Japan, and, after his death, edited by F. MAX MÜLLER and H. WENZEL. Small 4to., 7*s.* 6*d.*

Kâtâyana's Sarvânukrama*n*î of the *Ri*gveda.

With Extracts from Sha*d*guru*s*ishya's Commentary entitled Vedârthadîpikâ. Edited by A. A. MACDONELL, M.A., Ph.D. 16*s.*

Oxford

AT THE CLARENDON PRESS

LONDON: HENRY FROWDE

OXFORD UNIVERSITY PRESS WAREHOUSE, AMEN CORNER, E.C.